MIRRORING THE PAST

MIRRORING THE PAST
MIRRORING THE PAST

The Writing and Use of History in Imperial China

On-cho Ng and Q. Edward Wang

University of Hawai'i Press
Honolulu

Library of Congress Cataloging-in-Publication Data
Ng, On Cho.
Mirroring the past : the writing and use of history in
imperial China / On-cho Ng and Q. Edward Wang.
p.   cm.
Includes bibliographical references.
ISBN-13: 978-0-8248-2913-1 (hardcover : alk. paper)
ISBN-10: 0-8248-2913-1 (hardcover : alk. paper)
1. China—Historiography.   2. Historiography—China—
History.   I. Title: Writing and use of history in imperial
China.   II. Wang, Qingjia.   III. Title.
DS734.7.N4 2005
907′.2′051—dc22
2005008008

Designed by University of Hawai'i Press production staff

Printed by Integrated Book Technology

Contents

Prologue

This book was not written to resolve scholarly problems concerning historiography in imperial China; nor is it intended to advance technical discussions on the subject. What we offer is an up-to-date, reliable survey of imperial Chinese historiography, an account that we believe to be a reasonably comprehensive and truthful reconstruction of the parameters and patterns of historical production in a culture distinguished for its veneration of the past. We wrote this book because there is a great need for such a panoramic work.

Chinese civilization is well known for its long, continuous tradition of historical writing. Since antiquity, writing history has been the quintessential Chinese way of defining and shaping culture. As China forged a unified empire, dynastic rulers gradually but surely turned the production of history into a routine, bureaucratic business, as evidenced by the appointment of court historians and the institutionalization of the History Bureau in the seventh century. Indeed, from the third century B.C.E. onward, the writing of dynastic histories was undertaken as a matter of course. One central and inescapable task of a new dynasty was to compile the history of the previous dynasty. History was the textual manifestation of a new imperium, and control of the past, by imperial fiat, was part of the power and authority of the new regime. According to one estimate, in order to render the official dynastic histories, or "standard histories" (*zhengshi*), that have been compiled over more than a millennium into English, a total of some forty-five million words would be required (Dubs 1946, 23–43). And this total does not include an almost equally large number of private and unofficial histories that further testified to the Chinese predilection for ordering the past through historical narratives.

The study of Chinese historiography in the English-speaking world has never really flourished. Scholarly endeavor has been sporadic and intermittent, if not downright sparse. In 1938 Charles Gardner published, to our knowledge, the first systematic, book-length study entitled *Chinese Traditional Historiography,* a small volume of some hundred pages. It was followed in 1955 by Yu-shan Han's *Elements of Chinese Historiography* and W. G. Beasley and E. G. Pulleyblank's edited volume, *Historians of China and Japan*, in 1961. Pulleyblank later contributed a long article, "The Historiographical Tradition," to Raymond Dawson's anthology, *The Legacy of China*, which appeared in 1964. The three decades from the 1960s to the 1990s were apparently a fallow period except that 1975 witnessed publication of *Essays on the Sources for Chinese History*, edited by Donald D. Leslie, Colin Mackerras, and Wang Gungwu, a work that offers some coverage of the Chinese historiographical tradition. Otherwise, no major works on historiography in traditional China have appeared in English. Despite the immense value of the studies we have listed, these pioneering works are now out of print and outdated. Denis Twitchett's *The Writing of Official History under the T'ang*, published in 1992, was the first major study on traditional Chinese historiography to appear in a long time. It was followed by two monographs on Sima Qian, the great historian in the Han, written by Stephen Durrant and Grant Hardy. But all these studies are specific in scope and coverage. Twitchett's study focuses on the Tang, while those by Durrant and Hardy deal with only one historian, important though Sima was. However valuable individual studies on aspects and periods of Chinese historiography may be, they cannot adequately substitute for a continuous account. In short, there is no single, up-to-date English-language volume that offers a critical survey of the Chinese historiographical tradition.

This relative lack of attention to traditional Chinese historiography not only reveals a lacuna in the field of Chinese studies but also detracts from a general understanding of Chinese civilization, of which the charisma of history was integrally a part. Insofar as history, the storehouse of moral lessons and bureaucratic precedents, was the *magister vitae*—the teacher of life—to the Chinese literati, neglect of the historiographical tradition of China meant diminution of a broad view of Chinese culture. Accordingly, a current and comprehensive survey of traditional Chinese historiography, one that integrates and reflects the scholarship and academic interests of the past two decades, is necessary.

It may also be argued that this need is not a parochial one defined solely in terms of Chinese studies. The onslaught of poststructuralism, deconstructionism, postmodernity, postcolonialism, and other post-Enlightenment theories in the human sciences has underscored the multivalent and polyvocal loci of truths. Setting aside the question of the interpretive cogency and explanatory power of these theories, they have, at the very least, usefully demytholized the paradigmatic status of European Enlightenment values and world views. A variety of historical conceptions have been shown to be ideological constructions rather than cultural truisms. Thus, for instance, it has become de rigueur these days in academia to deuniversalize a host of notions that have hitherto been Eurocentrically construed and defined, such as modernity, or even the concept of culture itself. As the putative universality of the Western tradition of historiography wanes, it seems increasingly necessary for practicing historians and historiographers to come to terms with alternative perspectives. To the extent that every people has a legitimate history of history, the development of a deeper understanding of the historical profession and discipline as a whole may well require seeking insights and inspirations from the historiographical traditions of other cultures. In the recently published *A Global Encyclopedia of Historical Writings,* edited by a group of Western historians (Woolf 1998), for example, many of the entries pertain to non-Western traditions of historiography. Hence, even though this book on traditional Chinese historiography speaks to scholars and students of China, it should also appeal to historians of other parts of the world, if for no other than pedagogical reasons. While appropriate texts are abundantly available for the study of the historiographical traditions of Europe and America, instructors often find themselves at a loss to identify proper books for China. Many are forced to fall back on works published decades ago. Our work, at the same time that it traces the general contour of traditional Chinese historiography, is an advanced technical synthesis of the latest scholarship on the subject.

As befits an overview of traditional Chinese historiography, this book is organized chronologically, following the dynastic successions, beginning in antiquity, during which time the early forms of historical consciousness emerged, and ending in the mid-nineteenth century, when encounter with the West began to engender a fundamentally different historical outlook. This periodization corresponds with the conventional division of Chinese history that we find in much of the scholarly literature produced in the West. The main merit of this schema is that it strikes a chord of harmony with many existing books on other aspects of Chinese history. Readers can readily integrate the materials found here with information on the other historical developments from other works. The individual chapters detail the complexities and nuances of the unfolding historiographical tradition, revealing the roles that history and historians played in phases of Chinese history. For every period we explore and examine Chinese historiography on two levels: first, historiography as the gathering of raw materials and the writing and producing of narratives in order to describe what actually happened in the past—the compilation of history; and second, historiography as thought and reflection about the meanings and patterns of the past—the philosophy of history.

A continuous narrative in the form of a general survey often runs the risk of highlighting the trees while losing sight of the forest. In detailing the multitude of causal and crucial elements in the historiography of the various dynastic periods, a survey may blur the overarching themes. It may gloss over the metanarrative, as it were, neglecting the unyielding bedrock of logic and the assumptions that lie beneath and extend beyond and above the surface historical minutiae. A recounting of the historiographical endeavors and accomplishments of the individual dynasties that on their own become luminous with significance may in the end fail to illuminate the very substance and nature of historiography in imperial

China. Told in the form of a survey, the historiographical story may appear to be just one damned fact after another, much as happens in handbooks or encyclopedias. What integrated picture, then, do all the dynastic snapshots yield? What overall profile can be constructed out of the separate developments? What continuity flowed through the apparent disjunctions of epochal segmentation? What whole may be intuited from the accumulations of the parts? Our work aims to answer these questions and thereby demonstrate the main lines and themes of historiographical developments. To seek to demonstrate the whole is not to flatten out the diverse movements in Chinese historiography throughout the ages in the name of static coherence. It is not, as critics are wont to say these days, to essentialize what making history was all about in imperial China. What we do seek here, however, is an integrated view of Chinese historiography, one that reveals the continuity that persisted within particular periods.

Historical consciousness in early China germinated within a unique world view animated by an anthropocosmic commingling of Heaven and humanity, wherein human affairs and agency were at once the reflection and the embodiment of Heaven's will and action. Confucius, generally acknowledged as the author-editor of the *Spring and Autumn Annals* (*Chunqiu*), purposefully employed and manipulated historical retelling as educative disquisition. Otherwise a pedestrian chronological record, the *Spring and Autumn Annals* became in the hands of Confucius a powerful tool that infused moral purport into the writing of history. This didactic act of using the past to convey the moral messages and judgments vouchsafed by Heaven exerted an enduring impact on Chinese historiography. The making and writing of history came to be enmeshed in moral edification. And it was precisely because of this historiographical principle and practice of bestowing praise and levying blame (*baobian*) on personages and events of the past that history acquired its unmistakable charisma and authority.

The two acclaimed historians in the Han, Sima Qian (c. 145–85 B.C.E.) and Ban Gu (d. 92 C.E.), played remarkable roles in orienting historical writing in new directions. As a consequence, the grand enterprise of doing history began to depart from the antique model established by Confucius in terms of both scope and style. Yet notwithstanding their innovations that boldly forged new conventions and expanded the horizons of historical writing, Sima's intention to explore and reveal the relationship between Heaven and human affairs through history, and Ban Gu's concern with dynastic history and the ways in which knowledge of the past was preserved and presented, very much reflected earlier historiographical assumptions. Both asserted that the history of human knowledge and awareness of the past was, in its essentials, pragmatic knowledge, the practical purpose of which was demonstrated through distinguishing the good and excoriating the wicked. The pragmatic lessons of the past were most revealingly conveyed in the exemplary lives of individuals, and indeed, beginning with Sima Qian, the biographic form became the major narrative vehicle for bringing to light the deeds of the past. History was essentially the record of the operation and influence of moral forces and principles in the lives of past personages, whose behavior and agency were in turn brought to bear on the well-being of the state and society. Thus history was normative; it was a moral narrative guided by the principal didactic function of celebrating virtues and deterring vices (Pulleyblank 1961, 143–144; L. Yang 1961, 52; Moloughney 1992, 1–7). History was not only considered morally edifying, but it was also thought to be capable of proffering trustworthy socioeconomic and political precedents and analogies, so that it served as a most reliable guide for contemporary statecraft. The abiding historiographical conviction held that juxtaposing and probing similar events of past and present would yield invaluable practical insights crucial for the betterment of the state and society (Hartwell 1971, 694–699). It is small wonder that Etienne Balazs's famous characterization of Chinese historiography as history "written by officials for officials" has become a sort of adage that supposedly encapsulates the substance and import of historical production in imperial China (Balazs 1964, 132, 135).

An interesting related issue, or subtext, one that has increasingly engaged the attention of scholars working on the intellectual culture of the Renaissance and early modern Europe, needs to be mentioned here, and that is the question of readership. It may reasonably be argued that if the educative and moralizing stance on history of Sima Qian and Ban Gu — and for that matter of the later Chinese historians and historiographers as well — reflected their prerogatives and imperatives as authors, then we may assume that a world of readers existed where history was expected to be *read* in a certain manner. In other words, the Chinese historians authored history in a particular way because they assumed that history would and should be read in this manner. Just as writing about the past was purposefully intended to educate people, the state, and society, so reading about the past was a deliberate, goal-oriented act of learning pursued with practical aims. For instance, in the Song, reading and discoursing on history before the throne came to be institutionalized as imperial lectures through which rulers and officials were educated in the art of rulership and governance. In fact, testing the knowledge of history in the imperial civil service examinations was a clear example of the mindful and goal-oriented reading of the past (cf. Grafton 2001, 13–14; Jardine and Grafton 1990, 30–78; Hartwell 1971, 696–698; 703–709). Understood from the vantage point of both author and reader, history was normative and ameliorative, charismatically transformative.

Apart from its utility as statecraft and morality, history had its use in political legitimation and propaganda. In imperial China the compilation of a dynastic history served the political goal of confirming the legitimate succession of the new regime. The transition from one dynasty to the next was conceived and explicated in terms of the continuation of power and authority by a "proper" (*zheng*) ruler, who successfully forged "unity" (*tong*) — hence the ideal of *zhengtong*, the orthodox and systemic continua-

tion of power. By dint of its virtues, its moral excellence, not to mention
its political and military prowess, a new dynasty received the Mandate of
Heaven and assumed authority by legitimately displacing and replacing
the moribund predecessor. At the service of *zhengtong* history was supposed
to set the record straight by affirming orthodox transmissions of power
(L. Yang 1961, 46–48; H. Chan 1984, 19–48).

This unabashed and overt indenturing of history to ideological and
political orthodoxy and moral-ethical edification, while acknowledged as
a clear indication that the Chinese venerated the past, has been regarded
by many Western commentators as an unmistakable indication of the ultimate ahistoricity of the Chinese way of recording and interpreting the
past. Often evaluating imperial Chinese historiography in terms of modern Western historical standards, and frequently neglecting the substantive achievements of traditional Chinese historians, critics have frequently
reached simplistic and unjustified conclusions. Wong Young-tsu, in a recent article (2001), has rightly voiced his dissatisfaction with some of the
sweeping misconceptions of traditional Chinese historiography, which he
exposes and takes to task. Take, for example, the historiographical principle and practice of praise and blame. While historical didacticism and
analogies may have generally been accepted as working in the service of
moral and political certitude, they were by no means invariably crude
forms of moral hucksterism and ideological boosterism that ignored truth.
To praise and blame was to give credit where credit was due, an endeavor
that was informed by fidelity to what had actually happened. It was by preserving the veracity and authenticity of the past that history appropriately
and efficaciously served as the great teacher of life; and it was in the act
of truthful recording that moral lessons were pronounced and enshrined.
Likewise, with regard to the orthodox and legitimate assumption of power,
there was by no means consensus among Chinese historians as to which
dynasties were legitimate. Lively and vociferous debates on this issue occurred ever so often, as individual scholars rendered judgments on legitimacy, based on the historians' rigorous investigations and critical readings
of historical events (Wong 2001, 128–131; L. Yang 1961, 32; K. Hsu 1983,
435–436).

Indeed, we should realize that the desire to unearth the truth about
the past for its own sake is relatively recent in the West. The disinterested
quest for knowledge of the past and the cognitive approach to historiography, supposedly free of practical intent, came into being only with the
onset of European modernity. Before the sixteenth and seventeenth centuries the West was, like China, preoccupied with history as pragmatic
and usable knowledge (Iggers & Wang 2001, 21–35). In point of fact, we
may reasonably contend that any culture that values the past invariably en-
genders and sustains conceptions of history that embody larger meaning
and significance—paradigms of human actions, patterns of cosmic movements, and wills and purposes of providential forces. Even today, apprehension of the meaning and significance ensconced in history enables us

to shed light on the present and speculate about the future. History constitutes, to put it another way, a practical past (Graham 1997, 1–2; 201–202). Seen in this cross-cultural light, traditional China was hardly exceptional.

Moreover, post-Enlightenment, if not postmodern, thinking in the West has long acceded to and taken for granted the inexorable role of the present in the making of the past. The Rankean assertion of objective realism and scientific history—to write history as it has really been, shorn of the cultural and personal burden of the present—is as much a myth as the Confucian proleptic conception that present problems are reenactments of past problems—that history literally repeats itself. In our practice of history, we have come to accept the fact that the point of entry for historians is always present determinations and current events, an assumption, or more correctly, reality, which we may call presentism. The eminent French historian Lucien Febvre has famously declared that such presentism is the very bedrock of the reconstruction of the past: "The Past is a reconstitution of societies and human beings engaged in the network of human realities of today" (de Certeau 1988, 11). Thanks to the many works of literary critics such as Edward Said and historical theorists like Hayden White, which we need not belabor here, historians have become quite cognizant of the inherently constructivist and representational nature of any historical discourse. Narratives and interpretations of the past cannot be absolutely truthful presence of the past; they are perforce "a *re-presence,* or a representation" (Said 1979, 21). A historical narrative "is not merely a neutral discursive form that may or may not be used to represent real events," insofar as it entails the ideological and political stances of the narrator (White 1987, ix). In other words the conviction of historical truth premised on the assumption of a neat correspondence between what happened in the past and its recovery in historical research and retelling in historical narratives has been rent asunder. Of course, reference to such intellectual developments and sensibilities in the contemporary West does not suggest that imperial Chinese historiography was self-consciously aware in like manner of the ontological and epistemological condition in the representation, or re-presentation, of the past. Rather, it is to remind us that the Chinese conception of history as the repository of recoverable lessons for present and future actions is an instance of the inexorable presence of presentist motives in the endeavor to disinter the past.

But does it mean that this belief in the talismanic power of history swamped any serious concern with establishing what really did happen? Did the Chinese historians treat the past merely as a treasure trove of lessons and precedents to be placed in the midst of the present society? Was history simply memorialized with faith and memorized by rote rather than examined with zeal and reconstructed with imagination?

In addition, critics have frequently referred to the imperial patronage and control of the production of history in traditional China as a crippling impediment to telling the truth about the past. And it is true that the great majority of the dynastic histories were compiled under imperial aegis by scholars working in official capacities. From the fall of the Han dynasty in the third century to the rise of the Sui dynasty in the late sixth, the writing of dynastic histories received official endorsement, and they came to be known as the "standard histories" (*zhengshi*). With the consolidation of the venerable tradition of official historiography, the writing of history indeed seemed to be, as Balazs commented, undertaken by officials for officials (1961, 78–94). In the Tang dynasty, official patronage of historical writing became institutionalized when the imperial court established the History Bureau (*shiguan*). There, historians were given assistance and support for their research and writing, but they were also handed instructions and directives from supervising officials and emperors. As the making of history was institutionalized and coopted into the bureaucracy, so the reasoning goes, critical impulse and creative spirit were stultified. W. J. F. Jenner, for instance, has launched a withering critique of traditional Chinese historiography, especially official historiography, which he sees as a mere stratified stockpile of accumulated administrative experience, couched in rigid and conventionalized language, whose aim was to instill the right values in the minds of the bureaucrats. This invented past, invested with the imprimatur of imperial power, became a veritable cultural prison marked by the tyranny of a history that was the final arbiter of values and behaviors (Jenner 1992, 5–12). Interestingly enough, Jenner's evaluation was prompted by his desire to determine the reasons that explained the tragic events of Tiananmen in 1989 in relation to the nature of Communist rule. The irony is that his reconstruction of the Chinese historiographical past bespeaks the presentist origination of his project. He resorts and appeals to his usable past after all.

What is wrong with Jenner's portrayal? The principal problem is that it gives very short shrift to the Chinese insistence, perhaps even fixation, on truthfulness and veracity in the retelling of the past. Chinese historians had always been inspired and empowered by what Liu Yizheng has called the ideal of the "authority of history" (*shiquan*), whose very potency and persuasiveness came from its fidelity to what actually happened (1969, 19–35). Confucius himself was keenly sensitive to the availability of sources. He remarked to his disciples that he could discuss the rituals and ceremonies of the Xia and Shang dynasties but not those of the Qi and Song states because he found insufficient documents, physical artifacts, and oral traditions for the latter two. Confucius' distinguished pupil Zi Gong cast appropriate doubt on the traditional accounts of the reign of the last ruler of the Shang, and concluded that King Zou's decadence and turpitude might have been exaggerated. Mencius (c. 372–298 B.C.E.) warned that if one were to completely believe what the *Classic of History* (*Shujing*) said, then it would be better not to read it at all. Han Fei (280–233 B.C.E.) took a dim view of the stories of the legendary sage-rulers of Yao and Shun, the cultural heroes and paragons of Confucian China. But perhaps the foremost case of upholding the principle of truthful recording is that included in the *Zuo Commentary* to Confucius' *Spring and Autumn Annals*. In 568 B.C.E.

three brothers, all of whom were official historians of the state of Qi, were put to death one after another, because they insisted on recording a story truthfully, contravening and thwarting the wishes of those in power. The tale was told matter-of-factly, without pathos, clearly intimating that in ancient China, there was already the widely accepted and unyielding principle of upholding the truth about the past at all costs, even to the point of accepting death with equanimity (K. Hsu 1983, 432).

It is important to note that the Chinese themselves were very aware of some potential pitfalls in official compilations of history, carried out under imperial auspices and oversight. Thus, the institutionalization of the making of history also meant the installation of means to safeguard the truth by forestalling its corruption and compromise. In the Tang, when the History Bureau came into being, the emperor had no access to what the Bureau had written precisely because of the anticipation and fear of imperial interference. In fact, individual compilers did not share their writing with fellow compilers in order to maintain each writer's independence from undue influence and pressure. In Chinese history there were many cases of the official historians' courageous fight for truth, even at the risk of alienating their imperial overlord and losing their lives. Needless to say, there were also many cases of imperial meddling and political strong-arming such that compilation rules were violated and historiographical conventions subverted. Nonetheless, while it would be naïve to think that all official historians were men of principle and official compilations emerged unscathed from the briar patch of imperial whims and bureaucratic infighting, we must not lose sight of the elaborate mechanisms created in the Chinese officialdom to ensure and encourage the truthful preservation of past records. By the time the history of the Ming was compiled, the principles and iterations of thorough gathering of sources and impartial recounting of the past had become standard fare in the world of official historiography. These included the broad marshalling of materials, vigorous vetting of the sources, careful distribution and division of labor among the compilers, standardized rules of recording, faithful adherence to truth in recording, impartial evaluation, patient and painstaking effort in compilation, and narrative concision (L. Yang 1961, 55; J. Chen 1981, 38–47).

Moreover, we must not lose sight of the vibrant world of private historiography that consciously transcended the strictures of collective compilation under direct court patronage. The innovation and creative imagination in these works must not be ignored (Wong 2001, 133–137; J. Chen 1981, 56–68). Furthermore, we ought to pay heed to the myriad cautions issued by the Chinese historiographers and historians themselves with regard to the unreliability of official compilations. Liu Zhiji (661–721), for instance, an astute historiographer and philosopher of history of the Tang, extended his criticisms of the History Bureau to other important areas of historiography. He tirelessly argued for the critical evaluation of the sources and impartial reconstruction of historical narratives through truthful recording that conscientiously avoided concealment, embellishment, and distortion. At the same time that Liu maintained praise and blame as the paramount function of history, he reminded readers that such functionality was entirely contingent on the veracity of the historical accounts in the first place. It was only when accounts separated the authentic from the apocryphal, presenting both the good and wicked in equal measure, that histories could legitimately play the requisite and valued role of moral adjudicator (K. Hsu 1983, 435–438; J. Chen 1981, 47–56).

Besides the issue of truth, observers and critics in the West have questioned the nature and methods of historical records in imperial China. While most of them have been impressed by the voluminous and continuous records that do undoubtedly furnish crucial material for understanding the Chinese past, many have blithely and sweepingly characterized them as products of "scissors-and-paste," to borrow R. G. Collingwood's words, wanting in reflection on the nature and meaning of history. In other words, to many Western observers, much of Chinese historiography was mere mechanistic assemblage of congeries of lived stories and events, an encyclopedic parade of facts and information.

It is quite true that we may readily identify certain fairly standardized formats that dominated the writing of history in imperial China. First, there was the annals-biography, or composite, style (jizhuan) that most of the standard histories adopted. As mentioned above, the biographical essay formed the core of traditional historical writing, for the exemplary lives of individuals were seen and presented as the realization of the enduring principles and values embodied in the classics. The rise and fall of dynasties, and the complex unfolding of past happenings, were conveniently filtered through the lives of people of pivotal historical significance, through whom crucial insights into a past era could be developed. In addition, the biographic information and narratives were often complemented by brief comments (zan) that purposefully highlighted the importance of the lives depicted. The annals of the imperial rulers and princes, and the biographies of the notable officials and personages, together forged an educative catalog of evidence of the worthy and time-honored principles that were at work in history through individual lives. These paragons and role models became vivid guides to proper action and ethical conduct for posterity (Moloughney 1992, 1–13). Yet it is noteworthy that as early as Sima Qian and Ban Gu, biographies alone were deemed to be inadequate. Hence within the composite style, there was also the use of tables and the writing of monographs or treatises on specific topics. The tables were historical charts, and the treatises and monographs addressed issues that went beyond biographic details to covering a wide array of topics from geography, to astronomy, to flora and fauna, just to mention a few. In short, Chinese historians conscientiously studied various aspects of human activities but within a narrative style that crystallized around individual lives.

In contradistinction to the composite style, there was the chronicle (*biannian*). It was a chronological recounting of the past as a concatenation of events, sequentially ordered and arranged. One obvious shortcoming of this format was that events were recorded individually in isolation without a broad sense of situational context and circumstantial interconnection. While a chronicle had the distinct merit of providing a clear picture of temporal continuity, the spatial coherence of events was often in short supply. As a consequence there emerged a third style of narrative, known as "narratives from beginning to end" (*jishi benmo*). The goal of these histories was to reorder and reorganize the information culled from a chronicle by subsuming it under topics and themes. Materials on a particular topic or event, often scattered throughout the chronicle, were reassembled so that the development and trajectory of any one episode in history might be mapped, retraced, and reconstructed. In this format of recording, isolated parts would be brought together to constitute a cohesive whole, a full-fledged historical narrative with a beginning, middle, and end.

In addition to these three dominant styles, there were many variations, especially in the world of private historiography. Some focused on treatises or monographs; others were highly synoptic works organized by theme, such as institutional developments; still others were miscellanies. The point here is that notwithstanding the apparent uniformity of forms favored by the standard histories, there were many actual historical styles. Moreover, the manner of recording was by no means so highly conventionalized that the intrinsic drama was bleached out of events. They were not merely bland factual entries in a dry encyclopedic catalog of the human past (Wong 2001, 138–144).

Did format hamstring and constrain substance? Did rigid style mean conventional substance? In fact, if Chinese historiography had simply been generated by the scissors-and-paste method, and if format stultified substance, historical criticism would not have been such a prominent pursuit that inspired and engaged so many Chinese historians. Furthermore, these critics of history were not simply engrossed in isolated minutiae; their historical criticism did not target piecemeal particulars alone. Many were intent on rebuilding and refurbishing the factual foundation of ancient history through wholesale rigorous critiques. Liu Zhiji, for instance, tackled not only individual classics and texts but sought to reexamine the entire antiquity tradition, which to him was much entrapped in a penumbra of myth and fable. Liu questioned the accuracy of many entries in the *Spring and Autumn Annals* and doubted the veracity of Sima Qian's and Ban Gu's renderings of China's ancient past. Even the iconic story of the much-admired practice in ancient China of voluntary surrender of the throne—Yao selflessly yielding his position to the virtuous Shun, and Shun altruistically giving up his rulership in favor of the sagely Yu—was subject to skeptical interrogation.

In the Song, the growth of antiquarian studies further stimulated the critical and skeptical impulses within Chinese historiography. Ouyang Xiu (1007–1072), who complemented his historical research of textual material with investigations of ancient artifacts, showed that at least three of the "Ten Wings" (appendices explaining the moral significance of the hexagrams in the *Classic of Changes*) were not authored by Confucius but by later scholars. Zheng Qiao (1104–1062), who was equally adept at exploring the worlds of material culture and classical scholarship, scrutinized the Han classical commentary tradition and questioned the credibility of their descriptions and interpretations. Sima Guang (1019–1086) set up rigorous standards of determining and measuring truth based on comparisons of sources; he repudiated all manner of literary works containing the fanciful, bizarre, and fabulous.

In the Qing dynasty, spurred on by the exacting and meticulous methodology of evidential research (*kaozheng*), classicists and historians critically parsed the meanings of the sages' words and carefully determined the origins and authenticity of the ancient texts and artifacts. In short, there was a concerted reexamination of the classics and antiquity, whose roles in Chinese culture would be increasingly historicized—antiquity became a segment in time and the classics became objects of study. As the classics and antiquity came to be historicized, they were no longer viewed as transtemporal, universal, and therefore, immutable, but rather as products *in* and *of* history. This effort produced two historiographical developments. First, it yielded a remarkable improvement in the means by which historical sources and materials were read and examined. This in turn led to new understandings of previous historical scholarship. Second, it fostered a historicist sense, a historical-mindedness or consciousness—the awareness of the passage of time, the cognizance of anachronism, and the knowledge that the present and the past were qualitatively different. Wang Fuzhi (1619–1692), for instance, called for the critical vetting and verification of sources as he urged historians to cultivate a sense of anachronism, an awareness that the past and present "each has its own time, its own situation and its own emotions, values and reasons" (K. Hsu 1983, 443). Gu Yanwu (1613–1682), as he immersed himself in the study of ancient history and culture—language, phonetics, institutions and so forth—was bent on reconstructing the past in an unbiased and impartial fashion, guided solely by corroborated facts and evidence. In the eighteenth century, Dai Zhen (1724–1777) asked scholars "to explain the past with past meanings; neither infusing one's own opinions nor projecting ideas of later generations into the past" (K. Hsu 1983, 445). This epistemological stance culminated in Zhang Xuecheng's (1738–1804) bold and eloquent contention that the classics were all histories (K. Hsu 1983, 435–446).

Not only were Chinese historians insistent on ascertaining truth through exacting methods of verifying evidence, constructing narratives, and effecting interpretations, they were also keenly interested in espousing conceptual historical schemas that sought to give shape to the past. In other words, Chinese thinkers had their own grand overarching theories and philosophies of history. In the main, Chinese theories of the flow of history displayed three dominant, but interrelated modes of expression:

classicality, caducity, and continuity. Historical classicality refers to the conviction that the antique past established excellent criteria of achievement and values of judgment, and they therefore became the *classic* ones by which subsequent ages and cultures would have to be measured. The antique past, the golden age, was the wellspring and storehouse of moral and practical lessons. The corollary of historical classicality was historical didacticism, the idea that history was the charismatic teacher of life in all its diversity (Frykenberg 1996, 149–152). Historical caducity points to the related sense that time is degenerative; the present is perforce inferior to the ancient past. Historical continuity celebrates timeless universality as opposed to contingent particularities. The present is seen to be the same as the past, because both are essentially uniform in character. Without a sense of anachronism, perception of the difference between the past and presence is filtered through the lenses of classicality and caducity—the present divergence is the result of a fall from the glorious classical past (Burke 1969, 1–2; Logan 1977, 18).

Given the pervasive historicist conceptions of classicality, caducity, and continuity, the primary criteria for value in imperial China were generated by the past, and not engendered by present experience or anticipated future ideal (Mote 1976, 3–8). Even though the appeal to the classical need not mean blind aping of the past, the summoning of antique models did imply that the subsequent ages and the present were afflicted with a perennial pathology, that there was a besetting cultural degeneration as time marched on. The measurement of the present against the classical past also suggested their essential continuity, as the inferior present could be improved by retrieving the old, insofar as there was qualitative uniformity bridging the two. These perspectives of the past were very much reinforced by the Neo-Confucian grand unity of the cosmos and the social, cultural, and political polity. The abiding Way (*dao*), and its manifestations of Heaven (*tian*) and Principle (*li*), inhered in the cosmos and humanity as the ultimate authority. They embodied the universal norms and values that transcended time. Since its only function was to ratify the validity of the overall pattern and the overarching principle, the particular was rendered incidental and peripheral (Ng 1993b, 564–567). Since the present was not regarded as a period sui generis but merely a degenerate version of a past era, there was no epochal differentiation in the modern sense.

Nonetheless, within the three dominant modes of historical thinking—classicality, caducity, and continuity—the Chinese thinkers formulated their own epochal concepts as they sought to make sense of the past through historical schemas. In accordance with the historical vision of the Han New Script (*jinwen*) classical tradition, Dong Zhongshu (179?–140? B.C.E) espoused the idea of the "Three Beginnings" (*sanzheng*). Here he was referring to the legitimate succession of three regimes, the Zhou, the Shang, and the state of Lu, of which Confucius was the uncrowned king. Dong also postulated a cycle of Simplicity (*zhi*) and Refinement (*wen*), positing that the beginnings of dynasties were characterized by the institution of simple but pious rituals and rites, while their conclusions were steeped in extravagance and artificiality that sowed the seeds of eventual demise. From the Eastern Han exegete He Xiu (A.D. 129–182), we get a modified form of this tripartite succession, known as "Preserving the Three Systems" (*cun santong*), or "Linking the Three Systems" (*tong santong*), which was in turn associated with the "Three Ages" (*sanshi*). In the eighteenth century, followers of the New Script tradition, such as Zhuang Cunyu (1719–1788), offered their own interpretations and variations. But these epochal constructions and orderings all dealt exclusively with antiquity (Ng 1994, 1–32). In their essentials they buttressed the historical perspective of classicality.

In the early nineteenth century, other New Script scholars like Gong Zizhen (1792–1841) and Wei Yuan (1794–1856) added their own versions of the Three-Age schema. Gong actually offered several versions. They all aimed at explaining the general principles and shape of the flow of time, which no longer only applied to antiquity. But as Gong himself made clear, this temporal trichotomy was after all a repetition of the antique Three Ages, in that its ending point was the age of universal peace, an age which happily replicated that same great golden era of yore. In other words, the paradigm of historical classicality still held sway in Gong's historicism. Wei's Three-Age schemas also exceeded the bounds of antiquity, but they were by and large devolutionary and regressive in nature, thereby affirming the paradigm of caducity. Moreover, he injected a principle of constancy, variously described as the One (*yi*), the ideal of *wuwei* (nonaction), and the Way that revealed his conformity to the traditional paradigm of continuity (Ng 1996, 82–85).

There were other means of ordering the diachronic passage of time. In the Neo-Confucian vision of the transmission of the Way (*daotong*), antiquity, from the age of the ancient sages to the time of Mencius, was the golden age during which the Way was created and flourished. With the passing of Mencius, the Way was eclipsed and in decline, which ushered in a prolonged age of degeneration, when Buddhism, Daoism, and other heterodox ideas pervaded China. Then with Han Yu's (786–824) retrieval of the Confucian Way came the beginning of the age of regeneration, which was finally brought to fruition by a succession of Confucian masters from Zhou Dunyi (1017–1073) to Zhu Xi (1130–1200).

Another way of identifying periods, which acquired some currency in the Song dynasty, was based on the dominant mode of scholarship at a certain time. Late antiquity, that is, the Han period before what some writers regarded as the infestation of Buddhism, was characterized as a philological age. From then through the Tang was deemed to be a literary age, while the Song itself excelled in speculative contemplation and was thus the age of philosophy (Barrett 1998, 80, 87–88). Another notable epochal scheme is found in Buddhism, generated by the Buddhist millenarian idea of "the latter days of the law." According to this scheme, after the Buddha's demise, the world went through three eras: that of the True Law, the Imitative Law, and the Latter Days of the Law. The temporal flux was marked by the degeneration of the Buddha's teachings, until, in the final era, the world was engulfed in chaos and ruin because people had completely forsaken the Buddha's law. Just as medieval Europe was anxious about the end of the millenium, so in China there was a prevailing concern among the Buddhist devotees regarding the onset and chronology of the Latter Days of the Law. In fact, in medieval China, this age was believed to have started in A.D. 552 (Sato 1991, 287; Barrett 1998, 75–78; cf. Burke 1976, 137–152).

Perhaps the most common way of periodizing Chinese history was through the creation of reign names that were combined with the sexagesimal cycle system of calendrical reckoning, beginning with Emperor Wu of the Western Han in 114 B.C.E. He decreed that the year of his ascension to the throne (116 B.C.E.) ushered in the reign of *yuanding* (the beginning of the tripod *ding*, a figure of speech for assertion of rule). The practice was institutionalized so that henceforth the enthronement of a new emperor went hand in hand with the declaration of a new reign name. However, at times a special occasion would also initiate a new reign title. This dating system was overtly political in purpose, for it affirmed and symbolized the legitimacy, dignity, authority, and administrative ideal of each new ruler. In fact, the dominance of this scheme may have discouraged the formation of other segmenting devices to shape and order the past (Sato 1991, 275–301; Wright 1958, 103–106).

In terms of the modern sense of historicity, the various schemes all failed in the end to generate a full-fledged sense of anachronism, that is, a distinguishing of one period from another by ascertaining their uniqueness and particularity. Nevertheless, there were historical perspectives in the world of imperial Chinese historiography that demonstrated a keen appreciation for the contingent and particular in the passage of time. In the Song dynasty, some historians such as Ouyang Xiu (1007–1072) and Sima Guang (1019–1086) were quite aware of the anachronistic nature of sources as they explored causation in the rise and fall of dynasties. In the seventeenth and eighteenth centuries especially, as the study of the classics and ancient history gathered momentum and became prevalent, antiquity increasingly came to be viewed as a segment *in* time. Gu Yanwu, for instance, railed against obdurate adherence to old institutions, arguing for institutional changes that would meet the special needs of the time and rejecting the idea that the ancient texts could be applied wholesale to current problems. Likewise, Wang Fuzhi affirmed the inevitability of change as new conditions and circumstances (*shi*) continually arose (Teng 1968, 111–123; C. A. Peterson 1979, 12; Ng 1993b, 567–578). In the eighteenth century this historical sense may be summed up by Zhang Xuecheng's proclamation that the classics were all histories, in the sense that they were the records of the governance of the ancient rulers. In effect, Zhang suggested that the classical past was time-bound and therefore could not reveal what happened after antiquity (Nivison 1966, 141–142). Similarly, Dai Zhen resisted the totalizing Neo-Confucian claim of a universal principle by positing that the Way was simply the quotidian practices in human relations manifested in everyday activities (Ng 1993b, 572–578). In the nineteenth century Gong Zizhen and Wei Yuan favored the provisional in varying and changing historical contexts; human accomplishments and actions were related to temporal movement in a human world, not charted by providence or rigidly defined by classical model.

Thus Chinese historiography did contain historicist views that shaped and ordered the past, schemes that qualified the traditional historical perspectives of classicality, caducity, and continuity by deauthorizing and loosening the transcendence, omnipresence, and constancy of the Way. To some extent the present came to be distanced from the Ur present—the antique past—and thus escaped the ghost of the Way-above-history.

So far, we have sketched three dimensions of history in imperial China —the use and usability of the past, the form and format of recounting the past, and the shaping and ordering of the past. By teaching moral behavior through history and by employing historical analogies as sociopolitical guidelines, historians in imperial China asserted the intimate and organic relation between the past and culture. History was embraced for its heroic charisma, at once the agent of moral transformation and the embodiment of culture. History was the collective cultural memory through which philosophy (the quest for the first principles of being) and politics (the erection of the ideal of rulership and the implementation of governance) acquired intelligibility. Historical narratives (which assumed a variety of forms and style) and historical philosophies (which gave order and shape to the apparently amorphous flow of time) proffered eidetic illustrations of the enduring principles of cosmology (the workings of Heaven and earth) and anthropology (the flux and occurrence of human events and actions).

In the chapters that follow, we highlight the dynamic nature of Chinese historiography by noting innovations and changes during different historical periods. We show that historical writing in imperial China was by no means merely bibliographic logorrhea or uncritical amassing of information and that it was not entrapped in a static rehashing of the old as veneration of received traditions. By examining a wide array of historians and historical texts, including both official dynastic histories and private compilations, we hope to portray the diversity and heterogeneity of the Chinese world of historiography. Our framing of the Chinese historiographic past means, perforce, inevitable exclusions, even as we attempt to reconstruct a continuous and comprehensive account. In this account, our goal is to illustrate changes in the ways of conceptualizing and looking at the past and to show how these changes influenced and related to the writing of history itself.

However, more than comprehensive coverage, we aim to identify the dominant mode, or *Zeitgeist,* of historical thinking at a given time, and to explain its genesis and influence in terms of the contemporary sociopolitical and intellectual contexts. It is interesting to note that if the Chinese historians devoted themselves to the collating of human variety, and to the minute annotation of dynastic rise and fall, it was because of their faith in *Geist*—the Way, the Principle—the animating and guiding force of spirit, thought, and above all, culture. In this view, people died, regimes passed, institutions crumbled, things perished, matter decomposed, and colors faded. But the Way, the culture, and the patterns of the past persisted. They knew so because history served as the mirror that reflected and showed the enduring value of the Way and the age-old, time-honored patterns of culture. In the final analysis, the monumental and exacting historical works produced in imperial China mapped the contour of Chinese civilization, not for the sake of understanding the past as disembodied and theoretical learning, but for realizing the grand didactic and pragmatic purpose of teaching the world by mirroring and displaying the past, warts and all.

Because we now know history cannot be a purely empirical enterprise of transcribing past happenings, and our present determinations and concerns inexorably impinge on our historical reflection, perhaps we can join in spirit the Chinese historians in their excavation of a practical and usable past.

CHAPTER 1

The Age of Confucius

The Genesis of History

> The Grand *Shi* wrote in his records: "Cui Zhu assassinated his ruler." Cui
> Zhu had him killed. The Grand *Shi*'s younger brother succeeded to the post
> and wrote the same thing. He too was killed, as was another brother. When a
> fourth brother came forward to write, Cui Zhu finally desisted.
>
> Meanwhile, when the *Shi* living south of the city heard that the Grand
> *Shi* had been killed, he took up his bamboo tablets and set out for the court.
> Only when he learned that the fact had been recorded did he turn back.
> (Watson 1989, 147, modified transliteration)[1]

This dramatic, death-defying devotion to duty took place in 548 B.C.E.
and was recorded in the *Zuo Commentary* (*Zuozhuan*), a historical text
from the early Warring States period (475–221 B.C.E.). The *Zuo Commentary* tells us that Cui Zhu was a ruthless, ambitious minister in the
powerful state of Qi, which occupied a substantial part of North China
Plain during the Zhou dynasty (1066–256 B.C.E.). He murdered the ruler
of the state and replaced him, but gathered all power to himself. In other
words he engineered a bloody coup d'état. Though successful, Cui's perfidious behavior did not escape the attention of the *shi*, who, apparently
undaunted by the prospect of execution, insisted on "telling it like it is," to
use today's journalistic parlance. The incident, although coolly described
in the matter-of-fact language of the *Zuo Commentary*, nonetheless conveys
a profound and moving moral message—the ultimate triumph of the *shi*'s
dedication to his responsibility, which was to record the truth regardless
of personal cost. Who were these *shi* who persisted in recording a truthful
account of events?

The Origin of the *Shi*

In modern Chinese, the character *shi* means history. But in ancient China,
it referred to an official title held by a certain group of people, often from
the same family. We may properly call them historians, or scribes, to the

---

1. In quotations from other scholars, we have altered the transliterations of names to accord
with usage in this book.

extent that what they did was to enter data and keep records. However, neither historian nor scribe describes the full responsibilities borne by the *shi* in ancient China. Indeed, the meaning of the character *shi* has changed over time, from denoting an official title to embodying an abstraction (*Shixueshi* 1983, 111; Jin [1944] 2000, 29–31; Qu 1999b, 2–7). What caused this change? What were the origins of the *shi* and how did their duties and charges evolve over time?

As some scholars have noted (S. Wang 1997, 211–214; Inaba 1999, 30–31), the *shi*, or *gushi* (literally, blind historian), had existed even before writing was invented in China. Because of their exceptional memory, the *shi* took responsibility for remembering important events, and in the process recast and recited them in stories and poems. This image of the *shi* we may appropriately associate with that of Homer, the blind poet from ancient Greece who told and retold momentous events of the past. Once writing was invented, however, *shi* became an official position open to literate people with suitable talents and abilities. Interestingly enough, according to some sources, Zuo Qiuming, the alleged author of the *Zuo Commentary* and the *Discourses on the State* (*Guoyu*), was blind (*Shiji* 1988, 945). Zuo probably lived in the Spring and Autumn period (770–476 B.C.E.), a time when the office of the *shi* had become common. As the *shi* multiplied in number, a division of labor emerged. Most extant records show that in ancient China, *shi* was rarely a position held by only one person. Rather, it was a hereditary title retained in a family; once it was conferred, it could be passed on to junior members of the family and offspring. By the time this happened, the *shi* were probably members of the noble class (Li 1953, 5). However, whether or not the *shi* enjoyed a high status in the aristocracy of ancient China remains an open question. Nevertheless, the position remained hereditary well into the Han dynasty (206 B.C.E.–C.E. 222) and constituted an important part of government bureaucracy. Since a *shi* received his appointment not by virtue of military accomplishments but because of literacy and intellectual expertise, some modern Chinese scholars such as Liu Shipei (1884–1919), an influential intellectual in the early twentieth century, have argued that the *shi* were responsible for all scholarly activities in ancient China (T. Chen 1993, 7). Such a claim, exaggerated though it may sound, does seem to have corroboration in history. When the early Han dynasty recruited historians, the government required that the candidates know a minimum of 9,000 characters, a test that many college students in today's China would probably flunk (*Hanshu* 1962, 1721).

The number of *shi* began to burgeon in the Western Zhou period (1100–771 B.C.E.), a formative stage of Chinese civilization when an increasingly sophisticated literary culture came to be forged. Historical documents from this period show that the numbers of *shi* proliferated, reaching as many as a hundred. Most of their titles were distinguished by a prefix, such as *zuoshi* (left historian), *youshi* (right historian), *taishi* (grand historian), *dashi* (great historian), *xiaoshi* (small historian), *yushi* (court historian), and so on.[2] These prefixes, however, do not tell us much about their specific duties. For instance, we are unsure whether the *zuoshi* was responsible for recording the words and the *youshi* the deeds, or vice versa, because both were documented in early texts.[3] Although their responsibilities varied, the *shi* seemed to share a strong commitment to their primary assignment, the straightforward recording of what happened, regardless of political and personal risks. Their most important duty was to record the words and deeds of the king. "When the Prince had any fault," as an ancient source stipulated, "it was the duty of the historian to record it. . . . If he failed to record these faults, he was guilty of death" (Watson 1958, 73).

Perhaps because of the *shi*'s reputed dedication to his job, there were etymological explanations of the character *shi*, based on his exemplary, virtuous role. In the *Shuowen jiezi*, an etymological dictionary composed by Xu Shen (58?–147?) of the Han dynasty, for instance, we find that the word *shi* refers not only to a scribe but also to the idea of impartiality (*zhong*) that his work supposedly represents. Because the *Shuowen jiezi* was accepted as the authoritative lexicon that encapsulated Han scholarship on ancient culture, Xu's explanation stood largely unchallenged until the seventeenth and eighteenth centuries when there was a strong scholarly interest in studying ancient classical culture, especially the classical and historical texts. What came to be known as "evidential scholarship" (*kaozheng xue*), the dominant mode of learning of the time, combined the use of philology, phonetics, and history to establish the exact meanings of ancient texts. Some scholars began to dispute Xu Shen's etymology of the word *shi*. Jiang Yong (1681–1762), for example, argued that the meaning of *shi* was associated more with the recording tools the scribes used than with the idea of impartiality. Wu Dacheng (1835–1902), a scholar from the late Qing period, supported Jiang's proposition in his critical annotation of the *Shuowen jiezi*. Having found many appearances of the graph *shi* in the bronze inscriptions of the Shang period (1600–1100 B.C.E.), which preceded the Western Zhou, Wu believed that the character *zhong* (the seman-

---

2. Jin Yufu ([1944] 2000, 16–22) provides a table that lists more than thirty titles of historians found in ancient texts. Liu Jie (1982, 28–32) modifies the table with some additions. More recent studies show that in the oracle-bone inscriptions, *shi* has more than seventy different titles (T. Chen 1993, 5–6). Adding those in the bronze inscriptions, the number could be well over a hundred (W. Du 1993, 41–42). The best description of the *shi* in English appears in Hsu Cho-yun and Katheryn Linduff (1988, 244–247).

3. The "Yuzao" chapter of the *Classic of Rites* states that left historians recorded deeds and right historians recorded words (*Liji* 1993, 271). However, Ban Gu's *Hanshu* (Han history) states the opposite: the left historian recorded the words and right historian the deeds (Watson 1958, 73). Scholars of later times, such as Huang Yizhou of the Qing dynasty, pursued this matter with detailed study. Huang agreed with Ban Gu; in addition he pointed out that the left historian was also called *neishi* (inside historian) and the right historian was called *waishi* (outside historian); the former was responsible for drafting edicts and decrees for the king and the latter for recording important events and extraordinary natural phenomena (Cang and Wei 1983, 8–9).

tic basis of the character *shi*) symbolized the bamboo strips onto which the scribes put their writings.

Wu's study anticipated a new trend of classical study in the early twentieth century, as scholars extended their study from written texts to historical artifacts, especially the Shang oracle bones. Naturally, attempts were made to search for the original meanings of *shi* in the oracular inscriptions. Luo Zhenyu (1866–1940) and Wang Guowei (1877–1927), two prominent scholars of the oracle-bone script, provided new supporting evidence for Wu Dacheng by stating that the *shi* was an ancient bookkeeper. Wang Guowei (1997) ventured a more specific theory, claiming that the *shi* played specific ritualistic roles in royal ceremonies. Around the same time, Naitō Konan (also called Naitō Torajirō), an esteemed Japanese sinologist well known, inter alia, for his comprehensive study of the Chinese historiographical traditions, endorsed Luo's and Wang's research while offering his own interpretation. Together with Wang, Naitō noted the *shi*'s role on ceremonial occasions. He contended that in ancient times, military affairs tended to be more important than civil ones, and he believed that the *shi*'s initial assignment involved tallying the number of arrows shot at a ceremony. Thus in one way or another Luo, Wang, and Naitō suggested that a *shi* was a scribe responsible for administering protocols on important ceremonial occasions. Both Naitō (1949, 3–7), as well as Jin Yufu ([1944] 2000, 12), the author of the first complete survey of Chinese historiography in twentieth-century China, explicitly stated that Xu Shen's association of the character *shi* with the abstract idea of impartiality was not entirely convincing.

Naitō's observation about the importance of military affairs in ancient times is an interesting one. Etymologically speaking, the character *zhi* (knowledge)—a word and idea often associated with the work of the historian—consists of the characters of "arrow" and "mouth." The mouth component on the right indicates the pronunciation of the word, which is common in the construction of Chinese characters, and the arrow on the left suggests its meaning, which can mean "casting" and "directionality" (Hall & Ames 1987, 50). If the notion of knowledge is derived from the figurative trope of archery, it is reasonable to surmise that the *shi*, scribe/historian, often the most knowledgeable person in ancient society, would be responsible for tallying the shooting of arrows. In recent years Chinese and Japanese scholars have continued the etymological research on the character *shi*, although their findings are not radically different from those of their predecessors in the early twentieth century.[4] If the *shi* was a scribe appointed to administer and assist in state and religious ceremonies, it ex-

---

4. While these scholars offer different interpretations of the character *shi*, they all seem to place the *shi* at the scene of ceremonial occasions. Chen Tongsheng (1993, 3–4) discusses briefly some of the more recent interpretations of the word *shi*, whereas Inaba Ichirō (1999, 32–33) includes the new research done by Japanese scholars, and Hsu Cho-yun and Katheryn Linduff (1988, 244–247) do the same for Western scholarship on the subject.

plains the variety of its titles, for these ceremonies often followed complicated procedures, involving divinatory inquiries, sacrificial rituals, omen
interpretations, as well as entering records and bookkeeping.

These ceremonies required not only the presence of scribes/histori-
ans, but also the service of the *zhu* (priests), the *wu* (shamans) and, a bit
later on, the *ru* (masters of ritual dances and music, who were the proto-
Confucians). With their participation, the ceremonies involved invoca-
tions, incantations, prayers, as well as ritual dances and music. Shamanism
was indeed prevalent in ancient Chinese culture and society; ancient rulers
were perhaps shamans who practiced divination and made prognostica-
tions pertaining to governance, as evidenced by the oracle-bone inscriptions (K. Chang 1984, 46–47). These ancient kings with shamanic power
were aided by assistants, most of whom were *zhu*, who made up the core of
the priestly class at the time (Maspéro 1978, 112). There is evidence that
the Duke of Zhou (?–1094 B.C.E.), the peerless paragon of a selfless and
virtuous official who inspired Confucius (551–479 B.C.E.), served as the
dazhu (great shaman) (Ching 1997, 10–11, 16–17).

Shamanism was not a uniquely Chinese phenomenon; it was common
in ancient religious lives everywhere (Ching 1997, 14). What is of interest to
us is how shamanistic religious life was related to the emergence of historical consciousness in ancient China. In tracing the origin of the *shi*, many
scholars have found that in early texts, the *shi*, *wu*, and *zhu* worked side
by side in religious ceremonies, performing similar duties. In the *Classic
of Changes* (*Yijing*), for instance, the role of the *wu* and *shi* were indistinguishable with regard to the process of divinatory inquiries (Jie Liu 1982,
32–33). The *Zuo Commentary* mentioned the *zhu* and *shi* many times—such
as in Xianggong 27th year, Zhaogong 17th year, 18th year, 20th year, and
26th year—in the same breath and context for their ability of invocation
and recitation (*Zuozhuan* 1993, 524, 574, 576, 580, and 593). In addition,
there were instances in which the *shi* independently conducted divination
and interpreted its result for the prince (Watson 1989, 210). A more powerful testimony came from Sima Qian (145–87 B.C.E.), arguably the most
famous *shi* in early China, who will figure prominently in the next chapter.
While describing the duties his ancestors carried out at the court, Sima
Qian professed that what they did was something "close to the work of diviners and priests" (*Hanshu* 1962, 2732).

Even though the *shi* played roles similar to those of the priests and
shamans in religious affairs, their primary duty, as shown in the bronze
inscriptions of the Western Zhou period, was to record important events
(Hsu & Linduff 1988, 246). One inscription describes an occasion on which
a person named Song received his appointment from the king to be the
official in charge of various warehouses:

> It was the third year, fifth month, after the dying brightness, *jiaxu* (day 11);
> the king was at the Zhao (Temple) of the Kang Palace. At dawn the king
> entered the Great Chamber and assumed position. Intendant (*zai*) Yin to the

right of Song entered the gate and stood in the center of the court. Yinshi
received the king's command document. The king called out to Scribe (*shi*)
Guo Sheng to record the command to Song . . . . (Shaughnessy 1997, 3–4)

Important events included official investitures, as well as military campaigns, even disastrous ones. In another bronze inscription we see that
the king attended a hearing about a mutiny among his troops and asked
the *shi* to document it (ibid., 5). These inscriptions corroborate similar
references in written documents. The *Classic of Documents* (*Shangshu*) recorded instances where the *shi* were put in charge of preparing the texts
for prayers, holding documents, and composing announcements for various state and religious functions (ibid., 5–6). The image of the *shi* holding
documents on those occasions provides, some have argued, an etymological clue to the original meaning of *shi* (G. Wang 1997; Naitō 1949, 5–7).
The bronze inscriptions and the *Classic of Documents,* the earliest written
document in China, clearly showed that the *shi* were responsible for keeping records, although their responsibilities seem to have entailed multiple
functions at the royal court, a phenomenon that began in the Western
Zhou period and continued through the Han dynasty (Zongtong Li 1953,
3–4). Indeed, as part and parcel of the growing literate and civil cultures,
the *shi* had become "ubiquitous; everything done at court was now put in
writing: the investitures themselves, of course (copies of which were both
given to the investee and also apparently stored in the royal archives), but
also verdicts in legal cases, maps, and so forth" (Loewe & Shaughnessy
1999, 326). When Confucius passionately registered his admiration for the
cultural accomplishments of the Zhou—"The Zhou, as compared with the
two previous dynasties—how magnificent is its culture! I follow the Zhou"
(*Analects* 1997, 62)—he was paying tribute to a culture whose development
owed much to the instrumental roles played by the *shi*. Similarly, when the
late Herrlee Creel made the keen observation that "we simply have to accept the fact that the Chous were a people who liked to write books" (1937,
255), he paid homage to the work of the *shi*.

It is quite understandable that Confucius extolled the literary culture
of the Western Zhou. As the *shi* worked with the *zhu* and *wu* in state and religious ceremonies, they also came to be connected with the *ru,* or the proto-
Confucians, with whom Confucius was identified. According to Liu Xin (46
B.C.E.?–C.E. 23) in the Han, the origin of the *ru* could be traced to a government position. In the early twentieth century there was great interest
in identifying more specifically what this position was prior to Confucius'
time. Hu Shi (1891–1962), for example, examined the social origins of the
ru. He and his critics debated whether the *ru* constituted a social class, as in
the case of the *wu* and the *zhu,* who possessed special knowledge in ritual
ceremonies and skills in ceremonial dances and music (Eno 1990, 190–
191; Yao 2000, 18–19). Since the *ru*'s primary duty was the custodianship
of the rites of ceremonies and the performance of ritualistic dances, they
must have worked along with the *wu,* the *zhu,* and the *shi*. One important

ceremony was the ritual of rainmaking, which was of course "very central to an agricultural society dependent on natural beneficence" so that "the best-known dances are those devoted to rain-making" (Ching 1997, 18–19). While the principal figure in the rainmaking process was the shaman, recent etymological studies of the character *ru* ("cloud" above "sky") also place *ru* at the scene, suggesting their similarly important ritualistic role (Yao 2000, 19–20). The *ru* responsible for praying for natural beneficence were no doubt aided by the *shi*. The *shi* were ubiquitous and indispensable in court activities because they boasted knowledge in astrology, which enabled them to provide crucial assistance in and information on divinatory inquiries. They explained celestial phenomena, interpreted omens, offered prophecies, and, most important, designed calendars according to the movement of heavenly bodies. According to the "Yueling" chapter in the *Classic of Rites*, for instance, the king, on the advice of the *dashi* (great historian), who kept track of the movements of the sun, moon, and stars, held a ceremony to mark the arrival of spring (*Liji* 1993, 241). The *Zuo Commentary* (*Zuozhuan* 1993, 428, 601) mentions the *shi*'s prophecies of political misfortunes, based on their observations of irregular movements of the stars and planets. Since the *shi* were responsible for recording what took place in the surrounding world, including celestial phenomena, it was not surprising that they developed knowledge of astrology. Some scholars have even suggested translating *shi* as "astrologer," besides "scribe" and "historian" (Bauer 1976, 73; T. Chen 1993, 5–14; Cang & Wei 1983, 10–11). The *shi*'s responsibilities definitely included overseeing the movements of heavenly bodies, and compiling and maintaining an accurate calendrical system. This obligation remained unchanged through the early Han dynasty, when Sima Qian continued his family tradition by becoming *taishiling* (grand historian), whose title is more felicitously translated as the grand astrologer, according to a recent monograph on Sima (Hardy 1999, xi, 18).

The Emergence of History

While the *shi* played religious and ritualistic roles similar to those of priests and shamans, they also assumed a civil position as official scribes and historians of the court (Hsu & Linduff 1988, 244–247). This dual responsibility meant that the *shi* recorded not only significant human events but also extraordinary occurrences in nature. During the Shang and Western Zhou periods, there was not yet a keen awareness of the necessity to distinguish such events as happenings in two different and separate spheres of existence. So there are equally compelling reasons to translate *shi* as either astrologer or historian (Han 1955, 2–3; Schwartz 1985, 353). The *shi* operated within the world view of the Shang and Zhou, which saw the universe in holistic and correlative terms. To the extent that all things and affairs in the universe corresponded with one another, the ruler and the human political realm intimately followed and interacted with the cosmic order.

When assessing the role of the *shi* in the origin of Chinese historiography, it therefore behooves us to bear in mind the cosmological views and beliefs that guided their work. The multifarious responsibilities they bore were a very function and reflection of the organic integration of Heaven, earth, and humanity. The *shi*'s religious duties demanded knowledge of astrology and cosmology, through which they sought to understand the cosmos and interpret the omens and portents that were construed as messages to the human world. On the other hand, as court historians the *shi* prepared documents and preserved archives crucial for the efficient and effective operation of the central government, most notably the imperial edicts and ordinances. There was scarcely the need to distinguish the *shi*'s work as an astrologer from his endeavor as a historian.

In the *Classic of Documents*, the first classical anthology that collected examples of the *shi*'s work from the Western Zhou and earlier periods, there is much evidence of the fundamental idea that nature and humanity are inextricably related. Nature, as represented by Heaven (*tian*), is the cosmos that is totally integrated with human beings (*ren*) on earth, thereby forging an intimate Heaven-humanity relation (*tianren guanxi*). In this relationship Heaven is the superior entity whose agency and mandate are manifested in various natural phenomena that have a direct bearing on the lives of human beings. As a result, it is imperative for humanity to observe these phenomena, interpret their meanings, and detect Heaven's will. They must abide by the Mandate of Heaven (*tianming*). In the "Pan'geng" chapter of the *Classic of Documents*, for instance, King Pan'geng of the Shang is said to have moved the capital five times so as to follow the Mandate of Heaven revealed by oracle bones. In the "Tangshi" and "Taishi" chapters, frequently quoted by Chinese scholars in the past to explain the Shang's succession to the Xia (c. 2205–1600 B.C.E.) and the Zhou's succession to the Shang, possession of the Mandate of Heaven became the major validation of the legitimacy of rulership; lack of the Mandate provided justification for challenging a regime's authority (*Shangshu* 1993, 120; 123–124; 126–127). In the "Dagao" chapter, it is Heaven who supposedly supported the young King Cheng of the Western Zhou, with the assistance of the Duke of Zhou, in his precarious campaign against his rebellious and powerful uncles, despite the warnings of his senior advisors. King Cheng divined the Mandate of Heaven by means of the oracular turtle shell, and in its name he rebuked his uncommitted ministers:

> Stop! I the young son do not dare to disregard the command of the Lord on High, Heaven was beneficent to King Wen, raising up our little country of Zhou, and it was turtle-shell divination that King Wen used, succeeding to receive this mandate. Now Heaven will be helping the people; how much more so should it be turtle-shell divination that I too use. *Wuhu!* Heaven is brightly awesome—it helps our grand foundation. (Loewe & Shaughnessy 1999, 314)

Significantly, King Cheng not only used the Mandate of Heaven, received via turtle-shell divination, to justify his campaign and rally his people, but he also appealed to historical precedent to buttress his call to action. Interpretation of history thus complemented divination of the will of Heaven, an important conjunction discussed below. Suffice it to say here, this conflation of the historical and the divine constituted the core of the correlative world view—as the correspondence between the world of human events and the world of nature came to be firmly established, the world of nature was increasingly construed in anthropomorphic terms.

This correlative mode of thinking pervaded the ancient Chinese perception of their world, shaping cosmology in the most foundational way. In the words of John Henderson, "[c]orrelative thought is the most basic ingredient of Chinese cosmology," which "draws systematic correspondences among aspects of various orders of reality or realms of the cosmos, such as the human body, the body politic, and the heavenly bodies" (Henderson 1984, 1). In the *Classic of Odes* (*Shijing*), an ancient classic from the Western Zhou period, many poems acknowledge the correspondence between human misfortunes and natural dislocations. In describing a devastating drought, for example, the poem "Yunhan" registers the sadness.

> The drought has become so severe,
> That it cannot be stopped.
> Glowing and burning,
> We have no place.
> The great mandate is about at an end,
> Nothing to look ahead to or back upon.
> The host of dukes and past rulers
> Does not help us;
> As for father and mother and the ancestors,
> How can they bear to treat us so? (Loewe & Shaughnessy 1999, 336)

In what way was this correlative mode of thought related to the historical consciousness in ancient China? We have noted that King Cheng's interpretation of the Mandate of Heaven employed historical precedents to bolster his argument, which suggests that he might have been reminded of historical examples by some of his court historians. By the middle part of the Western Zhou period, court scribes and historians appeared to have greatly expanded their role in the sociopolitical arena. Many of them might have actually composed those elegiac poems in the *Classic of Odes* that underscored the correlative idea (Inaba 1999, 30). The authors of these songs came from the corps of scribes (*shi*), who "moved from singing about the rituals to the ancestors to singing about the deeds of the ancestors themselves" (Loewe & Shaughnessy 1999, 333). In singing about ancestral deeds, that is, happenings of the past, the historians-*cum*-scribes also promoted and disseminated the anthropocosmic idea of the interaction and correspondence between Heaven and humanity, examples of which abound in their writings (Schwartz 1985, 352–353).

By the middle period of the Western Zhou dynasty, the *shi* had expanded their role at the court, not only playing a religious role by singing ritual songs dedicated to the ancestors, but also assuming a more secular role by singing songs about the actions and affairs of the ancestors. How this transition took place is still an open question. There are doubts about whether there was a direct connection between the prevalent religious and shamanic practices in the Shang and the early Zhou periods, on the one hand, and the formation of the correlative mode of thinking evident from the mid-Zhou onward. Drawing on Lévi-Strauss, for instance, Benjamin Schwartz (1985, 351–352) argues that in religious rituals where divinatory inquiries are made, the human and the supernatural force themselves into consciousness as two separate domains, whereas in the idea of correlation, the cosmos is perceived and presented as an organic whole. Yet Schwartz also acknowledges that the doctrine of the Mandate of Heaven—a doctrine that is pervasive in both the *Classic of Documents* and the *Classic of Odes,* two anthologies attributed to the *shi*— is crucial in creatively and organically linking the spheres of the divine and the human.

As China's earliest written documents, the authenticity and authorship of these two works have attracted much interest over the centuries. Conventional wisdom holds that while many people contributed to these anthologies, it was Confucius who edited them and made them what they were. "In the time of Confucius," wrote Sima Qian, "the House of Zhou had declined and the rites and music had fallen into neglect. The *Classic of Odes* and the *Classic of Documents* had become defective." Then Confucius arranged the records and classified the events in the *Classic of Documents.* He also "played on the zither and sang the three hundred and five pieces [that comprise the present *Classic of Odes*]" (Feng 1952, I, 44, modified transliteration). Here Confucius is perceived as someone doing the principal work of the *shi:* preserving historical records. Given the parallel roles played by the *shi* and the *ru* in religious ceremonies in early China, this ought not be surprising. What concerns us is the way Confucius carried out this job of editing and reorganization. From conventional sources we know that Confucius, in compiling these anthologies, sought to celebrate and glorify the literary culture of the Western Zhou, which he ardently admired and desired to revive. In editing and arranging the records of the *Classic of Documents,* for instance, he paid great attention to those that would transmit the rites of antiquity, particularly the ritual culture of the Zhou. In compiling the *Classic of Odes,* Confucius was said to have expunged duplications and undesirable elements, retaining only those poems and songs that exemplified the rites and norms of ancient times (ibid). In the *Analects* (*Lunyu*), Confucius claimed that even though the *Classic of Odes* consisted of 300 pieces, they "may be covered in one phrase: 'without deviating' " (*Analects* 1997, 52), that is, they do not deviate from the constant and universal ideals of antiquity. In other words Confucius both relied on the extant literary culture established and preserved by the *shi* and assumed the role of the *shi* in reorganizing, modifying, and synthesizing this culture.

If Confucius was a cultural transmitter, what he transmitted was by and large the work of the *shi*, which, in the main, he viewed favorably. In the *Analects* there are indeed many references to the *shi*. However, in this well-known passage Confucius commented on their work rather critically:

> When simplicity (*zhi*) surpasses refinement (*wen*), one is a rustic (*ye*); when refinement surpasses simplicity, one is a scribe (*shi*). Only when refinement and simplicity are well blended can one become a gentleman. (*Analects* 1997, 83)

Here Confucius was not entirely satisfied with the work of the *shi*, who he thought valued refinement over simplicity. What perturbed him was apparently the overly literary quality of the *shi*'s work, with its finicky and ornate embellishment of human accomplishments. This problem might well have stemmed from their ritualistic role in religious ceremonies, sacrifices, and festivals, for the *shi* had to prepare the prayers, design the divinatory inquiries, and announce the results. It is certainly plausible that the *shi* might have to resort to euphemistic subterfuge and pedantic disquisition. By contrast, Confucius was intent on upholding the integrity of history by using simple and direct language to record the past. In the *Analects*, whenever Confucius praised the work of a *shi*, he was usually referring to his loyalty to the principles bequeathed by the past, regardless of changes in the surrounding circumstances. He admired a *shi* named Yu because Yu was "straight" (*zhi*) as an arrow: "When the state possessed the Way, he was like an arrow; when the state lost the Way, he was still like an arrow" (*Analects* 1997, 153). To be straight means to adhere to the principle, moral or political, to which the *shi* must subscribe. In Confucius' own historical practice, that is, the compilation of the *Classic of Documents* and the *Classic of Odes*, he selected or discarded materials so as to uphold incontrovertible political and cultural principles. Nonetheless, Confucius was much concerned with using adequate sources, as evidenced by this well-known statement:

> The rituals of the Xia, I can discourse on them. I went to Qi, but they could not provide enough evidence. The rituals of the Yin, I can discourse on them. I went to Song, but they could not provide enough evidence, either. That is because they did not have enough literature and worthy men left. If they did, I would be able to prove it. (*Analects* 1997, 61)

Apparently, even though Confucius was self-consciously and deliberately selective with his materials, he lamented their paucity. As a consequence he was deeply appreciative of the fact that the Zhou was replete with literary culture. To him, sources were the basic building blocks of all compilations of records of the past. It is also important to note that while

Confucius was no doubt concerned about the veneer of superficial literary refinement in the work of the *shi*, he did not go so far as to reject it. He clearly preferred "simplicity." But what was paramount to him was maintaining balance between the two approaches: judicious proportioning of literary refinement and unvarnished description of the past. A dialogue between Zi Gong, one of Confucius' disciples, and Ji Zicheng, illustrates the master's position. Ji Zicheng pronounced, "What the gentleman needs is simplicity; that is all. What does he need refinement for?" Zi Gong disagreed. "Refinement is as important as simplicity; simplicity is as important as refinement" (*Analects* 1997, 127). Zi Gong's answer reflected the teachings he received from Confucius, which avowedly comprised refinement/culture (*wen*), moral conduct, wholehearted sincerity, and truthfulness (ibid., 91).

Confucius built his cultural enterprise on the literary culture preserved by the *shi*, which was also to a great extent the cultural legacy that he inherited from the tradition of the *ru*. But he was also critical of some aspects of the *shi* culture. What then did he actually do to reformulate and enrich it? To answer this question, we should look again at the correlative conception of Heaven and humanity as a continuum and organic whole, paying attention to its role in shaping ideas about history and writing about the past in early China. In accordance with correlative cosmology, the ancient Chinese subscribed to a correspondence between the heavenly bodies, the human body, and the body politic, which ultimately yielded the idea of the Mandate of Heaven. As shown in the *Classic of Documents*, a ruler such as King Cheng, aided by the ingenious and resourceful Duke of Zhou, uses this Heaven-humanity correlation to his political advantage, staking his political fortune on the fact of his receiving the Mandate of Heaven, just as his worthy predecessors once had. The Mandate of Heaven is no longer an abstract and arbitrary idea stemming from a transcendent sphere beyond the reach of humans. Rather, Heaven is an active and intimate being who bestows a concrete blessing upon the Zhou people to reward their good deeds, especially those of their great leader King Wen. The bestowal of the Mandate of Heaven corresponds with the good behavior of the Zhou state and its people; it also corresponds with the bad deeds of the Shang state and its people. It verifies, validates, and corroborates the development of human history. In the *Classic of Odes* a poem entitled "The Mandate of Heaven" offers a clear illustration:

> The Mandate of Heaven,
> How beautiful and unceasing!
> Oh, how glorious
> Was the purity of King Wen's virtue!
> With blessings he overwhelms us.
> We will receive the blessings.
> They are a great favor from our King Wen.
> May his descendants hold fast to them. (W. Chan 1963, 6)

Just as the Zhou people earned the Mandate of Heaven because of their virtuous behavior, so the people of the Shang lost it because of their misdeeds, personified by their wicked last ruler, King Zhou.

There was, however, no assurance that the victorious and favored Zhou would not someday fall in the same way the Shang had; they might lose Heaven's sanction of their rule as a result of degeneration and corruption. "Heaven's Mandate is not constant," warned another poem. The Duke of Zhou, who once acted as the regent for the young King Cheng, was clearly aware of this and cautioned the king, "I dare not say with certainty that our heritage will forever truly remain on the side of fortune." He offered the advice that the Zhou must follow the great example of King Wen, who first brought the Mandate of Heaven to the Zhou people: "My way is simply to continue and extend the virtue of our peace-establishing king, and Heaven will not have occasion to remove the mandate received by King Wen." The Duke of Zhou made it abundantly clear that those who eventually lost the Mandate of Heaven were those who "could not practice and carry on the reverence and the brilliant virtue of their forefathers" (W. Chan 1963, 6–7). Here, into the theory of the Mandate of Heaven, the Duke of Zhou had inserted history and thus human agency—a harking back to and continuation of the virtuous deeds of the ancestors. From that which lay above and beyond the human pale, Heaven, he brought political and social legitimacy down to earth. Human future was concrete and malleable, and its control began with ancestor worship, where specific personages were identified (Pines 2002, 55–88).

What the Duke of Zhou did here might well reflect his cunning strategy for protecting his political stakes in the Zhou court (Shaughnessy 1997, 101–125). But this shift of attention from Heaven to ancestors marked a crucial turn in the course of intellectual development in ancient China, and accounted for the emergence and development of historical practice in the Western Zhou. Within the continuum of Heaven-humanity, Heaven admittedly occupied the superior position; it was the source of the Mandate after all. But Heaven was invariably mirrored in the behavior of the people, as the cosmic corresponded with the human. Because one could observe this correspondence only teleologically—recognizing the correspondence only in hindsight—one was naturally led to the worship of one's ancestors for they had experienced and realized Heaven's Mandate once before. In the documents from the period, we find complaints about not knowing whether Heaven will bless the people of Zhou the way it has blessed their forefathers. An inscription on the bronze vessel named Mao Gong Ding records such a complaint from King Xuan (r. 827–782 B.C.E.):

And so august Heaven unstintingly stood by us, watching over and protecting the Zhou. There was no danger that the former kings would prove unworthy of the mandate. [But now] pitiless Heaven rises awesome, and if I, a small child succeeding [to the throne] am inadequate, how shall the state be blessed? (Eno 1990, 25, modified transliteration)

Even a being as powerful as the king was unsure about his relationship with Heaven. It is small wonder then that ancestor worship appealed to the Zhou people. In this form of ancestor worship, to borrow the words of Grant Hardy, "the dead were conceived of as acting in the present, and the sense of their presence was given concrete form by the use of impersonators who took their places at the ritual feasts and sacrifices of a clan" (1999, 5). Here we may recall the reference to King Wen by King Cheng as well as the Duke of Zhou in their divination and interpretation of the Mandate of Heaven. This growing interest in appealing to the ancestors meant that the *shi* would have to change from singing about the rituals devoted *to* the ancestors to singing about the deeds *of* the ancestors (Loewe & Shaughnessy 1999, 333). In this crucial way, ancestor worship contributed to the rise of the study and practice of history in the Western Zhou. Inheriting the testaments from ancestors meant recording, preserving, and constructing the past. Not surprisingly, then, this period witnessed a proliferation of official historian positions, with the appearance of the grand historian and great historian, not to mention the left historian and right historian, and many other scribal-historical titles (Jin [1944] 2000, 16–23; Naitō 1949, 8–30). The first protohistorical text, the *Classic of Documents*, also came into being. In it the *shi* entered records and offered accounts of the accomplishments, together with the trials and tribulations, of the Zhou people, as well as those of their neighbors and predecessors.

Because Confucius deemed himself a transmitter of the Zhou legacy, he continued the honored tradition of recording and memorializing human deeds of the past. In the process he ushered in what some scholars have pointedly described as a significant intellectual development—the "rise of rationalism" or the "growth of humanism" in the ancient Chinese world view (Feng 1952, 30–42; W. Chan 1963, 3–48). In Confucius' own writings, he frequently referred to the Mandate of Heaven. His praise for the feats of Yao, an ancient sage-king, for example, bore remarkable resemblance to the admiration expressed by the Zhou people for their King Wen. "How great was Yao as sovereign!" Confucius exclaimed, "How lofty! Heaven alone is greatest! Yao alone could imitate it! How boundless! The people could hardly find words to praise him! How lofty were his achievements! How brilliant his cultural institutions!" (*Analects* 1997, 99). His equating Yao with Heaven suggests that he firmly subscribed to the correlative cosmology. As had the Duke of Zhou, Confucius also saw the realization of the Mandate of Heaven in the good deeds of human beings. But as Wing-tsit Chan points out, for Confucius, "Heaven is no longer the greatest of all spiritual beings who rules in a personal manner but a Supreme Being who only reigns, leaving his Moral Law to operate by itself" (1963, 16). In other words, Confucius added something new to the legacy and tradition inherited from the Zhou. Heaven, a supreme being who granted and withdrew fortune from humanity, no longer appeared as uncertain and unpredictable as it had been. Heaven could be readily understood and apprehended by morally cultivated people such as Confucius himself. In a frequently quoted autobiographical statement, he claimed the following:

> At fifteen, I bent my mind on learning; at thirty, I was established; at forty, I was free from delusion; at fifty, I knew the decree [Mandate] of Heaven; at sixty, my ears became subtly perceptive; at seventy, I was able to follow my heart's desire without overstepping the rules of propriety. (*Analects* 1997, 52)

Not only did Confucius believe that he knew the Mandate of Heaven, he also hinted that he possessed it. When pursued by Huan Tui, a military minister of the state of Song, Confucius boldly asked, "Since Heaven has endowed me with moral force, what can Huan Tui do to me?" (*Analects* 1997, 91) When he was entrapped in another predicament, besieged in Kuang, Confucius confidently proclaimed:

> King Wen being dead, is culture not lodged here? If Heaven had intended to exterminate this culture, I, a subsequent mortal, would not have been so involved in this culture. If Heaven does not intend to exterminate this culture, what can the man Kuang do to me? (*Analects* 1997,102)

Here he was explicit about the role Heaven entrusted to him — to transmit the culture of the Zhou.

How Confucius came to endow himself with such a mission is an interesting but highly complex question, and one that lies outside the purview of this study. For our purposes, what is important to note is that compared with his predecessors in the Western Zhou, Confucius, while maintaining his firm belief in the Heaven-humanity correlation, showed more confidence in and placed more emphasis on human agency. For this reason modern scholars have credited him with initiating a humanist turn in ancient Chinese thought (W. Chan 1963, 3–48). Not a few have remarked about the striking fact that "the *Analects* contains so few references to T'ien (Heaven)" (Eno 1990, 96). Of course, Confucius was not unconcerned with or unafraid of Heaven; he was very much so, as the *Analects* reveals. He once stated that a gentleman — the model human being, the *junzi* — ought to hold three things in awe: Heaven, great men, and the sage's words (*Analects* 1997, 163). Significantly however, he juxtaposed Heaven not only with the deeds of great men but also the words of the ancient sages. Viewed in this light, Heaven did not seem to figure as a prominent force in the philosophy of Confucius (Eno 1990, 98). More precisely, it was not that Heaven had become insignificant for Confucius, but that "the Way of Heaven must be cultivated in personal experience and social interchange" (Yao 2000, 154). In short, Heaven was to be comprehended and realized in terms of human deeds and actions.

If Confucius played down Heaven's omnipotent and transcendent role, he did so by emphasizing immanent human agency. Confucius believed that through education one can acquire the ability to know the world, and with this knowledge one can gain knowledge of the Mandate of Heaven, which is inexorably embedded and reflected in human deeds. The idea that Heaven's Mandate was reflected in the behavior of the people was of course an ancient one, but Confucius' emphasis on the rational capacity of humanity to know both itself and Heaven was something new and innovative. When his student Zizhang posed the question — "Ten dynasties hence, are things predictable?" — Confucius responded with this very revealing answer:

> The Yin followed the rituals of the Xia; what has been reduced and augmented is known to us. The Zhou followed the rituals of the Yin; what has been reduced and augmented is known to us. Whoever may succeed the Zhou, even a hundred dynasties hence, things are predictable. (*Analects* 1997, 57)

Here the word "predictable" (*kezhi*) can be translated as "knowable." Confucius' answer is interesting in at least two ways. First, it shows Confucius' tremendous faith in education as he assures his student that if one studies, one can come to know things. Moreover, elsewhere Confucius affirms that study is a joyous and communal pursuit — having schoolfellows with whom to share knowledge and learning is a pleasure (*Analects* 1997, 47). Second, Confucius posits that in order to know the future, "ten dynasties hence," one has to study the past because as time progresses, one adds to and takes from past experiences. The future is invariably mirrored in the past. In a nutshell, Confucius' conviction in the agency of history reinforces his confidence in human agency.

Forms and Ideas of Historiography

There is no better place to examine Confucius' confidence and faith in human agency than his *Spring and Autumn Annals* (*Chunqiu*), one of the Six Classics (*liujing*), which include the *Classic of Odes* (*Shijing*), *Classic of Documents* (*Shangshu*), *Classic of Rites* (*Liji*), *Classic of Changes* (*Yijing*), and the *Classic of Music* (*Yuejing*) that by the third century B.C.E. was no longer extant. The *Spring and Autumn* was the fruit of Confucius' practice of history. For him the actual events that constituted history illustrated the very ideas and ideals he fervently embraced and advanced: "If I wish to set forth my theoretical judgments, nothing is as good as illustrating them through the depth and clarity of actual events" (Watson 1958, 51). This famous pronouncement recalls the equally famous statement made by Dionysius of Halicarnassus (ca. 65–1 B.C.E.) — that history was "philosophy teaching by examples." Confucius not only ascribed pedagogic functions to history, but he also sought in it a sense of cultural belonging. Not long before his time the Western Zhou royal house had fallen, together with the established ritual tradition that Confucius held in awe and of which he, as a member of the *ru* group, had expert knowledge. Although his training as a *ru* did gain him a few government positions, sometimes even high-ranking ones, Confucius never held them for long. He blamed his unsuccessful career on the decline of culture and values of the Zhou. Many states in the Zhou feudal system had become powerful, and they fought among themselves for the title of *ba* (hegemon). As the Zhou royal house became increasingly weak and politically irrelevant, so did the rites and culture developed originally to maintain the system of enfeoffment.

For a long time Confucius kept his faith in the Zhou cultural system, hoping to restore it through moral suasion and intellectual revivification. He earnestly believed that Heaven had ordained him with this mission. To begin with, his approach was historical, insofar as he endeavored to preserve the Zhou rites and culture through education and writing. His work was quite comparable to that of the *shi* in earlier times. One motive behind Confucius' work on the *Spring and Autumn* was his conviction that the *shi* culture had declined steeply in his time, and as a result many historical records had been lost and ancient texts scattered (Jin [1944] 2000, 40). However, unlike the *shi*, Confucius was convinced that the best way to preserve the memory of ancient culture and institutions was not simply to maintain the records, but more importantly to nurture one's moral character, so that one became a gentleman of profound and superior qualities (*junzi*). "If a man is not humane," Confucius asked rhetorically, "what can he do with the rituals? If a man is not humane, what can he do with music?" (*Analects* 1997, 58) The cultivation of moral values in people would lead to restoration of the rites. To Confucius, these moral values included humanity, justice, righteousness, sincerity, filial piety, and truthfulness, but the central virtue was humanity (*ren*). What was humanity? In the *Analects* Confucius gave many definitions, but when asked whether it could be summarized in one single word, he answered, "It is perhaps 'like-hearted considerateness.' What you do not wish for yourself, do not impose on others" (*Analects* 1997, 156). In order to act in such a way, one needed to know both self and other. Learning therefore became an integral component in the teachings of Confucius. Such learning perforce included the knowledge of history, for Confucius believed that knowing the past helped predict what was to come (*Analects* 1997, 50).

But learning itself was not enough. "Learning without thinking," Confucius declared, "is fruitless; thinking without learning is perplexing" (ibid., 55). This certainly recalls his criticism of the work of the *shi*. In other words, although Confucius was engaged in the pursuit and study of history, from which valuable information on the ideal Zhou culture was gathered, he could never be content with being a *shi*, especially at his time when their achievements had significantly deteriorated and their roles considerably diminished. He lamented, "I was in time to see blank spaces in character books [historical records] and horse-owners seeking aid from another to break in a horse. Nowadays, there are no such people" (ibid., 156). The blank spaces he referred to were the places where the *shi* did not enter records because of uncertainty, which indicated to him that the *shi* were no longer as responsible, circumspect, and careful as their predecessors in entering historical records. They stood in sharp contrast to the *shi* of earlier times, such as Yu, who was straight as an arrow and to whom Confucius accordingly paid homage (ibid., 153).

Yet what prompted Confucius to turn to historiography was more than his dissatisfaction with the work of the *shi;* he had also come to the painful realization that he would be unable to fulfill the mission bestowed on him by Heaven—restoring the ritual culture and political order that had reached perfection in the Western Zhou. The last entry of the *Spring and Autumn Annals* recorded that in the spring of the 14th year of Duke Ai, a unicorn was captured in a hunt. When Confucius heard the news, he was greatly saddened, realizing finally that his life mission would be forever thwarted. The *Gongyang Commentary* (*Gongyang zhuan*) on the *Spring and Autumn* that appeared in the Warring States period proffers this explanation:

> Why did Confucius record this? Because he recorded unusual things. Why was this unusual? Because the unicorn is not a beast of the Middle Kingdom. . . . The unicorn is a beast of virtue. When there is a true king, it appears, but when there is no true king, it does not appear. Someone reported that there was a small deer with a horn. Confucius said, "Ah! For whom did it come? For whom did it come?" and, turning back his sleeve, he brushed his face and his tears wet his robe. . . . At the western hunt a unicorn was captured. Confucius said, "My way is ended!" (Watson 1958, 84)

The *Gongyang Commentary* is known for its deep and at times arcane reading of the *Spring and Autumn Annals*. According to its explanation, the capture of the unicorn forced Confucius to realize that he had lost his opportunity to complete his mission in his lifetime; someone else would have to take his place. What he should and could do now was to work on a history, namely, the *Spring and Autumn Annals*, through which he would offer the world and posterity his wisdom and experience. More precisely, since a text called the *Spring and Autumn* already existed, Confucius wanted to "bring the meaning out of the *Spring and Autumn* for a future sage, which is something a gentleman would be pleased to do" (*Gongyang zhuan* 1993, 747). This explanation provided by the *Gongyang Commentary*, a New Script (*jinwen*) classic, which highlights the prognosticatory nature and intent of Confucius' work, has been subject to dispute over the centuries. However, there is evidence in the *Analects* that Confucius did believe in portentous meanings associated with the appearance of certain animals. On an earlier occasion, he had complained about not seeing the phoenix, a divine bird that portended the great tranquility of the empire. "I am done for," he said with a somewhat ironic smile that underscored his disappointment (*Analects* 1997, 103). What he could bear with good humor in his prime years was painfully disappointing in his twilight years. Saddened though he was,

Confucius promptly developed a new sense of his reason for being. He embarked on the project of making available to the world a historical text replete with moral and political meaning. In his treatise on the Confucian school, Sima Qian, the great Han historian, concurred with the explanation given by the *Gongyang Commentary:* "At the western hunt a unicorn was captured. Confucius said, 'My way is ended!' Therefore he used the records of the historians to make the *Spring and Autumn*" (Watson 1958, 85).

For Confucius, "to make" (*zuo*) the *Spring and Autumn* was not a light task; it was a new mission ordained by Heaven. He might be bewildered by and even anguished over a Heaven that was apparently inscrutable, but he never ceased to savor the joy of participating in the Heaven-decreed moral mission entrusted to profound, superior, and noble men, namely, the *junzi* (Schwartz 1985, 127). Confucius fully understood that the accomplishment of Heaven's mission required human agency. Although he himself might no longer be the person who could restore peace and order, he could help prepare the coming of a new age by promoting and cultivating moral values in people. The best way to achieve this goal was to evoke the memories of the past by writing and teaching history, recalling the sagely rulers of yore who had exemplified and personified the cherished values of China. In a word, Confucius' "making" of the *Spring and Autumn* reflected his understanding of his ultimate role in the world—retrieval of the past through history.

In order to understand what Confucius actually accomplished in historiography, it is helpful to look at the characteristics of the *shi*'s historical practice in the Spring and Autumn period. Confucius, as we know, did not create a history out of nothing. Rather, he elaborated and augmented the preexisting *Spring and Autumn,* which was a *shi* work from his native state of Lu. The term "spring and autumn," as the ancient sources suggest, was a very broad one, referring to the historical records of all of the states at the time. But other names also existed, such as *Sheng* for the records in the state of Jin and *Taowu* in the state of Chu, as mentioned by Mencius (372–289 B.C.E.) (S. Wang 1997, 24; Mencius 1970, 327). Nonetheless, it seems that the term "spring and autumn" was the most popular. For instance, Mozi (fl. 479–438 B.C.E.), a philosopher who lived shortly after Confucius, claimed that he had seen the *Spring and Autumn* of hundreds of states (S. Wang 1997, 24). Although many annalistic records are no longer extant, the *Bamboo Annals* (*Zhushu ji'nian*), unearthed in the third century C.E., provides some clues to the general features and structures of these works that were comparable to the *Spring and Autumn*.

Why was the term, "spring and autumn," used to name historical works? The answer lies in the way the *shi* recorded events. Owing to the powerful influence of the correlative world view of Heaven-and-humanity, the *shi* paid close attention to the interrelations between phenomena of both the human and the natural spheres. Their knowledge of astronomy enabled them to make calendars, and in accordance with their astrological and calendrical reckonings, they offered portentous advice to their princes and kings. In the 14th year of Duke Wen in the *Zuo Commentary*, for example, Inside Historian Shufu, upon seeing a comet entering the Plough, predicted that the princes of the Song, Qi, and Jin would all die from internecine insurgencies within seven years (*Zuozhuan* 1993, 428).

The *shi*'s astronomical knowledge not only helped them prognosticate, but also formulate and formalize a sense of time. In designing the calendrical system, they divided, periodized, and even predicted the passage of time by associating it with a numerology based on the number of twelve with regard to the months and the number of four with respect to the seasons. The moon's orbit around the earth resulted in the notion of a month, and the idea of a year arose out of observation of the cyclical succession of the four seasons. The idea of the four seasons was essential to Shang cosmology because it coincided with the Shang's spatial notion of the world, which was characterized by the conception of the *sifang* (four quarters) and their relation with the center (Xueqin Li 1985). In early Chinese cosmography, there was a central notion of *tianyuan difang* (round-shaped heaven and square-shaped earth) that probably originated from the "theory of the covering heaven" (*gaitian shuo*) (Needham 1959, 3:210–216). Heaven was described as a round hat covering the earth, while earth was likened to a dinner plate placed upside down under the heaven. The Sifang idea suggests that this "dinner plate" was not only square-shaped but also had four quarters.

Just as the change of the four seasons helped shape the Shang's spatial notions of their world, so too it enabled the *shi* to organize their records within a temporal framework. A complete cycle of the four seasons gave them the unit of a year, which they subdivided into four seasons and twelve months. The months were added as more events were entered, requiring a more specific sense of time. Seasonal change also served to indicate the beginning of a year. Although the Xia, the Shang, and the Zhou had different beginning months for the new year, they all used the winter solstice as a pivotal point (Loewe & Shaughnessy 1999, 20). In other words, while the first month of a year varied in time, the spring season was always considered the first season. If spring began a year, then autumn marked the midpoint in the cycle of a whole year. Hence, spring and autumn were more instrumental than summer and winter in arranging historical records.

In addition, the *shi*, being appointed officials, developed a sense of civil time that they wove into the calendar. The accession of a king to the throne commonly marked the beginning of a year. In the *Spring and Autumn*, we find that the king always ascended to his position in the beginning of the year, or the spring season; hence the first month of the year, the "correct/upright" month (*zhengyue*), always fell in spring. This further attests to the importance of the spring season in marking time. It was for this reason that Du Yu (222–284) (1982, 11), a Jin scholar who studied both the *Spring and Autumn* and its commentaries, believed that the term "spring and autumn" was used to name the records the historians preserved in many states. A cursory survey of the *Spring and Autumn* gives the distinct impression that more entries were registered in the spring and autumn seasons.

This integration of natural and political notions of time in early China contrasts starkly with the Western experience and practice, where historical writing originated as "an operation against Time," to the extent that time was the totalizing force that threatened to engulf all events of the past, thereby destroying them as unique occurrences. It was for the purpose of saving the memory of events worthy of remembrance that history was written (Momigliano 1966, 15). In order to safeguard historical memory, Greek historians such as Herodotus (485?–425? B.C.E.) invented a narrative form wherein historical events unfolded according to their own causations. In ancient China, while the search for causation was not absent from historical practices, historians generally subscribed to a notion of time marked by the lunar calendar year, punctuated by the change of seasons. Thus annals (*biannianshi*), or the annalistic form as exemplified by the *Spring and Autumn*, naturally became established as the dominant form of early Chinese historiography. Their authors, the *shi*, always had the dual responsibility for keeping track of the changes in both natural time and human history (Q. Wang 1995, 70–71). In fact, the annals became the best form for the Chinese historians because they wished to shed light on the correlation between Heaven (nature) and humanity (history). But use of annals did not preclude the *shi* from describing changes over historical time, which is a crucial element in the development of historical consciousness. In summarizing the merit of the annalistic form, Du Yu remarked that the annals allowed "the recorder to link the event with the date, link the date with the month, link the month with the season, link the season with the year, then distinguish the remote from the recent and tell the similar from the different" (1982, 11).[5]

Combining their work on calendar and history, the *shi* were very much responsible for fostering and strengthening the correlative world view in early China, from at least the Spring and Autumn period to the early Han dynasty, when Sima Qian wrote his magnum opus, the *Records of the Historian (Shiji)*. In the documents written by the *shi*, there was abundant evidence of their interpretations of the intricate relationship between heavenly phenomena and earthly affairs. Benjamin Schwartz contends:

> In the recorded discourses of those specialized functionaries and wise men called *shih* [*shi*], who seem to combine the functions of astronomers, astrologers, calendar experts, and chroniclers, we do indeed find evidence of correlation of human events with the movements of the heavenly bodies. One

---

5. While annals provided the time frame for the *shi* to enter historical records, different orders existed in different historical periods. Inaba Ichirō (1999, 34–37), for example, states that in the oracle-bone divinations of the Shang, the *shi* recorded the date first, followed by the month and the year. But in the Western Zhou period, the order came to be reversed: the year, the month, and then the date.

> is indeed tempted to speculate that something like a rudimentary astrology provides the first most important applications of correlative cosmology in China, at least on the high cultural level. (Schwartz 1985, 353)

As we shall see in the next chapter, the *shi* not only preserved records in order to illustrate the human-cosmic correlation, but they also helped develop cosmological theories, such as the theory of the Five Phases (*wuxing*), to make sense of the major changes in China's political history from the fifth century B.C.E. through the first century C.E., that is, from the Warring States period, through the Qin, to the Han (A. Wang 2000, 80).

When Confucius decided to work on the *Spring and Autumn*, he could no longer see much sophistication in the works of the *shi*. Instead, he saw compromised quality as a result of the *shi*'s distracting interest in literary refinement. In his own work, therefore, Confucius focused on "reducing the literary excesses (*yueqi ciwen*) and removing the unnecessary repetitions (*quqi fanchong*) in order to establish the principle and rule (*yizhi yifa*)" (*Shiji* 1988, 145). He strove for a balanced relationship between refinement and simplicity. To him, literary excesses, or *wenci*, had a broad meaning; it referred not simply to rhetorical indulgence and extravagance. Upon hearing that the state of Song had held a great ceremony for reaching a truce with its enemy, Confucius described it as excessive *wenci*, implying that politics and governance had come to be dominated by rhetoric and was therefore lacking in practical substance (S. Wang 1997, 15).

One way to curtail literary excesses in historical writing was to promote and follow straightforwardness, which was Confucius' aim in his rendering of the *Spring and Autumn*. Yet we should not confuse the virtue of straightforwardness with modern historiographical ideas of impartiality or objectivity, although it does seem to adumbrate the latter (Q. Wang 2000b). When Confucius emphasized the imperative of straightforwardness, he was actually referring to the moral courage of the historian. Armed with such courage, historians would record whatever they felt was important or necessary, unfazed by the prospect of losing their lives while performing their noble task. Straightforwardness did not require historians to record everything, which would render their work indistinguishable from the work of the earlier *shi*. Rather, he hoped that historians would establish and illuminate the moral meanings and principles (*yi*) in history. To this end historians ought to be selective with their sources. Hence in working on the *Spring and Autumn*, or for that matter in editing the *Classic of Odes*, Confucius expurgated many records he deemed unimportant. Furthermore he singled out a particular period—from the first year of the reign of Duke Yin to the fourteenth year of the reign of Duke Ai (722 to 481 B.C.E.)—which he thought best demonstrated moral principles in history (S. Wang 1997, 24). Mencius (371–289 B.C.E.?), a Confucian of the Warring States period whose influence is generally considered only second to that of Confucius, affirmed the moral nature of the master's work on the *Spring and Autumn*.

The *Sheng* of Jin, the *Taowu* of Chu, and the *Spring and Autumn* of Lu were
books of the same character. The subject of the *Spring and Autumn* was the affairs of Huan of Qi and Wan of Jin, and its style was the historical. Confucius
said, "Its righteous decisions [principle] (*yi*) I ventured to make." (Mencius
1970, 327, modified transliteration)

In other words Confucius deliberately reformed the tradition of the
shi by injecting a moral intent into the historical records that he inherited
from them. What Confucius did with the *Spring and Autumn* marked a new
beginning in Chinese historiography. He not only preserved and expanded
the annals, along with the other classics, but he also added a new, moral
purpose to the pursuit of historical knowledge.

Although Confucius' insistence on investing historical writing with
moral values and meaning has elicited much criticism, especially among
modern historians, there is no denying that what Confucius achieved was
significant for his time. He transformed the historical culture, turning the
shi into historians. As many modern scholars have noted (W. Du 1993,
86; Zongtong Li 1953, 14–18; Q. Chen 1999, 46–48), it was highly significant that Confucius, albeit not a *shi* as such, produced a self-contained
historical record, providing an inspiring example to many later scholars
who pursued the study of the past. Although, as Etienne Balazs famously
contended, in the Chinese historiographical tradition, "history was written by officials for officials" (Hardy 1999, 10), there is ample evidence to
suggest that private initiatives for writing history were far from negligible
(H. Franke 1961), and many of these initiatives consciously harked back to
the morally driven historiographical ideals propounded by Confucius.

To be sure, there are still disputes about whether Confucius actually
wrote the *Spring and Autumn Annals,* but even among those who say that
Confucius had nothing to do with the compilation, there seems to be
agreement that during the fifth and the fourth centuries B.C.E., from the
late Spring and Autumn period to the Warring States period, historical
consciousness in China went through a transformation (Jie Liu 1982, 39–
42; T. Chen 1993, 38–47). This had much to do with the decline of the
Zhou royal house, which wreaked havoc in the political and social arenas.
A great anxiety arose among intellectuals, not the least of whom were the
followers of Confucius led by Mencius. They sought in the past and history
a sense of order; they hoped to develop a philosophy of history that could
facilitate their goal of restoring peace. As we shall see in the next chapter,
this fervid interest in pursuing history for the purpose of restoring order
and peace was shared by many thinkers at the time and yielded different
schools of thought that began to compete for prominence. The Confucian
view of history, with its emphasis on political hierarchy and moral excellence, was by no means the dominant one. However, its influence seemed
to have outlived that of many of its competitors, eventually furnishing the
theoretical foundation and moral presumptions for traditional Chinese
historiography.

According to Mencius, what prompted Confucius to work on the *Spring and Autumn* was his profound anxiety about the destruction of the political and moral order of the Zhou:

> The world fell into decay, and principles faded away. Perverse words and oppressive deeds waxed rife again. There were instances of ministers who murdered their sovereigns, and of sons who murdered their fathers. Confucius [was] afraid, and made the *Spring and Autumn*. What the *Spring and Autumn* contains are matters proper to the sovereign. On this account Confucius said, "Yes! It is the *Spring and Autumn* which will make men know me, and it is the *Spring and Autumn* which will make men condemn me." (Mencius 1970, 281–282)

In the *Analects* Confucius had already expressed his grave concern and grief over the fall of the Western Zhou royal house, which, to him, meant the destruction of the ideal political system of antiquity. The Way of rulership (*wangdao*), or simply the Way (*dao*), established in ancient times by the sage-rulers had begun to disintegrate.

> When the empire possessed the Way, decrees governing the rituals, music, and punitive expeditions were issued by the Son of Heaven. When the empire lost the Way, decrees governing the rituals, music, and punitive expeditions were issued by one of the various princes. . . . If the empire possessed the Way, state power would not be in the hands of ministers. If the empire possessed the Way, the common people had nothing to censure. (*Analects* 1997, 160)

For Confucius the existence of the Way of rulership was determined by whether the political hierarchy was maintained. He was distressed by what he saw and experienced, as the Way seemed increasingly out of joint. An expert on ritual culture, Confucius readily identified the offences and transgressions of his time. He found, for instance, that Ji Shi, a nobleman, hired eight rows of dancers to perform in his court. This clearly violated protocol because only the emperor was entitled to that—a person in Ji Shi's position could have no more than two rows. Thus Confucius questioned: "If this could be tolerated, what could not be tolerated?" (*Analects* 1997, 58) Confucius lamented that the disrespect of the feudal lords for their sovereign was so rampant in China that the situation was worse than that in the uncivilized neighboring states (ibid., 59). Since Confucius' sociopolitical hierarchical order was very much based on the cultural distinction between the civilized Chinese and the barbaric non-Chinese, his invective here was poignant and damning. To Mencius' way of thinking, Confucius had every reason to produce a historical text that espoused time-honored ideas and values that would serve the ultimate purpose of reviving the political and moral ideals of antiquity.

The best way to demonstrate how Confucius worked on his *Spring and*

Autumn would have been to compare his approach with that of the original. However, the complete text of the original *Spring and Autumn* has long been lost; there is only mention of it in other texts that mostly appeared after Confucius' own text. Nonetheless, we may safely conjecture that the original *Spring and Autumn* was a historical record kept by the *shi* in the state of Lu, and it covered a longer period than Confucius' *Spring and Autumn Annals*. In addition, if his text is compared with the contemporary *Bamboo Annals,* evidence suggests that Confucius expunged many records while forging his own (Suqing Zhang 1998, 147–148; S. Zhao 2000, 8–20). But it should be pointed out that Confucius apparently did make an effort to incorporate events that were not recorded in the original annals. He had asked his students to collect over a hundred annals to use as additional sources (*Shitong* 1978, 1:9). Confucius intended the *Spring and Autumn* to be a historical document of all of China, not simply for the state of Lu. However, he did not do an evenhanded job. Larger states and the states he visited certainly received a better coverage (Kennedy 1942, 48). In any event we may be quite sure that the *Spring and Autumn* we see today is probably the one that was handed down by Confucius. It is very likely that he did work on the *Spring and Autumn,* and his avowed purpose was to use it, along with the other classics, for pedagogical purposes (S. Wang 1997, 15–17), although whether Confucius actually considered teaching to be his new calling, as the *Gongyang Commentary* claimed, is a complex and intriguing issue that cannot be settled here.

Transformation is not, however, the same as creation, but creation was never Confucius' goal. "I am not one who knows it at birth," he declared, "but one who loves antiquity and assiduously seeks it." Elsewhere, he made it explicit: "I transmit and do not create. I believe in and love antiquity . . ." (*Analects* 1997, 90, 87). In his historical practice, where he revealed his love for antiquity, he closely followed the principle he set for himself, which was to expand rather than abandon the historiographical tradition established by the *shi.* In identifying the historiographical characteristics of the *Spring and Autumn,* "discriminating use of terminology" (*shuci*) and "arranging and comparing events" (*bishi*) were among the most apparent. These two defining characteristics, first mentioned in the *Classic of Rites,* have been considered by both ancient and modern scholars as the most representative of Confucius' approaches in the *Spring and Autumn* (W. Du 1993, 88–89; Qu 1999b, 137–138; Suqing Zhang 1998, 109–135). They therefore warrant close examination.

"Discriminating use of terminology" referred to the fact that Confucius, after weighing the various connotations and implications of available synonyms, would settle on the one that best described the nature of the event. "Arranging and comparing events" pointed to his attempt not only to arrange events in the right chronology but also to juxtapose them so as to facilitate comparison. To use terminology with discrimination was to make appropriate judgment about historical events and personages. Through words of praise and condemnation, the moral implications of

different events and deeds could be highlighted. Given Confucius' grave
concern with the widespread political disorder of his time, it is hardly surprising that he levied criticism through nomenclatural manipulation. In
Chinese historiography this came to be known as the "*Spring and Autumn's*
law of the pen" (*Chunqiu bifa*). That is, by recording history in a particular manner and employing the most felicitous language, the moral significance of the past might be brought to bear on the present. What disturbed
Confucius the most, as Mencius pointed out, was the all-too-common fact
that the "ministers murdered their sovereigns," a blatant violation of the
hierarchical political order that Confucius held dear. In the *Spring and Autumn*, therefore, Confucius used the term "to murder" (*shi*) to record such
incidents to express his condemnation and outrage. By contrast, other
annals often simply used the term "to kill" (*sha*). Obviously, "to murder"
implied greater moral censure. The *Spring and Autumn* records twenty-six
cases in which ministers took the lives of their princes, and it uses the term
"murder" twenty-five times. Only in one instance is the term "kill" used.
But interestingly enough, both the *Gongyang Commentary* and the *Guliang
Commentary* to the *Spring and Autumn* nonetheless interpret it as "murder"
(S. Zhao 2000, 31–33).

Confucius did not invent the "discriminating use of terminology." Although other annalists did not seem to be as meticulous as Confucius in
choosing words, they too exercised a good deal of care when entering
records. The *Spring and Autumn*, for example, records that in the 28th year
of the reign of Duke Xi, King Xiang of the Zhou was summoned by Duke
Wen of the state of Jin for a gathering in Wendi. When King Xiang arrived,
Duke Wen met him, along with the other dukes present. Duke Wen also
let King Xiang go hunting in Heyang. But the record made no mention
of the meeting, nor was there reference to Duke Jin's summoning King
Xiang. The record stated only that the "King went hunting in Heyang."
The *Zuo Commentary* recorded how Confucius explained the reason for the
omission:

> It was not a good precedent that a minister called up a king. Hence the
> *Spring and Autumn* records that [the] "King went hunting in Heyang"; all
> land is supposed to belong to the king, but here is no longer King Xiang's
> territory. In fact, it records this way to show the Jin's generosity. (*Zuozhuan*
> 1993, 410)

This case, with its deliberately incomplete entry and Confucius' explanation, has often been used as an example to elucidate the "law of the pen"
supposedly enacted by Confucius in the *Spring and Autumn*. But the contextual evidence actually shows that Confucius was not the one who entered
the record in the first place. The *shi* of the state of Lu who compiled the
original *Spring and Autumn* had done that. Confucius only endorsed the
manner of their recording. We may safely assume that the *shi* had already
applied, before Confucius, the practice of discriminating use of termi-

nology. In the *Bamboo Annals,* for instance, the same event was recorded in threadbare fashion; it simply tells us that "King Xiang of the Zhou met the dukes in Heyang," thus omitting the same fact that the king was asked to be there by Duke Jin (S. Wang 1997, 15). Both omissions were intended to spare the Zhou royal house humiliation by purposefully concealing the fact of its greatly diminished sovereignty.

But if Confucius did not invent the discriminating use of terminology, he did add something new, as we can see in the following example. At the beginning of the seventh century B.C.E. the Jin was ruled by Duke Wen's grandson, Duke Ling, who was assisted by an able minister, Zhao Dun, and his cousin, Zhao Chuan. Duke Ling was not a good and benevolent ruler. During his reign, he alienated his ministers and the people as a result of his wicked behavior, including shooting randomly at people from his terrace for entertainment. Zhao Dun remonstrated with him, but to no avail. Duke Ling was so annoyed by the remonstrations that he attempted to kill Zhao Dun. Zhao Dun escaped the assassination attempt, but Duke Ling was murdered by Zhao Chuan in a peach orchard. When this happened, Zhao Dun had not yet crossed the state border. Upon hearing the news, he returned to the capital. Grand Historian Dong Hu recorded: "Zhao Dun assassinated his ruler" and presented the document to the court. Zhao Dun said, "That is not true!" But the historian replied, as recorded in the *Zuo Commentary,* "You are the chief minister. When you fled you did not cross the border. Now you have returned you do not punish the culprit. If you are not responsible, who is?" As if this whole affair was not perplexing enough, Confucius was reported to have commented: "Dong Hu was a good historian of ancient times. In recording principles he did not conceal anything. Zhao Dun was a good official of ancient times. For the sake of the principle he was willing to receive a bad name. What a pity! If he had crossed the border he might have escaped the charge" (Watson 1989, 79, modified transliteration).

Both Dong Hu's recording and Confucius' comment have caused puzzlement and precipitated disputes for the past two millennia (Suqing Zhang 1998, 155–162). Why did Dong Hu blame Zhao Dun for something he did not do? Why would Confucius, a person who had praised the straightforwardness of the historian, endorse Dong's apparent falsification of the record? Why did Confucius praise Zhao Dun's acceptance of responsibility, but wish he had not? Although this is not the place to enumerate all the explanatory theories, we should look at some of them in an effort to illustrate Confucius' moral position in historiography. According to all three authoritative commentaries, Dong Hu blamed Zhao Dun because after he returned to the Jin, he did not persecute Zhao Chuan for murdering the duke, a dereliction of his duty as the chief minister. Moreover, although Dong Hu had no evidence that Zhao Dun was involved in planning the murder, his unwillingness to prosecute his cousin implicated himself. Therefore, in stating that Zhao Dun, instead of Zhao Chuan, murdered his duke, Dong Hu not only duly recorded this offense in history, but also suggested who ought to be blamed. In other words, by entering the record in this way, Dong killed two birds with one stone: recording the event and simultaneously passing judgment on it. This explains why Confucius praised him for being a good historian—while Dong might have distorted the record and gone beyond the usual duty of the historian, he achieved the ultimate goal of practicing history—pinpointing the moral significance of past events and deeds. As for Confucius' praise for Zhao Dun, it stemmed from the fact that although he might have committed a transgression, he did not attempt to usurp the duke's position, an offense that was not so uncommon in that period of history. Instead, Zhao remained a loyal minister to the state of Jin, performing his service regardless of his ruler's faults.

Confucius' praise of Dong Hu reveals again that while he appreciated the historian's straightforwardness, he did not advocate what we understand to be the idea of objectivity. To be straightforward meant taking the historian's moral responsibility seriously by pointing out the wrong and the right, regardless of political pressure. It is, to be sure, a value-laden approach, quite different from the idea of objectivity, which is supposed to be value free, "*wie es eigentlich gewesen*," in Ranke's words. The Confucian approach considers historical writing to be a normative practice, whereas the Rankean one views it as descriptive (Q. Wang 2000b, 163–164). In Confucian historiography, the agency of history is demonstrated not so much in telling what really happened as in showing what should have happened, something that the historian brings to light. The historian's responsibility "is not only to show what has already been done but also to suggest, whenever appropriate, what other possibilities may have existed and why the failure to realize them has led to disastrous consequences" (W. Tu 1993, 7–8). To maintain one's responsibility and to be straightforward was not as easy as we may think. Given the *shi*'s foremost responsibility of preparing documents and keeping records, there were cases in Confucius' time, as recorded in the *Zuo Commentary*, where they were offered bribes to conceal facts. Dong Hu not only did not conceal, but he also made an effort to reveal more. When Dong said that it was Zhao Dun who assassinated Duke Ling, he at once preserved the events in the records and set a moral example for posterity. This was exactly what Confucius wanted in a historian. As Ye Shi (1150–1223), a Confucian of the Southern Song dynasty (1127–1279), commented, given the seriousness of the murder, it was widely known at that time that Zhao Chuan was the perpetrator. But Dong Hu wanted history to mirror more than the mechanics of an event. Later generations needed to know both the incident itself, and, more important, the person who was ultimately responsible for it (Suqing Zhang 1998, 160–161). The *shi* had a dual duty—"[t]hey were trying both to get the facts right in all their specificity and to see the rightness in the facts," to borrow David Schaberg's words (2001, 18).

Yet we may still wonder why Dong Hu did not tell the whole story. To explain this, we must consider the annalistic format. While annals have the advantage of connecting time and history, they do not offer much space for detailed records. A typical entry in the *Spring and Autumn* contains only a few brief statements, as we can see in one concerning the third year of the reign of Duke Yin:

> The 3rd year, the spring's second month, the day of *jiyi*, the sun had an eclipse. The 3rd month, the day of *gengxu*, the Heavenly King [King Ping of the Zhou] passed away (*beng*).
> The summer's 4th month, the day of *xinmao*, the Lady Jun died (*zu*).
> Autumn, the son of Lady Wu came [to the state of Lu] for funeral gifts [for King Ping's death].
> The 8th month, the day of *gengchen*, Duke Song died (*zu*).
> The winter's 12th month, Earl Qi and Count Zheng allied in Shimen.
> The day of *kuiwei*, Duke Song was buried. (*Zuozhuan*1993, 345)

Although the annalist did not employ many words for this one year, he recorded many events that were both significant and related. The sun's eclipse, for example, portended the death of King Ping of the Zhou, indicating the correlation of the cosmos and humanity. Although the king died in the spring, he did not receive a proper burial right away because in the fall the son of Lady Wu was still asking for funeral gifts. But this might not be that unusual since Duke Song's burial was also not arranged until a few months after his death. Deaths, as we can see, were a predominant theme in this year's records. Yet the way in which these deaths were recorded varied. To record the king's death, for instance, the word *beng* was used, whereas the word *zu* was used in the case of Lady Jun who, although without a title, was the mother of Duke Yin. *Zu* was also used in the case of Duke Song. The finer distinctions of meaning connoted by these two words need not concern us. Suffice it to note that the historians entered these records thoughtfully so as to convey what really happened, in keeping with their moral judgments. Given the space limitations imposed by the annalistic format, they developed an exacting historiographical technique and fine hermeneutical art.

Despite space constraints, the *Spring and Autumn Annals* recorded events that covered a wide range of areas, from extraordinary natural prodigies and calamities to the intricacies of political life, while identifying their temporal and chronological location. When the *Annals* recorded various kinds of death, it indicated the time of their occurrence. As George Kennedy's study reveals, "105 entries have the exact day, 23 the month only, 16 the season only" (1942, 43). The practice of precise dating of an event on record can be traced back to the divinatory inquiries of the Shang period. But the diviners, many of whom were *shi*, did not follow a specific chronological order, as did the *Spring and Autumn* (Inaba 1999, 34–35; Q. Chen 1999, 56). In the *Spring and Autumn*, there was the "mechanical arrangement" that every event was marked by the season of a particular year and frequently also by the month or even the exact day, together with the corresponding cyclical signs (Kennedy 1942, 41). If we assume that Confucius sought conformity in the use of terminology, it was also likely that he developed this uniform dating system, especially in light of his effort to incorporate into the *Spring and Autumn*—via the practice of "arranging and comparing events"—events that took place in states other than the Lu. The practice of incorporation demanded a more systematic chronological ordering.

Its phraseological uniformity and chronological precision notwithstanding, the *Spring and Autumn Annals* is a dull and dry text, as many of its critics past and present have remarked. The quest for narrative uniformity perhaps made the problem worse, rendering the presentation of events much less imaginative. We should also consider the fact that at the time the *Spring and Autumn* appeared, the Chinese were still writing on silk and bamboo strips. The unwieldy nature of the writing materials may well have encouraged verbal parsimony. Yet a more probable cause may be found in the ancient Chinese historiographical tradition itself, in which the *shi* were assigned specialized tasks in the general process of keeping records. The *Classic of Rites* informs us that "when the emperor acts, the Left Historian records it; when he speaks, the Right Historian makes a record" (Watson 1958, 73). Perhaps, as the Han historian Ban Gu (C.E. 32–92) explained, it was the case that while the *Spring and Autumn Annals* recorded the deeds, the *Classic of Documents* kept the words, and hence the latter contained more descriptive and expositive writings (Watson 1958, 73). As we shall see, these two ways of recording the past would converge.

CHAPTER 2

From the Warring States Period to the Han

The Formation and Maturation of Historiography

I n his famous *Comprehensive Perspectives on Historiography* (*Shitong*), Liu Zhiji (661–721), the eminent Tang historiographer and historical theorist, surveyed all the stylistic and narrative forms employed by historians up till his time and concluded that there had been, all in all, six of them. The *Spring and Autumn Annals* (*Chunqiu*) was one.

> By the time Confucius worked on the *Spring and Autumn*, he observed ancient laws and rites of the Zhou and inherited the records of the Lu historians. He accorded human affairs to its Way, making clear what ought to be punished and what ought to be rewarded. He also ascertained the calendar according to the sun and moon, and confirmed rituals and music for court meetings. Although he made subtle statements and entered enigmatic records, what he said is absolute and has perpetual value. This is why his work has become the only one of its kind, which has lasted throughout the many centuries. (*Shitong* 1978, 1:7)

Narratives and Interpretations

As one of the few annals surviving today, the *Spring and Autumn Annals* sheds considerable light on China's early historical culture, especially the work of the *shi*. While this classical text may be stylistically dry, Confucius' followers earnestly believed that it contained enigmatic but profound meanings and even prophesies. As early as the Han period, the *Spring and Autumn Annals* had already become "the pivot of classical studies." Some ten centuries later, in the Song period (960–1279), studies of the *Spring and Autumn* continued to be "the main current of classical scholarship in that era" (Henderson 1991, 13). From the mid-fourteenth century onward, the *Spring and Autumn* received even higher praise. The eighteenth-century classicist Liu Fenglu (1776–1829), for example, considered it the master key to understanding all the classics. Echoing Liu, the late Qing reformer Kang Youwei (1858–1927) remarked that "although the Six Classics are very voluminous and divergent, their guiding principles can all be found in the *Spring and Autumn*." What drew their attention to the *Spring and Autumn* was that compared with the other classics, it was historical in approach and content. Moreover, it offered a historiographical philosophy based on the principle of teaching by historical examples. The text recorded "real affairs," Shao Yong (1011–1077) of the Song explained, "[and] thus good and evil take on concrete forms in it." Cheng Yi (1033–1107), another eminent Song Confucian thinker, described and praised the usefulness of the *Spring and Autumn* with this powerful metaphor: if the classics were medical prescriptions, then the *Spring and Autumn* was the medicine prescribed to cure diseases (ibid., 16–17).

But perhaps these accolades misrepresented the basic attributes and contents of the *Spring and Autumn*. To many of its readers, including Wang Anshi (1021–1086), the *Spring and Autumn* was merely a "fragmented and incomplete court report" (*duanlan chaobao*). It neither offered sufficient information on the period of history it supposedly covered, nor provided many helpful clues to the hidden moral meanings and political messages. To understand how the *Spring and Autumn* ascended to such a towering position among the Confucian classics, we must look for reasons beyond the text itself. We must look at the other forms of historical writing mentioned by Liu Zhiji, especially the styles adopted by the *Classic of Documents* and the *Zuo Commentary*.

The *Classic of Documents* contains the earliest historical records from China's high antiquity. It represented, according to Liu Zhiji, the discourse form that focused on recording words (*jiyan*), thus preserving the kings' edicts and announcements, as well as their conversations with their subjects. Such emphasis on recording words differed from the central concern of annals, which sought to record events (*jishi*) (*Shitong* 1978, 1:2–3). But the documents in the *Classic of Documents* were not all discourses (W. Du 1993, 80–81). Apart from verbal disquisitions and pronouncements, many of them gave fairly detailed narrative descriptions of events. The "Yaodian" chapter, for instance, describes the feats of Yao, the legendary sage-king, and the "Yugong" chapter the accomplishments of Yu, another legendary sage-ruler who successfully controlled disastrous flooding. The "Guming" chapter vividly depicts events around the death of King Cheng of the Zhou. Their apparent departure from the general norm of recording words has caused scholars throughout the ages to question the veracity of these descriptive passages. These chapters, according to skeptical scholars, were probably written in the Spring and Autumn or the Warring States periods. In fact, the question of the authenticity of the *Classic of Documents* became a central polemical issue for many Confucian scholars from the Han period onward, as evidenced by their polarization into two classical schools of commentarial learning—the so-called New Script (*jinwen*) and the Old Script (*guwen*) schools. The debates between these two camps on the *Classic of Documents* exerted considerable impact on historical writing, especially during the late imperial period, as the issue of reliable sources and original materials took center stage. What is worth noting here is that most of the documents about which scholars argued recorded events rather than words, often in a narrative form. If these documents were indeed written in later times, then we have reason to suggest that there appeared in historical writing a gradual convergence of the tradition of recording words with that of recording events in the late East Zhou period. This convergence, couched in the format and style of the chronicles, apparently occurred in the Warring States period (Lewis 1999, 131–132).

Traditional scholarship holds that the *Spring and Autumn Annals* and the *Classic of Documents,* the two earliest historical texts, pioneered two different genres of historical writing: the recording of events versus the recording of words. This division of labor, argued Liu Zhiji (*Shitong* 1978, 1:1–25), was still very much alive in the Warring States period when the *Spring and Autumn Annals* and the later *Zuo Commentary* were compiled. As the *Zuo Commentary* expanded on the *Spring and Autumn,* the *Discourses on the State,* generally believed to have appeared around the same time and have been written by the same author, Zuo Qiuming, continued the effort of recording the words of historical personages. Recent studies have found that both the *Zuo Commentary* and the *Discourses on the State* adopted similar narrative techniques in historical description (Schaberg 2001, 6–7). By the Warring States period attempts had been made to modify and enrich the style and format of the annals by incorporating more substantive narratives.

The *Zuo Commentary* is a perfect example. While principally organized as a chronicle, it may be regarded as China's first narrative history (Watson 1989, xi). Although its narratives are often desultory and isolated, lacking any apparent cohesion, Ronald Egan believes that they "consistently give the reader a sense of the larger, causal context of particular events" (1977, 324). In order to account for the *Zuo Commentary*'s anecdotal style as well as its intrinsic but latent historical coherence, we have to look at how and why it was written.

Conventional wisdom has long held that it was written by Zuo Qiuming, a *shi* of the state of Lu and contemporary of Confucius. He compiled it because after Confucius' death, his disciples' teachings of his ideas varied, as they worked mostly within an oral tradition that resulted in a good deal of internal confusion, dissension, and contradiction. Sima Qian explains Zuo's motivation:

> The Lu gentleman Zuo Qiuming feared that the various disciples, differing in their biases, would be content with their own opinions and lose what was genuine. Therefore, taking Confucius' scribal records as his basis, he put in order all their words and completed the Chunqiu of Master Zuo [*Zuo Commentary of the Spring and Autumn*]. (Schaberg 2001, 318; modified transliteration)

Sima Qian's view of the provenance of the *Zuo Commentary* and its authorship has long been a bone of scholarly contention. Recent scholarship tends to challenge the notion of Zuo Qiuming's sole authorship and argue instead that the *Zuo Commentary* went through many hands during its composition, and hence represents a transmitted tradition rather than the product of a single author (Kamata 1993). Specifically, these critics say that the forging of this tradition involved the merging of parallel traditions: the oral transmission of Confucian teachings and the preservation of written historical records by the *shi* (Watson 1989, xiv–xv; Schaberg 2001, 315–324; Lewis 1999, 132). By the time the *Zuo Commentary* and its sister text, the *Discourses on the State,* were written, the traditional historiographical division between recording deeds and recording words had lost its currency.

This change had a twofold implication. It illustrated the decline of the role of the *shi*. In broader terms it reflected the decline of what may be described as the official historical culture of the *shi* that had flourished in the Western Zhou. And it heralded a new stage in the development of Chinese historiography that culminated in the Han period in the magisterial innovative works of Sima Qian and Ban Gu. There were several reasons for the decline of the official historical culture. First of all, the decline and fall of the Zhou political order generated a profound sense of cultural malaise among the *shi,* whose work was predicated on the existence of a stable, powerful order and its supposed correspondence with the Mandate of Heaven. The *shi* entered historical records concerning both political-civil time and natural time, but the disintegration of Zhou suzerainty meant the disappearance of the requisite civil order. In the *Spring and Autumn Annals* Confucius took great pains to remind his contemporaries of the Zhou political calendar, honoring, for example, the "king's upright month" (*wang zhengyue*), which was often placed in the beginning of a year. In the Warring States period this political-civil time became virtually nonexistent, as the political irrelevance of Zhou royal house became all too clear.

Second, the disintegration of the Zhou ruler's power meant a decline of the shamanic political culture, which in turn helped transform the work of the *shi*. The ancient kings may be regarded as chief shamans who conducted divinations and interpreted oracles, and it was the *shi* who managed and officiated at those religious activities. During the Warring States period, constant warfare and complex diplomatic maneuvering demanded considerable human ingenuity, making human agency seem more reliable than divine intervention that appeared remote at best and capricious at worst. While religious activities still provided solace for the psyche, they no longer played the same practical role in the court and government. The *shi* had therefore to make adjustments in their work. Although they held on to their fundamental belief in a correlative universe where Heaven and humanity were integrated, and continued to make cosmic observations, predictions, and prophecies according to their astrological knowledge, they no longer focused their activities narrowly on legitimizing the king's rule and his personal well-being. Rather we find, in the *Zuo Commentary,* that the *shi* applied their knowledge to predicting the outcomes

of battles or offering prophecies concerning misfortunes about to befall
the state. At the same time, together with other philosophers, they also
began to ponder questions about the nature of history and propound interpretive theories about the *Spring and Autumn*. "[D]uring the Warring
States period, with regard to Heaven-humanity correlation, the *shi* by and
large centered their activities on theoretical creation, not Heaven worship"
(T. Chen 1993, 12).

The *Zuo Commentary* documented this transformation. By incorporating narratives, it enriched and expanded the genre of annals forged by
the *shi*. But it also espoused a distinct, Confucian conception of history,
through which moral precepts were expounded for the practical purpose
of bettering the individual, the society, and the state. There were questions, especially those posed by the New Script Confucians who embraced
the *Gongyang Commentary*, of whether the *Zuo Commentary* was written originally as a commentary on the *Spring and Autumn Annals*. But even if it had
not been, there is still no denying the philosophical and ideological affinity
between the two texts (S. Zhao 2000; Suqing Zhang 1998; Schaberg 2001).
For those who believe that Zuo Qiuming was the author of the *Zuo Commentary*, the *Analects* provides clear evidence of the affinity between Confucius
and Zuo:

> Sweet words, a pleasing countenance, and excessive respectfulness—Zuo
> Qiuming deems it shameful; I also deem it shameful. To conceal one's
> resentment against a person and befriend him—Zuo Qiuming deems it
> shameful; I also deem it shameful. (*Analects*, 78)

To the extent that Confucius considered Zuo Qiuming his kindred spirit,
it is hardly surprising that the *Zuo Commentary* shared Confucius' moral
stance. However, if we do not believe that a single author, Zuo Qiuming
or otherwise, wrote the *Commentary*, we have to delve into the text itself
to see how it illustrates Confucian moral principles. In so doing, we may
also address another claim about its provenance—that the *Zuo Commentary*
was written as an independent historical text, not a commentary. Proponents of this claim usually also cast doubt on Zuo Qiuming's authorship.
The reasoning is that if Zuo were the author and Confucius' contemporary, he could not have recorded events that occurred some seventy years
after 481 B.C.E., the ending year of the *Spring and Autumn;* nor could he
have corroborated the prophesies and employed phrases that would not
be used until the late Warring States period (S. Zhao 2000, 73). There are
also a number of records found in the *Zuo Commentary* but not in the *Spring
and Autumn*, and vice versa.

In spite of these inconsistencies that seem to support the claim that the
Zuo Commentary is independent of the *Spring and Autumn*, there is plenty
of evidence to the contrary. The doubts about Zuo Qiuming's authorship
actually attest to the fact that the *Zuo Commentary* belongs to the Confucian hermeneutic tradition, which arose gradually after Confucius' death

and centered on the teaching of the *Spring and Autumn Annals* (Henderson 1991, 11–19). If the *Zuo Commentary* had been written by a single author intent on producing an independent history, it would have been unnecessary for him to belabor the rules and principles found in the *Spring and Autumn*. Of all the entries in the *Zuo Commentary*, 1,300 were written directly to explain records in the *Spring and Autumn*, and 100 or so more are closely related to entries in the *Spring and Autumn*. Entries that appear to be independent of the *Spring and Autumn* amount to about 300, or less than 20 percent of the work (S. Zhao 2000, 59–60). Significantly, even those independent passages tend to address the same moral issues that the *Spring and Autumn* addresses (Egan 1977, 340–352), an important fact we shall examine in greater detail.

The commentary entries seem to fall under three categories: phraseology, meaning, and events. As we have noted, the *Spring and Autumn* is known for its discriminating use of terminology, which demonstrates both the space constraints of annals and Confucius' nuanced revelation of his moral and political stance on historical events. The *Zuo Commentary* covers a longer period than the *Spring and Autumn*, but it begins with the same year, Duke Yin 1st Year, or 722 B.C.E. In the *Spring and Autumn*, the entry reads: "The first year's spring; the King's upright month." The *Zuo Commentary*'s entry is slightly different: "The first year's spring; King Zhou's upright month." Here "the first year" refers to the beginning of Duke Yin's reign in the state of Lu—his ascendancy to the throne was explained in the *Zuo Commentary* (*Zuozhuan* 1993, 343). What is more interesting is the mention of King Zhou. The *Zuo Commentary* underscores the point that the *Spring and Autumn* uses the Zhou calendar and not those of previous dynasties, since the "upright month" is associated with different months in the other dynastic calendars (Suqing Zhang 1998, 43–44; Loewe & Shaughnessy 1999, 20). While this seems a trivial matter, it actually shows that the *Zuo Commentary* shares Confucius' desire to promote the Zhou sovereignty.

In fact, the *Zuo Commentary* seems not only to share the same political positions and moral judgments as those of the *Spring and Autumn Annals*, but it also appears to have thoroughly understood their import. When the *Spring and Autumn* omits certain words and events, it is not due to space requirements but because of moral disapproval. In those instances the explanations provided by the *Zuo Commentary* and other commentaries become essential to our understanding and appreciation of the *Spring and Autumn*. Let us look again at the entry of "Duke Yin, 1st Year." Why does the *Spring and Autumn* not mention Duke Yin's accession (*jiwei*)? The *Zuo Commentary* explains that the *Spring and Autumn* "does not record that Duke Yin succeeded the position because he was just a regent." As we recall, after the death of Duke Hui, the previous ruler, Duke Huan, Duke Yin's younger brother, became the head of the state and Duke Yin became the regent (*Zuozhuan* 1993, 343). In other words, while Duke Yin was the de facto ruler of the state of Lu at the time, he did not officially occupy that position. In omitting Duke Yin's ascendancy to power, Confucius upheld the principle of "correct use of names" (*zhengming*), which shows "how linguistic order corresponds to moral behavior and administrative practice" (Schaberg 2001, 50). And indeed, in 682 B.C.E., when Duke Huan reached his majority and came to power, his accession (*jiwei*) was duly recorded in the *Spring and Autumn* (*Zuozhuan* 1993, 353).

While emphasizing the practice of correct use of names, the omission does not show a strong moral condemnation of Duke Yin's coming to power; rather, it hints at the expectation of his eventually returning power to the rightful ruler, his stepbrother Duke Huan. There are, however, cases in which the omission of names is clearly meant to be a moral censure. In 597 B.C.E., or Duke Xuan 12th Year, the *Spring and Autumn* records that ministers from the states of Jin, Song, Wei, and Cao met in Qingqiu and formed an alliance. But it mentions neither the purpose of this alliance nor the names of those who attended. This is inconsistent with the *Spring and Autumn's* "law of the pen," according to which the names of the ministers are supposed to be mentioned in the records. The *Zuo Commentary* explains that the alliance was for the purpose of "assisting those states that were in need of help and attacking those that were disloyal." But because few states in the alliance actually took any concrete action, the *Spring and Autumn* omitted the ministers' names in order to criticize not only the failure of the alliance but also the hypocrisy of those who initiated it (*Zuozhuan* 1993, 443, 447). The same strategy is used elsewhere. In Duke Cheng 2nd Year (589 B.C.E.), ministers from various states came to Shu and formed an alliance. Again the *Spring and Autumn* did not record their names because, as the *Zuo Commentary* explains, this alliance was formed out of expediency, not sincerity. Moreover, the *Spring and Autumn* left out the fact that the dukes of the states of Cai and Xu also participated. It did so to show disapproval not only of their involvement in the meeting but also of their riding in horse chariots belonging to the state of Chu. In Confucius' opinion, these two dukes failed to follow the rules of propriety appropriate to their status (ibid., 456).

The *Zuo Commentary* also points out that the *Spring and Autumn* excluded certain facts because it intended to mitigate the negative moral or political implications associated with the events. In Duke Xuan 7th Year (602 B.C.E.), for example, Duke Xuan went to Heirang to join an alliance with other states. Instead, he was taken hostage by the state of Jin because in the year before, when Duke Wen of Jin ascended to power, Duke Xuan had chosen not to attend the ceremony, nor did he send anyone in his place to congratulate Duke Wen. After paying a ransom, Duke Xuan was eventually released. In order to save the face of Duke Xuan, the *Spring and Autumn* chose not to mention the Heirang alliance meeting at all (ibid., 439). A couple of decades later, in Duke Cheng 10th Year (581 B.C.E.), Duke Cheng of the state of Lu attended the funeral of Duke Jing of the Jin state. However, he found no other princes were there to pay homage to the deceased. Because the Lu people considered this incident a shame to their state, the *Spring and Autumn* ignored Duke Cheng's attendance at the funeral (ibid., 465). This kind of omission was prompted by a supposed contravention of appropriate propriety (*li*), which Confucius took pains to uphold by writing the *Spring and Autumn*. Just as dukes Xu and Cai should have prepared their own chariots, so Duke Cheng of Lu, being an equal of Duke Jing, was not supposed to be there for Duke Jing's funeral. But the sad reality was that such incidents happened frequently in the Spring and Autumn period because the political hierarchy established by the Western Zhou was falling apart. Not only were heads of small states such as Lu subjected to humiliation by more powerful states such as Jin, but even the Zhou royal family was not spared. The best-known incident involving the Zhou, mentioned in the previous chapter, took place in 632 B.C.E., when King Xiang was called by Duke Wen of Jin for a meeting in Heyang. In order to minimize the devastating implication of this incident—the king being summoned to a meeting assembled by a duke—the *Spring and Autumn* noted instead that the king went hunting in Heyang (ibid., 410). The *Spring and Autumn* used this method of "appropriate concealment" to preserve and promote the image and status of three kinds of historical personages: the honorable, the closely related, and the worthy (L. Yang 1961, 51). Such purposeful concealment explains many of the omissions and euphemisms in the *Spring and Autumn*. The king belonged to the category of the "honorable," and the dukes of the state of Lu belonged to the group of the "closely related" because the entries were entered by someone from the same state. Both, according to Confucius, merited special treatment.

It is noteworthy that as the *Zuo Commentary* offered illustrations of such moral exercises, it also sought to affirm the historicity of the text by explaining away the inconsistencies and mistakes committed by either Confucius or its original author. Unlike the *Gongyang Commentary* and the *Guliang Commentary*, the other two extant commentaries on the *Spring and Autumn*, whose principal goal was to expound the moral principles and political ideals embedded in the classical text, the *Zuo Commentary* was particularly interested in history and historiography. It revealed, for instance, that although the *Spring and Autumn* intended to record the deaths of the kings, dukes, and other dignitaries, it often failed to record them accurately or completely. This is because, as the *Zuo Commentary* contended, the *Spring and Autumn* entered those records according to the date and time when the death was announced or reported (*congfu* or *conggao*), and not in accordance with the date and time of the actual occurrence (S. Zhao 2000, 115–120). If a death was not recorded, it was often because it was not reported in the first place. The reason *Spring and Autumn* relied on those reports or announcements, explained the *Zuo Commentary*, was because of its emphasis on propriety—once a dignitary died, it ought to be properly announced. Failure to do so was an act of negligence that was an offence against propriety. The failure to record those deaths, or record them accurately, was meant to be a warning to those who neglected their duty (*Zuozhuan* 1993, 427). This kind of explanation shows a discernable bias that favors Confucius, the putative author of *Spring and Autumn*, a sage who deserved to be excused from factual mistakes and omissions. But the *Zuo Commentary* was also a history intent on keeping the record straight and so it was obliged to point out inconsistencies even while explaining and justifying their presence. By the same token, when the *Zuo Commentary* recorded eclipses missed by the *Spring and Autumn,* it chose to blame the negligence on the original author or authors, the Lu *shi,* not Confucius (ibid., 364, 394).

The *Zuo Commentary* was able to identify and rectify errors and omissions because, unlike other commentarial works, it made use of contemporary sources — nearly all of them long since lost — and was written for the expressed purpose of supplying historical details to elaborate the terse account in the *Spring and Autumn.* Offering substantive historical narratives was its main contribution to the Confucian hermeneutic culture (Suqing Zhang 1998, 17–19). Since the laconic prose of the *Spring and Autumn* often failed to offer adequate explanations for the principles it promoted, it was up to historical works like the *Zuo Commentary* to "make the text of the classic fully comprehensible (and comprehensive)" (Henderson 1991, 143). In contrast to the *Spring and Autumn,* the *Zuo Commentary* offered many rich and complex historical narratives. Its composition shows a sharp departure from the previous historiographical tradition, ushering in, as Liang Qichao (1873–1929) described it, a "historiographical revolution" ([1922] 1980, 58). In fact, it set a new standard for subsequent historical works. When Sima Qian set out to write his historical magnum opus, he had in mind the style and substance of the *Zuo Commentary* (Hardy 1999, 122–123).

Many of the narratives in the *Zuo Commentary,* whether elaborate or curt, were undoubtedly written to expound Confucian moral principles. In Duke Yin 1st Year (722 B.C.E.), for example, a brief record is entered: "Summer, in May, the Earl of Zheng defeated Duan in Yan." This threadbare entry belies a complex and bloody court struggle between two brothers, the details of which are supplied by the *Zuo Commentary.* The conflict began when Duke Zhuang, the earl of Zheng, was born:

> In the past, Duke Wu of Zheng had taken a bride from the state of Shen, known as Lady Jiang of Duke Wu. Lady Jiang gave birth to the future Duke Zhuang and to his brother, Duan of Gong. Duke Zhuang was born wide awake and consequently greatly startled Lady Jiang. Therefore she named him Born Awake and came to hate him. But she loved his younger brother Duan and wished to have him declared heir to the throne of Zheng. Repeatedly she begged Duke Wu to do so, but he would not agree. (Watson, 1989, 1–2; modified transliteration)

After the death of Duke Wu, Duke Zhuang became the earl of Zheng. At his mother's repeated request, he also enfeoffed his brother Duan with a city called Jing, so Duan came to be known as *taishu* of Jing. Encouraged by his mother, the *taishu* developed an insatiable appetite for power. First he expanded the city walls, violating the regulations set by the former kings.

Although Duke Zhuang was advised by his officials to punish the *taishu*, he chose to do nothing, saying, "Lady Jiang would have it that way—how can I avoid danger?" But one official warned him:

> "There is no end to what Lady Jiang would have! Better tend to the matter at once and not let it grow and put out runners, for runners can be hard to control. If even plants that have put out runners cannot be rooted out, how much more so the favored younger brother of a ruler!"
>
> The Duke said, "If he does too many things that are not right, he is bound to bring ruin on himself. I suggest you wait a while." (ibid., 2; modified transliteration)

Since the duke did nothing, the *taishu* became more aggressive. He asked other regions in the state to acknowledge fealty to him apart from the duke. The duke did nothing to stop it. The *taishu* then took control over those regions and greatly expanded his fief, almost dividing the state in half. Still the duke did nothing:

> The Taishu completed the building of his walls, called together his men, mended his armor and weapons, equipped his foot soldiers and chariots, and prepared for a surprise attack on the capital of Zheng. Lady Jiang was to open the city to him. When the duke learned the date planned for the attack, he said, "Now is the time!" He ordered the ducal son Lu to lead a force of two hundred chariots and attack Jing. Jing turned against Taishu Duan, who took refuge in Yan. The duke attacked him at Yan, and on the day *xinchou* of the fifth month, Taishu fled the state and went to Gong. (ibid., 3; modified transliteration)

By providing this background history, the *Zuo Commentary* greatly expands the terse entry in the *Spring and Autumn*, which simply noted the occurrence of a battle in Yan, but glides over the fact that it was actually a civil war between two brothers. The concealment was deliberate, according to the *Zuo Commentary*, because Confucius intended to leave the impression that this was a war between two states, as opposed to an internecine conflict. He did not mention that Duan was the younger brother because such behavior was unacceptable. Nor did he refer to Duke Zhuang because he failed to act in a timely fashion to thwart Duan's plan and fulfill his duty as the head of the state. Instead, Confucius called him *bo*, or earl, which can also mean elder brother, ridiculing him for his failure to educate his younger brothers, and thereby causing the civil war (*Zuozhuan* 1993, 344). In fact, by entering the record in that particular manner, Confucius insinuated that Duke Zhuang had planned all along to kill or expel his brother. The *Zuo Commentary* understood the insinuation and hence provided the detailed prologue—Duke Zhuang's repeated refusal to heed the advice of his officials.

Using elaborate narratives to explain an otherwise unremarkable incident, the *Zuo Commentary* fulfilled its commentarial function; it supplied
the causes for events recorded in the *Spring and Autumn*. Without the *Commentary's* explications, it would be almost impossible to appreciate Confucius' veiled criticism of both Duke Zhuang and his brother Duan. As
David Schaberg remarks, reading of the *Spring and Autumn* "is dependent on narratives of the sort collected in the *Zuozhuan;* without these we
would know neither the names of actors nor the events that reveal their
moral status" (2001, 174). The *Zuo Commentary* therefore does seem tightly
bonded with the *Spring and Autumn* (Suqing Zhang 1998; S. Zhao 2000;
Henderson 1991).

In glossing the *Spring and Autumn,* the *Zuo Commentary* also established
causality in history, premised on the moral principle of recompense (*bao*)
(Schaberg 2001, 170). As Egan puts it, "[T]he abiding lesson of *Zuo Commentary,* a lesson that is illustrated by hundreds of its narratives, is that
rulers who are wise and who are dedicated to their people's welfare pros-
per, while those who are evil or foolish come to a bad end" (1977, 326).
The *Zuo Commentary* also explained the effect of events mentioned in the
Spring and Autumn. Confucius' goal in compiling the *Spring and Autumn,* as
Sima Qian maintained, was to "call good good and bad bad," to honor the
worthy and condemn the unworthy" (Watson 1958, 51). Using historical
incidents, the *Zuo Commentary* demonstrates outcome of conduct in terms
of recompense—good behavior would be rewarded; evil behavior punished—which "is continuous with, but more encompassing than, the ideology of ritual propriety" (Schaberg 2001, 170). The younger brother, Duan,
failed to follow propriety, which caused him to lose the battle, the fief, and
everything else in his native land. There is more to the story, however. If
Duan was at fault, so were his elder brother and perhaps even his mother.
As the principle of recompense was all-encompassing, the *Zuo Commentary*
also tells us what happened to these other characters. Having expelled his
younger brother, Duke Zhuang now turned to his mother, confined her
and vowed: "Not until we reach the Yellow Springs [underworld] shall we
meet again!" But he later regretted the vow:

> Ying Kaoshu, a border guard of Ying Valley, hearing of this, presented gifts
> to the duke, and the duke in turn had a meal served to him. He ate the meal
> but set aside the meat broth. When the duke asked him why, he replied,
> "Your servant has a mother who shares whatever food he eats, but she has
> never tasted your lordship's broth. I beg permission to take her some."
>
> "You have a mother to take things to. Alas, I alone have none!" said
> the duke.
>
> "May I venture to ask the meaning of that?" said Ying Kaoshu.
>
> The duke explained why he had made the remark and confessed that he
> regretted his vow.
>
> "Why should your lordship worry?" said the other. "If you dig into the

earth until you reach the springs, and fashion a tunnel where the two of you
can meet, then who is to say you have not kept your vow?" (Watson 1989,
3–4; modified transliteration)

So the mother and son met in a tunnel and reconciled. The *Zuo Commentary* concludes, "Ying Kaoshu was a man of utmost filial piety. He loved his
mother, and succeeded in inspiring a similar feeling in Duke Zhuang. Is
this not what the *Book of Odes* [*Classic of Odes*] means when it says: 'While
filial sons are unslacking, forever shall you be given good things'" (Watson
1989, 4; modified transliteration).

In recounting this story the *Zuo Commentary* employed three techniques characteristic of its historiography. First was the use of dialogues
to propel the narrative. Second was the interjection of an independent
anecdote—Ying Kaoshu's account of his filial relationship with his mother
—that, while historically insignificant, dramatized the ongoing narration and underscored its meaning (Egan 1977, 332–333). Third was the
commentarial protocol of quoting the master and hence the ubiquity of
phrases like "the gentleman remarks" or "Confucius remarks." All three
techniques were adopted by later historians and exerted a far-reaching influence in Chinese historiography.

The *Zuo Commentary's* use of dialogue recalls the early practice in the
Classic of Documents and the *Discourses on the State* (a text also attributed to
Zuo Qiuming) of recording the words of political figures. As Schaberg remarks, "Both works record speeches solely in the context of anecdotes, and
in both works the centerpiece of most anecdotes is the formal speech or
dialogue" (2001, 6). By the Warring States period there was no longer a
clear division between recording affairs and recording words; instead, the
tendency was to integrate speech into action. The *Zuo Commentary* exemplified this integration, which would be completed in Sima Qian's *Records of
the Historian*. Discourse alone no longer played such an essential role, as
the multivalent strategies of the *Zuo Commentary* indicate. Liu Zhiji contended that the discourse form went out of style around the third century
(*Shitong* 1978, 1:1–7, 14–16). What the *Zuo Commentary* did was to create a
cascade of multilayered narratives, a practice perfected by Sima Qian, who
was fond of injecting anecdotes into narratives, thus constructing "multiple narration" (Hardy 1999, 61–85). These "dramatized incidents" in the
Zuo Commentary enhanced both the aesthetic and factual components of
the historical record (Egan 1977, 332–333). They helped the author or authors complete the narration and explain its didactic meaning. They also
help readers anticipate the outcome of the unfolding event. The intrusion
of the episode where Ying Kaoshu describes his filial relationship with his
mother paves the way for the reconciliation between Duke Zhuang and his
mother.

Ying Kaoshu's story represents a recurrent motif in the *Zuo Commentary*, one that has been called the "filial diner" (Watson 1989, xxxiii). In
607 B.C.E., for instance, Zhao Dun, a minister of Jin, almost lost his life

in a conspiracy planned by his ruler. While describing the critical scene where Zhao fights his way out, the *Zuo Commentary* inserts a flashback by telling a filial-diner story. In it Zhao fed a hungry man. Like Ying Kaoshu, after receiving food from Zhao, the diner wanted to go home first and give the food to his mother. Now, as Zhao faced extreme danger, the diner repaid his debt by saving him—an example of the principle of recompense (Egan 1977, 344–346; Watson 1989, 78). By inserting this story, the *Zuo Commentary* not only prepares readers to understand the outcome of this event—good behavior would be rewarded—but it also reiterates the Confucian theme of filial piety, a cornerstone of Confucian moral and social teachings. While independent and sometimes even disruptive of the main narrative, these stories serve a larger normative purpose embedded in the *Zuo Commentary*'s moral historiography.

The *Zuo Commentary*'s innovative use of formal, independent "comments" on recorded events was also significant in the development of Chinese historiography, insofar as "comments" were to become a standard feature of almost all the dynastic histories. Using comments based on quotes from Confucius was a creation of the *Zuo* and other commentaries. All historical works up to the Warring States period, including the *Zuo Commentary*, had no visible author, a fact in stark contrast to the Greek tradition in historiography (Schaberg 2001, 258). However, by adopting the form of "Confucius remarks" or "the gentleman remarks," the *Zuo Commentary* moved a step closer to revealing authorship. Even though the author or authors remained invisible, he/they at least could make comments through Confucius' mouth. In fact, remarks attributed to Confucius appear eighty-four times in the text (Watson 1989, 4 n. 9). By the time Sima Qian wrote his work, he no longer deemed it necessary to borrow the words of Confucius or others; he simply stated: "The grand historian remarks." Sima's example was followed by later historians and became a part of the dynastic and many other histories.

Historical Prophecy and Political Legitimacy

The *Zuo Commentary* was just one text among many that registered the transformation of the ancient historical culture in the Warring States period. Often described as the golden age of philosophy, China in the fifth and fourth centuries B.C.E. witnessed a proliferation of schools of thoughts and ideas. Confucius was a pivotal figure who spearheaded this "major intellectual breakthrough" (Hsu 1999, 583), and in terms of historiography, his achievements lay in his innovative reworking of the *Spring and Autumn*. The burgeoning of intellectual culture went hand in hand with the rise of a new social class or group, the *shi* (intellectuals/schoolmen), to which the *shi* (historian/scribe) came to belong. These *shi*, or "schoolmen" (Lewis 1999), originated from the Zhou nobility, but as times went on, they came to include many talented and educated of obscure backgrounds. Increasingly, the term *shi* referred to a person of moral and intellectual excellence, connoting cultural status rather than social origins (Hsu 1999, 584). Unlike the Western Zhou and earlier periods when the *shi* (scribes) constituted the core of the literate elite as appointed officials, the new *shi* (intellectuals) consisted of members from various walks of life. There were two main reasons for this expansion. On the one hand, the Zhou court was no longer able to absorb all the educated people and monopolize the intellectual culture; many educated and talented people had to seek employment in the feudal states. There were also increased opportunities for education and upward social mobility. Confucius played an essential role in democratizing, as it were, educational opportunities; he offered his teachings to all regardless of social origin. Confucius, although a pioneer, was not alone; many others established schools of thought. The knowledge of history appeared to be an important component in many of the schools. The *Zuo Commentary* documented many cases where the *shi* (intellectuals), including the *shi* (historians/scribes), used historical examples to articulate and enhance the persuasive power of their ideas. Many distinct views and practices of history emerged, resulting in one of the most creative periods in historical thinking and writing.

After Confucius' death, interpretations proliferated around Confucius' ideas and ideals, especially those manifested in his *Spring and Autumn*. Such intellectual endeavors unquestionably contributed to the growth of Confucianism as a whole. As Burton Watson reminds us, "when Chinese scholars talk about the *Spring and Autumn Annals* they do not mean simply the brief, dull text of the Lu chronicle, but the text as interpreted in the light of this [Confucian] tradition" (1958, 78–79). Indeed, the word *zhuan* can well be translated as "tradition," as opposed to the more common "commentary"—hence the *Zuo Tradition*, as opposed to the *Zuo Commentary*—so as to convey the literal meaning. In addition to the *Zuo Commentary*, there were, as pointed out, the *Gongyang Commentary* and *Guliang Commentary* (or *Gongyang Tradition* and *Guliang Tradition*), the other two extant commentaries on the *Spring and Autumn*. All three works sought to explicate, extend, and disseminate Confucius' ideas and doctrines. Compared with the *Zuo Commentary*, the *Gongyang* and the *Guliang* aimed at illuminating the moral meanings and political messages that Confucius invested in the original classical text. With regard to Duke Yin 1st year (722 B.C.E.), the beginning point of the *Spring and Autumn Annals* and the three commentaries, the *Zuo Commentary* explained that Confucius did not mention Duke Yin's ascension to the throne because he was only a regent and continued with an elaborate narrative about the fratricidal conflict between Duke Zhuang and Taishu Duan. By contrast, both the *Gongyang Commentary* and *Guliang Commentary* elaborated on the rationale behind the omission of Duke Yin's ascension. The *Gongyang Commentary* has this to say:

> Why didn't it speak of ascendancy? Because it was to follow the duke's intention. Why did the duke have such an intention? Because he intended to give the state to Huan afterwards. Why did he want to give it to Huan? Because

though Huan was younger, he was more honored than his elder brother
Yin. All the people in the state knew very well that Huan was honored and
Yin was humbled, even though Yin was not only older but also nicer. Ministers would like to make Yin the head of the state. Yin had thought about
declining the offer but accepted it after all because he was worried if he
did not do so, then Huan might not be able to ascend to the throne in the
future because these ministers might not trust him. So Yin became the
duke for Huan's sake. Since Yin was not only the elder but also nicer, why
didn't he become the official throne? Supposedly the heir ought to be the
elder regardless of character; yet the parent could favor a son regardless of
age. Huan was honored because of his mother's preference. Why so? Because a son's honor comes from his mother and vice versa. (*Gongyang zhuan*
1993, 646)

This elaborate explanation utilizes a very different strategy in expounding the Confucian principle of filial piety. Bypassing extensive historical
narrative, the *Gongyang Commentary* went straight to the point, explaining
why filial piety took priority. Even if the parent was wrong, there was still
no reason for disobedience because "a son's honor comes from his mother
and vice versa." This statement drove home the ideal social order anchored
on the parent-child relationship, in which parents were to be obeyed by
children.

Notwithstanding the imperative of obedience and respect for the familial hierarchy, children needed to understand the difference between
right and wrong. This was the often overlooked aspect of filial piety that the
Guliang Commentary addressed in the same entry. Adopting a strategy similar to that of the *Gongyang Commentary*, the *Guliang Commentary* offered discussions rather than narratives. Instead of concentrating on the mother's
preference, it discussed the role of the father, the deceased duke of Lu,
and pointed out that faults also lay with Duke Yin, and this explained why
Confucius did not mention his ascendancy. Besides filial piety there was
also the *dao*, the Heavenly Way, which revealed right and wrong. Huan was
honored because his father had favored him—the *Guliang Commentary* did
not mention his mother—but it was wrong. "A filial son should expand his
father's virtue, not his wrong," the *Guliang Commentary* claimed, "and to
honor his father's will by giving power to Huan was not correct, but a mistake. The father eventually righted his wrong by letting Duke Yin be the
regent. But Duke Yin wanted to give the throne to his brother because
he thought it had been his father's intention. What he did would have repeated his father's wrong." The *Guliang Commentary* concluded that by preparing the throne for his younger brother, Duke Yin neither realized the
profound values of the Way nor understood the true meaning of filiality
(*Guliang zhuan* 1993, 748). Here we are offered not only a different reading on Duke Yin's coming to power, but also another interpretation of the
principle of filial piety.

Apart from its liberal use of narratives, the *Zuo Commentary* also differed from the other two commentaries in terms of interpretations. Although it by and large shared Confucius' worry about rampant political disorder and social unrest, the *Zuo Commentary* actually endorsed certain changes taking place. It ridiculed the quixotic behavior of Duke Xiang of Song, who, while engaging in a battle with his enemy in 638 B.C.E., fastidiously followed propriety by not allowing his army to strike the enemy before it came into position, an action that eventually cost him the battle and his newly acquired status as the hegemon (*Zuozhuan* 1993, 400). The issue here was anachronism. By the time the three commentaries appeared, there was no longer any realistic hope that the Zhou royal house might regain its suzerainty, as Confucius had wished several decades earlier. As most of these historical texts were not written by official *shi* of the Zhou court, it is understandable that some took unorthodox positions regarding the relevance of Zhou ritual culture. In fact, there seemed to be a consensus among the *shi* (intellectuals) that the challenge for them was not to figure out how to preserve or revive the Zhou ritual culture but to find a way to capture the essence of the old culture. The *Gongyang Commentary's* explanation of the capture of the unicorn reflected this consensus—the Zhou system had come to an end, which disheartened Confucius, but a new ruler would soon emerge from its ruins (*Gongyang zhuan* 1993, 747).

The *shi* (intellectuals) no doubt proposed different ways to explain the changes and to build a new order that would reflect and accommodate changed realities. But their efforts collectively seemed to lead to "a historical leapfrogging into an imagined antiquity that had the twin virtues of being sufficiently distant from received practices to allow for a critique, and sufficiently lacking in documentation that one could assign to it whatever practices one desired" (Lewis 1999, 123). In short, the past—the antique past, to be more precise—came into prominent play. Descriptions of this antiquity varied a good deal, so did interpretations of its relation to the present time. Mencius, for example, seemed to agree with the *Gongyang Commentary's* pronouncement that there was a critical historical juncture in Confucius' time. He went further to argue that the time in which he was living was just like others in the past, in which the sage-kings ruled according to the will of Heaven. However, there were 500-year intervals between these junctures, when governance was less than ideal. Mencius described this schema of historical development:

> From Yao and Shun down to Tang were 500 years and more. As to Yu and Gaoyao, they saw those earliest sages, and so knew their doctrines, while Tang heard their doctrines as transmitted, and so knew them. From Tang to King Wen were 500 years and more. As to Yiyin and Laizhu, they saw Tang and knew their doctrines, while King Wen heard them as transmitted, and so knew them. From King Wen to Confucius were 500 years and more. As to Taigongwang and Sanyisheng, they saw Wen and so knew his doctrines, while Confucius heard them as transmitted, and so knew them. From Confucius downwards until now, there are only 100 years and somewhat more. The

distance in time from the sage is so far from being remote, and so very near
at hand was the sage's residence. In these circumstances, is there no one to
transmit his doctrines? Yea, is there no one to do so? (Mencius 1970, 502;
modified transliteration)

Here Mencius advanced a cyclical view of historical movement, in which
ancient ideals were renewed and transmitted periodically—the sage-kings
had established the doctrines of governance and bequeathed them to posterity. Every 500 years or so, a new sage-king would appear to renew the
ancient doctrines and values. But there was a problem in Mencius' theory:
Confucius was not a ruler, and yet without him the 500-year cycle did not
hold. Mencius had to find a way to put Confucius on a par with the other
wise rulers. His solution was to develop a new criterion of governance,
based on the Heaven-humanity correlation. Replying to Wan Zhang's question whether the sage-king Yao gave the throne to Shun, Mencius gave a
surprising answer:

"No. The sovereign cannot give the throne to another."
"Yes; but Shun had the throne. Who gave it to him?"
"Heaven gave it to him . . . ." [the dialogue continued. Wan Zhang appeared
puzzled and asked if Heaven gave specific injunctions. Mencius answered in
the negative, claiming that Heaven's will is manifested in people's conduct]
"The sovereign can present a man to Heaven, but he cannot make Heaven
give that man the throne. . . . Yao presented Shun to Heaven, and Heaven
accepted him. He presented him to the people, and the people accepted
him. Therefore I say, 'Heaven does not speak. It simply indicated its will by
its personal conduct and its conduct of affairs.'" (ibid., 354–356; modified
transliteration)

Here Heaven and humanity became interchangeable. While Heaven indicated its acceptance of a ruler through its conduct, its conduct was shown
and manifested in the behavior of the people (*min*). Mencius pointed out
that after Yao's death, people went to Shun for leadership, and not to Yao's
son. So it was the people's action that made Heaven accept Shun. Mencius
referred to a statement from the *Classic of Documents:* "Heaven sees . . . as
my people see; Heaven hears . . . as my people hear" (ibid., 357). What
Heaven and people wanted from a ruler was benevolence (*ren*). Because
Confucius embraced benevolence in his teachings and personified it in his
deeds, he showed that he had received the Mandate of Heaven and hence
was an "uncrowned king" (*suwang*). In fact, according to Mencius, Confucius' status was higher because he was not an ordinary sovereign king, but
a sage-ruler like Yao and King Wen.

Mencius developed a theory of political legitimacy that reformulated
the idea of the Mandate of Heaven. To him, the Mandate of Heaven was not
an abstract idea, much less a convenient justification of the authority of a
reigning ruler. Rather, it was something realized in a benevolent govern-

ment: "It was by benevolence that the three dynasties gained the throne, and by not being benevolent that they lost it. It is by the same means that the decaying and flourishing, the preservation and perishing, of [s]tates are determined" (ibid., 293–294). Benevolence was, in essence, humanity; as Mencius proclaimed, "Benevolence is the people." In other words, if the sovereign treated people as his first priority, he established a benevolent government; and if the government was benevolent, it would endure: "There are instances of individuals without benevolence who have got possession of a single [s]tate, but there has been no instance of the throne's being got by one without benevolence." Mencius regarded the people as being prior to the ruler: "The people are the most important element . . . ; the spirits of the land and grain are the next; the sovereign is the lightest" (ibid., 483–485).

Mencius' emphasis on benevolent and munificent government seemed idealistic in an era when the warring states, sometimes numbering a couple of hundred, were engaged in ferocious warfare dominance, or in the case of the smaller states, for survival. However, his idealism had enormous appeal. In many illuminating narratives the *Zuo Commentary* championed Mencius' idea that "people are the root" (*minben*) (Q. Chen 1999, 65–71). In 520 B.C.E., for instance, Yanzi, an envoy from the state of Qi, had a conversation with his host on a visit to the state of Jin. When asked about the situation in Qi, Yanzi answered frankly that it was not good because the ruler showed no benevolence toward his subjects. By contrast, the ruler of Chen, the neighboring state, exercised benevolence and as a result would soon annex Qi. Yanzi elaborated, "If the ruler loves people like his parents, then the people will follow his rule as naturally as the flow of water" (*Zuozhuan* 1993, 544). Mencius used the same metaphor: "The people turn to a benevolent rule as water flows downwards" (Mencius 1970, 300).

Because the people were the first priority in governance, the *Zuo Commentary* held that some of the political changes taking place at the time were justified. When Duke Zhao was the ruler of Lu, he felt threatened by an able minister named Jishi. Duke Zhao conspired to kill him but did not succeed because Jishi had already garnered enough support in Lu. Instead, Duke Zhao had to flee from his own state and eventually died in exile. In his absence Jishi ruled Lu and exercised benevolence toward the people. As a consequence, a *shi* named Mu commented that Jishi was a gift from Heaven so that Lu would enjoy beneficent rule. Although he was not a prince, his position was justifiable because he had the support of the people. "The spirits of land and grain," Mu concluded, "do not require a permanent worshipper, nor is one's throne permanent. This has always been the case since antiquity" (*Zuozhuan* 1993, 602). To put it another way, expedient change was acceptable, if it served the people. Although the comment came from one individual, it nonetheless shows that the *Zuo Commentary* endorsed certain political changes, as opposed to Confucius' insistence on restoring the Zhou ritual system. What concerned its author or authors, as well as Mencius, was whether the changes would in fact benefit the people. For them, history would accommodate expedient change as long as it conformed to some enduring principle.

The idea of the primacy of the people was also shared by Xunzi (318–238 B.C.E.), another leading Confucian who was otherwise considered an opponent to Mencius' interpretations of Confucian teachings (Qu 1999b, 162–163). While sharing Mencius' empathy for the people, Xunzi appeared less nostalgic about the past. Mencius' cyclical view of history placed a notable emphasis on retrieving the past. Xunzi was more concerned with recent experiences. "If one would like to observe the traces of the sage-kings, one can simply look at the later kings because they elaborated on them" (W. Du 1993, 143–144). He also had a more realistic view of historical change; the earlier the times were, the more obscure their records became, and hence they were less relevant and valuable. His observation brings to mind Confucius' remark that he could discuss the rituals of the Xia and Yin, but not that of the Song because of lack of evidence (*Analects*, 1997, 61). However, Xunzi's expression was not as sentimental. Confucius wished he had the evidence so he could talk about all the ancient rituals. Xunzi hinted at the idea of progress or evolution in history, whereas Confucius' interest in the ancient ritual system and normative tradition, *li*, presumed a regressive view of historical change. In the *Classic of Rites*, a compendium of the Zhou ritual culture, Confucius supposedly introduced two concepts — "great unity" (*datong*) and "small prosperity" (*xiaokang*) — to describe the origin of *li*. Confucius posited that an ideal past once existed, an age of great unity, when everyone lived in peace and harmony without the need of *li*. In the following age of small prosperity, however, *li* was created by the sage-kings to sustain the social and political order. Sadly, in subsequent ages *li* fell into oblivion (*Liji* 1993, 256–257). Though regressive, Confucius' periodization of history in terms of great unity and small prosperity would prove to be inspirational to many later Confucians, fueling their imagination of an ideal future. By turning Confucius' scheme on its head, the age and ideal of great unity could be projected onto the future as a sort of alluring utopia.

Confucian interpretations of historical change were not the only theories available at the time. Mozi (468–376 B.C.E.), a major critic of Confucian teachings, found fault with the determinist, or naturalist, tone in the Confucian idea of history (Puett 2001, 55–56). He played down the role of Heaven in human affairs, disdaining the Confucian idea, especially the Mencian cyclical view, that "might encourage a hope for the future based on Heaven's presence in history" (Schwartz 1985, 162).

It was Han Fei (279–233 B.C.E.), a leading Legalist, who articulated a more optimistic view of history. Although he respected Confucius, Han Fei regarded Confucian teachings as anachronistic, irrelevant, and even detrimental. To Han, change was not only inevitable but also necessary. To expound his argument, he divided history into four periods: the ancient past (*shanggu*), the middle past (*zhonggu*), the recent past (*jingu*), and the contemporary age (*dangjin*). He contended that each age had its unique needs and problems, requiring the specific service and talents of particular heroes and sages. In ancient times when people were struggling with the wild and natural elements, it was fitting that a sage would help them build houses for protection. Another sage would teach them to make fire to cook foods, thereby improving their health. In the middle past when the great flood occurred, the sage Yu tackled the problem. As each age faced particular challenges, different sages appeared. Han Fei concluded, "Those who praise the way of Yao, Shun, Tang, and Yu to the present age will certainly be laughed at by the new sages. The sage does not assign truth to high antiquity, nor take as law any constant proprieties. He assesses the affairs of the age and prepares himself in response to them" (Lewis 1999, 39). In the contemporary age there must be sages with new insights appropriate to the time, given that the experiences of the past sages are dated and no longer relevant.

Convinced of historical evolution, Han Fei took it for granted that a new age would succeed the old, even though he did not quite explain how a new order might come into being. Nevertheless, in an era of feudal warfare and political strife, there was the yearning to ascertain control over the future. The ability to make prophecies about historical change had great appeal. Traditionally this had been the job of the *shi* (scribes); it was now assumed by many others of the *shi* (intellectual) social group, which included a wide variety of talents—religious experts, bureaucratic officials, military specialists, and even physicians (A. Wang 2000, 78–81). Mencius, Mozi, Xunzi, and Han Fei were not *shi*, nor was Zou Yan (305–249 B.C.E.), the alleged founder of the Yin-Yang and Five-Phases school, but all of them speculated on history and historical change with thoughts of what the future might hold.

Zou Yan articulated the most complete and complex theory of historical change, which was later appropriated to justify the establishment of the Qin dynasty (221–206 B.C.E.) as the legitimate power that unified China. Zou was a hotly sought-after and successful advisor in his time, honored by powerful lords and rulers wherever he traveled (Schwartz 1985, 356). Though exceedingly popular, however, none of Zou Yan's writings, if he ever produced any, survived the Qin period. What little we know of them comes from Sima Qian. Zou Yan owed his popularity and influence to two things: his elaboration of correlative cosmology with the theory of the Five Phases (*wuxing*) and his ingenious use of this theory to interpret and predict historical change. By correlating natural phases with patterns of history, he created a highly appealing theory because of its putative predictive value (ibid., 362–363).

The predictive power stemmed from a supposed regularity and precision in the workings of the five phases. The Five Phases (or elements or agents) of earth, wood, metal, fire, and water were mutually reinforcing and negating, such that fire melted metal, metal cut wood, wood made fire, fire was extinguished by water, water was absorbed by earth, and so on. To the extent that the interaction of these phases followed a predetermined pattern, everything in the universe was predictable. Zou Yan integrated this system of naturalistic and cosmic movement into history by identifying one historical period with one element and then constructing a pattern of succession from the past, through the present, to the future. According to Zou's theory, since the Yellow Emperor, the legendary ancestor of the Chinese, represented the element of earth, the succeeding Xia dynasty was naturally associated with wood, as wood penetrated earth. From this correspondence we know the Xia's succession was legitimate because it conformed to the cosmic pattern of change. The Xia was later replaced by the Shang, which was associated with metal. The Shang was supplanted by the Zhou, which embodied the fire element (Schwartz 1985, 362). The plausibility of this theory depended on the *a priori* association of one element with a dynasty, which set in motion the chain of replacement. Zou Yan and his disciples developed an elaborate system in which emblematic colors, ritual acts, and paraphernalia of all sorts played roles to advertise and justify the authority of a regime. The entire complex of rituals that linked political change with cosmic-natural movement became the defining ceremony marking a new ruler's ascendancy and symbolically signaling the legitimacy of his new government.

It should be noted that neither the Five Phases nor the correlative idea were Zou's invention. The *Classic of Documents* had mentioned them and discussed their interrelations (Henderson 1984, 7–8). Nor was Zou Yan the first to use these elements and phases to make predictions. The *Zuo Commentary* recorded many such prophecies made by the *shi* (historian/scribe). For instance, in Duke Zhao 9th Year (533 B.C.E.), a fire broke out in the state of Chen; whereupon Pi Zao made a prophecy based on it—the state of Chen would regain its sovereignty from the state of Chu because the former was symbolized by water and latter by fire, and water extinguishes fire (*Zuozhuan* 1993, 559). We are not sure about Pi Zao's occupation, but it is likely that he was a *shi*. Several decades later, in Duke Ai 9th Year (486 B.C.E.), three *shi* advised the ruler of Jin not to attack Song in his effort to help Zheng. He should attack Qi instead.

> Ying [the surname of the Jin ruler] is a name of Water, Zi [the surname of the ruler of the Song] is the position of Water. To put the name and the position in antagonism is not to be attempted. Yan Di had a Fire master, from whom the house of Jiang is descended. Water conquers Fire. According to this you may attack the states with the surname of Jiang. (A. Wang 2000, 84)

Here we see a good example of how the elements were correlated. In this case they were associated with the names of the persons involved. It is also noteworthy that not all five elements were involved, as the numerology of five was only one among several commonly used enumeration orders (Henderson 1984, 7). There were numerologies of three, four, six, eight, and others. Yet by the Han era, Five-Phase numerology had eclipsed its rivals (ibid., 9–10). The shift from the numerology of four, which found expression in the idea of the Sifang (four directions), to that of five reflected a change in the political realm. The rise of the theory of the Five Phases "transformed the ancient Sifang-centered cosmology and dismantled the previous mode of cosmology integrated with political power" (A. Wang 2000, 92). In the Sifang theory, the cosmos was perceived in terms of four, as in the four directions, so there was the presumed center that radiated power to the four poles. In the Five-Phase system, the center disappeared and change became utterly cyclical. The absence of a power center mirrored in a trenchant way the situation of the Warring States period. More specifically, it reflected the fact that rulers had by then lost their shamanic monopoly in divination. They had to rely on the advice of the *shi* (intellectuals) for guidance (ibid., 75ff). All this helped account for the popularity of Zou Yan's Five-Phase theory.

Zou Yan's genius lay in his systematization of the Five-Phase cosmology into a sophisticated correlative theory that could be brought to bear on human history (Schwartz 1985, 366). He not only associated historical periods with the various Phases, but he also related the rise and fall of polities with extraordinary natural occurrences, which he construed as omens and portents. The rise of the Yellow Emperor, linked with the earth element, was announced by the appearance of a yellow dragon and a great earthworm. The ascendancy of the Xia, embodying the wood element, was heralded by the appearance of luxuriant vegetation. The rise of the Shang, representing the metal element, was predicted by the appearance of a sword blade in water. All the dynasties assumed emblematic colors correlated with their elements—the Yellow Emperor was yellow, the Xia green, the Shang white, and the Zhou red (A. Wang 2000, 138–139). The Zhou's replacement of the Shang was foretold by the unusual presence of red birds. Although these ingenious associations were after-the-fact explanations of dynastic successions, Zou Yan's theory, by virtue of its seeming command and comprehension of dynamic cosmic-historical patterns, laid claim to explanatory potency and cogency.

Toward the end of the Warring States period, his theory found a powerful proponent in Lü Buwei (?–235 B.C.E.), the chief political advisor of Yin Zheng, prince of the state of Qin and future First Emperor of the Qin dynasty. In *Master Lü's Spring and Autumn* (*Lüshi chunqiu*), a work composed by a group of schoolmen under Lü Buwei's patronage, Zou Yan's theory came to be increasingly couched in political language. It was used not only to explain dynastic successions of the past but also to predict future ones, that is, to lay the grounds for Qin's ascendancy. Although Zou Yan died long before the Qin dynasty (221–206 B.C.E.) came into existence, he had prophesized, according to *Master Lü's Spring and Autumn*, that the dynasty succeeding the Zhou would be associated with the water element and black color, in keeping with the natural cosmic pattern of the succession of the Five Phases. After the Qin was established, all that remained to be done was to associate the new dynasty with the predetermined emblematic color and element, thereby justifying its historical succession and legitimizing its political rule. In the initial years of the Qin dynasty, the new ruler and his advisors undertook with great gusto and fanfare this task of consolidating legitimacy by appropriating all the cosmic signs and asserting symbolic control over the natural forces.

The World of Sima Qian and His Magisterial History

In 221 B.C.E., the Warring States period finally came to an end. Having overpowered the six other contending states through military conquests and diplomatic maneuvers, the state of Qin, which had risen in the northwest, now occupied the power center. The Qin unification marked a new beginning in Chinese history, and the influence of its rule and institutional innovations were far-reaching (C. Huang 2002). The Qin dynasty was actually short-lived, even though the founding emperor dreamed of creating an eternal regime, a goal reflected in his draconian policies. In addition to implementing unifying measures, such as adopting a standard script, a uniform width of highway, and imposing thought control—the last culminated in the notorious episode of burning undesirable books and burying Confucian scholars alive—the Qin ruler enthusiastically appropriated Zou Yan's Five-Phase theory to affirm his legitimacy. Aligning his reign with Zou's cosmic scheme, the First Emperor adopted water as the ascendant element and black as the emblematic color. His ambition to create a new era in history was underscored by the fact that water represented the fifth and final phase, so it was the Qin that brought a closure to the succession of the powers (Puett 2001, 144). Zou's theory also justified the emperor's embrace of Legalism, a school of thought that prevailed in the late Warring States period. Through strict use of the legal apparatus, the emperor established a regimented and coercive sociopolitical order associated with the water element, which was animated by the *yin* force characterized by "the severity of winter and darkness" (Schwartz 1985, 363). Thus cosmological theory provided the underpinning of policies that strove to order the world. But mythic-cosmic thinking could not explain away the fact that the Qin subjects lived in misery under repressive rule. Not long after the emperor's death, in face of widespread rebellions, the Qin collapsed almost as quickly as it rose. From the ruins emerged the Han dynasty, during which historical and historiographical achievements reached unprecedented heights.

The Han in many ways inherited Qin institutions, but the precipitous rise and fall of the Qin also presented a serious question: how was the Han to reckon with the Qin in history? More precisely, how should both the Qin and Han be situated in terms of Zou Yan's scheme of dynastic succession? To answer these questions was to determine the legitimacy of the Han. Since the Han rose initially as a rebel force against the Qin, the early rulers, such as Liu Bang (256/247–195 B.C.E.), who became the founding Emperor Gao, simply considered the Han dynasty to be the rightful replacement of the Qin. No sooner had he founded the dynasty than Emperor Gao decided to take over the emblematic color and element of the Qin—black and water—in order to make the Han the legitimate successor to the Zhou (fire). The Han rejected the legitimacy of the Qin in dynastic history, turning it into a mere interregnum by an illegitimate usurper. Emperor Gao simultaneously reversed the harsh Legalist policies of the Qin. He grounded his rule in the Huang-Lao (Yellow Emperor and Laozi) school of Daoism that favored "nonaction" (*wuwei*). As a consequence the early years of the Han were by and large characterized by an unobtrusive government that levied moderate taxes and corvée.

Yet Emperor Gao and the early Han rulers were no less interested in centralizing power. As self-proclaimed successors of the Zhou, they were nevertheless ambivalent about the Zhou's enfeoffment system (*fengjian*). Emperor Gao initially revived the system, but he quickly changed his mind and waged campaigns against the newly enfeoffed kings. These campaigns were not entirely successful—Emperor Gao died in one of them—because they failed to destroy the power of the fiefs. But the desire to centralize persisted, which may explain the early Han rulers' lukewarm reception of Lu Jia's (c. 206–180 B.C.E.) proposal that the Han rule in accordance with the Confucian classics. It was not until the reign of Emperor Wu (r. 141–87 B.C.E.) that a new direction was taken. Many later Confucian scholars were ambivalent about the legacy of the Emperor Wu. He was an ambitious and aggrandizing ruler who pressed for territorial expansion and power consolidation. He waged aggressive internal campaigns against rebellious local powers and external ones against hostile nomadic tribes north of the border. As a result, within a few decades, the Han dynasty had forged a highly centralized empire of unprecedented size. But Emperor Wu, unlike his predecessors, took an avid interest in Confucian learning despite its disapproval of government pursuit of centralizing policies. In 136 B.C.E., because of the emperor's interest and patronage, acclaimed Confucian scholars were endowed with professorships to teach the various classics, and in 124 B.C.E. these classics were established as the core curriculum in the newly founded imperial academy, leading to a fundamental philosophical and ideological shift from Huang-Lao Daoism to Confucianism.

The key figure credited by most Chinese scholars for effecting this transition was Dong Zhongshu (179–104 B.C.E.), a proponent of New Script classical Confucianism. Like his predecessors Lu Jia and Jia Yi (201–168 B.C.E.), who desired to integrate Zou Yan's Five-Phase theory into the Confucian moral vision of history and in this fashion reject the legitimacy of the Qin, Dong Zhongshu argued that the Han should sever its ties completely with the Qin by adopting a new symbol. Lu Jia, drawing on Zou Yan's correlative theory without accepting the implication that the succession of power meant the triumph of one element over another, had put forth a grand moral cosmology of Heaven-earth-humanity guided by the *dao*, the universal moral Way. Lu contended that the transmission of power was achieved ultimately in response to the moral principles patterned on Heaven, which was the *dao* illuminated by the sages in the classics, the *Spring and Autumn Annals* in particular. In other words, the Han acquired power because it had apprehended the moral Way. Following Lu Jia, Dong Zhongshu revised the Five-Phase system with a competing theory, the Three Systems (*santong*), which referred to the succession of the first three dynasties of Xia, Shang, and Zhou. The dynamic force behind dynastic succession was the Mandate of Heaven, responsible for all transmissions of authority. By introducing this theory of Three Systems that promoted the eternal Way mandated by Heaven, Dong rejected "the implication of [the] Five Powers [phases] theory that there are different ways of government, each legitimate: rule by force and rule by virtue." Instead, Dong maintained that "the Dao of Heaven is the only legitimate and permanent way of government" (A. Wang 2000, 150).

Although no convincing evidence suggests that Emperor Wu's decision to change the dynastic symbol from water to earth indicated his acceptance of Dong Zhongshu's proposal—Michael Puett (2001, 169) has argued that Dong's theory had little to do with Emperor Wu's decision—by adopting the earth symbol, performing the *fengshan* sacrifice, and creating a new calendar, Emperor Wu clearly intended to project the image that he was a reincarnation of the Yellow Emperor, the legendary ancestor of the Chinese and the first power in the Five-Phase system. In other words he wanted his reign to be the start of a new era, making a clean break from the Qin, a move championed by Dong Zhongshu. Similarly, when Emperor Wu adopted the Xia calendar, the first dynasty in Dong's theory of the Three Systems, he might also be subscribing to Dong's position that the Qin be expunged from the legitimate line of dynastic succession. But the emperor's adoption of the earth element could also mean that he did recognize the Qin's position in history and did acknowledge the Han as its successor because earth was the symbol that immediately followed the Qin symbol of water. Such contradictions illustrate why Emperor Wu's legacy is open to different interpretations.[1]

The ambiguity and complexity of Emperor Wu's era characterized the world of Sima Qian, commonly, and with justification, regarded as imperial China's greatest historian. Indeed, Sima's entangled relationship with Emperor Wu left a profound imprint on his life and work. In many respects Sima Qian was a true son of his age, and his presentation of history was as complex as the age itself. His magnum opus, the *Records of the Historian* (*Shiji*), portrayed in detail a "microcosmic world" or "a world in miniature," marked by inconsistencies, uncertainties, and contradictions (Hardy 1999). Sima Qian wanted to make sense of his world, which, for

---

1. Michael Puett (2001, 174–175) argues that Emperor Wu, animated by a sense of historical continuity, was intent on acknowledging the Qin as a predecessor, whereas Aihe Wang (2000, 151) seems to suggest that the emperor more or less shared Dong Zhongshu's stance and was intent on denying Qin's place in dynastic succession. Michael Loewe (1986, 103–106) points out that these two positions represented two conflicting political forces in the Han court. During the reign of Emperor Wu the one represented by Dong Zhongshu began to gain an upper hand.

him, spanned from his own time back to the remote beginnings of high antiquity. Sima, in his earnest effort to understand the past, created a historical tradition that was utterly different from the ones he inherited. He developed new styles and forms that would exert lasting influences on Chinese historiography.

Sima Qian was born into a family bearing the hereditary title *shi*, or *taishi* (grand historian/astrologer). However, he was not particularly interested in offering predictions and warnings to the emperor based on readings and interpretations of prodigious celestial phenomena—examples of these duties and activities abound in the *Zuo Commentary*. The young Sima Qian studied with Dong Zhongshu, an expert on correlative cosmology and an outspoken proponent of the theory of the "unity of Heaven and humanity" (*tianren heyi*). Dong's influence, especially his interpretation of the *Spring and Autumn*, is identifiable in Sima's *Records*. Like Dong, Sima registered his immense admiration for the *Spring and Autumn* in his writings. But as Stephen Durrant contends, there is "no indication that Sima Qian accepted Dong Zhongshu's idea that one had to go well beyond the words of *Spring and Autumn Annals* to find the text's cherished 'principles'" (1995, 65). In fact, while Dong and Sima were both interested in the *Spring and Autumn* and shared Confucius' belief in the efficacy of expounding abstract ideas through past events, they had divergent views of history. Dong was ultimately interested in establishing a "moral-politico-metaphysical system that transcends or even negates historical changes," and this diverged quite sharply from the intentions of the historically minded Sima Qian (W. Li 1994, 354).

What were Sima's historical ambitions and views? Even though Sima was born into a family of *shi*, he did not seem to have planned originally to do what he eventually did—produce a magisterial history. Even by the time Sima's father inherited the title and position of *shi*, priorities had changed because the official historical culture had been transformed, as we have shown. Certain of their responsibilities had been taken over by others and the office had lost some of its traditional cachet and prestige. The Qin did restore a few of the *shi*'s activities, but owing to the brevity of the dynasty, their prestige was not revived significantly. The Han likewise reestablished *shi* positions at court, but at the same time, some bearing the old title were asked to perform duties in the executive and legal branches of the government. In addition, certain traditional *shi* duties, such as calendar-making, were assigned to officials other than the *shi* or *taishi*. In fact, it was not until Emperor Wu's reign that the position of *taishi*, whose primary responsibility was to design and administer the calendar, was resurrected (Niu 1999, 36–39). In a letter to his friend Ren An, Sima Qian admitted that "the *shi*, with his knowledge of literature, history, astrology and the calendar, is close to being a diviner and shaman-priest." While this description recalls the *shi* of old, by Sima's time the *shi* had long suffered diminished prestige and importance. Sima lamented that the *shi* of his time, like court jesters, performed their tasks merely to entertain their masters (X. Chen 1998, 32–34).

Sima Qian would not be content with the status quo; nor was his father, Sima Tan, who had high expectations and hopes for his son. The elder Sima ensured that his son received a solid education, immersing him in the learning of the various schools. His intensive study in his formative years must have stimulated a good deal of intellectual curiosity, for as a young adult, Qian embarked on an investigative tour. He traveled widely, visiting many historic places seeking to gain firsthand knowledge of the country's typography, geography, and diverse cultural traditions. Not long after his return, his father died. On his deathbed Sima Tan recalled the family's honor and responsibility as court historians in the past:

> Our ancestors were Grand Historians for the house of Zhou. From the most ancient times they were eminent and renowned when in the days of Yu and Xia they were in charge of astronomical affairs. In later ages our family declined. Will this tradition end with me? If you in turn become Grand Historian, you must continue the work of our ancestors. (Watson 1958, 49; modified transliteration)

Sima Tan obviously intended to encourage his son to renew the glorious family tradition, but his advice was based on an anachronistic belief, to the extent that the office of Grand Historian had lost much of its former luster (X. Chen 1998, 32–34). Sima Tan's own experience had illustrated the sad decline of the status of Grand Historian. One factor contributing to his death seemed to have been the great shame and resentment he felt as a result of his exclusion from the *feng* and *shan* sacrifices on Mount Tai in 110 B.C.E., the first of its kind ever performed by a Han emperor (Satō 1997, 58–60). Traditionally, as the Grand Historian, Sima Tan would have been in charge of the ceremony. Instead, he had to stay behind in court, deprived of the opportunity to participate in the grand ritual.

Sima Tan's high expectations and deathbed injunction no doubt influenced Sima Qian's work and engendered an identifiable "tension" in his writings (Durrant 1995, 1–28). This tension arose not only because father and son had different ideas of history, but also because of the difference in the planning and direction of their careers. Early on in his life Sima Qian had planned a different career for himself. After his tour of the country, the main goal of which was to look for vestiges of great heroes and their exemplary accomplishments, but before his father's death, he entered government service as a *langzhong*, an officer in the imperial retinue. Aspiring to establish a name for himself through martial achievements, he took part in several military expeditions and led one to Bashu (Sichuan) on the dynasty's southwestern border. But when his father passed away, Sima gave up his military life and followed the old man's exhortation to continue the family's historical tradition. Instead of *ligong*—achieving political power and bureaucratic merit—he would devote himself to *liyan*—establishing a lasting tradition of words and writings (X. Chen 1998, 31–95).

Sima left no record of what he thought about this midlife career change, but judging from his father's words, we have reason to believe that Sima had little choice. As Tan pointedly reminded Qian that he would inherit the position of grand historian, he also gave his son a lesson in filial piety:

> After I die, you will become Grand Historian. When you become Grand His-
> torian, you must not forget what I have desired to expound and write. Now
> filial piety begins with the serving of your parents; next you must serve your
> sovereign; and finally you must make something of yourself, that your name
> may go down through the ages for the glory of your father and mother. This
> is the most important part of filial piety. (Watson 1958, 49)

Sima Qian was told in no uncertain terms that his quest for achievements must include fulfillment of filial obligations to his parents. He was given no choice but to continue and complete the historiographical project that his father had started. Upon hearing his father's words, Sima made this pledge: "I, your son, am ignorant and unworthy, but I shall endeavor to set forth in full the reports of antiquity which have come down from our ancestors. I shall not dare to be remiss!" (Watson 1958, 49–50)

Sima Tan's urging his son to continue his work raises another question. Had Tan's historical project stemmed from his own personal interest, or was it an assignment that came with his title of *taishi*? There is no question that the work of the *shi* in the Han differed tremendously from that in earlier times. The *taishi*'s primary responsibility fell within the area of calendar design and administration. As grand astrologer, it is reasonable to assume that Sima Tan studied history largely out of his own interest (Hardy 1999, 18; X. Chen 1998, 33–34). However, it is also possible that the project may not have been a completely private one, because apparently at that time the *taishi* was not yet a position that dealt exclusively with the calendar, as it would later become (Niu 1998, 46–48). Whatever the case, Sima Tan, out of admiration for the ancient *shi* tradition, probably aspired to write a history of his age, imposing on himself the duty of an "official historian" (Inaba 1999, 97). Undoubtedly Tan held a very high regard for his own age and was loath to let the glorious accomplishments of the time fall into oblivion: "Now the house of Han has arisen, and all the world is united under one rule. I have been Grand Historian, and yet I have failed to set forth a record of all the enlightened rulers and wise lords, the faithful ministers and gentlemen who were ready to die for duty. I am fearful that the historical materials will be neglected and lost" (Watson 1958, 49).

Although his intention as a *shi* seemed resolute and unequivocal, Sima Tan's general intellectual position was ambiguous. There was an "apparent discrepancy" between Sima Tan's injunction to his son and his own writings, specifically a piece entitled "The Essential Meaning of the Six

Schools" (Lun liujia yaozhi) (Durrant 1995, 7–8). In enjoining his son, Tan not only drew on the Confucian idea of filial piety but also went so far as to compare his project, which Sima Qian was to take over, with that of the Duke of Zhou and Confucius. But in his essay on the Six Schools, which was perhaps the only essay written by him and kept intact in the *Records,* he clearly advocated the Huang-Lao Daoist position. The lack of sources does not allow us to surmise the reasons for Tan's expressed elevation of Daoism over Confucianism. But the fact remains that he greatly appreciated the accomplishments of his own age and of Emperor Wu, and therefore commanded his son to do what Confucius had done for his age, namely, to organize the historical records. Tan pointed out that since the last capture of the unicorn, there had already been a lapse of nearly five hundred years. Following Mencius, he believed that the time was ripe for the appearance of another sagely figure who would do what the Duke of Zhou and Confucius had done for their times (Durrant 1995, 6–7).

Although Sima Tan's chronological calculation was inaccurate and the analogy farfetched, Sima Qian understood his father's wishes and was resolved to continue his mission to produce and bequeath to posterity a historical work of lasting value, one comparable to Confucius' *Spring and Autumn Annals.* In fact, he aspired to surpass the achievement of the master and establish a literary tradition of his own. Sima did not, however, develop this ambition overnight. He would first experience a great personal calamity before he finally devoted himself wholeheartedly to his avowed enterprise. Three years after his father's death, as the old man had predicted, Sima became grand historian. His first major assignment, at his own suggestion, was to design a new calendar, the Taichu (grand beginning) calendar, to complement Emperor Wu's adoption of the earth element and the new emblematic color of yellow. This calendrical design was to mark the reign as a new beginning in history. This amicable relationship with Emperor Wu did not last long. Heedless of his father's advice that the grand historian should not become involved in civil affairs, Sima, in 99 B.C.E., hazarded a remonstration on behalf of General Li Ling, a person with whom he was only casually acquainted. His action ended in tragedy. Not only was he unable to save the general, who was executed for having been taken prisoner in a battle, but Sima himself, having angered the emperor, was condemned to the punishment of castration.

Sima Qian regarded his punishment as a great personal shame. But instead of committing suicide, he was determined to stay alive to complete the historical work that his father had instructed him to compile. He told his friend Ren An, "If I concealed my feelings and clung to life, burying myself in filth without protest, it was because I could not bear to leave unfinished my deeply cherished project, because I rejected the idea of dying without leaving to posterity my literary work" (Hardy 1999, 24). Having suffered calamitous humiliation, Sima Qian had nothing left but his writing in which he could realize himself and achieve something truly significant in the remainder of his life. If at his father's deathbed, he took on the project out of filial fealty, he now regarded it as his own calling that gave his life meaning. This incident, as some have argued (D. Zhang 1994, 144–145; Satō 1997, 361ff), left visible marks on Sima's approach to and organization of the *Records*. As he brooded over his painful experience, Sima Qian found himself, much to his comfort and solace, in good company:

> In former times the count of the West was arrested at Qiangli and developed *Changes of Zhou* (*Zhou yi*). Confucius was in distress in the region of Chen and Cai and created *Spring and Autumn Annals*. Qu Yuan was banished and wrote "Encountering Sorrow" ("Li sao"). Zuo Qiuming lost his sight, and then there was *Discourses of the States* (*Guoyu*). Master Sun had his legs amputated at the knees and elucidated *Military Tactics* (*Bing fa*). Buwei was removed to Shu and generations have passed down his "Overviews of Lu" ("Lu lan"). Hanfei was imprisoned in Qin and we have "The Difficulties of Persuasion" ("Shuo nan") and "The Frustrations of Standing Alone" ("Ku fen"). The three hundred pieces of *Poetry* were, for the most part, written as a result of worthies and sages expressing frustration. In all these cases, men had ideas that were stifled. They could not manage to communicate their doctrines [in their generation]. Therefore, they narrated past events and thought of people to come. (Durrant 1995, 13)

The creative lives of these historical figures convinced Sima that "literary power springs from a prodigious, frustrated energy that makes constraint and control all but impossible" (ibid.). Confucius especially stood out. What the master sought to achieve epitomized the ultimate goal of writing—preserving for subsequent ages memories of the past. Confucius was no doubt the most important inspiration for Sima, who evidently modeled his work after the sage.[2] In the *Records* almost one-fourth of his personal comments refer directly to Confucius, and the number escalates to one-third if references to texts ascribed to Confucius are counted (Hardy 1999, 116). Sima once claimed that he would end his history in the year 122 B.C.E., when another unicorn was captured. He deliberately harkened back to the previous capture, whose symbolic importance had prompted Confucius to work on the *Spring and Autumn Annals*. Sima also stated that he would leave his finished work at a famous mountain so that it would be read by future sages who would fully appreciate his words and thoughts. This calls to mind Confucius' perception of his work. As explained in the *Gongyang Commentary*, Confucius saw himself living in a time when his ideas were poorly understood and he pinned his hope on the future.

When Sima located the temple of Confucius in the former state of

---

2. It is worth noting that although Sima Qian used materials from the *Zuo Commentary* and imitated its style, he only mentions Zuo Qiuming as the author of *Discourse on the States*, not as the author of the *Zuo Commentary*. This could mean either that he, as Wai-yee Li (1994, 352–353) notes, regarded the *Zuo Commentary* as part of the *Spring and Autumn* tradition, or that he considered the *Zuo Commentary* to be a text written by more than just Zuo Qiuming himself (Schaberg 2001, 317–320).

Lu, he "wandered about awestruck, unable to leave," and vowed, "The tall mountain, I look up to; the high path, I try to follow it" (Hardy 1999, 119–120). His deep reverence for Confucius stemmed from his conviction of the value of the *Spring and Autumn*. In a long conversation with Hu Sui, a colleague who had helped design the Taichu calendar, Sima voiced his belief that the *Spring and Autumn* was the "most helpful" guide to government:

> [I]t distinguishes what is suspicious and doubtful, clarifies right and wrong, and settles points which are uncertain. It calls good good and bad bad, honors the worthy, and condemns the unworthy. It preserves states which are lost and restores the perishing family. It brings to light what was neglected and restores what was abandoned. In it are embodied the most important elements of the Kingly Way. (Watson 1958, 51)

Sima wanted to emulate Confucius in preserving lost states and restoring perished families by reconstructing the past. He revealed to Ren An, "I have gathered together the old traditions of the world which were neglected and lost, and investigated their deeds and affairs. I have searched into the principles behind their successes and failures, their rises and declines, [making] in all, 130 chapters" (Hardy 1999, 195).

However, unlike Confucius—or more precisely the Confucius represented by such New Script Confucians as Dong Zhongshu—Sima Qian did not intend his work to be solely a moral critique delivered through history. He distanced himself "from the attempt to distill from the *Annals* an abstract, absolute, and atemporal moral system—in brief, the ahistorical tendency of the dominant Han interpretation of the *Annals*" (W. Li 1994, 361). He broached something new by departing from the ahistorical tendency of early Han thinking, as represented by his former teacher Dong Zhongshu. Dong had sought to circumscribe monarchical power by subjecting it to the dictate of the Mandate of Heaven, whose interpretation was now the responsibility of intellectuals and not of the kings themselves. In his "Three Expositions on the Way of Heaven and Human Affairs" (*Tianren sance*), Dong expounded the Heaven-humanity correlation. Heaven would not only reward those who followed its Mandate, but also warn those who misbehaved by issuing portentous signs and punishing them if they did not heed these warnings. Dong used this activist and rational Heaven to condemn usurpers such as the First Emperor of Qin and to affirm the necessity and legitimacy of Han's ascendancy to power. Dong claimed that it was from his study of the *Spring and Autumn* that he learned about the point at which "the realm of Heaven and the realm of man meet and fuse" (*Hanshu* 1962, 2498; W. Li 1994, 403). While it ingeniously connected history with politics, thereby promoting the status of Confucianism, Dong's theory was in the end ahistorical. It denied real historical change, regarding it simply as reincarnation of a previous period in a predetermined cycle, and hence transforming human agency into a passive response to the will of Heaven (W. Li 1994, 353–358). Moreover, according to Dong, dynastic changes were merely means by which Heaven exhibited the qualities it wanted to promote in human society: the Xia embraced honesty, Shang reverence, and Zhou cultivation. The Han, by following the Xia, would also honor honesty. These qualities were represented respectively by the reigns of the ancient sage-kings, and all their successes and achievements were recorded in the *Spring and Autumn* (A. Wang 2000, 148–151).

By contrast, Sima was determined to establish the authority of history itself, significantly adding to Confucius' endeavor of asserting moral authority through historical precedents (W. Li 1994). He refuted Hu Sui's comparison of his work with the *Spring and Autumn* by asserting that such a comparison would "mistake their true nature" (Watson 1958, 54), even though Sima admired and was inspired by Confucius. Living in an "encyclopedic epoch" (Lewis 1999, 287ff), he aimed to deliver a comprehensive account of history that no one had ever attempted before, and in the process he would fulfill the basic mission of a historian: remembrance. As with Confucius, he intended to "transmit" (*shu*) rather than "create" (*zuo*). Although his primary duty as grand historian was not to write history, the position apparently gave him full access to government documents and archives. Sima took full advantage of this privilege. In his own preface to the *Records,* he tells us that he "drew from" (*chouyin*) various historical records and books placed in the "stone rooms and metal caskets," by which he meant not only government archives but also writings on history, the Six Arts, philosophies, poetry, military matters, astrology, the calendar, divination, medicine, and registries, not to mention drawings and folktales (X. Chen 1998, 114–117). He relied heavily on these sources, which he incorporated, often without much alteration, into his *Records.* This produced the two main characteristics of his work. On the one hand, the *Records* preserved many valuable historical sources that included, most notably according to Ban Gu, the *Genealogical Origins* (*Shiben*) and the *Spring and Autumn of Chu and Han* (*ChuHan chunqiu*), which were lost after the Han, and such extant texts as *Discourses on the States* and *Intrigues of the Warring States* (*Zhan'guoce*) (*Hanshu* 1962, 2737). On the other hand, Sima's work featured a unique "multiple narration," in which the same event or character would appear in different contexts (Hardy 1999, 73–85). This manner of narration stemmed from Sima's intent to maintain the integrity of the sources while revealing the plurality of human existence.

Sima Qian was fascinated by history's capriciousness, contingency, and complexity. In order to unravel its mystery, he needed "to explore the boundary between the realm of Heaven and the realm of humanity, to comprehend the process of changes in times past and present, and to establish the tradition of one family" (*Hanshu* 1962, 2735). Whereas Dong Zhongshu highlighted the convergence and harmony of Heaven and humanity, Sima Qian explored the uncertainty and fluidity of their boundaries; he was unsure about any direct or immediate correspondence between the two spheres. To characterize Sima's approach in this way is not, however, to suggest that he emancipated history from moral judgment.

Sima very much inserted his moral views into his reading of history, criticizing what he deemed to be improper behavior, including that of Emperor Wu. On one level Sima's work was "an engine of war of a subject against his prince," fueled by his "desire for self-justification and triumph over his adversary [Emperor Wu]" (Lewis 1999, 316). Sima also revealed his unstinting sympathy for heroic and righteous figures in history, especially those defeated, tragic heroes with whom he strongly empathized, as they reminded him of his own plight. His voicing of moral opinions was typical of the Confucian historiographical principle, and he emulated Confucius by making moral judgment through rhetorical means, "integrating judgment with narration" (*yu lunduan yu xushi*), in the words of the Qing savant Gu Yanwu (1613–1682) (S. Bai 1999, 80–98; D. Zhang 1994, 177).

Furthermore, to facilitate the injection of his moral arguments, Sima created a standard form of commentary in the *Records,* which began with the clause "The grand historian remarks." Setting his comments apart in this fashion allowed Sima to express his moral views without infringing on the integrity of the narrative. There are, in total, 137 commentaries, which amount to about 6 percent of the book. In these passages, Sima Qian comments on historical events, critiques historical figures, highlights the gist of narratives, and underscores the meaning of different stories (D. Zhang et al. 1995, 102–112). Thanks to Sima's example, commentaries became a permanent fixture in Chinese historiography until the beginning of the twentieth century.

We should also note Sima Qian's appeal to the notion of "transmission," which reminds us of Confucius' claim that he was engaged with "transmission" rather than "creation" (*shuer buzuo*). Indeed, Sima consciously identified himself with Confucius, to the extent that his *Records* and the master's works were both forged in the cauldron of life experiences marked by frustration, rejection, and misunderstanding. The irony was that in dwelling on and lamenting the lack of appreciation for their work, both Confucius and Sima Qian were hinting at their radical newness — they were ignored because they were offering innovative ideas that most people could not comprehend. The absence of recognition was paradoxically a result of their creative genius. In this sense Sima — and Confucius too — could in some ways see himself as a "creator" or "an unrecognized sage" (Puett 2001, 178–179).

If Sima Qian was ever a "creator," his major creation was undoubtedly the annals-biographic style (*jizhuan ti*) of historiography. Even though Sima was keenly interested in exploring the boundary between the realms of Heaven and humanity, he was ambivalent about Dong Zhongshu's theory of "Heaven-humanity resonance" (*tianren ganying*) because he refused to subject all historical changes to the will of Heaven, as many of his contemporaries, especially the Yin-Yang magicians (*fangshi*) whom Emperor Wu trusted, were wont to do. Sima respected the Mandate of Heaven and even believed in the possible intervention of Heaven in human affairs. But his ideas differed fundamentally from the pantheistic idea of

Heaven's agency in the human world (T. Chen 1993, 183). By utilizing the annals-biographic style, Sima was able to prominently feature the diversity of human actions in history as well as their consequences.

Sima's *Records* consists of five major sections: "Basic Annals" (*benji*), "Chronological Tables" (*biao*), "Treatises" (*shu*), "Hereditary Houses" (*shijia*), and "Arrayed Biographies" (*liezhuan*). Assuming different functions, these sections constitute the ways in which Sima Qian presented the variety and hierarchy of human lives. The twelve basic annals present "kingly traces" from the Three Dynasties through the Han as one complete thread. The ten chronological tables delineate the lineages of royal and noble families, and the thirty hereditary houses describe the lives of ministers. The largest category, the seventy arrayed biographies, record various people who "established merit or fame throughout the world." Finally, the eight treatises, which stand alone and constitute a different genre, examine the "interchanges between Heaven and humanity," tracing the vicissitudes of the multifarious human institutions (ritual, music, pitch-pipes, calendars, and sacrifices) in connection with the realm of Heaven. The treatises provide the general institutional backgrounds for the activities described in the biographies (*Shiji*, 1988, 956).

Even taking a cursory glance at the *Records'* structure, one is struck by its comprehensiveness. Covering over three thousand years, from China's legendary past up till his own time, Sima produced a universal history of encyclopedic proportions, a heroic endeavor which perhaps mirrored the intellectual climate of his age. The structure, particularly that of his twelve basic annals and eight treatises, may have been inspired by the structure of *Master Lu's Spring and Autumn,* an encyclopedic work readily available for his reference (D. Zhang 1994, 162). But the latter is "more philosophical than historical" (Hardy 1999, 54) and is composed mostly of short essays. The *Records* is also known for its inclusiveness. While the "kingly traces" are the guiding thread of the entire work—supposedly showing Heaven's granting and withdrawing its Mandate—they by no means cover the wide scope of Sima's interests. In the arrayed biographies, for example, Sima studies the lives of a wide variety of people, ranging from officials, diplomats, generals, philosophical masters, scholars, and poets, to merchants, manufacturers, diviners, assassins, and bandits. His treatises focus on the evolution of rituals, music, law, and calendar, without ignoring changes in economics and commerce. This inclusiveness attests not so much to the totalizing philosophy of the Heaven-humanity correspondence as to the particularities in history. While Sima intended to present the general pattern of historical movement, he was intrigued by exceptions to the general rule. Historical contingencies and particularities animated him, and they account for the enduring historical value of his work. For more than two millennia, the characters recorded in the *Records*—many were neither heroic nor glorious—have come to vivid and imperishable life in the minds of readers. Seen in this light, Sima indeed fulfilled the task he assigned to himself, that is, to "transmit" culture. His success, as many have noted

(W. Li 1994, 365–391; Durrant 1995, 123–143), derived from his empathy for the people he wrote about and his "love of the wondrous or unique" (*aiqi*). His *Records* created a vivid world—a "microcosmic world" fraught with all the uncertainties and inconsistencies that we encounter in the real world. Indeed, Sima's approach to the past subverts the kind of coherent master narrative that characterizes many Western historical writings (Hardy 1999).

As Dong Zhongshu's erstwhile student, Sima agreed with Dong's general theory about the change of history, particularly with regard to the succession of dynasties. After recounting the life of Emperor Gao, the founding emperor of the Han, Sima remarked:

> The government of the Xia dynasty was marked by honesty, which in time deteriorated until mean men had turned it into rusticity. Therefore the men of Shang who succeeded the Xia reformed this defect through the virtue of reverence. But reverence degenerated until mean men had made it a superstitious concern for the spirits. Therefore the men of the Zhou who followed corrected this fault through cultivation. . . . It is obvious that in the late Zhou and Qin times the earlier cultivation had deteriorated. But the government of the Qin failed to correct this fault, instead adding its own harsh punishments and laws. Was this not a grave error? Thus when the Han rose to power it took over the faults of its predecessors and worked to change and reform them, causing men to be unflagging in their efforts and following the order properly ordained by Heaven. (Watson 1969, 145–146; modified transliteration)

By associating such virtues as honesty, reverence, and cultivation with the Three Dynasties and noting their cyclical succession, Sima (albeit only once in the *Records*) extended Dong Zhongshu's theory of the Three Systems. Sima here also seemed to have accepted Dong's position of rejecting the Qin's place in the dynastic successions because of its adoption of Legalist policies. However, in the basic annals, where kingly lines are traced back to legendary times, the First Emperor of the Qin is included, as are Empress Lü, the wife of Emperor Gao of the Han, and Xiang Yu, the archrival of Emperor Gao, before the latter founded the Han dynasty. Xiang Yu, defeated by the future Emperor Gao, committed suicide and did not found a dynasty. Not only did Sima Qian place these figures of failure on a par with the Yellow Emperor and Emperor Wu, his own master (whose chapter is unfortunately lost), but he also showed great sympathy for their lives, empathized with their mistakes, and lamented their failures.

Significantly, Sima Qian did not attribute the failure of his protagonists to the will of Heaven. Instead, he explained their defeats by carefully unfolding causal factors. His chapter on Xiang Yu is a good example. At the beginning of the account, Sima relates the foreboding story in which the young Xiang Yu remarks, upon seeing the First Emperor of the Qin who is visiting his native place, that the ruler is not irreplaceable. This serves to pique the readers' curiosity about the future development of this ambitious young man. Joining his uncle in a rebellion against the Qin, Xiang Yu quickly rises through the ranks and makes himself, after the death of his uncle and the murder of his lord, the supreme commander of a powerful force with which he defeats the Qin army. But in spite of this astonishing success and his physical prowess, Xiang Yu eventually loses to his rival, Liu Bang, the future Emperor Gao of the Han, in their bid for power. Again, to prepare readers for Xiang's ultimate failure, Sima tells in intricate detail a story that takes place at Hongmen, where Xiang invites Liu, who is at that time inferior to him, to a banquet where he plans to kill him. But Xiang's residual "good-heartedness" causes him to abort the plan, which portends his final defeat. Xiang, however, blames his tragedy on Heaven. At the end of his life, he proclaims to his remaining horsemen that he still has the ability to kill any enemy they want him to, but this desperate last-ditch posing does not save his cause. Xiang bemoans his fate: "It is because Heaven would destroy me, not because I have committed any fault in battle." Painfully aware of Heaven's plans to abandon him, Xiang jettisons any thought of returning to his home region and reassembling his forces. As a final dramatic stand, Xiang commits suicide instead (Watson 1969, 68–104).

After telling this powerful story, Sima Qian refused to accept Xiang Yu's failure as a predestined event. To him, Xiang was "deluded" in thinking that he should blame his fate on the will of Heaven; he should instead have "woken up to accept responsibility for his errors." Xiang's errors boiled down to his blind faith in brute force and his tyrannical way of rule (ibid., 104). Sima's trenchant criticism reveals his disapproval of ready appeal to the correlative idea in historical explanation. He was more interested in demonstrating the power and potency of human agency in shaping history. Heaven, of course, played an undeniable role in human history, but in the *Records,* he urges us "not to legitimize such a turn of events as inevitable or as the palpable unfolding of a rational Providence, but rather to register the difficulty of explaining what were for him the recent . . . unpredictable, unprecedented, and cataclysmic changes" (W. Li, 1994, 405). In a word, Heaven became the trope through which Sima expressed the uncertainty, contingency, and exigency that characterized and animated history (W. Li 1999).

It is also noteworthy that while Sima intended to preserve and transmit ancient culture, he was skeptical about his sources, such that he diligently searched for evidence, sometimes by visiting actual sites. At times he reminded the readers of his uncertainty, and where there was doubt, he would inform readers of his inconclusive investigations. The most common way in which Sima expressed his doubt was his use of the expressions "it was said" (*yun*) and "or it is said" (*huoyue*). These qualifying words appeared most frequently in his chapter on Emperor Wu's *feng* and *shan* sacrifice, showing his disapproval of the superstitious nature of the ceremony (*Shiji* 1988, 204–224; W. Li 1999, 50–51). Moreover, using the commentary attached to the end of a chapter, Sima expressed his skepticism regarding some of the most honored cultural figures. His comments on the chapter about the Five Emperors, with which he began the *Records,* are a good example. Being legendary figures, these emperors, including the Yellow Emperor who was then worshipped not only as the ancestor of the Chinese but also the progenitor of Huang-Lao Daoism, left no written records. Sima attempted to verify their existence by visiting their alleged birthplaces and checking with the oral tradition, but he was unable to reach a definitive conclusion. Therefore, even though he decided to include them, he conveyed his doubts about their historical authenticity, which could also be construed as a veiled critique of the Han worship of them (*Shiji* 1988, 7–8; W. Li 1994, 370).

Just as commentaries enabled Sima to express his opinion, so his "multiple narration" allowed him to present the multifacetedness of history and the plurality of human life. This method was described as "mutual illumination" (*hujian fa*) by the Song scholar Su Xun (1009–1066) (D. Zhang 1994, 178). Using this method, Sima presented stories on the same subject culled from a number of different sources to shed light on different sides of a historical figure or an event. The resulting complexity permitted him to offer subtle and nuanced judgments. In Sima's chapter on the "First Emperor of the Qin," for instance, he voiced his overt disapproval of the Qin's Legalist philosophy and policy that led to suffering, unrest, and eventually dynastic collapse. But when he mentioned a failed assassination attempt on the First Emperor by Zhang Liang, a rebel who later assisted in founding the Han, he brushed it aside, stating simply that the emperor was disturbed by a bandit. The details of the incident appeared in Zhang Liang's own biography (*Shiji* 1988, chapters 6, 55). Sima's narratives on Emperor Gao adopted a similar approach—the emperor was depicted in more positive light in his own chapter than in other chapters where he was present (*Shiji* 1988, chapters 8–9, 53–57, 92–93, 97–99). Sima's goal was to show important personages in different perspectives. In their own chapters they appear as bona fide rulers, whereas elsewhere they are perceived by others as ruthless tyrants, capricious masters, or even rustic bumpkins.

Ban Gu and the Emergence of the Dynastic History

Sima Qian followed the *Discourses on the States,* selected material from the *Genealogical Origins* and the *Intrigues of the Warring States,* incorporated the text of the *Spring and Autumn of Chu and Han,* and added an account of recent affairs, bringing his history down to the era Tianhan. His discussions of Qin and Han are very detailed. . . . With his diligence he had browsed very widely in books, threaded his way through the Classics and commentaries, and galloped up and down from the past to the present, covering a period of several thousand years. Yet his judgments stray rather often from those of The Sage. In discussing fundamental moral law, he venerates the teachings of Huang-Lao school and slights the Six Classics. In his introduction to the

"Memoirs of the Wandering Knights" he disparages gentlemen scholars who
live in retirement and speaks in favor of heroic scoundrels. In his narration
on "Merchandise and Prices" he honors those who were skilled at making
a profit and heaps shame on those in poverty and low station. It is these
points which mar his work. Yet Liu Xiang, Yang Xiong, and other men of
wide learning and copious letters all praise Qian as a man of excellent ability
as a historian and testify to his skill in setting forth events and their causes.
He discourses without sounding wordy; he is simple without being rustic.
His writing is direct and his facts sound. He does not falsify what is beauti-
ful, nor does he conceal what is evil. Therefore his may be termed a "true
record." (Watson 1958, 68; modified transliteration)

This comprehensive appraisal of Sima Qian's *Records* can be found in the
Han History (*Hanshu* 1962, 2737–2738), China's first dynastic history. It appeared in the late first century, about a hundred years after Sima Qian had
completed his masterpiece. The *Han History* was written mostly by Ban Gu
who, like his predecessor, took the project over from his father, Ban Biao
(3–54). After Ban Gu's death, his sister Ban Zhao (45/51–114/120) completed the work. Some have conjectured that it was Ban Biao who composed the above appraisal, but regardless of its authorship, it represented
the opinion of the Ban family and revealed the cultural climate at the time.
Although only a century had elapsed, the world of the Bans was different
from Sima Qian's. Just a few decades before Ban Gu was born, it was a trying
time in Han history, marked by Wang Mang's (45 B.C.E.–C.E. 23) usurpation that almost ended the Liu family royal line. Fortunately for the Han,
Wang Mang's regime did not last, as his attempt to dislodge the Han was
thwarted by the so-called "Guangwu Restoration." A powerful member of
the royal Liu family clan from outside the court reestablished the Han imperial order. But this crisis generated a strong sense of urgency among the
literati to reaffirm the legitimacy of the Han through history-writing.

Sima Qian's coverage ended with the reign of Emperor Wu. During the
transitional period from the Former Han (206 B.C.E.–23 C.E.) to the Later
Han (25–220), a number of works sought to pick up where Sima had left
off (*Shitong* 1978, 2:338; Qu 1999b, 199), including the Ban family's *Han
History*. In a way, the *Han History* was conceived as a sequel to the *Records*.
However, judging from the Bans' appraisal, they had reservations about
their predecessor, especially with regard to Sima's view of history (Park
1994, 51ff). Specifically, they criticized Sima for not fully embracing the
Confucian idea of history, that is, for not fully subscribing to the power of
Heaven in human affairs. Sima had great personal respect for Confucius;
he gave him and his teachings extensive coverage, and he placed Confucius' biography in the section on hereditary houses, violating his own rule
because Confucius bore no hereditary title. He also wrote two chapters in
the arrayed biographies to describe Confucius' disciples and followers. But
Sima did not believe in a perfectly neat correspondence between Heaven
and humanity. According to the Bans, "[i]n discussing fundamental moral

law, he [Sima] venerates the teachings of the Huang-Lao school and slights the Six Classics." Sima's "veneration" for Huang-Lao Daoism was derived from his respect for human agency in history and his interest in the constancy of change in both the human and natural worlds. Sima's fascination with the flux of history also reflected his receptiveness to the *Classic of Changes*, a major text in both the Daoist and Confucian traditions at the time (T. Chen 1993, 284ff). Seen in this light, Sima Qian's admiration for Confucius did not quite preclude his attraction to Daoism. It is plausible to argue that his view of history was a sort of Daoist-Confucian eclecticism (Crawford 1963).

Nowhere was Sima Qian's eclecticism better expressed than in the "Biography of Boyi and Shuqi." It is surprising that Sima chose this particular chapter to inaugurate the arrayed biographies as it describes the lives of two unconventional figures from the late Shang period. Most of the tale, however, is devoted to commenting on the meanings of their lives, as opposed to a straightforward recounting (Durrant 1995, 20). Boyi and Shuqi were both exemplars of morality, marked by their disinterest in political power. They were distinguished by their "readiness to relinquish the power" (*guirang*) they had and their willingness to die for their belief in righteousness. These were virtues highly praised by Confucius, as Sima Qian tells us. However, contrary to Confucius' description, Sima did not think that Boyi and Shuqi maintained their equanimity in the face of adversity and death because they expressed their rancor in the song they sang on the last day of their lives. Moreover, while Sima was moved by their moral courage and tragic deaths, he questioned the ultimate correlation between Heaven and humanity: "The so-called Way of Heaven, does it exist? Or does it not?" In the end, Sima sought comfort in the fact that although the deaths of Boyi and Shuqi cast doubt on the existence of a rational Heaven, thanks to Confucius' praise, these two brothers achieved fame in history (Watson 1969, 11–15). In stating that Confucius had misplaced his admiration for Boyi and Shuqi's equanimity, where there was actually none, Sima's comment may be seen as a veiled critique of Confucius and Confucian values. Yet at the same time, he also departed from the Daoist value of detachment by stressing that these two brothers justifiably showed rancor at the end of their lives (W. Li 1994, 381). Apart from demonstrating Sima's unwillingness to adhere to the values of one school, the biography of Boyi and Shuqi may also be seen as a lament of his own fate. This chapter is most likely a later addition, written after Sima's castration, mirroring his own desires, frustrations, and hopes (Satō 1997, 584–587).

Such accommodating eclecticism and interpretive individualism are found nowhere in the *Han History*, despite its purported aim of extending the *Records*. Even though the *Han History* inherited a great deal of content and form from the *Records*, it was written for quite a different purpose, and, in fact, some sections of the *Han History* were "clearly intended as refutations." Thus "comparison of these two great histories throws into clear relief the philosophic position of both authors" (Crawford 1963,

406). In contrast to Sima Qian's highly syncretic and personal interpretations, which contributed to his overt endorsement of the early Han rulers' laissez-faire government and his covert critique of Emperor Wu's authoritarianism, Ban Gu had one paramount goal: to legitimize the position of the Han dynasty in history. To this end he unequivocally supported Dong Zhongshu's theory of "Heaven-humanity resonance" and employed it time and again to promote Han legitimacy. He also enthusiastically endorsed the centralizing policies of Emperor Wu and his successors. Ban regarded such moves as the only effective way to maintain social order and achieve economic prosperity. Moreover, he and his father were ardent supporters of Confucianism as the official ideology, regarding it as the foundation of good government and the reason for the successes of the Han dynasty.

Despite these obvious differences in their views of history and political ideology, Ban Gu's life bore some interesting similarities to Sima Qian's. Both were born into a learned family and received a good education, but both were thwarted in their desire to establish a name for themselves either in a military or political career. Although Ban Gu never suffered the humiliating experience of castration, his life was overshadowed by the brilliant military career of his brother Ban Chao. He was also incarcerated twice and died during the second imprisonment. Both men also embarked on their projects initially as a result of private and personal incentive. Ban Biao could not boast, as could Sima Tan, a distinguished lineage in history-writing, but he did bequeath a worthy project to his son. Although both Sima's and Ban's work began as private projects, they each later received support from the government, which enabled them to gain access to official documents, archives, and various other materials. And finally, in pursuing their projects Sima Qian and Ban Gu both encountered unexpected mishaps as well as serendipitous turns, so that the compilation processes themselves became dramatic stories.

We do not quite know how Ban Gu actually took over his father's project. We are told only that Ban Biao started the project somewhat late in life. By the time Biao died, he had completed several fascicles, tentatively entitled "Later Biographies" (Houzhuan), which belonged to the categories of annals and biographies, but not the hereditary houses. His children decided to preserve this practice, so the completed *Han History* contains no biographies of the hereditary houses.

Ban Gu's continuation of his father's project did not proceed smoothly. Shortly after he began his writing, he was arrested and thrown into prison, charged with the crime of "writing and altering national history privately" (*si gaizuo guoshi*). Through the intercession of his brother Ban Chao, Emperor Ming (r. 58–75) took an interest in his case. After reading what Ban Gu had written, Emperor Ming not only ordered his release but also appointed him, in C.E. 62, a court historian, first as the *lantai lingshi* (command historian of the Orchid Mound) and later as the *jiaoshu lang* (attendant of book collation). These two positions gave Ban Gu unfettered access to government documents and library holdings, and allowed him to devote more than twenty years to the compilation of the *Han History*. During this period Ban Gu seems to have enjoyed prestige and power, thanks to his close association with Dou Xian, who dominated the court. However, in C.E. 92 when Dou was killed by a political enemy, Ban Gu was thrown into jail and died shortly afterwards, leaving the unfinished work to be completed by his sister Ban Zhao.

Although Ban Gu and Sima Qian shared some common experiences, there was a key difference. In spite of his initial misfortune, Ban Gu was able to complete the bulk of his work under auspicious conditions, and this no doubt influenced his view of history in general and of the Han dynasty in particular. In addition, because of Wang Mang's usurpation, which his father personally lived through and which almost ended the rule of the Han, Ban felt a compelling need to buttress Han legitimacy. Because of this personal motivation and ideological consideration, his work departed from Sima Qian's, even though the *Records* was the initial model.

Ban Gu's *Han History* also differs from Sima Qian's in being a dynastic history, covering only the period of the Former Han dynasty (206 B.C.E.–23 C.E.). This focus, needless to say, is consistent with Ban Gu's purported aim of exalting the Han in history. Ban Gu complained that Sima Qian's ambition to deliver a general account of historical changes diminished the greatness of the Han dynasty, making it appear to be a mere sequel to the past glories of hundreds of previous kings. Moreover, the Han had been placed in the company of brutal reigns of such evil rulers as the First Emperor of Qin and Xiang Yu. Drawing on Dong Zhongshu's theory of the Three Systems, Ban Gu proclaimed that the Han was a reincarnation of the sagely times of Yao and Shun. He thus entitled his work *Hanshu*, emulating the *Shangshu*, or the *Classic of Documents*, which recorded the events of those resplendent times (Qu 1999b, 201).[3]

Ban Gu's blanket criticism of Sima Qian missed the important fact that the bulk of the *Records* covers more recent periods. Those fascicles on the history prior to the Han constitute no more than 30 percent of the work, whereas the part on the Han, which covers less than a hundred years, comprises more than one half of the *Records* (Jin [1944] 2000, 64). In addition, since Ban Gu intended to cover the history of the dynasty after Emperor Wu's reign (or, more precisely, after the introduction of Sima Qian's Taichu calendar in 104 B.C.E.), he relied on the *Records* to cover the early part of Han history, repeating its many chapters verbatim. The *Records* provided "the skeleton and the flesh" of the *Han History*, and for the most part, Ban Gu made only "merely minor variations in the complexion and added the tints" (Sargent 1944, 129).

---

3. Lien-sheng Yang (1947) pointed out that by using "*shu*" in his title, Ban Gu set the example for using that word for dynastic histories, whereas the word "*shi*," used by Sima Qian, came to be conventionally applied to general histories in which coverage was not confined to a single dynasty. For lack of better terms, however, we follow conventional practice and translate both *shi* and *shu* as "history."

The *Han History* divides its hundred fascicles into four categories: "Imperial Annals" (*diji,* fascicles 1–12); "Tables and Charts" (*biao,* fascicles 13–20); "Monographs" (*zhi,* fascicles 21–30); and "Arrayed Biographies" (*liezhuan,* fascicles 31–100). It differs from the *Records* in two areas: nomenclature, such as changing "Treatises" into "Monographs" and "Basic Annals" into "Imperial Annals," and deletion of the category of "Hereditary Houses." Except in the early years the Han did not confer hereditary titles on its generals and ministers (Jin [1944] 2000, 62), a move by the Han to centralize authority. This was a policy that Sima Qian disapproved but one that Ban Gu supported.

Unlike his predecessor, Ban Gu adhered very strictly to his categories while writing the *Han History.* Sima Qian periodically broke his own rules by including some otherwise "unfitting" figures in certain categories, such as Confucius and Chen She, a rebel leader at the end of the Qin, in the hereditary houses. Ban Gu, on the other hand, punctiliously upheld his rules, conscientiously placing his heroes in appropriate categories. In the imperial annals, for example, he included only the Han emperors and one empress, Empress Lü, wife of Emperor Gao. Such anti-Qin figures as Chen She and Xiang Yu, who had abetted to some extent the founding of the Han, were placed in the arrayed biographies where they were no longer in competition with their fellow rebel, Liu Bang, who was to become Emperor Gao. If in Sima Qian's presentation, the so-called "world of bamboo" (historiography) and the "world of bronze" (history) were somewhat in contention—Sima intended to re-present history through historiography (Hardy 1999)—in Ban Gu's *Han History* the two worlds had merged: historiography not only corresponded with history, or the real world, but it also idealized history by setting up a normative order that was more apparent than real. Ban Gu's intention was to celebrate and promote the Han, and for many centuries after he wrote his work, his historiographical system and especially his principled, consistent application of it, proved exemplary for many dynastic historians. Liu Zhiji, the great Tang historiographer, praised the *Han History* for establishing the archetype in dynastic historiography and considered it a new and better genre than Sima Qian's universal history (*Shitong* 1978, 1:19–22).

Ban Gu's brazenly ideological goal of promoting the Han legitimacy also meant that he was enthusiastically applying the theory of the resonance between Heaven and humanity to explain the Han ascendancy to power. In his description of early Han rulers such as Emperor Gao, Empress Lü, and Emperor Wu, he borrowed liberally from Sima Qian, but he made some notable alterations. In the case of Emperor Gao (Liu Bang), for instance, Ban Gu, almost word for word, repeated Sima's depictions of Liu Bang's early life, including the many auspicious signs that surrounded and followed him, such as those "wonderful sights" or the "misty emanation" that hovered above him, which allowed him to drink and eat for free, and which enabled his wife always to locate him wherever he was in hiding. Ban Gu also repeated the story Sima told that Liu Bang once killed with his sword a giant serpent, which turned out to be the son of the White God, so his slaying of the beast suggested that he was the Red God. But Sima and Ban told the story with different purposes in mind. Sima's inclusion does indicate that he was influenced by the idea of Heaven's intimate correlation with humanity, but he may simply have wanted to use this fanciful story to satisfy his own, or the readers', curiosity for the unique and the wondrous. At the end, by way of eulogy, he wrote that Emperor Gao "rose from the humblest beginnings to correct a discordant age and turn it back to the right. He brought peace and order to the world and became the founder of the Han" (Watson 1969, 144). In the final analysis Sima was interested in Emperor Gao's human, albeit spectacular, accomplishments. By contrast, in the *Han History*, Ban offered an entirely different version of the eulogy: "The line of descent of the Han Emperor is traced from the Emperor Tang (Yao). Coming on down to the Zhou, in the Qin it became the Liu family. . . ." Having presented such a majestic genealogy, Ban proceeded to make the following claim:

> From the foregoing accounts we infer that the Han succeeded to the fortunes of Yao; its virtues and the happiness recompensing it are already great. The cutting in two of the snake, the auspicious omens which appeared, the banners and pennons which emphasized the color red in harmony with the virtue of fire, were responses which came of their own accord, thereby showing that Emperor Gao secured the rule from Heaven. (Dus 1938, V:1, 149–150)

This juxtaposition throws into sharp relief the two men's divergent interpretations of Han history. Whereas Sima was primarily interested in Liu Bang's ability and achievement as a leader, Ban adopted Dong Zhongshu's cosmic-historical theory to bolster Han legitimacy. Liu Bang's killing of the snake now became a prophetically auspicious omen that portended his eventual triumph. In order to expound the Heaven-humanity correlation, Ban also wrote the "Monograph on the Five Phases" (Wuxing zhi), one of four monographs—the others being on penal law, geography, and arts and literature—he added to the category, expanding and revising Sima's treatises. Creation of this fascicle enabled Ban Gu to introduce the major figures who subscribed to the religious, philosophical, and cosmological thinking of the Five Phases, among them many Han intellectual luminaries such as Dong Zhongshu, Liu Xiang (79–8 B.C.E.), and Liu Xin (46 B.C.E.–23 C.E.). It also permitted him to record many specific examples that supposedly attested to the Heaven-humanity correspondence, according to which human actions cohered with cosmic and natural forces. Ban's addition of this monograph reflected the popularity of such beliefs in his time (W. Du 1993, 287–288).

Ban Gu did not refrain, however, from reproving certain Han events and figures. He had an unwavering belief in the value of Confucianism, or rather the Han orthodoxy of Confucianism tinged with enough Qin Legalism to justify the policy of centralizing power (Crawford 1963, 406). Ban Gu praised Emperor Wu's initiative in promoting Confucianism in government. He believed the emperor fared better than his predecessors, Emperors Wen and Jing, and his "grand achievements" were even comparable to those of the Three Dynasties. However, Ban also pointed out implicitly that, unlike his predecessors, Emperor Wu did not pay sufficient attention to the welfare of the common people (Dus 1938, V:1, 119–120; W. Du 1993, 267), a criticism that echoed Sima Qian's sentiments in his own chapter on Emperor Wu. Ban Gu's position was typically Confucian, similar to that of many Confucian scholars in the famous "salt and iron debate" (81 B.C.E.) where they challenged the Han government's apparent interest in profit-making. Ban Gu's ambivalent attitude toward Emperor Wu's reign suggests that he did not disregard his duty of being a staunch moral critic.

Ban Gu was also known for his erudition (S. Bai 1999, 120–124; W. Du 1993, 271ff). He sought to produce an encyclopedic history of the Former Han dynasty, as evidenced not only by the length of the *Han History*—although it covers a period of only two hundred years, it is more than one and half times the size of Sima Qian's *Records*—but also by the broad coverage of subjects. Ban's monographs, which expanded on Sima Qian's treatises, covered some of the same subjects, such as those on rivers and waterways, sacrifices, and calendars (albeit with different titles). But he created many others. More important, in the monographs Ban did not confine his research and writing to the Han. Instead, he strove to provide a comprehensive account of a subject. In the "Monograph on Penal Law" (Xingfa zhi), for example, Ban traced the origins and changes of the Han military and legal systems back to Zhou times. The "Monograph on Commodities" (Shihuo zhi) augmented Sima Qian's treatise on the same topic with many more details because Ban surveyed the evolution of economic life from ancient times to the Han. Two of these monographs stand out. One was the "Bibliography of the Arts and Literature" (Yiwen zhi), and the other was the "Records on Geography" (Dili zhi). The former expanded Liu Xin's *Seven Summaries* (*Qilue*) and offered a comprehensive survey of extant books in the government libraries, in addition to discussing the origins and development of the various forms of scholarship. The latter contained valuable information on geography, typography, demography, ethnology, imperial administration, and diplomacy. The last part, on Han foreign policy, dovetailed with some of the fascicles in the arrayed biographies. Together they fashioned the Chinese imagination, image, and conception of the world at the time (Q. Wang 1999). The monographs were emulated by many later historical works (S. Bai 1999, 121).

Finally, the *Han History*'s section on tables also attests to its encyclopedism. The "Table of People of Ancient and Modern Times" (Gujin renbiao), most likely the creation of Ban Gu's sister Ban Zhao, listed the names of many people, especially those in times prior to the Han, and hence this section provided an up-to-date and comprehensive biographic dictionary, a "who's who," as it were.

The *Han History*'s encyclopedism came not only from Ban Gu's erudition but also his fastidious use of sources. Ban was indebted to many authors of the Han period, including Sima Qian, Lu Jia, Liu Xiang, Liu Xin, and Wang Chong (27–100). Wang, an acclaimed philosopher, was a close friend of Ban's family. Ban's position as a court historian also gave him access to the library, the imperial archives, and government collections. In addition, since Ban's father had connections and experiences with the Han government, Ban might have based some of his writings on oral sources, as he could still have had access to many eyewitnesses to the events he was describing. The accomplishment represented by the *Han History* owed much to Ban's ability as both a historian and a compiler who effectively organized, selected, and processed all the sources available to him, weaving them, almost singlehandedly, into a tightly knit narrative. He fulfilled not only the historian's ancient role of preserving and transmitting culture, but also the task of turning history into a useful tool of political and moral education.

Ban Gu's conscious use of history reflected the climate of the Later Han dynasty. Although he died in prison before he could complete the book and witness its reception, Ban produced a work that was well received by contemporary Han scholars as well as many emperors of the Later Han. In fact, while written initially as a sequel to the *Records,* in the many centuries since its completion, the influence of the *Han History* has rivaled that of its predecessor. It won acclaim almost overnight for two main reasons. One was its dynastic focus. The work provided a model that was easy to follow, especially for those who were involved in collective projects, as was often the case in later times. The second reason was its overt goal of using history to serve the reigning government. Naturally, this appealed to rulers, which often translated into imperial sponsorship of historical writing.

What was the immediate influence of the *Han History* in the Later Han? While Ban Gu was working on his *Han History,* the emperor ordered a collective project, the composition of a history of the Later Han (Du 1993, 288–290). Although official historians had been fixtures in government since antiquity, rarely had the court commanded them to compose a contemporary history. The main duty of court historians had always been to preserve government documents and collect historical records. Because most of the compilation and writing took place in the Eastern Pavilion (Dongguan), where the Han government kept its documents and archives, the product of this collective endeavor, which took several decades to complete, came to be known as the *Han Records of the Eastern Pavilion* (*Dongguan hanji*). In its later stages the project fell very much under the supervision of Cai Yong (133–192), an acclaimed historian of his time. However, Cai's participation did not save him from imprisonment and death for his alleged connection with Dong Zhuo (?–192), an ambitious minister responsible for undermining the Han imperium. Although Cai pleaded for his life, citing the example of Sima Qian, so that he could finish his own work on the Later Han history, he did not succeed. The *Han Records of the East-ern Pavilion* fared hardly better; only 24 fascicles have survived, out of the original 143.

Buoyed by their keen awareness of the use of history, the emperors of the Later Han became interested in acquiring historical knowledge for themselves, especially the history of their immediate predecessors in the Former Han. Ban Gu had provided a good text, but his erudition and the imposing size of the *Han History* also intimidated them. Thus in 198, Emperor Xian (r. 189–220) asked Xun Yue (148–209) to produce an abbreviated version. In about two years Xun Yue completed a work entitled the *Han Annals (Hanji)*. Although it was based almost entirely on material from the *Han History*, it did not preserve the annals-biographic form but reverted to the annalistic form, modeling itself on the *Zuo Commentary*. This allowed Xun Yue to highlight the royal successions, a stylistic move that would please the emperors. Basically Xun Yue left out most of the sections other than the imperial annals, although he incorporated some of their contents into the annals, as he saw fit. Using Ban Gu's fascicles in the imperial annals, he also reorganized them and associated the recorded stories with the year, month, and date on which they occurred. In cases when he could not find or ascertain the dates, he put these events in places where similar events took place or where there seemed to be a sensible connection or causation. At the cost of compromising the integrity of most of the stories, Xun Yue achieved the effect he wanted, which was to feature the royal family prominently, giving the impression that everything revolved around it. Unfortunately, however, neither the political wisdom in his work nor the Emperor Xian's interest in history saved the dynasty. In 220, twenty years after Xun Yue completed and presented his work, Emperor Xian was dethroned and subsequently killed, marking the end of the Han dynasty. Though Xun Yue died before this regicide, and while he believed in the "sacrosanctity of the imperial order," Xun realized that the Han order "was no longer viable" (C. Chen 1975, 99).

In producing the *Han Annals,* he reiterated all the occurrences recorded by Ban Gu that were presumably proofs of the intimate correspondence between Heaven and humanity, but he also expressed serious doubts about this cosmic-historical idea and its practical efficacy. His conclusion was somewhat agnostic. At times Heaven's blessings could lead one to success, and sometimes success could be achieved through one's own effort; but at other times, nothing could be achieved, no matter how hard one tried (S. Bai 1999, 125–127). Perhaps the fall of the Han validated Xun Yue's conception of fate.

Historical Schemas and Philosophy in the New Script Classical Tradition

One important aspect of the Han historiography was the emergence of periodizing schemas, which germinated within the New Script exegetical tradition based on the *Gongyang Commentary* to Confucius' *Spring and Autumn Annals*. The *Commentary* sought to "[reveal] the profound principles [concealed in the] subtle language" (*weiyan dayi*) of the classics—the illumination of the profound values embedded in the abstruse words of the sages. It should be noted that the *Spring and Autumn Annals* was viewed by both the Old Script and New Script scholars as containing great principles (*dayi*) that were intimately concerned with proper political and social behavior. However, as we recall, the Old Script school, identified with the *Zuo Commentary*, explicated the principles in the *Spring and Autumn* largely in terms of historical examples and precedents. The New Script school showed more interest in plumbing the profound meanings of Confucius' actual words, many of which were seen to be messages of suprahistorical and cosmological significance. To New Script scholars, every word, or even the absence of words in many cases, was fraught with meaning. The imperative task of a commentary was to reveal the principles and meanings concealed in the *Spring and Autumn*'s cryptic language. Such language had been necessary because Confucius had had to avoid offending the ruler while propounding his ideas of institutional changes, and a literal reading would lose sight of the essential meanings. A tradition grew up, therefore, that sought to make manifest the great principles implied in subtle language of the classics, and this tradition was much animated by its conception of China's ancient history (Q. Chen 1997, 19–38).

He Xiu (129–182), the great Later Han New Script exegete, said that the *Gongyang Commentary* embodied the great principles of the "three categories" (*sanke*), subdivided into the "nine points" (*jiuzhi*). The first category was "Preserving the Three Systems" (*cun santong*) or "Linking the Three Systems" (*tong santong*), under which were subsumed three "points": (1) "taking the Zhou dynasty as the immediate predecessor," (2) "recognizing the state of Song as the descendant of the more remote predecessor [of the Shang]," (3) "establishing the king envisioned in the *Spring and Autumn Annals* as the new king."

The second category was "Unfolding of the Three Ages" (*zhang sanshi*), embodying another three points: (1) "recording what was personally witnessed with different language," (2) "recording what was heard through contemporary accounts by the elders with different language," (3) "recording what was heard and known through transmitted records with different language."

The third category was "Distinguishing the Inner from the Outer" (*yi nei'wai*), consisting of the final three points: (1) "treating his [Confucius'] state [of Lu] as the inner and the rest of the Chinese hegemony as the outer," (2) "treating the Chinese hegemony as the inner and the outlying barbarian tribes as the outer," (3) "the barbarian tribes becoming part of the feudal hierarchy" (Ng 1994, 3–10).

Such schematic conceptions were, in effect, historical depictions of the political and cultural developments in ancient China. "Preserving the Three Systems" referred to the succession of systems of rule in ancient

China. According to the New Script tradition, the state of Lu in the Spring and Autumn period had established itself as a legitimate dynasty, succeeding the Zhou dynasty, which followed the Shang, whose descendant was the state of Song. Thus appeared a line of legitimate dynastic succession: the Shang (or Song), then the Zhou, and then finally the Lu. Dong Zhongshu, who first explicated this tripartite succession, regarded Confucius as an uncrowned king. Dong interpreted the last entry in the *Spring and Autumn Annals*—the capture of a unicorn—as evidence that Confucius had secured the Mandate of Heaven to rectify the flaws of the moribund Zhou dynasty and erect new institutions. The initiation of a new regime required its proper legitimation, and hence "Preserving the Three Systems" of the Shang, Zhou, and Lu. The Shang and Zhou descendants legitimately shared the title of king with the ruler of the state of Lu. But descendants of the Xia dynasty before the Shang would be relegated to the realm of the Five Emperors. To explain this the New Script tradition generated the following related notions: "relegating the Xia," "taking the Zhou as the immediate predecessor," "taking the Song as the more remote predecessor," and "establishing the king envisioned in the *Spring and Autumn Annals* as the new king." In addition, Dong postulated an alternating cycle of Simplicity (*zhi*) and Refinement (*wen*). The beginning of a dynasty was identified with Simplicity, which emphasized the spirit and piety underlying the rites and ceremonies. Simplicity gradually gave way to Refinement, an obsession with external objects and artificiality that eventually led to decadence. Happily, the rise of the new state of Lu signaled restoration of the cycle of Simplicity. The notion of "Preserving the Three Systems" and the alternation of Simplicity and Refinement legitimated a line of dynastic succession and dramatized the distinction of the newly instituted dynasty as a new historical beginning (Elman 1990, 173–174; Q. Chen 1997, 8–26).

According to the other major New Script precept, "Unfolding of the Three Ages," Confucius had subtly separated the history of the twelve reigns (722–481 B.C.E.) of the house of Lu into three ages. The events of the first age he had heard and knew of through transmitted records; those of the second he had heard through contemporary accounts by the elders still alive; those of the third he had personally witnessed. Significantly, he used different language to record events in each different time period. For distant events, dearth in detail was unavoidable and proper. But for more recent events, especially those Confucius personally witnessed, more complete details were proffered. However, the location of people and events in time did not alone determine narrative style and language; moral consideration also played an important role. Dong made it clear that Confucius used his chronicles as a vehicle for his moral adjudication, lavishing praise and levying blame. Such was the "law of the pen" enacted in the *Spring and Autumn Annals*.

He Xiu further elaborated this three-stage succession of the Lu house. He identified the age that Confucius knew through transmitted records as the age where there was order arising out of decay and disorder. The age which Confucius learned about through oral testimony was that of "approaching peace," when the internal core of Chinese culture gradually enveloped the peripheral barbarian cultures. Finally, the age that Confucius personally witnessed was the epoch of "universal peace," a time of political maturation and cultural expansion, when China and the barbarians merged to form a great unity (Elman 1990, 231–237; Q. Chen 1997, 40–49).

In the Han, in addition to the significant advances in the compilational and narrative technique evidenced by the accomplishments of Sima Qian and Ban Gu, a philosophy of history was born and matured, a systematic vision of political and cultural developments showing the ancient Chinese past as a diachronic progression, whose zenith was "universal peace," an ideal realizable in the here and now (Ng 1994, 3–10). But perhaps such schemas were ahistorical in the final analysis; for, as we have pointed out, their totalizing account of historical progression tended to swamp the particularities and diversities that Sima Qian so valued in his reconstruction of the past. The rise of New Script school represented an important intellectual development in Confucianism that had a far-reaching influence on the Chinese view of their past. The climate of Later Han Confucian culture was characterized by the interest in textual criticism, advanced and exemplified by the works of Ma Rong (79–166) and Zheng Xuan (127–200), both leading Old Script scholars. Their exegetical studies, as well as those of their disciples and followers, provided indispensable assistance to later scholars in understanding the Confucian classics. However, in the Later Han this high level of textual criticism neither altered the fate of the Han nor enhanced the vitality of Confucianism as a social and political philosophy.

CHAPTER 3

The Age of Disunity

Proliferations and Variations of Historiography

The death of Emperor Xian of the Later Han in 220 marked not only the collapse of an empire, but also the end of an era. Like the fall of the Roman Empire, the fall of the Han Empire plunged China into a period of division, the medieval age in Chinese history, as it were. Although different in terms of duration and characteristics, this Chinese period of division, spanning almost four centuries until the founding of the Sui dynasty in 581, bore some superficial resemblances to the Middle Ages in European history (Holcombe 1994, 6–24). Just as medieval Europeans remained fascinated with the Roman Empire, so the Chinese and other peoples who occupied China proper at the time—the Han Chinese and various non-Han ethnic groups known as the Särbi (Xianbei in Chinese)—made "persistent efforts to reconcile the present with ideas of the past" (Pearce, Spiro, & Ebrey 2001, 3). In short, they lived "in the shadow of the Han" (Holcombe 1994, 6). This cultural nostalgia was clearly reflected in historical writing. Indeed, post-Han China witnessed a boom in historical pursuits, especially official dynastic historiography. There appeared many valiant and at times vain attempts by court historians of the various regimes, often commissioned by their emperors, to forge dynastic and lineage ties with the Han. Both the exiled regimes established by the Han Chinese in the south and the newly founded Särbi domains in the north sought legitimation through historical reconstruction.

The Historiography of Legitimation

This enthusiasm for reliving the Han imperial dream unquestionably contributed to the historiographical boom in the Age of Disunity, but it also masked cruel historical realities. The sad fact was that after the collapse of the Han, no regime was able to establish a strong, unified empire on the Han imperial model. The ruins of the Han spawned the establishment of three kingdoms, none of which was powerful enough to unify China. The Wei (220–265), whose foundation was laid by Cao Cao (155–220), a former general of the Later Han who delivered the final blow to the already tottering empire, occupied the Yellow River basin, the old power center of the Qin and Han Empires. But Cao Cao's southern campaign, which could

have realized his ambition to become the successor of the Han, ended dis-
astrously in the battle at Chibi. His adversaries, the Shu (221–263) in the
southwest and the Wu (222–280) in the southeast, formed a coalition and
fought off Cao's advance. After Cao Cao's death, however, the Shu and Wu
were equally unsuccessful in their campaigns against the Wei. The Shu,
established by Liu Bei (161–223), a relative of the Han royal family, claimed
legitimate succession to the Han throne. It launched five consecutive expeditions under the leadership of its able minister Zhuge Liang (181–234), a
reputed strategist, but in the end the campaigns were futile. After Zhuge's
death in 263, the Shu state was taken over by the Wei, but two years later
the Wei fell into the hands of the usurping Sima family (no relations with
Sima Qian). The Sima family established the (Western) Jin dynasty (265–
316) and conquered the Wu in 280. But unification under the Jin was short-
lived. A bloody civil war in the early fourth century not only led to the
dynasty's downfall but also an invasion of the non-Han "barbarians," the
Särbi and Tabgatch (Tuoba in Chinese). The Sima family, along with a number of hereditary houses, retreated south of the Yangzi River and resumed
its regime as the Eastern Jin (317–420). Toward the end of the fourth century, the various Särbi/Tabgatch kingdoms in the north were unified by the
Northern Wei dynasty (386–534). Chinese history thus entered the period
of the Northern and Southern dynasties. The Eastern Jin lasted only a century. Its territories in the south came to be controlled successively by the
(Liu) Song, Qi, Liang, and Chen dynasties, whose respective tenure was
even shorter. The Northern Wei dynasty also faced enormous challenges
and succumbed to the domination by a few powerful military families. One
emerged to become the founder of the Sui dynasty (581–618), which would
eventually unify north and south to end this long period of division.

During this age of political disintegration, however, despite frequent
dynastic changes, there were notable continuities in the domain of historical production. Dynastic historiography flourished. It carried on the Han
legacy of linking history with politics. If Sima Qian's historical endeavor
was motivated largely by his private interests, Ban Gu charged historical
production with a more direct, pragmatic political mission. His overt goal
was to help the rulers locate valuable lessons from the past that they might
apply directly to the current situation. One of the major political issues addressed by historical writing was that of legitimacy in dynastic and royal
succession (*zhengtong*). Ban Gu had become preoccupied with this question when he looked at the crisis brought on by Wang Mang's attempted
usurpation. In the *Han History* Ban offered a detailed biography of Wang
Mang, describing Wang's pernicious machinations and declaring that like
the First Emperor of Qin, Wang Mang was not destined to receive sanction from Heaven. Thus Ban used history to dispense judgment on political
legitimacy. Since Ban believed that Wang lacked the Mandate of Heaven,
his regime could not be legitimate. When Xun Yue received the Emperor
Xian's commission to abridge the *Han History*, he essentially offered a political apologia for the Han imperial order by harking back to the Confu-

cian wisdom of history (C. Chen 1975, 84ff), celebrating the legitimacy of
the Han by virtue of its securing the mandate from Heaven to rule.

Xun Yue *Han Annals* merely indulged Emperor Xian's delusion that he
was the beneficiary of the blessings of his mighty ancestors; it did not save
the empire. Nor did his appeal to Confucianism stave off dynastic collapse.
In fact, by the end of the Han period, Confucian learning had become a
victim of its own success. Having received official sponsorship and patronage, Confucian scholars devoted most of their energy to exegetical studies,
hoping to extract exact and authentic meanings from ancient texts and
turn them into reliable compendia that would serve as practical guides to
ritual ceremonies and government operations. While this textual scholasticism performed an important service to scholars of later times, it also
caused vociferous controversies at the time between, for example, the Old
Script and New Script Confucian textual traditions. Such highly academic
debates consumed much intellectual energy, and classical studies became
sterile textualism with little bearing on actual life.

Consequently, there was the gradual loss of vitality and interest in Confucianism. Many literati began to seek spiritual solace and intellectual out-
let in Neo-Daoism (*xuanxue*) and also, increasingly, in Buddhism. Indeed,
after the fall of the Han, China's political and cultural life experienced
dramatic changes. But Confucianism did not become irrelevant and its emphasis on political legitimacy remained a vitally paramount concern. In
fact, the downfall of the Han greatly sharpened subsequent rulers' awareness of political legitimacy and heightened their vigilance against anyone
who coveted their positions. History came to be their primary tool for
expounding and consolidating legitimate political succession (*zhengtong*).
Following the exemplary practice of the Han, especially the compilation
of the *Han Records of the Eastern Pavilion*, rulers appointed official historians and sponsored similar projects (Jie Liu 1982, 68–71). The examples of
Sima Qian and Ban Gu inspired the production of private history as well.
Scholars not only participated in official projects, but many also embarked
on their own projects, seeking to extend and improve upon existing works.
There thus appeared a "high tide" of historical production, particularly
the writing of dynastic history, which revealed great fascination with Han
history (Qu 1999b, 227–234).

The fervent enthusiasm for writing history owed much to the rulers'
interest. Emperor Xiaowen of the Northern Wei remarked, "Princes [are
often inclined to] abuse power to benefit themselves. If historians don't
record their [evil behavior], what else can they be afraid of?" (W. Du 1998,
20) This warning was quite commendable, coming from the ruler himself. Most likely, it resulted from his ministers' repeated remonstrations
and admonitions. Not every ruler, of course, felt comfortable enough to
allow historians to record their deeds and behaviors without discrimination. An intriguing tension existed between the prince and his ministers.
While ministers were supposed to serve and obey the prince, it was also
their responsibility to instruct him in moral values and imbue him with

political ideals, lest he fall victim to the manipulations by his in-laws and eunuchs, for by the time Ban Gu's successors compiled the *Han Records of the Eastern Pavilion*, the emperor's throne was not only threatened by ambitious ministers and generals, but also by court intrigues involving imperial in-laws. History was both politically instrumental and morally didactic, and thus played an important role in the education of the prince.

Royal patronage of history at the time resulted in an extremely important development, that is, the compilation in the court of the "diary of activity and repose" (*qijuzhu*), or court diary, a practice that originated in the reign of Emperor Xian (r. 189–226) of the Later Han, one of the most historically minded emperors of the dynasty. During the period of disunity, the court diary gradually became "the standard chronological record compiled for each reign" (Twitchett 1992, 8). This practice of recording in detail what happened at court and imperial audiences would be continued as a standard historiographical practice in subsequent ages. The compilation of the court diary marshaled the raw materials on which the dynastic histories would be based. In some periods female historians (*nüshi*) recorded the lives of the inner court (Y. Jin [1944] 2000, 114). Another notable development was the affirmation of the importance of contemporary history that resulted, no doubt, from the desire of rulers and scholars to use history as a tool of political legitimation. The *Han Records of the Eastern Pavilion*, a work based on court diaries, was considered to be on a par with Sima Qian's *Records* and Ban Gu's *Han History*. Collectively these model works of historiography came to be known as the "Three Histories" (Sanshi) (*Shixueshi* 1983, 14).

The first historical masterpiece that appeared in the Age of Disunity was by Chen Shou (233–297). Although not a court-appointed official historian, Chen has been much praised for his *History of the Three Kingdoms* (*San'guozhi*), identified as one of the masterly "Four Histories," putting it in the illustrious company of the works of Sima Qian, Ban Gu, and Fan Ye (398–445) (*Shixueshi* 1983, 108). While writing this history, Chen benefited from various court diaries and contemporary historical writings. There had already been numerous contemporary histories compiled in the reigns of the Three Kingdoms (Qu 1999b, 229), but Chen's work outshone and outlasted them all. Although Chen employed individual chronological segments within the period of division and wrote separate histories of the kingdoms, he took pains to paint a global picture and construct a narrative that connected the age as a whole. This novel achievement received high praise and was imitated by later historians (S. Bai 1999, 161; Qu 1999b, 250–251).

That Chen Shou succeeded in producing such a panoramic historical vision had a good deal to do with his background. Born and raised in the state of Shu, Chen studied with Qiao Zhou (c. 201–270), an acclaimed scholar known for his erudition in both the classics and history. Though Chen excelled in his study—his fellow students compared his accomplishments to those of Confucius' own disciples—he did not have a smooth political career. He held several different positions in government but failed to realize his greater ambition because of the factional strife and intrigues at court, which was then under the sway of powerful eunuchs. At midlife Chen was embroiled in fractious court politics and thrust into a whirlwind of power struggle and dynastic change as the Shu were being conquered by the Wei (Yang & Wu 1998, 31–34). He did not quite give up his political and bureaucratic ambitions, but he experienced many twists and turns before he landed a decent position under the new ruler of the Jin dynasty that had grown out of the Wei. As an attendant of composition (*zhuzuo lang*) at the Jin court, Chen had access to libraries and archives, even though he was not assigned the task of composing a history. In some ways Chen's life reminds us of Sima Qian's. Inspired by Sima, Chen, at the age of forty-eight, began writing the *Three Kingdoms*. Frustrated by his trying experiences in politics and government, he devoted himself to historical scholarship and developed a burning desire to make his name through his writing. Like Sima, Chen did not expect his contemporaries to appreciate his work. He placed his hope in the future, convinced that posterity would one day recognize its value (ibid., 47–51). In actuality, neither Sima nor Chen had to wait long before others came to appreciate their works, but while Sima was apparently honored and enjoyed a comfortable life after finishing the *Records,* Chen did not get to personally relish his success. Shortly after he completed his work, he died of an illness. Almost immediately after his death, his friends presented his work to the court where it promptly received official and popular recognition (Yang & Wu 1998, 51; S. Bai 1999, 158; W. Du 1998, 93).

It is instructive to compare Sima Qian's and Chen Shou's respective positions on the issue of *zhengtong,* that is, the question of legitimate dynastic succession. As we recall, Sima sympathized with such tragic heroes as Xiang Yu and Chen She, who, although never becoming rulers, were accorded some legitimacy, and Sima promoted their status in his *Records.* Chen Shou had more rigid criteria. As a student of Qiao Zhou, who had written what was possibly the first systematic work of historical criticism, *Examinations of Ancient Histories* (*Gushi kao*) (Y. Lu 1998, 76–77), Chen Shou seemed uninterested in following Sima's example. Qiao had criticized Sima for deviating at times from Confucian moral standards by embracing figures such as Xiang Yu, and in so doing he failed to promote properly and explicitly the Han's legitimacy. Chen was thus cautious in his treatment of controversial historical figures, lest sympathy with them be construed as violation of Confucian standards. He was particularly consumed by one central question: how to maintain a delicate balance in treating the relationships among the Three Kingdoms and their relations with the Han dynasty? He regarded the Jin dynasty, which replaced the Wei, as the "legitimate" successor to the Han, and so he recorded the lives of its rulers under "Imperial Annals," whereas the lives of the Shu and Wu rulers were described in the biographies. In order to show the integrity of this Wei-Jin legitimacy, Chen also omitted the imperial coronations of both the Shu and Wei rulers (Cutter & Crowell 1999, 70–71). The arrangement of his *Three Kingdoms* fully reveals his position on political legitimacy. It starts, in thirty fascicles, with the history of the Wei, beginning with the imperial annals, followed by the biographies. The work then devotes fifteen fascicles to the Shu and twenty to the Wu. Unlike Sima Qian and Ban Gu, Chen Shou composed neither treatises nor monographs, probably due to a shortage of time.

But beneath the interpretive patina that asserted Wei-Jin legitimacy was Chen Shou's deep sympathy for the Shu, his former homeland, and even in some respects, for the Wu. In the case of the Shu, although Chen did not refer to its rulers with imperial titles, he called them "former princes" (*xianzhu*) and "later princes" (*houzhu*), and their wives, "princesses" (*hou*) and "madams" (*furen*). With regard to the Wu, he simply used the individuals' names. Moreover, while Chen omitted records that dealt directly with the Shu coronation, by using Sima Qian's methods of "multiple narration" or "mutual illumination," he described in detail the events around it, such as how the Shu officials initiated the process and repeatedly and earnestly memorialized the prince. He also included documentation related to the ceremony as well as to the *feng* and *shan* sacrifices. All this textual maneuvering was intended to hint at what actually took place. By contrast, even though Chen mentioned the Wei and Jin coronations, he kept their descriptions very brief, concealing all the fanfare and ceremony (Yang & Wu 1998, 57–61). Notwithstanding his acknowledgment of Wei-Jin legitimacy, his text conferred on the Shu a certain degree of historical respectability and importance. Chen's sympathetic treatment of the Shu is not surprising. First, although he became a Jin official, he was a Shu native and may be forgiven his nostalgia for the Shu and his lament of its downfall, which he lived through. Second, the Shu was founded by a member of the Liu clan, which had established the Han dynasty. However, despite this and the fact that Ban Gu had argued vigorously that only the Liu family was entitled to legitimate sovereignty, Chen did not directly affirm the legitimacy of the Shu. In any event the Liu family legacy did not last, as the Shu had the shortest duration of the three kingdoms.

Chen was not entirely consumed by his nostalgia for the Shu; nor was his valuation of Wei-Jin legitimacy an ideological straitjacket. Chen refused, in the end, to be bogged down by the issue of legitimacy in writing dynastic history (Lei 1990, 298ff). Like Sima Qian, Chen was first and foremost interested in preserving memories of the past through truthful historical recording, despite political pressure. He wrote the history of each state independently—his work acquired its title, *History of the Three Kingdom*, posthumously. By presenting each kingdom separately, he acknowledged the fundamental historical reality of the time, namely, that the unified Han Empire was no more and in its place were three equally powerful kingdoms (Y. Jin [1944] 2000, 86). Hence he spent almost an equal amount of time describing the history of the Wu, a kingdom that seemed to lack royal pedigree as well as the means and will to overpower its rivals, as he did with the histories of the Shu and Wei. In this respect Chen Shou differed from Sima Qian, Ban Gu, and many of his contemporaries who remained enthralled with the glories of the Han; nor was he completely encumbered by the ideal of China as a unified empire. In that sense Chen was perhaps unique among compilers of dynastic history in imperial China, for their works almost always celebrated the ideal of political and territorial unification.

Chen's realistic representation of the history of the Three Kingdoms was a product of his time. Whereas Ban Gu and Xun Yue wanted to elevate the image of the reigning court, Chen sought to promote the aristocratic lineages (*shizu*) and the great magnate families (*haozu*). At times Chen's biographic-historical recounting, far from being a dispassionate exercise, lapsed into hero-worship (S. Bai 1999, 162). Of course, the admiration for heroic individuals and deeds was not new—Sima Qian and Ban Gu had glorified their heroes—but Chen seemed to shape history around dramatic accounts of the thrilling deeds of his historical protagonists, which did successfully set readers' hearts aflutter. While he showed an interest in Heaven's will and intervention, he was more intrigued with heroic deeds and majestic feats. Since history, to him, illustrated heroic actions, the history of the Wu could well be placed on a par with those of the Wei and Shu because all three kingdoms produced heroic personages. Chen took pains to describe the era's many extraordinary figures and, interestingly, often associated their achievements with Heaven's intervention. For Chen, Heaven's dictates were decisive, but their significance could be illuminated only by the scintillating feats of heroes in history (ibid., 164).

Nor was Chen Shou interested only in successful heroes. His work outlived others of its kind precisely because it offered animated descriptions of historical figures, including tragic ones who failed to realize their intentions. As a result, many of Chen Shou's stories have become engraved not only on the cultural memories of the Chinese, but also on those of the peoples in East Asia generally. It was therefore not surprising that Luo Guanzhong (fl. 1330–1400) decided to rewrite these stories as a historical novel and produced the literary masterpiece *Romance of the Three Kingdoms* (*Sanguo yanyi*), arguably the most widely read historical novel in late imperial and modern China. One innovation of Chen Shou's style can be seen in his introduction of a figure, in that he often described the individual's physical appearance in conjunction with that person's character. Luo Guanzhong incorporated all of these descriptions into his novel, much to his readers' delight. Chen Shou's vivid individual portraits and heroic view of history perhaps reflected the political and social culture of this period of division, which had an enhanced appreciation for the individual. Some scholars have characterized it as an age that witnessed the "discovery of the individual" (Holcombe 1994, 4; Yü 1980 & 1985).

Chen Shou made a point to include heroic personages from a wide variety of backgrounds, many of whom did not possess aristocratic or royal pedigrees. A case in point is the story surrounding Liu Bei, the founder of the Shu and Chen Shou's former master. To begin with, Liu Bei himself is described as having unusually big ears and long arms, hardly a flattering image. As a member of the Liu clan, or the Han royal family, Liu Bei lays claim to the throne, a claim with which Chen implicitly sympathizes. But Chen shows that Liu's success in founding the Shu is less the outcome of his own talent than the result of the collective efforts of his assistants, among the most prominent of whom are Guan Yu, a horse merchant, Zhang Fei, a butcher, and most important, Zhuge Liang, a recluse of high intelligence recruited by Liu after repeated visits and invitations. Although Zhuge looms large in Chen's account and emerges as a sympathetic figure of great abilities, Chen criticizes Zhuge's ultimate inability to attract able military generals to him, which contributes, in Chen's opinion, to Zhuge's failure to defeat the Wei. Nevertheless, Chen's evocative depiction of Zhuge's multifaceted talents and lively praise for his achievements established the principal components of the Zhuge Liang legend in the popular imagination (Henry 1992). Thanks to Chen's historical account and Luo Guanzhong's later novelistic embellishment, Zhuge Liang figured vividly and conspicuously in the Chinese popular historical lore as a paragon—the paradigmatic statesman blessed with superior power and charisma, endowed with a personality that distinguished him from his humdrum social peers.

Despite Chen Shou's sympathy with Liu Bei and his cause in renewing Han legitimacy, Chen tried to be as realistic and objective as he could regarding Liu's successes and his failures, revealing not just the virtues but also the shortcomings of his hero. This historical "realism" elicited criticism from those who were adamant about preserving the Han political legacy and legitimacy through the state of Shu. For instance, a century or so after Chen's death, Xi Zuochi (?–384) denigrated Chen's *Three Kingdoms* precisely because of Chen's view on the Wei succession. Xi Zuochi, who wrote the *Spring and Autumn of the Han and Jin* (*Hanjin chunqiu*), connected the Eastern Jin to the Han, bypassing the Wei. He maintained that after the death of Emperor Xian, Han sovereignty continued in the state of Shu, but in 263, when the Sima family of the Wei annexed the Shu, there was a transition of power from the Han to the Jin. Consequently, Xi Zuochi considered the Wei to be the usurper, an illegitimate successor to the Han, and hence did not deserve a position in the line of dynastic succession based on the Liu bloodline.

Xi Zuochi's indictment is quite understandable. Xi wrote his work in the Eastern Jin, an émigré regime that had retreated to the south after losing control of the Yellow River basin. His theory was a valiant, albeit self-serving and ideologically driven, attempt to promote the legitimacy of his own dynasty (Jie Liu 1982, 74) in face of its redoubtable opponent in the north, the Särbi regime of the Northern Wei dynasty. It should be noted that by naming their dynasty the Northern Wei, the Särbi ruler was clearly interested in claiming legitimacy as a successor to the earlier Wei dynasty. There was, therefore, every reason for Xi Zuochi to condemn the

Wei as illegitimate. One may well argue that Xi's attempt to connect the Jin to the Han was a move that ran counter to historical reality and thus lacked historical validity. But what Xi did was to devise a cultural, as opposed to historical, argument to buttress his position, and this move was to have a far-reaching influence. He based his theory of political legitimacy on what we may call a conception of culturalism. He argued that because the Jin dynasty had inherited the Han's ritual culture, the Jin was politically legitimate; the barbarous Northern Wei, in contrast, was an uncivilized regime, and its political power was therefore unjust and unjustifiable. Xi established cultural tradition and cultural strength as the principal criteria for determining political legitimacy. In short, culture took precedence over, and could offset or compensate for, the loss of territorial space. This culture-driven, or culturalist, theory of *zhengtong* would be expanded by the later Song historians as they dealt with regimes of conquest in northern China (Q. Wang 1999; W. Du 1998, 87–89).

Xi Zuochi was not the only historian of the southern dynasties who showed a keen interest in legitimacy, or *zhengtong*. It was in fact a pervasive issue throughout the entire era, with which anyone who wrote history had to engage (Lei 1990, 355–356). The cases of Shen Yue (441–513) and Xiao Zixian (487–537), two historians also known as accomplished poets and essayists, are particularly instructive. In addition to literary fame, Shen and Xiao enjoyed successful official careers, both serving in positions close to the power center. While their high status at court facilitated access to official documents, it could have adversely affected their ability to write objectively. Shen was born into a military family that had served the (Liu) Song, the Qi, and the Liang, which Shen himself had helped to establish. Xiao Zixian's family background was equally impressive, as he was the grandson of Emperor Gao of the Qi. A distant cousin of Emperor Wu of the Liang whom Xiao served, he enjoyed prestige for his royal pedigree and was esteemed for his literary talents. However, as both men were commissioned by the reigning court to compile a history of the previous dynasty, both faced the same problem as Chen Shou did when tracing the lines of dynastic succession. Thanks to many preexisting works that they used liberally, and perhaps more important, thanks to their outstanding literary skills, Shen and Xiao finished their assignments quickly. But evidence of concealment (*hui*) of facts, due to political pressure and their own sense of ethical propriety, are apparent in their accounts. After all, they had complex personal relations with their subject.

Shen Yue composed the *Song History* (*Songshu*), a work that explained the rise and fall of the (Liu) Song dynasty (420–479). He benefited tremendously from earlier works written by Xu Yuan (394–475) and others, all of which were contemporary histories compiled under the patronage of the Song court. Although they were valuable as firsthand accounts, they also often concealed and even distorted facts in depicting the transition from the Eastern Jin to the (Liu) Song. Shen Yue noticed their flaws and lamented that "when dealing with contemporary events, these records were most likely not factual" (W. Du 1998, 137). But he made little effort to rectify the problem, and even himself made similar attempts to conceal bad behavior on the part of the Qi rulers who had dislodged and replaced the (Liu) Song.

Xiao Zixian's challenge was even more daunting. His *Southern Qi History* (*Nanqi shu*) dealt with the dynasty founded by his own ancestors. By the time he was ordered to compile its history, the Qi had been replaced by the Liang. Xiao strove to embellish and celebrate the actions of his ancestors in wresting power from the (Liu) Song and in founding the Qi. But he had to point to the ills of the last Qi reign in order to please his new master, Emperor Wu of the Liang dynasty. Xiao was forced to manipulate and interpret history in such a way as to prove that the Liang's replacement of Qi was legitimate. Therefore, although both works are painstaking in their efforts to describe the dynastic fortunes from the Song to the Liang, historians past and present have not regarded them highly, precisely because the authors submitted rather blatantly to political expediency and ideological imperative (*Shitong* 1978, 1:116, 187, 199; S. Bai 1999, 153; Qu 1999b, 256–263; W. Du 1998, 142).

Yet Shen Yue and Xiao Zixian fared far better than Wei Shou (505–572), whose *Wei History* (Weishu) was dismissed by Liu Zhiji as "foul history" (*huishi*) (*Shitong* 1978, 2:365). Liu Zhiji's assessment may not have been entirely fair, for according to Qing scholars (W. Du 1998, 143–146), Liu may have relied on inaccurate information when he accused Wei Shou of demanding bribes from those who wanted their ancestors included in his history. In actuality, while serving as a court historian under the Särbi/Tagbatch regimes in north China, Wei Shou apparently enjoyed the support of emperors who preferred and encouraged factually sound recording of their reigns (Qu 1999b, 263).

Despite the fact that these northern dynasties were traditionally regarded as culturally inferior to the southern dynasties, their rulers were no less serious in emulating the Han model of dynastic historiography. The support Wei Shou received for his compilation of the *Wei History* was a good example. Based on a rich corpus of contemporary sources culled by court historians, the *Wei History*, comprising 131 fascicles, may justifiably be characterized as an encyclopedic work. The work contains imperial annals, arrayed biographies, and monographs, and on the whole it is much more comprehensive than its contemporaneous counterpart, Xiao Zixian's *Southern Qi History*. Wei Shou was adamant in asserting the political legitimacy of the northern dynasties as the rightful successors of the Han Empire. He referred to the southern peoples as "island barbarians" (*daoyi*), a term connoting their isolation from the cultural mainstream in the north. Wei viewed the southern dynasties as usurping regimes and attributed to the northern ones not only political but also cultural legitimacy. A contemporary source described an episode in which a northerner harangued a southern general for a contemptuous remark he made about northern culture, which suggests that Wei's cultural pride and confidence may have accurately reflected the self-perception of the northern regimes (Pearce, Spiro, & Ebrey 2001, 18–19). By the sixth century, the northern dynasties had already rivaled their southern counterparts in cultural development, a fact apparently corroborated by the number of historical texts produced. Between the fall of the Han and the founding of the Tang, as many as 140 dynastic histories appeared. If we disregard those by historians about the Western and Eastern Jin dynasties, we find that the northern historians contributed exactly as many works as their southern counterparts, that is, thirty-six (Inaba 1999, 186).[1]

Remembering the Han through History

The appointment of court historians and the introduction of court diaries were important factors contributing to the proliferation of dynastic histories, but a more important reason appeared to be the fall of the Han itself. The seemingly new practices in historiography were really extensions and modifications of Han precedents such as the *Han Records of the Eastern Pavilion*. In addition, the Han Empire loomed large in the political, cultural, and historical memory of the following era. The persistent preoccupation with political legitimacy, as shown in the works of Chen Shou, Xi Zuochi, and others, underscored the perennial relevance of the Han to historians. Indeed, this paramount concern with legitimacy became a central feature of Chinese historiography. Chen Shou and Xi Zuochi might diverge in their views of history, but they shared the same passion in studying the fall of the Han and its aftermath. Prior to the *Song History*, Shen Yue had written a *Jin History* (*Jinshu*). No longer extant, it described Jin's ties and succession to the Han. In addition to his *Southern Qi History*, Xiao Zixian wrote a *Later Han History* (*Houhan shu*), which was also lost. All these endeavors suggest that the authors' interest in history had a good deal to do with their intent to enshrine and perpetuate the memory of the Han.

These scholars were by no means exceptions. Historical interest in the Han persisted throughout the Age of Disunity. To some extent it was exactly this fervent interest that generated the first waves of dynastic histories. The *Han Records of the Eastern Pavilion*, while unprecedented when it appeared and paradigmatic in its influence, was incomplete, for it came to a halt in the last turbulent years of the Han. After the Han collapse, many historians sought to complete it, and eight of these efforts are still extant (Qu 1999b, 228–229). Although some were written by official historians, many were private initiatives. Moreover, a few by official historians were not official assignments. Sima Biao's (?–306) *A Sequel to the Han History* (*Xuhanshu*) was a good example. Attendant of the Secretariat (*mishu lang*) at the

---

1. If we add the works by Jin historians — twenty-six titles — then southern historians produced more, but it is unknown how many of them were by Eastern Jin historians in the south. Inaba's table may not be complete, however, if we compare the titles in his table with those mentioned by Qu Lindong (1999b, 227–234). Qu does not, however, provide a table.

Jin court, Sima Biao was inspired by Ban Gu's *Han History* to write a sequel. The result was a complete history of the Later Han in eighty fascicles that followed Ban's model and consisted of three sections (annals, biography, and monograph). Unfortunately, most of the work is lost. Only eight monographs have survived, numbering thirty fascicles. While the coverage of these monographs conformed to Ban's original design, they did examine new subjects, such as bureaucracy (*baiguan*), and chariots and costumes (*yufu*). In addition, Sima Biao revised Ban's "Monograph of Geography" into the "Monograph of Counties and Districts" (Junguo zhi). These additions and modifications were not simply indications of shifts in interest but were a direct result of Sima Biao's design. His primary goal was to explore the causes of the Han's downfall. The annals-biographic style did not allow him to explain, much less articulate, these causes, except perhaps by dropping a few hints in the commentary sections. But since these were lost, along with the annals and biographies, we are uncertain whether Sima provided any political analyses in the comments. We do know that the monographs served this purpose. By creating separate monographs on the bureaucratic system and its protocols and culture, Sima Biao drew attention to the imperial administration that to a large extent defined the political order. He emphasized how important it was for a prince to maintain an aura of majesty (*junwei*), while ministers must observe appropriate protocol (*chenyi*), an emphasis stemming from his view that the Han fell because of the collapse of the ruler's majesty and the failure of ministers to abide by the rites. But he did not find only this fault. In his "Monograph on Sacrifices" (Jisi zhi), he launched a veiled attack on emperors who spent lavishly during their reign and praised the virtue of frugality. To Sima, exorbitant spending also contributed to the tragic end of the Han.

Sima Biao's emphasis on a strong, ritualistically correct political order reflected a genuine practical concern, for his own era was characterized by chaos and disorder. This contributed to a nostalgia for the halcyon days of the glorious Han Empire and explains the enthusiasm for writing the history of the Han.

By the time Yuan Hong (328–376), an aristocrat of the Eastern Jin, embarked on his project on the Han, he had already seen many works on the great dynasty, several of them penned by his contemporaries. Yuan had grown up under the Eastern Jin, an admittedly lesser dynasty founded by the survivors of the bloody civil war known in history as the "Rebellion of the Eight Princes" (*bawang zhiluan*, 291–306), in which eight royal relatives revolted against the reigning emperor (Holcombe 1994, 3). Yuan's family was forced to leave the land where they had flourished under the Han, and although Yuan was born well after the war, his enterprise was impelled by his acute nostalgia for a lost time and place. His interest in his own lineage, as well as Han history in general, plunged him into assiduous study of the voluminous histories that had appeared. But the more he read, the more he became dissatisfied with their quality. His complaint was twofold. First, while these histories often contained rich information about the Han, they frequently failed to provide a clear outline of its history. Second, many historians were content with merely amassing, collecting, and preserving the sources on the Han. They often fell short in verifying and vetting those sources. Therefore in their works, there were many factual contradictions and mistakes (S. Bai 1999, 167).

In order to produce a clearly delineated outline of Han history, Yuan Hong decided to model his work on Xun Yue's *Han Records;* hence the title, the *Later Han Records* (*Houhan ji*). Like the *Han Records,* Yuan's *Later Han Records* is a chronicle that traces a succession of emperors. As we have seen in the case of Xun Yue, this chronicle style need not be as dry and terse as the *Spring and Autumn Annals* but could feature rich narratives. Even though Yuan Hong focused on the reigns and lives of the emperors, he made a point to incorporate many pertinent events and personages; he situated his narratives about the court and emperors in the broad contexts of surrounding events. Xun Yue had composed his work by relying primarily on Ban Gu's *Han History,* but Yuan Hong consulted numerous extant works in piecing together his account. As a result his work is longer and more substantial than Xun's, even though both produced thirty fascicles. It is also richer in descriptive details, including not only the emperors and their immediate associates but also various figures who were influential at the time. Not only did he preserve more detailed records for posterity, but he also made a notable modification in the annalistic form, which now integrated elaborate biographic narratives into the annals (S. Bai 1999, 168). Therefore despite the continued existence of both annals-biography (*jizhuan*) and annals-chronicle (*biannian*) (Naitō 1949, 174–175), there was increasingly a tendency to merge and modify them, as Yuan Hong did. In any event, the annals-biographic style became the predominant form in Chinese dynastic historiography, subsuming and absorbing the chronicle format (Jie Liu 1982, 82–93; Lei 1990, 553ff).

Like Sima Biao and others, Yuan Hong also turned to Han history because he hoped to extract from it usable lessons for his contemporaries. To him, historical writing ought to center on the "teachings of names" (*mingjiao*), by which he meant teaching people to understand the social hierarchy by having them learn the names of their positions in order to understand how those names fit into the overall structure. Having understood their "names," or socially defined titles and labels, then they must properly fulfill the roles and obligations that these names prescribed, and in so doing, they would "rectify" the political situation. Yuan Hong even criticized the works of Sima Qian, Ban Gu, and Xun Yue for supposedly failing to pay sufficient attention to the rectification of individuals' roles and positions. Although he admired his predecessor' accomplishments in historiography, Yuan Hong believed that his own work would present history as a mirror that reflected the correct social norms and proper political order. As a consequence, Yuan Hong held Cao Cao and his associates accountable for the end of the Han, because Cao, as a Han official, did not use his power and ability to help the young and inexperienced Emperor

Xian. Instead, by abusing his influence and position, he expanded his own power at the expense of the Han imperium. Cao failed to live up to his "name," his role and position, as a Han official. His action was a breach of trust that violated the existing political order and eventually caused the fall of the Han.

Yuan's view on the transition from the Han to the Wei was therefore different from Chen Shou's but similar to Xi Zuochi's. In fact, like Xi, Yuan also had a personal and political ax to grind when he condemned Cao Cao. At the time Yuan wrote his *Later Han Records,* the Eastern Jin court faced the potential danger of usurpation by Huan Wen (312–373), its most powerful minister. This greatly alarmed Yuan, who refused to write a panegyric on Huan Wen's father. When challenged by Huan Wen, he wrote a veiled mockery of Huan (S. Bai 1999, 173). Yuan's judgment of Cao Cao, a manipulative minister who usurped power, was a warning against contemporary usurpation.

Yuan Hong's idea of the "teaching of names" obviously grew out of his admiration for such time-honored Confucian principles as political loyalty exemplified by the ruler-minister relationship and filial piety expressed in the father-son relationship. But Yuan went further to ascertain the ontological foundation of the names. He argued that first there was the ontological principle of the *dao,* the Way, which was all-encompassing and pervasive, both in the human and natural worlds. As the relationships between the ruler and minister, and father and son, constituted the Way—the foundation of names and the social hierarchical order—they were immutable and eternal, just as mountains and rivers were durable and long-lasting. Yuan Hong's search for the ontological origin of names suggests a gradual shift away from the main philosophical and cosmological assumptions of Han Confucianism that his predecessor Xun Yue had taken pains to uphold. Xun Yue operated within a highly mechanistic, correlative universe, in which everything had its concrete correspondence and Heaven ultimately correlated with humanity in tangible ways, as revealed in history. By contrast, Yuan was more interested in exploring the first principles that defined humanity. His metaphysics was partly shaped, without doubt, by the tenets of Neo-Daoism, an esoteric and speculative philosophy that melded Daoist metaphysics with Confucian ethics and learning. It was all the rage among the literati, and we shall look at it in greater depth below. Just as many Neo-Daoists embraced the supremely spontaneous *dao* as the ultimate reality, while retaining a healthy and sober respect for the social norms taught by the perfect sage, Confucius, so too Yuan espoused the teachings of names in the very name of the authoritative principle of *dao,* according to which the universe operated and functioned. Yuan may also have been influenced by Buddhism. In his *Later Han Records* Yuan Hong gives a fairly detailed and enthusiastic introduction to Buddhism, which is apparently the "earliest formal mention of Buddhism in Chinese historiography" (S. Bai 1999, 175).

While Buddhism had certainly entered the Chinese cultural world by then, it did not yet enjoy wide currency. Among its many opponents was Fan Ye (398–445), arguably the most talented historian of the era. Fan Ye's steadfast objection to and harsh criticism of Buddhism may suggest that by his time Buddhism had already succeeded in expanding its influence in society and, more importantly, at court. Fan could no longer be indifferent to this import from India. There is ample evidence of the inroads that Buddhism had made into the state. Emperor Wen of the (Liu) Song (r. 424–453) showed a keen interest in this foreign import, believing that Buddhism promoted goodness (*shan*) and was therefore beneficial to the development of human moral character and social mores (S. Bai 1999, 145 ff). Emperor Wen's interest may have been practical and political rather than spiritual and religious, for he saw the religion as a useful ideological prop of his regime. But some at his court were genuine Buddhist converts, such as He Chengtian (370–447), an official historian charged with compiling the history of the reigning dynasty. He Chengtian believed in reincarnation and considered it the foundation of Buddhist teachings; by striving to improve one's karma, one was led to goodness that benefited both the individual and society.

Fan Ye, by contrast, vehemently opposed the idea of reincarnation. His opposition may have been a manifestation of his Confucian disinterest in the other world, but it may also have reflected his understanding of his own tumultuous life. Although born into a distinguished family, Fan Ye was the son of a concubine; it was said that his mother gave birth to him on the bathroom floor. Even as a child, he demonstrated extraordinary literary talents, which only stimulated jealousy among his more respectable siblings. Growing up to inherit a title from a childless uncle, he entered the officialdom, where he served in various positions and eventually became an attendant for the Secretariat of the Board of Officials (*libu shangshu lang*). His upward move in the bureaucracy came to a halt when he was in his mid-thirties, the result of his supposedly immoral behavior. He was demoted and became the magistrate of Xuancheng. Frustrated by this setback, he turned to the study of history and produced the *Later Han History* (*Houhan shu*). Although he later regained his position in court and even impressed Emperor Wen with his ability, he antagonized some of his powerful colleagues. In 445, when he was forty-seven, he was put to death for treason for his alleged involvement in a court conspiracy.

Fan Ye, following Sima Qian's example, took up the writing of history as a way to vent his frustrations in life and career. More important, Fan was very much influenced by Sima's perspective of history. To be sure, Fan Ye consulted many sources and had a model (Ban Gu's *Han History*) on which to pattern his work. But he was greatly inspired by Sima Qian, who had striven to establish a tradition of his own. Fan wanted to engage the past from his own unique understanding and perspective (S. Bai 1999, 133–134). In a letter to his nephews, Fan stressed, "I have always believed that in expressing oneself thought should be made primary and words should merely be used to convey the thought" (Egan 1979, 340). Unlike many of his predecessors and contemporaries preoccupied with the question of political legitimacy after the Han, Fan concentrated on the causes for dynastic collapse. Even though he wrote his work at a time when his political career was in the doldrums, he sought to enlighten himself with the lessons of Han history, aware that understanding of the present could come with knowledge of the past. His ruminations on history did not save him from the perils of court politics, but they did yield distinctive insights that made his work far superior to the many others. Like Sima Qian, Fan felt unappreciated. Although he had successfully come to grips with "the principle of historical writing," he had few listeners. "I have told it to others, but most were unable to appreciate what I said: perhaps because they look at things differently" (Egan 1979, 340–341).

One major difference between Fan's work and, for example, Yuan Hong's *Later Han Records,* is that in addition to his anti-Buddhist stance, he diverged from Yuan with regard to the teachings of names. Yuan asserted the immutability of the political order and social hierarchy with historical examples, Fan realistically acknowledged changes in history, including those that seemed to have violated the teachings of names. He was interested in confronting those changes and analyzing the various contexts in which they occurred, rather than simply subjecting them to moral censure. To be sure, Fan did have his own morally based standards for judging historical figures and evaluating historical events, but he derived this standard from his personal views on history; he did not necessarily adhere rigidly to the Confucian hierarchical social order and the values therein. Like Sima Qian and, to some extent, also Chen Shou, with whom Fan Ye shared a keen appreciation for historical change, Fan paid special attention to such qualities as "integrity" (*jie*) and "righteousness" (*yi*) when he described and judged historical personages. He praised those who demonstrated these characteristics, regardless of their origins and their eventual success or failure, and denounced those who were deficient in these virtues, even if they were of high social status. For this reason, despite his commendation of Ban Gu's erudition, which he thought was unsurpassable, he criticized Ban for failing to endorse those who demonstrated integrity and righteousness in their behavior, even though they were not allies of the Han. In such matters Fan believed that Ban Gu was inferior to Sima Qian (*Hou Hanshu* 1965, 1646–1647).

By emphasizing integrity and righteousness, Fan Ye expressed his doubts about the putative immutability of the sociopolitical order dearly valued by Yuan Hong and Ban Gu. In Fan's view, the sociopolitical structure was neither predetermined nor static, but a product of historical chance and change. Those who came to power did not necessarily possess superior moral traits, and those who failed often showed good and heroic characters. In fact, Fan found that those who held power often abused it and became morally corrupt. This was because, he suspected, they came to power fortuitously and not because of a predestined fortune. Under different circumstances they might have become quite ordinary or even abjectly poor individuals (*Hou Hanshu* 1965, 820–821). This kind of comment may have been a product of Fan's frustrations over his own setbacks, but it blazed a new trail away from mainstream dynastic historiography, which was anchored in a faith in the existing social order.

In exploring historical causation, Fan examined events from different perspectives. He concurred with the general consensus that the Han imperium was toppled as a result of the crippling abuse of power by court eunuchs, compounded by the political machinations of unscrupulous imperial in-laws. But unlike his predecessors who simply condemned these developments on grounds of moral corruption, Fan went further. "The causes of such catastrophes," Fan opined, "have long been discussed by historians, but the case of the fatal 'crack' originating with eunuchs may yet bear some comment." In order to examine the origin of the "fatal crack," he analyzed the psychology and experience of the eunuchs and found that

> . . . [t]he corporeal mutilation of eunuchs makes them defective human
> beings: their name and fame have no way to reflect gloriously upon their
> family, and their flesh and blood can never be passed on to an heir. Their
> evils are not detected even after scrutiny, and their propinquity to the ruler
> wins them his trust. Furthermore, in time they become steeped in court af-
> fairs and acquire expertise in formal precedents and usages. Hence young
> rulers depend upon their dutiful and proven service, and regent Empresses
> rely upon them to promulgate decrees; sovereigns consult them without any
> suspicion and become intimate with them because of their pleasing mien.
> (Egan 1979, 347–348)

But Fan Ye hastened to point out that not all eunuchs were perverse and baneful. There were plenty of honest and loyal ones who did not indulge their "evil nature." The problem, according to Fan, was endemic and institutional. It lay in the sad fact that once eunuchs became an integral part of the court, their domination took on a life of its own and grew disproportionately, resulting in "the crack for usurpation and seizure of power." Consequently, "faithful and worthy men were outwitted, and the altars of earth and grain were demolished and became ruins." Fan concluded, "When we trace the true causes of the dynasty's fall, it surely is not something that came about in one day or night" (ibid.). This sort of detailed and systematic historical analysis appears mostly in the "Introductions" (*xu*), "Disquisitions" (*lun*), and "Eulogies" (*zan*), placed at the beginnings or ends of the annals (*ji*) and biographies (*zhuan*).

While planning his *Later Han History,* Fan had intended to write a hundred fascicles, of which ten would belong to the monograph section. However, his writing process was later interrupted by a promotion that consumed much of his time, such that he finished only ninety chapters and was unable to complete the planned monographs (*zhi*). After his death, there was the attempt to couple his work with Sima Biao's monographs, since the annals and biographies in Sima's work had been lost. But incorporating

Sima Biao's monographs would not have been consistent with Fan Ye's ambition of making his work a worthy sequel to Ban Gu's *Han History,* for Sima had left out quite a few headings found in Ban's monographs (S. Bai 1999, 134–135). But even in its incomplete form, Fan Ye's work was considered a most valuable contribution to the study of Han history, especially his introductions, disquisitions, and eulogies (Qu 1999b, 242 ff). These sections were not Fan's innovation; they can be traced back to a long tradition beginning with Sima Qian, if not the *Zuo Commentary.* However, as Bai Shouyi contends (1999, 140), Fan's commentaries surpassed those of his predecessors, including those by Ban Gu, Chen Shou, and even Sima Qian, in both quantity and quality. Fan's commentaries amounted virtually to "historical essays" (Egan 1979, 346). As demonstrated by his analysis of the Han eunuchs, Fan Ye did not follow presupposed precepts, as Yuan Hong did, in his effort to distinguish the good from the bad, and the right from the wrong. He arrived at his judgments empirically, only after he had considered the facts from different angles.

His discussion in "Disquisition on Scholars" on the growth of learning and the evolution of scholarly community in the Later Han is another good example of Fan Ye's thorough historical analysis. It begins with the observation that scholarly life flourished as a result of the court's patronage. "Wherever a master of the classics happened to reside, there were those who did not regard a thousand-mile journey thence as too distant. Whenever a lecture hall was opened even for a short time, there were always hundreds or even thousands who carried their own provisions on their shoulders to make the trip." However, this initial burst of energy and creativity soon gave way to mediocrity and complacent repetition of established learning, not to mention the growth of fractious sectarianism among scholars. Tersely but trenchantly, he sums up the sad situation: "It is gabbling scholarship, in which each man sedulously apes his master." Scholarship ossified with established schools and factional polemics took the place of genuine scholarship exchange. Nevertheless, even though Fan was mightily dissatisfied with the way Han scholarship evolved, he declares in the end that the "effect of school learning" was on the whole positive, in that the growth of learning played a role in prolonging the rule of the Han (Egan 1979, 387–389). In addition to his interpretive perspicacity, Fan Ye boasted superb literary skills. He was adept at using parallelism in exposition—"Wherever a master of the classics happened to reside . . . Whenever a lecture hall was opened . . ."—in order to enhance the literary quality of the narrative. Fan Ye also frequently used binomes and four-character phrases in contrast or in parallel for the same purpose (Egan 1979). But since his main purpose was to present his arguments, he refused to become enslaved by rhetorical forms. "I never wanted to become a mere literary embellisher," he declared and warned that "in writing, there is the danger that the substance will be overshadowed by the outward appearance and that the sentiment will be cramped by ornamentation, that literary conventions will hamper the writer's purport and that rhythm will distort his thoughts" (Egan 1979, 340). Though blessed with literary talents, Fan Ye wanted only to use them to deliver powerful historical accounts. His *Later Han History* eclipsed many of its competitors, even those of later times by others famed for their literary gifts, such as Xiao Zixian. After the Tang period Fan Ye's *Later Han History* replaced the *Han Records of the Eastern Pavilion*, which by then had lost most of its chapters, to become one of the famed and respected "Three Histories," along with Sima Qian's *Records* and Ban Gu's *Han History* (*Shixueshi* 1983, 14).

Fan Ye also showed an ability to marshal sources that impressed not only the eighth-century Tang historiographer Liu Zhiji, but also historians of modern times (*Shitong* 1978, 2:343; Qu 1999b, 241–242; S. Bai 1999, 135–140; W. Du 1998, 113–116). Preserving historical documents had always been a main responsibility of the historian in imperial China, and Fan did a remarkable job of it. Fan Ye and Yuan Hong are usually paired with regard to Han history because one used the annals-biography style and the other the annals-chronicle style. But Fan's works unquestionably surpassed Yuan's in both informational coverage and historical interpretation. Writing his work several decades after Yuan, Fan Ye was of course indebted to him and others not only for information but also for the inspiration they offered on approaches and styles. The organization of his work resembled Yuan Hong's—both of them attempted a thematic, rather than chronological, approach when grouping historical figures in the biographies. This allowed them to put figures of different time periods under one heading and compare and contrast their actions and behavior (Qu 1999b, 241). But Fan Ye did a far better job, primarily because Yuan Hong adhered rigidly to established values and protocols while Fan was far more realistic about accommodating historical change. In the annals section, for example, he created chapters on all the empresses, which would have been unthinkable by Yuan Hong's standards. While this inclusiveness was not entirely Fan's invention, it nevertheless revealed, along with his fair-minded observations about the role of eunuchs, his acknowledgment of historical reality in Later Han court politics. Whatever our views on eunuchs and imperial in-laws, they were undeniably formidable forces in the later years of the Han and contributed to the dynasty's downfall. Because this was so, they needed to be studied in detail, with cool detachment.

Variance and Variety

From Sima Biao through Yuan Hong to Fan Ye, a continual line of historical works appeared that represented improvements in historical writing and historiography, especially with respect to Han history. The period of prolonged political uncertainty between the Han and Tang not only witnessed a high tide of dynastic historiography, but a proliferation of historical writings in general. As many scholars have observed, it was during this period that historical study gradually gained status as an independent form of learning. It began to cohere into a distinct discipline, independent from the study of the classics and other branches of learning. Both scholars and bibliographers began to treat history as a separate category in classifying books, and the court decided to make history one of the four core subjects at the national academies. In his bibliographic "Monograph on the Arts and Literature" (Yiwen zhi), Ban Gu had lumped historical works together with the classics and their commentaries, showing that in the Han times, historical study was not considered an independent arena of learning (Y. Lu 1998, 66). Ban Gu considered his own writing an attempt at expounding Confucian precepts, and he treated Sima Qian's *Records* as an extension of the classical tradition of the *Spring and Autumn Annals*. But after the Han, Sima Qian's work began to be known as the *Records of the Historian*, a title which replaced the original *Book of the Eminent Grand Historian* (*Taishigong shu*), suggesting a different take on the historical import of the work. By calling it the *Records of the Historian*, a rather generic title applicable to all previous historical records, Sima Qian's work was now considered the fountainhead of a new genre, rather than one individual's scholarly cogitations, as its original title might have suggested (ibid., 67).

Even though *Records of the Historian* still retained the original meaning of the term *shi*—that is, court official—the term itself began to acquire a new meaning after the Han period. Instead of denoting a position held by an official (and hence a person), *shi* now referred to a product, the writings of a historian. During the period of the Three Kingdoms, Qiao Zhou's *Examinations of Ancient Histories* (*Gushi kao*) explicitly used the term *shi* to refer to historical writings. Others also began to use the term in the same manner (*Shixueshi* 1983, 111). In addition, the term "Three Histories" became widely known. These three masterpieces became exemplars for anyone who aspired to produce works about the past. Historical writing attained status as a distinct and valued discipline, on a par with classical study and earning a combined reference with the classics (*jingshi*). From the Three Kingdoms period onward, both history and the classics were regarded as crucial components of educational and intellectual excellence.

The sheer number of historical works produced in the post-Han period demonstrated rising status of historical study. Ban Gu mentioned only twelve titles in history, that is, works that he considered to be of similar nature to the *Spring and Autumn Annals*, whereas the "Monograph on Classics and Books" (Jingji zhi) of the *Sui History* (*Suishu*), a dynastic history completed in 656, registered 874 titles of historical works. Of these, 817 were available at the time, amounting to a total of 13,264 fascicles. While some were written by historians of the Later Han, most appeared between the Han and Sui. Of all the books registered and abstracted in the *Sui History*, nearly 20 percent fell under the rubric of history, which constituted more than one-third the total number of fascicles (historical titles often had more fascicles than other genres) (Qu 1999b, 224–225). As the number of historical writings increased, bibliographers had little choice but to establish an independent classification for history. In the *Sui History*'s "Monograph on Classics and Books," history (*shi*) joins the classics (*jing*), philosophy (*zi*) and belles-lettres (*ji*) (Zeng 2000). By then the term *shi* referred more to the writing of history than to the title of historian. Even earlier, Ruan Xiaoxu (479–536), a bibliographer of the Liang dynasty (502–557), had already used *shi* to refer specifically to works of history as distinct from the classics (Lei 1990, 431). It should also be mentioned that the attempt to catalogue books using the quadripartite classification scheme of classics, history, philosophy, and belles–lettres had been first used by Xun Xu (?–289) and later by Li Chong (fl. 317–343) (C. Chen 1975, 173–174).

This classification scheme received court sanction. As history became a formal category in bibliography, historical learning, or historiography (*shixue*), was also established as one of the four subjects, along with Neo-Daoism (*xuanxue*), Confucianism (*ruxue*), and literature (*wenxue*), in the official learning promoted by Emperor Wen of (Liu) Song (r. 424–453). He also ordered court historians to compose a history of the previous dynasty, which marks the first time a reigning dynasty tapped official resources to compile a history of the previous dynasty (Lei 1990, 430). Earlier works of its kind, such as Ban Gu's *Han History*, had been private initiatives. But Emperor Wen was not the first ruler to establish historical study as an independent subject of learning. A century before, Shi Le (274–333), a Särbi general whose troops, along with other nomadic tribes, overran north China, had already turned historical study into one of the four forms of learning in his court. Despite ethnic differences, the Särbi rulers were equally, if not more, interested in using history to legitimize their regimes (W. Du 1998, 21–22; Lei 1990, 390–391).

Court interest in history was a double-edged sword, however. Although it no doubt promoted and energized the writing of history, the lives of the historians became hazardous as they increasingly faced imperial censure and censorship. As might have been expected, the court often brought political pressure to bear on the compilers, since those in power naturally tended to sanction only one "standard" version of history. Writings that deviated from official expectations and the imperial ideological bent often faced proscription. In the post-Han period, there were several infamous incidents in which historians were persecuted for the dissenting views in their writings (Lei 1990, 381–382). But there was also heroic resistance, such as the case of Sun Sheng (302–373), who refused to make revisions to cater to royal whims and decided to hide his work in a safe place for posterity. In order to promote the official view of historiography, Emperor Yuan of the Liang (r. 552–555) began to use the term "standard histories" (*zhengshi*) to identify those he regarded as authoritative. Emperor Yuan did not rule long, but the term he created endured. It was used to designate officially approved major works, many of which were histories of a single dynasty produced under court patronage. By the nineteenth century twenty-four works were included in the pantheon of standard histories (L. Yang 1947, 1961), which Homer Dubs described as "the world's greatest repository of historical information" (1946, 23).

Dynastic histories were only one sort of historical text. The "Monograph on Classics and Books" of the *Sui History* lists thirteen subheadings in the history section. In addition to standard histories, there were miscellaneous history (*zashi*), court diaries, ancient history (*gushi*), miscellaneous biographies (*zazhuan*), genealogy (*puxi*), gazetteers (*dili*), and others. Liu Zhiji, in his *Perspectives on Historiography,* divided historical works into ten genres, including informal records (*pianji*), anecdotes (*yishi*), family history (*jiashi*), county history (*junshu*), and informal biography (*biezhuan*) (*Shitong* 1978, 1:273). Clearly there were many local, family, and individual attempts at writing history. The post-Han period, then, saw parallel developments in historical writing (Y. Lu 1998, 15–20). Of the new genres, the miscellaneous biographies or informal biographies were the most representative in this period (ibid., 6–7), as we shall see below.

The growth of and substantive variations in historical writing may be attributed to a host of developments. Rulers wished to use history to legitimize their regimes; and appeal to the past was the means to explain and buttress the present political order. At the same time, the decline of classical Confucianism and the corresponding rise of Neo-Daoism encouraged focus on the self as a liberated and spontaneous individual, which gave rise to the popularity of informal and miscellaneous biographies. Other social and cultural factors were at work. The invention and dissemination of papermaking technology in the Later Han may have facilitated the writing and distribution of books, but we must note that while paper was used in great quantity during the third and fourth centuries, a large number of books were still written on silk and bamboo (Tsien 1962; S. Bai 1999, 156).

One social factor of particular significance was the rise of aristocratic lineages and magnate families. Their growing sense of self-importance motivated them to chronicle their pasts and leave other sorts of testaments; hence the proliferation of local and family histories, not to mention biographies. Although these great families had begun to acquire social and political influence in the Later Han, it was after the Han that they assumed visible roles in shaping political and social life. The System of the Nine Ranks and Impartial Judges (*jiupin zhongzheng zhi*), first introduced by Cao Cao in the early third century and continually implemented through the fifth century, contributed to the furtherance and consolidation of their power. This system had originally been intended to screen and recruit local talent for the central bureaucracy. But it came to be monopolized by magnate families, the regional elite and local aristocracy that had consolidated into a formidable force (Grafflin 1990, 148). As a result, the system functioned less as a meritocracy than a plutocracy, for it watered down the criteria on which the local talent were supposedly judged and blatantly favored those with genealogical cachet. Especially in the émigré regimes of the southern dynasties, the problem of favoritism, nepotism, and unfair grading was greatly exacerbated by the absence of a strong central power. With almost no exceptions, high ranks in the system were awarded to the members of the hereditary families, whereas members of the "impoverished families" (*hanmen*), given low ranks, were excluded from the official-

dom. As aristocratic pedigrees and noble lineages became the criterion
for selecting officials, there emerged an unprecedented interest in docu-
menting family history. It was in every noble family's interest to maintain
its illustrious status, and writing its history was a sure way to preserve the
name and stature of the clan. Moreover, there was also a noticeable change
in the structure of the biographic section in many official historical works.
In Shen Yue's *Song History* and Wei Shou's *Wei History,* for example, many
biographic chapters were organized around one family and described as
many as sixty members of that family across several generations (Clark
2004, 239–243; Qu 1999b, 274–277; Y. Lu 1998, 10–11). In addition to
enhancing family prestige, genealogies, family histories, and biographies
provided crucial background information on family members who could
be recommended to the government. Moreover, they furnished references
when families needed to procure appropriate matches in marriage. Not
surprisingly, the genre of "family instructions" (*jiaxun*) also proliferated,
such as the famous *Family Instructions for the Yan Clan* (*Yanshi jiaxun*), which
offered advice to all clan members on the ways they could maintain and
improve their social status.

The decline and unraveling of Confucianism had also fueled the rise
of a world view centered more around the individual, so informal or miscellaneous biographies also became popular. As Yü Ying-shih (1980, 1985)
has shown, the influence of Confucianism began to wane in the later years
of the Han for both political and intellectual reasons. The manipulation
of power by the eunuchs and imperial in-laws at court thwarted the ambitions of Confucian scholars. Many developed interests in politically safe
but intellectual sterile textual and philological studies that diminished
and obfuscated the practical value of Confucianism as vital learning. In
the post-Han period of political disintegration and social anomie, Confucianism lost its relevance for many people. It no longer seemed to function effectively as the ideological foundation for the sociopolitical order.
Attention shifted from the external world of society and politics to the
internal world of individual self-cultivation, encouraging the growth of
Neo-Daoism (Holcombe 1989). Neo-Daoism promoted the idea of "natu-
ralness" or "spontaneity" (*ziran*), which nurtured the ideal of the individual. A new cultural phenomenon of "pure conversation" (*qingtan*) consumed much of the intellectual energy in the post-Han period, in which
metaphysical and ontological discussions took priority over the practical
matters of state and society customarily favored by the Confucians. To participate in these pure conversations, participants had to show their famil-
iarity with such Daoist texts as the *Classic of Changes, Laozi,* and *Zhuangzi,*
but also to demonstrate quick wit, rhetorical excellence, and social acumen. This stimulated a strong interest in characterology (Yü 1980, 1985).
While the art of characterology was used primarily for making recommen-
dations in the Nine Ranks System, it also promoted the self-awareness of
the individual, and it exerted influence in historiography. In Chen Shou's
description of historical figures, for instance, he drew attention to both

their physical appearance and mental qualities, a move consistent with the practice of characterology and the newly emerged interest in portraiture. Experts often evaluated an individual's personality on both physiognomical and psychological levels (Yü 1985, 126–127; Qu 1999b, 286–290).

Nowhere was this self-awareness of individuality better shown than in *A New Account of Tales of the World* (*Shishuo xinyu*), a quasi-historical text that appeared in the mid-fifth century. It vividly records stories about 626 characters who flourished during the previous two centuries. "For most incidents and remarks," as Richard Mather tells us, "allowing for literary embellishment and dramatic exaggeration, there is no good reason to doubt their reality. Only a small minority pose problems of anachronism, contradiction of known facts, gross supernatural intrusions, or apparent inconsistencies" (2002, xiv). Almost all the characters described in the book were real historical figures who appeared in contemporary historical writings. Moreover, though the work was not deliberately written as a history, it was certainly not composed as a purely literary account. To attempt to draw such a clear line is to be anachronistic, however, since no clear division was made between history and literature until the sixth century (Y. Lu 1998, 69). It is therefore hardly surprising that when Liu Xie (465–522), a literary critic of the period who wrote the famously important *The Literary Mind and the Carving of Dragons* (*Wenxin diaolong*), reflected upon literary theories, styles, and genres, he included a chapter on "Historical Writings" (Shizhuan). This chapter, although part of a literary text, critically surveyed the traditions of historical writings up to its time, comparing and evaluating the works of major historians, and, more important, discussing the nature of historiography, the tasks of the historian, and the functions of their writings. Succinct and reflective, this essay yields important information on and insights into the history of Chinese historiography.

Just as the classics and history were not clearly separated in ancient China, so the boundary between literature and history was often not sharply drawn. But as Denis Twitchett points out, the historians' high moral concern and the government's involvement in official historical writing did eventually sharpen a critical awareness of the distinction between history and literature. The case of biographical writing is interesting and instructive. Ever since the time of Sima Qian, biographical writing had figured centrally in the reconstruction of the past. But according to Twitchett, such writing also planted "the seeds of fiction writing" (1961, 97). Indeed, as Twitchett contends, it was during the post-Han period that "semi-fictional and folklore element[s], which found no place in an official history compiled from adequate documentary sources, led a separate existence on the borderline between history and literature" (ibid., 98–99). The *Tales of the World* straddled precisely such a borderline, with its vivid portrayal of lives and deeds. Despite the fact that it was unofficial—or perhaps because of it—the work contained much candid information about the cultural milieu. As such, it was a crucial historical source. In the section entitled "Speech and Conversation," for instance, we see interesting examples of the quick-wittedness appreciated at the time, as in the case of Deng Ai (197–264):

> Deng Ai had a speech impediment, and when talking would refer to himself as "Ai-Ai." Prince Wen of Jin, teasing him, said, "How many Ai's are there, anyhow?" He replied, "When Jie Yu sang, 'Phoenix! Phoenix!' naturally there was only one phoenix. (Mather 2002, 40; modified transliteration)

Some of the conversations reveal changes in the intellectual culture at the time:

> All the famous gentlemen of the Western Jin court once went together to the Luo River on a pleasure excursion. On their return Yue Guang asked Wang Yan, "Did you enjoy today's excursion?" Wang replied, "Pei Wei is good at conversing on Names and Principles (*mingli*); his words gushed forth in a torrent, but with an air of refinement. Zhang Hua discussed the *Records of the Grand Historian* and the *Han History;* his words were slow and deliberate, well worth listening. Wang Rong and I talked about Fu Cha and Zhang Liang; our words, too, were totally transcendent, abstruse but lucid. (ibid., 43; modified transliteration)

Here, three currents of scholarly interest were juxtaposed—Confucianism with its emphasis on rites and principles, history with its anchor in factual accounts, and Neo-Daoism with its celebration of the transcendent—suggesting that in third-century Western Jin, Confucianism was no longer the dominant philosophy in society.

In the section titled "The Free and Unrestrained," we find the literati deliberately challenging Confucian social conventions, as they increasingly championed the free spirit of the emancipated individual. Ruan Ji (210–263), one of the famous Seven Worthies of the Bamboo Grove (*zhulin qixian*), known for their wisdom, erudition, and wit, ignored the accepted propriety prescribed by Confucian teachings. He saw himself as one who had broken free of the trammels of ordinary decorum:

> Ruan Ji's sister-in-law was once returning to her parents' home, and Ji went to see her to say good-bye. When someone chided him for this, Ji replied, "Were the rites established for people like me?" (ibid., 402; modified transliteration)

On another occasion when Ruan was supposedly in mourning for his mother, he got drunk and sat "with disheveled hair, his legs sprawled apart, not weeping." His friend Pei Kai came to pay his condolences and instead of frowning upon his misbehavior, Pei Kai remarked, "Ruan is a man beyond the realm of ordinary morality and therefore pays no homage to the rules of propriety" (ibid., 403; modified transliteration).

Of course, not everyone could display such outrageous behavior without incurring moral censure, even in this age of rampant individualism. Ji Kang (223–262), Ruan Ji's friend and another worthy of the Bamboo Grove, lost his life after being charged with perversion of public morals. Chen Shou and Fan Ye were also reproved for failing to follow proper mourning protocol (Yang & Wu 1998, 43, 49; W. Du 1998, 110). But the many incidents recorded in the *Tales of the World* convincingly show a dramatic cultural transformation, which was reflected in the burgeoning of miscellaneous and informal biographies, through which individuals sought corroboration and validation of their immortality and self-worth. Such solipsistic absorption also bred stylistic changes in how histories portrayed individuals. In the arrayed biography in Fan Ye's *Later Han History,* a work contemporaneous with *The Tales of the World,* several innovative chapters were included. Entitled "Ideal Behaviors" (Duxing), "Recluses" (Yimin), and "Exemplary Women" (Lienü), they record unusual anecdotes of free-spirited men and women (S. Wang 1997, 69). Historiography, in other words, was expanded in its portraiture of historical figures so as to provide a more comprehensive index of a multitude of personalities.

Although Fan Ye was well known for his anti-Buddhist stance, the extraordinary figures he recorded in his work may well reflect the influence of Buddhism. After all, this period witnessed a tremendous growth in the popularity of Buddhism, which came out of "a civilization with a strong epic tradition and a distinct taste for individual characters" (Twitchett 1961, 111). Interestingly enough, not long after *The Tales of the World* appeared, Chinese monks began to establish their hagiographical tradition, producing collective hagiographies with titles such as *Biographies of Famous Monks (Mingseng zhuan)* or *Eminent Monks (Gaoseng zhuan).* Their style and structure are very much in keeping with the tradition of secular biography established by Sima Qian and Ban Gu (Kieschnick 1997, 5), so we may argue that Chinese historiographical conventions exerted an influence on Buddhist biographic writing. Similarly, it is also valid to surmise that Buddhist interest in thaumaturgy penetrated the tradition of Chinese historiography, so that even people like Fan Ye began to take note of unconventional individuals whose unique behavior defied societal protocol and moral propriety. In fact, some of these individuals were Buddhist monks. *The Tales of the World* makes many references to the famous monk Zhi Dun (314–366), who appears almost as frequently as such prominent statesmen as Wang Dao (276–339) and Xie An (320–385). Thanks to this book, the monk Zhi Dun became one of the most celebrated personalities of his time (Holcombe 1994, 112).

The interest in biographical writing also shaped regional histories and local gazetteers, another form of historical writing that began to flourish during this period. Although few have survived, several extant ones, such as the *History of the Land of Huayang (Huayang guozhi),* offer glimpses of their content and structure. Arguably "the most representative work in local history-writing of this period" (Qu 1999b, 267), the *History of the Land of Huayang,* compiled by Chang Qu (ca. 291–361), recorded the history of western and southwestern China from the remote past to the fourth century. Chang Qu was a native of Sichuan, the region on which his work focused. He traveled widely, serving first as a literary attendant in the court of the Cheng-Han regime, a short-lived local polity in Sichuan from the early to the mid-fourth century, and later as a minor military advisor under the Eastern Jin dynasty. The *History of the Land of Huayang* has a unique structure. Its first four fascicles are monographs that give general descriptions of the culture, history, geography, population, transportation, customs, agriculture, folklore, and governments of the land, which offer rich and rare information for modern historians interested in the cultural and ethnic traditions and exchanges in this frontier area (Kleeman 1998). The rest of the book is conventionally structured around the lives of individuals, suggesting that Chang Qu was profoundly influenced by the exemplary works of Sima Qian and Ban Gu and other Han historians (Qu 1999b, 269). Official writings on Han history were one of the three main sources that Chang Qu drew upon. In addition, he consulted many local histories, few of which have survived, including those written by famous historians from the region such as Qiao Zhou and Chen Shou. But he also amassed material through his own research. As a court official, it is to be expected that Chang had access to the Cheng archives (Kleeman 1998, 110). However, although he duly recorded a short history of the Cheng-Han regime, he maintained his political loyalty to the Jin. This may explain his caution in using these Cheng documents. Because it contains such valuable information on the non-Chinese peoples living in the frontiers, the *History of the Land of Huayang* has received much attention from modern scholars and been praised, along with Wei Shou's *Wei History* and Cui Hong (?–525)'s *Spring and Autumn of the Sixteen Kingdoms* (*Shiliuguo chunqiu*), as representative writings in ethnic history (*minzu shi*) (Qu 1999b, 271).

Pondering on historiography itself also made noticeable progress in this period, as we can see not only in Liu Xie's reflections but also in Pei Songzhi (372–451)'s annotation of Chen Shou's *Three Kingdoms*. Pei's work began as an official assignment to annotate and gloss Chen Shou's highly acclaimed work. But he ultimately accomplished more than what he was asked to do. Using the *Three Kingdoms* as the basic framework, Pei marshaled all sources to which he had access and created an invaluable study in its own right, one that could be described, in modern parlance, as a historiography of the history of the Three Kingdoms. Its original title, *Annotations on the Three Kingdoms* (*Sanguozhi zhu*), does not fully convey the nature of his work. When Pei completed the *Annotations on the Three Kingdoms* in 429, it turned out to be a text larger than Chen Shou's original because Pei had consulted over 200 works and incorporated them as he saw fit into his account (Cutter & Crowell 1999, 68). Pei concentrated on four areas: addition (*buque*), comparison (*beiyi*), correction (*chengwang*), and disquisition (*lunbian*). The first two were assigned by Emperor Wen of the (Liu) Song, but the other two were created out of his own interests (Yang & Wu 1998, 240). In the first two areas, Pei first entered an excerpt of Chen

Shou's work, and then he compared it with other sources to allow readers to gain multiple perspectives, thereby creating a historiographical context. In Chen Shou's account of Liu Bei's recruitment of Zhuge Liang, for example, it states that Liu visited Zhuge's thatched hut three times in order to acquire his service. But in earlier sources Pei found that it was Zhuge Liang who first approached Liu Bei, expressing the wish to work for him. Though this finding contradicted Zhuge's own recollection, Pei remained convinced that it was credible (Henry 1992, 593ff). If Pei was correct, then Chen Shou's omission of Liu's and Zhuge's first meeting sheds important light on the cultural change taking place at the time—Chen's deliberate presentation of Zhuge as a recluse reflected the prevailing cultural climate of the era, in which disdain for politics and political activity was the vogue among the literati (Holcombe 1989).

If Pei Songzhi's effort reflected, as Chen Yinke (1890–1969) suggested, Buddhist influences in scriptural translation and exegesis (Yang & Wu 1998, 242), his interest in corrections and disquisitions expanded the Chinese historiographical tradition (Y. Lu 1998, 14–15). While Pei generally had high regard for Chen Shou's work, he remained somewhat critical of Chen's treatment of the Three Kingdoms' history. This was not directed solely at factual mistakes, but also at Chen's inconsistencies in executing his own historiographical plan and his concealment of certain events and behavior because of political pressure. As we have discussed earlier, Chen Shou wrote his work under the Western Jin, but he remained emotionally attached to the Shu. Much of Chen's concealment and many of his inconsistencies resulted from this tension. The situation in which Pei annotated Chen's work was similar, but Pei was more adamant that the historian had a sacred duty to keep the record straight. He seemed to have been convinced that what made history a useful mirror for the advancement in government was primarily its factuality. The idea that history told the truth was keenly appreciated by rulers and historians of his time, and this belief in the factual veracity continued to loom large in both official and private history and historiography in the Tang period.

CHAPTER 4

The Tang

The History Bureau and Its Critics

Upon hearing of the death of Wei Zheng (580–643), his former comrade-in-arms and chief advisor, Emperor Taizong (r. 626–649), one of the most admired emperors of the Tang dynasty, wept and said,

> Bronze as mirror to straighten one's clothes and cap; the past as mirror to illuminate dynastic rise and fall; and individuals as mirror to rectify our judgment—we have always known these three mirrors. . . . Now that Wei Zheng is gone, one of these mirrors has disappeared. (*JiuTang shu* 1975, 8:2661)

Emperor Taizong employed the much-used metaphor of the mirror to underscore the importance of Wei Zheng precisely because, through talented men and the past, we may see reflections of truth and knowledge. The mirror metaphor was certainly not the emperor's creation—it had been in use since the early days of Chinese civilization and had become a cliché by the Tang times—but it nevertheless revealed Taizong's keen awareness of the contemporary utility of history. Compared with Emperor Wen of the Sui (r. 589–604), for instance, who reunified the empire, Taizong's historical mindfulness and unstinting patronage of history were proverbial (Lei 1990, 608ff). Emperor Wen had been highly suspicious of history writing. In 593, he had decreed that the court tightly control all writing and teaching of history and that private history be strictly forbidden. His tight rein on historical production curtailed what had been a tremendous historiographical growth in the previous periods.

This situation did not persist, however; nor did the Sui dynasty itself. After a couple of decades of relative peace and prosperity, Emperor Yang (r. 605–617), the dynasty's second ruler, launched a military campaign against Korea that proved to be expensive and fruitless. Instead of expanding his domain, the wasteful expedition, exacerbated by other internal developments, spawned widespread rebellions that contributed to the dynasty's downfall in 617. Out of its ruins rose the Tang dynasty, founded by Li Yuan. However, no sooner had Li Yuan, who reigned as Emperor Gaozu (r. 618–626), consolidated his power base than he was forced into retirement by his second son, Li Shimin, who would reign as Emperor Taizong.

Shimin, in 626, staged a bloody coup that exterminated his two brothers, one of whom had been the crown prince. Although Taizong rose to power as the result of a brutal usurpation, he quickly proved himself to be a successful and admired ruler, and "inaugurated the first high point of Tang history" (Wechsler 1985, 38).

The History Bureau

Of the many institutions introduced by Emperor Taizong to legitimize the Tang dynasty, not to mention his own coming to power, official history writing stood out as one of the most salient. As Twitchett's (1992) detailed study has shown, the writing of official history under the Tang was built upon a time-honored tradition. Moreover, the Tang also enjoyed the advantage of a rich historiographical legacy. Prior to the Sui, historiography had flourished, and there had been much court sponsorship of historical writing and learning. Many bureaucratic offices and positions related to the writing of history in the Tang court were modeled on precedents, such as the Bureau of Literary Composition (*zhuzuo ju*), a subdivision of the Imperial Library (*mishu sheng*) established by the Northern Wei dynasty. This office had secured the service of such distinguished historians as Chen Shou and Fan Ye, whose historical accomplishments we have examined. However, its name, Bureau of Literary Composition, suggests that it may not yet have been an independent History Office as such (W. Du 1998, 183). In addition, before the Tang the court diarists, whose titles included "attendants of activity and repose" (*qiju lang*) and "residents of activity and repose" (*qiju sheren*), had been officials responsible for keeping track of events at court.

While a host of antecedents can be identified, the History Bureau (*shiguan*) was a Tang innovation that formally became "a separate bureau in the palace in 629" (Twitchett 1992, 13). This institutional innovation meant that henceforth the writing of official history would follow a more rigorous procedure, beginning with the compilation of the court diaries, through the composition of the daily calendar (*rili*) and the "veritable records" (*shilu*), to the completion of the national history (*guoshi*). The need to produce a national history—an earlier example was the *Han Records of the Eastern Pavilion*—was the raison d'être of the History Bureau. By this time, there was an unmistakable awareness of the paramount need to record the history of the contemporary reign. At the same time, there was an ongoing urge to uncover the history of previous ages (McMullen 1988, 160). The establishment of the Tang History Bureau was the logical culmination of an ever-increasing interest on the part of dynastic rulers to sponsor the compilation of official versions of history, a phenomenon that had been gaining momentum since the Later Han.

Although most of the materials produced by the Tang court diarists and "attendants of literary composition" are no longer available, some remnants provide glimpses of their practice of history. Let us first look at the compilation of court diaries. This practice can be traced back to the days when the count appointed left and right historians to record the words and actions of the ruler. The attendants and residents of activity and repose assumed responsibilities that clearly recall the old tradition. The attendants were responsible for recording "the emperor's acts" and the residents "the emperor's utterances" (Twitchett 1992, 35). Even their physical positions at court were consistent with tradition; attendants of activity and repose stood to the right of the throne, and residents of activity and repose to the left (W. Du 1998, 192–193). After an audience, they would enter their notes as formal records, usually in the format of a chronicle. They also consulted with the staff of the Imperial Secretariat (*zhongshu sheng*) and the Imperial Chancellery (*menxia sheng*) to ensure accuracy, since decrees and edicts were often drafted by these two departments. While we know from sources how court diarists worked at the Tang court, none of their records have survived, except for a work entitled *Court Diaries of the Founding of the Great Tang* (*Da Tang chuangye qijuzhu*), written by Wen Daya (ca. 572–628), an invaluable source on the early Tang. It recorded Li Yuan's successful uprising against the Sui and the founding of his own regime, which Wen observed intimately because of the close association between his family and the Li family. Nonetheless, the provenance of this work as a court diary remains dubious. Even though Wen did serve at the Tang court, he was not officially a diarist, nor did he intend to write a work according to the form of a court diary. As a consequence, from the Tang onward, bibliographers have rightly and consistently placed his work under such categories as "miscellaneous histories" (*zashi*) or "annalistic histories" (*biannian shi*) (Twitchett 1992, 41–42).

Another record of life in the inner palace was the "inner palace diary" (*nei qiju zhu*). This diary was needed because many important decisions were made outside of formal court assemblies, especially when the emperor was less than conscientious in attending court. Although the inner palace diary did not appear formally until the early eighth century, it actually had a history dating back to the Han. Moreover, from Han times forward, the responsibility for recording the lives of the inner quarters often fell to female historians. The Tang court inherited the tradition and, in one famous instance, successively appointed three sisters of the Song family, beginning with Song Ruoxin (?–820) (Twitchett 1992, 49–50).

If the inner palace diaries shed light on the emperor's private life and his relationship with his family, they were of little help with regard to the emperor's private meetings with his ministers where major decisions were made. To fill this lacuna, Yao Shou (632–705), then prime minister, memorialized the court in 693 about the need to make records of the meetings between the emperor and his ministers, both civil and military, as they deliberated on important administrative affairs. Yao's memorial led to establishment of the "records of current administration" (*shizheng ji*), usually written by the prime minister himself and sent to the History Bureau at the end of every month. In theory an important practice that ensured the keeping of complete court records, compilation of the record of administrative affairs was not regular; nor was it always factual, for the prime minister often took the opportunity to embellish or exaggerate his role in the meetings with the emperor (W. Du 1998, 194). But its very introduction and periodic compilation shows that the ideal of maintaining complete historical records had become a prevailing bureaucratic value in the Tang court.

The ideal of keeping records appealed to the Tang rulers and their ministers in different ways. Rulers embraced the ideal and the practice because they could thereby transmit their legacy to posterity. By recording and celebrating their feats and successes, rulers might acquire a sort of immortality through history. This notion of immortality through historical preservation had persisted since the time of Confucius and Sima Qian, but became particularly salient in the post-Han period, a fact that doubtless contributed to the proliferation of the writing of history (W. Du 1998, 26). According to Confucius' famous adage, there were three ways to attain immortality (*buxiu*): demonstrating great virtues (*lide*), achieving success in governance (*ligong*), or establishing scholarly traditions (*liyan*). Unlike their predecessors who might be content with one or another kind of immortality, Tang rulers such as Taizong desired to achieve all three. Taizong's active sponsorship of and serious engagement with history were unquestionably inspired by his fervent desire to enshrine his name in the annals of time.

For the ministers and historians who realized Taizong's interest in history, the keeping of historical records served a more urgent, immediate function—it set up an effective moral check against the abuse of royal power. Writing history exerted moral leverage by influencing the sovereign's decision-making. When the recordkeeping process was done correctly, in keeping with the established administrative statutes, the emperor was not supposed to have access to what the court diarists were recording, presumably making it possible for them to be impartial and independent. Concerned about his image in the records, Taizong once asked to look at the court diaries, only to be rebuffed by his ministers. As a result he apparently became very cautious in making any remarks in front of his court diarists, for fear that his infelicities and improprieties would forever be etched in the annals of history (ibid., 173–174). However, political exigency often trumped the ideals of historical independence, and history acted as only a check on imperial power. Taizong may have represented a paradigmatic monarch who respected the independence and integrity of history, but many of his successors found it hard to live up to his example and had no qualms interfering with the process of compilation.

Nonetheless, despite admitted violation and attenuation of the ideals, the Tang did establish a rigorous system that sought to ensure the comprehensive, unbiased recording of what took place at court. Establishing complete records constituted only the first step, however. The real contribution of the Tang dynasty, one that was regarded as exemplary by later scholars and commentators, was its systematic, institutionalized approach to the national history. It was to this end that the History Bureau was established. Its procedures represented a significant departure from the established tradition of historical writing in early imperial China. Unlike earlier works that fell under the category of "standard history"—a term that gained wide acceptance under the Tang—official histories in the Tang were a collective endeavor, supervised by chief ministers and commissioned by the emperor. Whereas Ban Gu, Chen Shou and Fan Ye, not to mention Sima Qian, had embarked on their projects individually and independently on their own private initiative, court-sponsored works compiled collectively became the norm in the Tang. Twitchett describes the primary duties of the History Bureau:

> The historiographers (*shiguan*) are responsible for the compilation of the National History. They may not give false praise, or conceal evil, but must write a straight account of events. . . . The historians should base themselves on the Court Diary and the Record of Administrative Affairs to make a Veritable Record, setting this out in chronological form and incorporating the principles of praise and blame. When this is completed it is to be stored in the official storehouse. (Twitchett 1992, 13–14)

Given the enormous interest of the Tang rulers in their own legacy, the History Bureau assumed a weighty task. It was viewed not simply as one element in the officialdom but as an integral part of the highest level of government. In the formative years of the Tang, the Bureau was located in a building adjacent to the Imperial Chancellery, under whose direct supervision it was placed. Later, when the Imperial Secretariat gradually became the most important organ of Tang government, the Bureau was relocated so that it would be in close proximity to the Secretariat, the new supervising office (ibid., 17–19). The Bureau was always under the oversight of the highest office in the land. The primary function of the Bureau was to marshal extant court sources, such as the court diaries, into a chronological account, first as a veritable record and then as a national history. There were only three or four compilers on the regular staff, who were given the title of staff writer (*xiuzhuan*) if they held concurrent official positions; if they held exclusive positions within the Bureau, they would be appointed under the title of staff member (*zhiguan*). They were aided by a few assistants, the "commanded historians" (*lingshi*) and several secretarial assistants, such as transcribers and bookkeepers.

Since the final product was a national history, the compilers had to cover not only court life but also the workings of the government as a whole in order to present a complete picture of an emperor's reign. This meant the compilers had to examine a variety of government documents. As soon as the Bureau was established, a systematic reporting procedure was set up. Various documents and sources—memorials, accounts of receptions of foreign guests, information about taxation and the census, lists of official appointments, evaluations, obituaries, and so forth—were brought to the historian-officials' attention, allowing them to record the details of the administration of government at various levels. Accounts of extraordinary events, including astronomical and terrestrial phenomena perceived to be significant and portentous, were also transmitted to the Bureau (W. Du 1998, 186–187; Twitchett 1992, 27–29). Although the veritable records and national histories principally featured the administrative details of an emperor's reign, they included information on a host of diverse subjects; they are invaluable sources for the study of Tang history in general.

As each veritable record was designed to record what happened in one emperor's reign, its compilation usually began immediately after the royal death. It was not a complicated task for the compilers. They needed only to organize and incorporate the material presented to them in the established narrative template, that is, the annals-biography form. Sources pertinent to the emperor and the empress were used to compose the basic annals, whereas those related to the ministers and other important personnel were utilized for the arrayed biographies. Upon completion, the veritable record was placed in the Imperial Library. Evidence suggests that the Tang veritable records were not sealed and declared off limits to any readers until it was time for the compilation of the dynastic history, as was the practice in later ages. Veritable records produced after the Tang were treated as classified and confidential sources, but Tang texts were circulated widely, available not only to the heir apparent, who would supposedly learn lessons of governance from them, but also to high-ranking officials, who could make copies of the chapters related to their ancestors and themselves (Twitchett 1992, 122–123). Some copies actually circulated in the provinces and were even taken abroad to Japan. Inspired by the Tang, Japanese historians compiled similar kinds of records, collectively known as the *Six National Histories* (*Rikkokushi*), which are the oldest historical works available in Japan today. Thanks to circulation outside of the court, some Tang veritable records are still available today, such as the *Veritable Records of Shunzong's Reign* (*Shunzong shilu*) preserved in the collected works of Han Yu (768–824), an eminent Tang scholar who helped edit it. There is even an English translation of this compilation (Solomon 1955). Other records were used by later historians who incorporated them into their own works, such as Sima Guang's (1019–1086) *The Comprehensive Mirror of Aid in Government* (*Zizhi tongjian*), a Song masterpiece we shall examine. But owing to the destructive civil war sparked by the An Lushan rebellion in 755, which led to the ransacking of the Tang palaces, a great number of these veritable records were lost, along with court diaries and inner palace diaries. After the rebellion, compilation of veritable records resumed, but few have survived. In the Tang period as a whole, the History Bureau compiled a total of twenty-five veritable records, consisting of 785 fascicles and covering sixteen imperial reigns, from Emperor Gaozu to Emperor Wuzong (r. 841–846) (W. Du 1998, 187). It was a prodigious textual output.

The veritable records were intended to furnish the materials for the national history. This history followed the same organization and style of the veritable records; it consisted of two sections, basic annals and arrayed biographies. In many respects it was simply an extension of the veritable records. But whereas each veritable record recounted the events of one reign, the national history was cumulative, meant to cover all the reigns from the beginning of the dynasty to the time of compilation. Compilation of the veritable records was routine business for the History Bureau, but composition of the national history seems to have been an ad hoc affair. During the early Tang, there were several occasions on which the national history was commissioned. The first, a work in thirty fascicles, was done in 627 under the editorial leadership of Yao Silian (?–637), an acclaimed historian who also wrote other histories. In 656, during Gaozong's reign, there was the second compilation, led by such chief ministers as Changsun Wuji (?–659) and Linghu Defen (583–666), who expanded the earlier work into fifty fascicles. During the reign of Wu Zetian (r. 684–755), the only crowned empress in imperial China, the size of the national history had increased to 110 fascicles. By her imperial fiat, Liu Zhiji and others condensed it to eighty fascicles, only to have it expanded again after her reign to 113 fascicles under Wei Shu (?–757), and still later to 130 fascicles under Liu Fang (fl. 690–750). Because the parts were scattered during the An Lushan rebellion, the national history came to a halt, and work was not resumed on it under the Tang (W. Du 1998, 188).

Despite the loss of many texts and compilations, however, a sufficient amount survived to enable historians to compile a Tang history after the dynasty's downfall. The *Old History of the Tang* (*Jiu Tangshu*) was completed in 945 and presented to the throne of the Later Jin dynasty (936–946). But because of the general political instability that plagued the Later Jin and other regimes of the post-Tang period, the process of compiling Tang history was by no means smooth. There were many interruptions and frequent changes of those in charge. All this instability and lack of continuity affected its quality, and in the Song there would be the rewriting of the Tang history, as we shall see. Nevertheless, the *Old History of the Tang* remains valuable since it preserved important original sources, that is, works penned by the Tang official historians. Many fascicles contain passages copied verbatim from the Tang veritable records and national history, thereby preserving them for posterity. Moreover, the compilers not only gathered surviving volumes from the capital Chang'an, but they also culled some veritable records from the provincial capitals. In addition, the compilers put together eleven monographs, covering topics ranging from calendars and rituals to finance, geography, customs, and equipage. Following the model laid down by Sima Qian and Ban Gu, the *Old History of the Tang*, which survives today with all 200 fascicles intact, was a well-structured dynastic history. What it lacks in interpretive insight and narrative coherence is compensated by its preservation of primary Tang materials.

The Compilation of Standard Histories

Significantly, the History Bureau was also charged with composing histories of the previous dynasties. Under Emperor Taizong, histories that covered almost all the dynasties in the post-Han period were compiled. Eight dynastic histories were produced in the first century of the Tang, and they were officially endorsed as standard histories. While the Tang unquestionably continued the much-cherished Han tradition of historical writing, the attitude of both the Tang rulers and scholars toward the Han was ambivalent. On the one hand, they aspired to emulate Han achievements in both imperial administration and intellectual culture; on the other hand, they saw the Tang as a worthy rival of the Han, capable of replacing it as the most important era in Chinese history. Animated by a healthy competitive spirit, the Tang saw itself as the most glorious chapter in the unfolding story of the noble civilization that was China. Emperor Taizong, for instance, entertained the ambitious goal of producing a historical compilation that would compare favorably with the two magisterial Han histories (McMullen 1988, 163). Interestingly enough, however, Tang historians did not work directly on compiling a history of the Han, perhaps humbled by the dazzling success of Sima Qian and Ban Gu. But they did engage in intensive critical analysis of the works of these two historians and their successors. They focused much energy on interrogating Ban Gu's *Han History,* which had eclipsed Sima Qian's work by the Tang times. To compete with the Han meant first extending the life of their dynasty and understanding the lessons of the past. The histories completed by Tang scholars therefore covered almost all the dynasties in the long period between the Han and Tang, regardless of the length of their existence. At the same time, Tang fascination with Han history and historiography, which came to be known as the "study of the *Han History*" (*Hanshu xue*), also helped to define the parameters of Tang official historiography, namely, it circumscribes their main interests within a dynastic frame. The overwhelming majority of the many histories penned by the Tang historians were dynastic ones, and study of Ban Gu's *Han History* (Qu 1999b, 292–293) became a specialized field of historical inquiry. With the inclusion of the *Han History* in the core curriculum in the National Academy, knowledge of Ban and his work became almost a sine qua non for office at the Tang court, especially after Wei Zheng included several excerpts from it in his popular compendium, *Essentials of Good Administration from a Host of Books* (*Qunshu zhiyao*). It is not surprising that many scholars, such as Yao Silian, who led the compilation of the first Tang national history, emulated Ban Gu in writing dynastic history.

It should be pointed out that Ban's popularity may also be attributed to his conspicuous and unequivocal embrace of Confucian values, as opposed to Sima Qian's eclectic blend of Confucianism and Huang-Lao Daoism. Indeed, Confucian scholasticism flourished in the Tang. Taizong decided to follow the Sui example of reforming the process of official recruitment by institutionalizing the system of civil service examinations. The Confucian classics, which constituted the core of the examination curricula, were again canonized. As with the Han, the Tang promoted the Confucian classical texts as official learning. Under the leadership of important scholars such as Kong Yingda (574–646), classical studies and commentaries prospered, and many devoted their talents to producing authoritative glosses. Such scholastic endeavors also stimulated historical studies. Confucian scholars such as Yan Shigu (581–645), who claimed descent from Yan Hui (521–481 B.C.E.), Confucius' most loyal disciple, coupled exegetical classical study with history. In addition to his significant contributions to establishing definitive versions of the Confucian canon, Yan Shigu (whose name means "to learn from the ancients") produced a detailed gloss on the *Han History*. Both Kong Yingda and Yan Shigu lent crucial support to Wei Zheng when he was in charge of compiling the *Sui History* (*Suishu*). Their assistance contributed to the high quality of the work, which one modern scholar hails as "a model of collectively written official histories and one of the first-rate Standard Histories" (W. Du 1998, 215).

While Ban Gu's work was greatly admired as an exemplar of dynastic history, the Tang effort to compile the histories of the previous dynasties harked back to Sima Qian's ideal of providing a panoramic view of Chinese history. Unquestionably many Tang scholars were inspired by Sima's ideal and practice of universal history. Already in the early Tang, there was a perceived need to systematically reconstruct China's past, beginning with the six dynasties that had come before the Tang. In 622, shortly after Li Yuan (Emperor Gaozu) established the dynasty, he issued an edict in response to Linghu Defen's suggestion to commission the project. The announced rationale was that although the short-lived dynasties fell rapidly, there were great lessons to be learned from them and outstanding figures to be commended for their accomplishments (*Tang Huiyao* 1955, 1090–1091). The message of edict was clearly driven by a political purpose — providing a historical explanation for the rise of the Tang — but it was also stimulated by history's didactic function — that enduring lessons and principles might be distilled from the rise and fall of dynasties. The Tang would learn from the past so as not to repeat old mistakes.

Equipped with historical hindsight, the Tang historians came in time to draw parallels between the Qin and Sui, and the Han and Tang. The first pair established a unified empire but suffered precipitous fall; the second set reaped the fruits of unification and built durable dynasties. At the time Emperor Gaozu issued his edict, he had no way of knowing how long his regime would last. His decision simply reflected his strong interest and faith in history, which many rulers believed was the bedrock of governance. But it is also significant that his endorsement of history was a departure from the Sui policy of proscribing the writing of history for fear of its subversive power. The Tang emperor was well aware of the possibilities resulting from control of history. In fact, the establishment of the History Bureau and the systematization of official history-writing in the reign of Emperor

Taizong were direct consequences of the throne's desire to oversee the shaping of the past.

The Tang History Bureau ushered in new practices that departed from the earlier traditions and models, even though court diaries and inner palace diaries had their antecedents in the Han. What was notably new in the Tang was the institutionalization of two sequential phases in the writing of history: the recording of history (*zhuji*), followed by the writing of history (*zhuanshu*). It would now be the formal, bureaucratic procedure that the court diarists would record events, and then it would be up to the staff of the History Bureau to transform the raw material into history, specifically, the national history. Moreover, as the importance of writing history grew, court diarists no longer had the auxiliary duties of recording celestial observations and calendar-making. Although the process of specialization may have begun as early as the Later Han (Naitō 1949, 237; Jie Liu 1982, 131), Tang officials raised it to a new level. There is little question that by Tang times the idea of history had come to be construed differently from the way it was conceived in the Han. The exclusive focus of court historians on human actions hinted at the fact that the Tang no longer viewed a direct correlation between Heaven and humanity as the propelling factor in history. The study of history had matured into an independent, even autonomous, subject with pragmatic sociopolitical applications. Unlike their predecessors who beseeched Heaven to bestow blessings on their human reigns, the Tang rulers seemed more interested in learning practical historical lessons that could help guide their rule. In brief, there was growing emphasis on human agency manifested in human history.

The establishment of the History Bureau also indicated another salient characteristic of Tang historiography: the collective composition of official history (Jin [1944] 2000, 101; Cang & Wei 1983, 182). However, this general observation needs some qualification. As noted earlier, the Tang practice of collective compilation of the national histories was based on previous models, particularly the *Han Records of the Eastern Pavilion*, but in practice, few worthwhile (and now extant) histories written after the Han were composed collectively until the Tang. During the Tang there was conscious restoration and expansion of much of the Han apparatus of official historiography, including sponsorship of collective writing of contemporary history, but even after the establishment of the History Bureau, collective writing did not immediately take root; nor were all the histories completed in the Tang products of the Bureau. In fact, the first group of histories was produced by the staff of the Imperial Secretariat, when the Bureau was under supervision of the Imperial Chancellery (Niu 1999, 223). At its inception, the Bureau was specifically charged with compiling the veritable records and national history; it had not yet been given the assignment of compiling other histories.

Because of fratricide among his sons, which resulted in his own forced retirement, Emperor Gaozu was unable to execute the project he decreed in 622, a history of the previous six dynasties. It was during Taizong's reign that the project was resumed and by 636 five histories had been completed, dealing with the dynasties of the Liang, Chen, Qi, Zhou, and Sui. Collectively, they were known as the *Histories of Five Dynasties* (*Wudai shi*). Only five histories were completed because Taizong and the chief compilers saw no compelling need to duplicate Wei Shou's *Wei History* and Wei Dan's (fl. 560–610) similarly titled work. These two works, completed under the Sui, were deemed competent accounts of the Northern Wei dynasty.

Of the five histories, only two, the *Zhou History* (*Zhoushu*) and *Sui History* (*Suishu*), were composed collectively, supervised by Linghu Defen and Wei Zheng respectively. The other three were written individually by imperial fiat—Yao Silian wrote the *Liang History* (*Liangshu*) and *Chen History* (*Chenshu*), and Li Baiyao (565–648) composed the *Northern Qi History* (*Bei Qishu*). But as Wei Zheng wrote the general introduction to both Yao's and Li's works, it would appear that Wei acted as general supervisor for all five histories. The general consensus has been that the histories by Li Baiyao and Yao Silian, although both were distinguished scholars, are of inferior quality to the three produced collectively (Qu 1999b, 296–297). Li and Yao were excellent narrators, extremely skilled in composing biographies, but they fell short in providing a sense of the broad context; the collectively authored works succeed in presenting a panoramic overview of pre-Tang history. Of the five histories, the *Sui History*, composed under Wei's direct supervision with the assistance of Yan Shigu and Kong Yingda, renowned classical exegetes, was deemed the best by both Tang contemporaries and modern scholars (ibid.; W. Du 1998, 214–215).

While the quality of these five histories varied, viewed as a whole, they shed considerable light on the changing perception of history during the Tang. Although unusual heavenly phenomena still draw attention, the focus now centers on human actions and their ramifications. It is also noteworthy that when these histories were completed in 636, there was no monograph section; they consisted of annals and biographies only. In addition, unlike earlier histories, which focused on issues of legitimacy in the dynastic succession (*zhengtong*), Tang historians spent considerably less time and space distinguishing legitimate from illegitimate dynasties. By and large they adopted a neutral stance toward their predecessors, accepting what happened as simply an integral part of history. In earlier writings the southern regimes had often derided the northern regimes as "barbarian captives" (*suolu*) and the northern regimes had described the southerners as "island barbarians" (*daoyi*). But Tang historians dropped these pejoratives and treated the north and south equally. Some Tang histories even included chapters on relations with non-Han Chinese peoples, showing a strain of cosmopolitanism in Tang high culture. The authors of these histories, especially Wei Zheng, who wrote most of the interpretative pieces that strove to reveal the lessons of history, tried overtly to compare the Tang with the Han and to draw parallels between the Qin and the Sui. Tang historians urged their rulers to learn from the errors of the tyrannical Qin and Sui and to emulate the successes of the Han.

Drawing on Confucian precepts, Wei Zheng concluded that the difference between the Qin and Han, and hence the Sui and Tang, lay in their diametrically opposed policies: one exploited their subjects and the other appeased them. By emulating the Han, the Tang would bring peace and well-being to the people (*Suishu* 1973, 55–56, 95–96). And finally, almost all of the Tang authors regarded Buddhism favorably, which suggests that by the seventh century Buddhism had become fully integrated into Chinese culture and society. The Tang position contrasted sharply with Fan Ye's anti-Buddhist stance two centuries earlier, and testifies to the "Buddhist conquest of China" (Zürcher 1972; S. Bai 1999, 179–180).

There were some obvious shortcomings in these histories, many of which also existed in the other histories compiled by the History Bureau. Whether individually or collectively compiled, they were composed under the aegis of the court and closely supervised by the chief ministers. As a result none displayed the sort of distinctive authorial characteristics, much less originality, that distinguished the works of a Sima Qian, Ban Gu or Chen Shou. Many of the biographies were written formulaically, with much space devoted to all the various official titles an official held, along with those of his father and grandfathers. Little attempt is made to describe a person's character and personality (S. Bai 1999, 179; Qu 1999b, 296). This problem, to be sure, was not confined to the Tang. Many earlier histories were also preoccupied with the distinguished genealogies of magnate families and their members. But in the Tang histories the formula seemed to be more rigid. Probably because of the desire to achieve a certain level of consistency among all the biographies, compilers preferred to include standard genealogical information rather than describe distinctive individual characters.

Another obvious deficiency was that the *Five Histories* included no monograph section. This was a glaring lacuna, especially if the Tang wished to establish parity with the Han. For the *Five Histories* to be included among the standard histories, a monograph section had to be added. In 643 Taizong mandated precisely that addition. Supervision of this endeavor was assigned to Chu Suiliang (596–658/9), a chief minister at court whose role was comparable to Wei Zheng's, and the actual compilation was to be done by the staff of the History Bureau. This was the Bureau's first assignment that involved writing about previous dynasties. Despite turnovers at the supervisory level—oversight went successively to Chu Suiliang, Linghu Defen, and Changsun Wuji—work proceeded smoothly without disruption, probably owing to the fact that the History Bureau had by then attained a high level of consistency and routinization. Changes at the top exerted minimal impact on the ground, as it were. The monographs, completed in 656, were integrated into the *Sui History,* for the obvious reason that since these topically based treatises examined long-term developments, they fit best at the end of the overall history. The monographs tackled ten main topics: rituals and protocols, the calendar, astrology, the five phases, ritual music, commodities, penal law, bureaucracy, geography, and books. Whereas the first five subjects were clearly modeled on the Han precedents established by Ban Gu and suggested a residual interest in Heaven's influence in human affairs, the remaining five focused unequivocally on human institutions and literary accomplishments. Clearly Tang historians were increasingly separating the domain of Heaven from the Way of human history as two separate spheres in the field of historical epistemology (Qu 1999b, 298–299).

With regard to the Tang recording of human accomplishments, one area especially deserves attention—the bibliographic treatise on books, entitled the "Monograph on the Classics and Literature" (Jingji zhi). It was a systematic attempt to classify knowledge by putting books into four categories—classics, history, philosophy and belles-lettres—which were further divided into thirteen subcategories. Such a painstaking taxonomic effort aimed to encompass the variety of writings that had appeared prior to the Tang, and to register and abstract a total of 6,520 titles. The effort contained 56,881 fascicles; those classified under "History" constituted 874 titles with 13,264 fascicles. Although many of these recorded books are no longer extant—some had already been lost at the time of their inclusion—the monograph itself amounts to a valuable "history of the book," showing the general contours and development of scholarly activities in imperial China. The Tang classificatory scheme of "classics, history, philosophy, and belles-lettres" became standard in Chinese bibliographical ordering, kept intact with only minor changes in the subcategories until the late eighteenth and even early nineteenth centuries (Zeng 2000).

In 648 the History Bureau also produced the Jin History (Jinshu) in 130 fascicles. It contained ten basic annals, twenty monographs, seventy arrayed biographies, and thirty contemporaneous records (zaiji). The last category was first used by the compilers of the Han Records of the Eastern Pavilion to record the histories of short-lived fiefdoms and was adopted here to describe the sixteen Särbi kingdoms in the north that existed simultaneously with the two Jin dynasties. Apart from the fact that it was the only dynastic history compiled officially by the Bureau, the Jin History boasts another special feature. Because it examines the frequent rise and fall of the many regimes in the post-Han period—the relative stability achieved by the Jin was only a foil to the violent dynastic changes taking place elsewhere—the Jin History commanded Taizong's special attention. The monarch was particularly fascinated by the lessons to be gained from a deep knowledge of great turmoil. The emperor personally contributed four fascicles, making it the only work with "royal authorship" among all the standard histories (S. Chen 1968, iii). Perceived as an "exemplar history" (Rogers 1968), the Jin History was presented as a gift by Taizong to his crown prince and Korean diplomats (Tang Huiyao 1955, 1091–1092).

By the end of Taizong's reign the History Bureau had already become an important office that produced work of high quality. But it did not monopolize official history writing. In the mid-seventh century, Li Yanshou (fl. 600–665), an official historian who had worked on the Jin History, produced two histories on his own: *History of the South* (*Nanshi*) and *History of the North* (*Beishi*). Emperor Gaozong (r. 650–682) actually wrote a preface commending his accomplishment upon the work's presentation to the court. Li was indebted to both his father, Li Dashi (570–628), who initiated the project, and works compiled by his fellow official historians, on which he relied heavily for sources and ideas. Although Li Yanshou's enterprise reminds us of Sima Qian's, Li was no match for the Han historian. While Li attempted to tell a broad continuous story in these two accounts, he did so by cutting and pasting previous texts, creating what R. G. Collingwood would have called "scissors and paste history" (1946, 274–282). But if Li Yanshou's rather mechanical approach earned him no accolades as an imaginative historian, his work has been well regarded by both his contemporaries and later scholars, primarily because it preserves sources from the period under investigation. In addition, Li did stitch together a somewhat coherent picture of the tangled history between the fall of the Han and the rise of the Tang, and it does serve as a historical introduction to the reunification of China under the Sui and Tang (McMullen 1988, 169).

Other private individual endeavors also persisted, as in previous times, but after the Tang, the dominant historical form was the official history compiled collectively (S. Wang 1997, 88). If, however, we are to pinpoint the Tang contribution to the development of Chinese historiography, it was not the introduction of new formats for compiling official historiography; nor was it the creation of the History Bureau, as both were continuations of earlier prototypes. Rather, the Tang gradually institutionalized the writing of official history, transforming it into an integral part of the imperial bureaucracy. The compilation of official history became, as it were, a "state-operated enterprise" (*guoying qiye*), in the words of Du Weiyun (1998, 195). And this bureaucratic institutionalization of history went hand in hand with another major Tang project—implementation of the civil service examinations. Both were political and cultural measures of immense lasting influence. Through them the Tang rulers strove to consolidate their dynasty by creating less coercive intellectual and ideological mechanisms of control (Wechsler 1985, 2). History and merit examinations proved to be the enduring twin legacy of the Tang, embraced faithfully by later regimes, whether Han Chinese or not. Official compilation of the standard history of the preceding dynasty became a matter of course, a time-honored tradition to be upheld by the reigning dynasty, and following the Tang model, such a history would usually be undertaken as a collective project with direct court sponsorship.

Liu Zhiji and Historical Criticism

Collective compilation under the aegis of the court was intrinsically prone to imperial censorship and interference, and critical scrutiny appeared almost immediately following establishment of History Bureau in the Tang. One important contemporary critic had actually worked in the Bureau, making his criticisms all the more cogent. This was Liu Zhiji, arguably the most perspicacious historical mind of his age, if not of all of imperial China. His most acclaimed work is *Comprehensive Perspectives on Historiography* (*Shitong*) completed in 710. This sharply insightful historiographical treatise predated by six and a half centuries Ibn Khaldûn's (1332–1406) highly praised *Muqaddimah* (1377), a work often hailed as the earliest critical study of history in the West. Liu wrote several other works and was involved in various projects at the History Bureau. Though few of his other writings have survived, the *Comprehensive Perspectives on Historiography* by itself has ensured his hallowed place in the annals of Chinese historiography.

Du Weiyun aptly describes the work as a "critical historiography" (*pipan shixue*), in which Liu examines different schools, styles, and ideas, delineating their changes and developments while assessing their contributions and shortcomings (1998, 251–252; Sanxi Zhang 1992). Although the work was a general study of historiography, Liu had one central purpose in mind: to criticize the practice of collective historiography in the History Bureau. In the "Self-Preface" (Zixu), Liu recalls his experience working as a staff historian in the Bureau and remarks that "while holding the right position, I was unable to do what I wanted to do; while delighted with the appointment, I could not achieve my grand goal. I became depressed and frustrated with myself, unable to express my true feelings. . . . I therefore decided to resign from the position and wrote the *Comprehensive Perspectives on Historiography* on my own so that I could realize my calling" (*Shitong* 1978, 1:290).

Liu voices the recurrent motif in the biographies of many Chinese historians: dedicating oneself to the writing of history as the answer to one's frustrations and thwarted desires. Liu in fact compares himself with earlier scholars by noting their similar experiences and motivations. As with Sima Qian, he professes his spiritual debt to Confucius. He hopes to achieve in history what the sage had done with the classics—to fully reveal and apprehend the nature of history, with its theoretical underpinning and practical manifestation, so as to ascertain its sacrosanct status as a canonical form of writing. On this score, Liu Zhiji's aspiration may also be likened to Liu Xie's. Liu Xie, in his masterful *The Literary Mind and the Carving of Dragons,* sought to illumine the profundity of literary pursuits, elevating them to the stature of the classics (Kang-i Chang 2001). He actually devoted one fascicle to historical writing, and in some ways, his brief historiographical cogitations furnished the point of departure for Liu Zhiji's full-fledged systematic contemplation. Liu Zhiji's authorial ambitions no doubt found support and justification in the historical examples of Confucius, Sima Qian, Liu Xie and others, because he initially viewed his own idea of a treatise on history with trepidation. But his unsatisfying experience in the History Bureau was the last straw, the coup de grâce that ended his self-doubt and convinced him to write the *Comprehensive Perspectives on Historiography* (*Shitong* 1978, 1:289–290).

The *Comprehensive Perspectives on Historiography* was meant to be a summation of Liu's life-long thinking about history. Prior to this, Liu had developed quite an impressive record of historical writing. Born into a distinguished family noted for its literary success, Liu showed an interest in historical studies very early. It seemed to be the only subject in which he excelled, as he was quite indifferent to study of the classics. Having passed the civil service examinations at the age of twenty, Liu landed a minor government position. Serving there during the next two decades, he built a solid knowledge base for his later historical work. Since his official job was not a taxing one, he spent considerable time at the libraries in the nearby capital of Luoyang. As his scholarly reputation grew, he was called upon by the court to take on positions that allowed him to pursue his interest in history, which resulted in many works that he either wrote by himself or with others. These covered a wide range, from family histories to compilations of the veritable records and national history, a range that amply demonstrates the breadth of his knowledge and versatility of his talents.

But Liu became increasingly alienated from his official tasks, especially while working in the History Bureau. His work was interrupted several times, due to the unstable political situation brought on by the death of Empress Wu Zetian and the frequent change of the Bureau's supervisors. In 708 he tendered a letter of resignation, which is included in the *Comprehensive Perspectives on Historiography*. In the letter, Liu outlined five reasons why it was a bad idea to compile history collectively at the Bureau. First, it was inefficient—the writing process involved too many people. Second, historians had difficulty gaining access to the archives because they first had to have permission from the chief ministers. Third, as the staff historians now worked as insiders in the court, they were released from their public responsibility of keeping the records straight. Fourth, because Bureau historians were supervised by different officials, the work often lacked consistent standards and uniform quality. Finally, some staff historians treated their positions as sinecures and whiled away their time doing nothing (*Shitong* 1978, 2:589–594; Hung 1969).

The poor quality of the court historians was Liu's main target. He held up the examples of Sima Qian, Ban Gu, and Confucius to indicate the high expectations one should have of historians. When asked why there were many literary writers but few historians, Liu Zhiji made the famous statement that a good historian had to possess three qualities: talent (*cai*), knowledge (*xue*), and insight (*shi*). As it was rare that one could cultivate all three qualities, there were few good historians, and seldom were they found at the History Bureau. Once the Bureau was established in court, Liu observed, official historians occupied a prestigious position. They got to enjoy working in an elegant office building; they had ample access to sumptuous food and excellent wine. Blessed with a good life and comfortable job, many stopped doing any work. Only one or two out of ten actually did real, substantive writing. Just as the office of the historians became ossified, so the nature of historical writing came to be obfuscated. If his-

torical writing were to be revivified, Liu thought, it would have to take up
the basic two-step process with renewed vigor: first, there had to be faithful, diligent recording and preservation of sources, and then these sources
had to be gathered into coherent accounts by historians of later times endowed with both knowledge and insight, such as Ban Gu (*Shitong* 1978,
2:318–327). The Bureau's dereliction of duty and the scarcity of historians
of true acumen were constant sources of Liu's discontent. It should, however, be said that Liu Zhiji's concern owed something to both his pride and
his prejudice (S. Bai 1999, 203–205). As a scion of a distinguished gentle
lineage, he looked down on some of his colleagues who lacked aristocratic
and scholarly pedigree. Liu's family background explained his great passion for family history. Not only did he write a genealogy of his own family
but he also suggested that a "monograph on the gentle lineages" (*shizu zhi*)
be added to the standard histories.

His prejudice aside, there is no doubt that what prompted Liu Zhiji to
write the *Comprehensive Perspectives on Historiography* was a much larger and
more crucial issue—factuality and truthfulness in the writing of history.
In both the History Bureau was remiss. This concern was the leitmotiv of
his book, constantly informing Liu's evaluations and criticisms. His work
is divided into thirty-five "Inner Sections" and thirteen "Outer Sections,"
with a total of forty-nine fascicles. With this organization, Liu deliberately
harked back to the similarly structured *The Literary Mind and the Carving of
Dragons* by Liu Xie, a work he both admired and wished to rival and surpass (Hung 1969, 13, note 3). The "Inner Sections" dealt with various subjects in historiography whereas the "Outer Section" proffered supplementary material and case studies. Liu's work discusses the many schools and
styles of historical writing, covering the arrangements, structures, and formats of the standard histories, as well as related subjects such as nomenclature, source selection, commentaries, supplements, narration, language,
and classification. His evaluations revolved around one central theme: how
to record and write truthful history. Liu devoted two specific fascicles to
this: "Straight Writing" (Zhishu) and "Crooked Brush" (Qubi). The former
commended those who kept the records straight and the latter disparaged
those who distorted history.

"Straight writing" (*zhishu*) is precisely the term many modern Chinese historians use to render Ranke's famous dictum, "*wie es eigentlich gewesen*" (to write as it essentially was). Coupled with "straight writing" was
the notion of "veritable recording" (*shilu*), a term that appears "more
than forty times in fourteen of the essays" in the book. These two notions
may be considered the "registered trade marks" of Liu Zhiji's idea of history (K. Hsu 1983, 435). To be sure, it was a time-honored practice to
use the word "straight" (*zhi*) to describe the historian's character. Confucius praised the historian named Yu for his "straightness." But for Confucius, being straight meant possessing moral courage—exposing evils to
the world regardless of personal risks—rather than attempting to achieve
historical factuality. However, when Liu Xie used the word "straight" in

The Literary Mind and the Carving of Dragons, it did connote genuine concern for the veracity of facts. Liu Xie pondered the difficulty of producing straight history in his contemplation of integrating factual history with moral censure. Daunted by the magnitude of such an endeavor, Liu Xie seemed finally to conclude that the intrinsic tension between the two was such that even great historians such as Sima Qian and Ban Gu failed to resolve it. In the final analysis, even Zuo Qiuming succeeded only in evoking beauty and eloquence in historical writing; he, too, failed to display "the courage of calling a spade a spade" (*Wenxin diaolong* 1983, 183). Liu Xie's lament anticipated Liu Zhiji's more strident critique of the ancient masters, although needless to say, his harsher invectives fell on lesser works and historians.

In *Comprehensive Perspectives on Historiography* Liu took pains to explicate the nexus between writing truthful history and the historian's moral responsibility. It was through upholding and promoting the principle of "straight writing" that the moral function of history in society could be demonstrated. In the chapter "Crooked Brush," he bemoaned the fact that historians often practiced "concealment" when telling of their kin or of worthies or the honorable, omitting events and deeds that might tarnish their reputations. Liu acknowledged that such might be expedient means to maintain the social order, but they grossly violated the principle of "straight writing" (*Shitong* 1978, 1:196); he repudiated the practice. In the chapter "Doubts on the Classics" (Huojing) in the "Outer Section," he even called into question Confucius' concealment, stating that if history was indeed a mirror, it should reflect everything—virtue and evil, good and bad. Only in that sense was a historical account a "veritable record" (*shilu*) (ibid., 2:402). Liu did not see "straight writing" as incompatible with a historian's moral judgment, but he gained much notoriety for daring to take Confucius to task, pinpointing instances in the *Spring and Autumn* where moral censure and concern inappropriately trumped truthful recording. To Liu, it was a historiographical imperative to critically parse and evaluate "individual statements contained in established texts," including those in the *Spring and Autumn,* but as Charles Gardner pointed out in his classic on traditional Chinese historiography, this was not a practice commonly assumed by Chinese scholars (Gardner 1938, 64). In his brief survey Gardner did not fully grasp the importance of Liu's project, mentioning only that "since the seventh century, a few bold, independent spirits have evolved the elements of historical criticism," but also quickly adding that "their results were ignored or frowned upon by the orthodox" (ibid., 3). In fact, Liu's book may be regarded as a systematic evaluation of existing histories.

Thanks to E. G. Pulleyblank (1961) and Hsu Kwan-san (1983), Liu's important contributions have been brought into much sharper relief. Both have shown that Liu Zhiji not only extended and augmented the existing critical tradition established by scholars such as Liu Xie, but he also strongly influenced the later practice of historiography, as we can see in the Song masterworks by Sima Guang (1019–1086) and Zheng Qiao (1104–1162). Liu's insistence on factual history was also endorsed by the eminent Tang scholar Han Yu, who lived a century or so after Liu. Han remarked that as "the *Spring and Autumn Annals* had already made it clear what ought to be commended and what to be condemned, the task of later historians would simply be to record what had actually happened so that the good and the evil would readily reveal themselves" (W. Du 1998, 317). Like Liu Zhiji, Han Yu believed that readers already knew, by reading the *Spring and Autumn*, what was right and wrong, and so historians need not belabor them. What readers needed was the delivery of facts.

Liu Zhiji's contributions to historical criticism were twofold. He evaluated historical works and their authors in a critical but dispassionate manner, and he stressed the need to scrutinize historical sources rigorously. Liu readily admitted that he was often unsparing in his assessment of his predecessors whose works, in his view, left much to be desired. He stated in the "Self-Preface" that he "often ridiculed the previous masters and was fond of revealing their mistakes" (*Shitong* 1978, 1:292). But he also tried hard to be fair. On Wang Shao (fl. 575–620), a Sui official historian, Liu showered accolades for his "straightness." But he also criticized Wang for "taking slander as straightness" and for incorporating too many trivial details into his accounts (K. Hsu 1983, 436). Conversely, Wei Shou was Liu's *bête noire,* "against whom he inveighs on every possible occasion," but he also commended Wei for his innovations in historiography (Pulleyblank 1961, 149; K. Hsu 1983, 436). In other words, Liu gave credit where credit was due.

In the area of source criticism, Liu Zhiji's ideas and insights are praiseworthy. He was aware of the difference between primary and derivative sources, and he brought this understanding to bear on his evaluation of historical works. Of the three commentaries on the *Spring and Autumn Annals,* for instance, Liu preferred the *Zuo Commentary* to the *Gongyang* and *Guliang Commentaries* because, in addition to its narrative elegance, the *Zuo Commentary* offered coherent descriptions of events, whereas the other two commentaries concentrated on explaining and interpreting words, whose authenticity they took for granted. Liu argued that historians should not rely excessively on verbal reports in recording, citing both the *Spring and Autumn* and *Classic of History* as bad examples of overdependence on hearsay. Historians ought to base their writings on firsthand observations as best they could (*Shitong* 1978, 2:379ff). Liu especially liked the *Zuo Commentary* because to the extent that Zuo Qiuming was the author—and there was no compelling evidence to reject his authorship entirely—Zuo, as a contemporary of Confucius, could have been an eyewitness to events that Confucius observed. It was logical to assume that his judgments were consonant with the sage's, and hence that Zuo was in a much better position than Gongyang and Guliang to expound the meanings of the *Spring and Autumn* because the latter two "were born and raised in a different place and in a later time." Liu asked rhetorically, "How could those based on legends and oral traditions compete with the one written with eye-witness experience?" (ibid., 418–419).

In addition Liu advocated broad but judicious employment of primary sources, especially government documents and archives. He also valued many nonofficial sources, such as the informal records (*pianji*), individual records (*xiaolu*), prefectural histories (*junshu*), and family histories (*jiashi*), because by and large they were produced by contemporaries (ibid., 273ff). Whatever the sources were, however, the historian had to analyze them carefully before using them.

Liu's source criticism embodied an external dimension and an internal one (Inaba 1999, 224–229). External criticism examines the style in which the sources were written. Liu recommended that historians use a normal prose style, for he thought verbal plainness facilitated the factual reconstruction of history because of its accessibility and intelligibility. He himself, however, perhaps due to Liu Xie's influence, used antithetical rhythmic prose (*pianwen*), a relatively flowery, ornate form, in the *Comprehensive Perspectives on Historiography*. Liu Zhiji's recommendation actually anticipated the rise of the "ancient prose" (*guwen*) movement that from the mid-Tang onward became the rage among many literati. Of course, it was not Liu's primary goal to rigidly promote a particular style in writing history; he simply wanted to ensure historical factuality. Liu thus objected "to the use of euphuistic fine writing" and advocated inclusion of realistic colloquial speeches in historical reconstructions. As Pulleyblank describes it, Liu "pours scorn on those historians who made barbarian rulers speak in high-flown phrases full of classical allusions and praises those who retained vulgar expressions at the expense of elegance." Liu maintained that "if things are all to be recorded without error the words must be close to the actual ones, so that one may almost dwell with the men of the past" (Pulleyblank 1961, 146–147). He also suggested that historians adopt a concise (*jianyao*) and eclectically nuanced style (*yonghui*) in narration, eschewing the literary flourishes that had been fashionable before Tang times (*Shitong* 1978, 1:165ff).

Not only was Liu intent on employing a style that mimetically captured what had actually happened, but he was also much consumed with factual content. He was particularly wary of the authenticity of the Five Phases theory as it was applied to history. Liu favored human explanations for affairs that took place in the human world (Pulleyblank 1961, 145). He did not oppose the recording of celestial phenomena in history, nor did he refute the possibility that these phenomena might have bearing on human history. He was willing to concede that in certain cases a correlation between Heaven and humanity seemed to have indeed occurred, but he was unwilling to endorse wholesale the assumption that every major change in history was due to Heaven's will. He criticized Sima Qian for using the correlative idea indiscriminately in explaining the rise and fall of regimes in the Warring States period. He also had reservations about Ban Gu's zeal for matters astronomical (ibid.; Lei 1990, 575–578).What disturbed him was the pervasive, often far–fetched use of the Heaven–humanity correlation in historical writing from the Han to his own times. His historiography was rationalistic and naturalistic.

As a history of histories, the *Comprehensive Perspectives on Historiography* also conscientiously evaluated the forms and styles historians used. Liu first placed all preexisting histories under the two main categories (*erti*) of annals-biography and chronicle. He then subdivided them into six schools (*liujia*), which he discussed in turn, regarding their origins, development, and prospects. Although he seemed to believe that these forms and schools had in general exhausted the ways in which historians presented history, he did see possibilities for modification and addition. In considering the monographs in the standard histories, for example, he suggested eliminating or drastically revising the format of those on astronomy, bibliography, and portents, as they were often either inconsistent with the general coverage of a standard history or unhelpful in forging a sound understanding of historical changes. At the same time, he recommended adding three new monographs: one on cities (*duyi zhi*), one on gentle clans (*shizu zhi*), and the last on the exotic plants and animals presented as tributes to the throne (*fangwu zhi*) (Pulleyblank 1961, 145). His appeal had some success. Although most standard histories retained the monographs that Liu wanted to expunge, his recommended additions were adopted by later scholars such as Du You and Zheng Qiao (S. Bai 1999, 196).

Historical Encyclopedias

Liu Zhiji's ideas regarding monographs influenced the compilation of Tang historical encyclopedias. In 801, a century after Liu completed the *Comprehensive Perspectives on Historiography*, Du You (735–812) finished his *Comprehensive Compendium* (*Tongdian*) and invented the encyclopedic form of institutional history. Du's intention to compose privately a comprehensive account of the histories of institutions recalls Liu Zhiji's aspiration to produce a comprehensive reflection on historiographical issues. But Du's innovation transcended Liu Zhiji's conception of the forms and formats in historiography, even though Du was undoubtedly inspired by Liu's thinking. Du excluded such topics as astronomy, the Five Phases, and portents from his work. Du's work was based on a similarly structured book by Liu Zhi (fl. 700–758), Liu Zhiji's son, entitled *Administrative Compendium* [*on Institutions*] (*Zhengdian*), written some twenty years earlier. In the *Comprehensive Compendium*, Du You also included the *Military Directives* (*Wuzhi*) written by Liu Kuang (fl. 700–760), another son of Liu Zhiji (McMullen 1988, 185–186). Furthermore, like Liu Zhiji, Du was attracted to the idea of writing a general history (*tong shi*). During the reign of Emperor Yuan of the Liang dynasty in the sixth century, the court had commissioned historians to compile a *General History*, the completed final version of which comprised 600 fascicles. Although it did not survive, the compilation may have inspired both Liu Zhiji and Du You, as both of them used the key word "comprehensive" or "general" (*tong*) in their titles.

As a seasoned official who had joined the government at the age of twenty and rose through the ranks to become a chief minister in his later years, serving three emperors consecutively, Du You was well qualified to conduct a comprehensive study of government institutions. Besides his personal interests and experiences, the political situation in the mid-Tang may also have prompted him to write the *Comprehensive Compendium*. Several decades after Liu Zhiji had completed his work, the Tang dynasty suffered great upheaval that resulted from the An Lushan rebellion, which almost toppled it. Serving in government during this tumultuous period, Du had much direct experience with an immense variety of political and administrative crises. He wanted to commit to writing his painfully fresh memories and in the process illuminate the perils that faced the Tang. His goal was to distill and highlight the valuable lessons from the past in order to ascertain the best ways to prolong the life of the dynasty. Hence the genesis of an encyclopedic work that took over three decades to complete. Du You's work was emblematic of a dominant trend in Tang historiography—that having knowledge of and understanding the past would directly benefit current governance (W. Du 1998, 326–331).

What underlay this pragmatic historiography was a heightened sense of the utility of history. This did not mean taking liberty with the past so that historians selected or distorted past examples to illustrate current situations. Rather, it meant an abiding interest in finding human explanations for what had happened in the past. This in turn diminished an interest in the supernatural and the occult as forces in history. One of Du You's foremost goals was to produce a comprehensive institutional history that loosened the ties between human development and heavenly mandate. Du even hinted at the idea of evolution, casting doubt on the entrenched belief that the ancients were superior to the moderns and challenging the age-old dictum, "the right ancient and the wrong modern" (*feijin shigu*). Du not only acknowledged that historical change was necessary and inevitable, but he also deliberated on the causes for and patterns of such change. He came to the conclusion that every age had its "circumstances" (*shi*) and "patterns"(*li*), and the best way to cope with them was to embark on change through adaptation and adjustment (*biantong*), or in his words, "catching up with the times" (*shishi*).

Although neither a historical theorist nor philosopher, Du You did influence other Tang scholars. Most notably, Du's idea of evolution was later elaborated and expanded by Liu Zongyuan (773–819). Liu is known in history mainly as a towering literary figure in the Tang, but he also wrote several significant essays on historical change as manifested in institutional evolution. In *On Enfeoffment (Fengjian lun)*, for instance, Liu maintained that the ebb and flow of fiefdom represented an irrevocable historical trend, and he analyzed why this was so. In *Critique of the Discourses of the States* (*Fei Guoyu*), a piece most representative of Liu's historical thinking (Qu 1999b, 430), Liu enumerated the reasons why it was no longer necessary for historians to subscribe to the idea of a correlation between Heaven and humanity. He dismantled the stories recorded in the *Discourses on the States* which supposedly recorded Heaven's manifest interventions in human affairs. Liu rejected the idea of the Mandate of Heaven and its impact on human history, arguing that humans were solely responsible for their own actions. He commended those in history who adapted to changing times and condemned obscurants who, clinging to the belief in Heaven's blessings, opposed the march of time and thus consigned themselves to the dustbin of history (Zongyuan Liu 1979, 1268–1269, 2308, 2310–2311).

In his *Comprehensive Compendium* Du You clearly advanced the idea that history was useful not because it revealed a correlation between Heaven and humanity, but because it encapsulated human accomplishments in all their glory. By examining the most comprehensive account of history, we may see how things develop and understand the dynamics of change. Du You not only excluded chapters on the Five Phases, astrology, and the calendar, but he also organized the book in such a way as to forcefully present his interpretation of human history. According to David McMullen, Du aimed to "sustain a polemical outlook." While visibly indebted to the many previous monographs, Du deliberately departed from them, presenting materials in different order and investing in them a different historiographical intention (1988, 203).

Du was not the first to demonstrate interest in institutional history. Prior to the An Lushan rebellion, the Tang court had commissioned the *Six Institutions* (*Liudian*), a compendium of Tang bureaucratic apparatuses. It delineated government in accordance with the six bureaucratic divisions prescribed in the Zhou ritualistic compendium. Du You's *Comprehensive Compendium* was not modeled on any precedent. It was divided into nine sections, beginning with foods and goods, followed by civil examinations, offices and posts, rituals, music, war, punishments, administrative geography, and ending with border defense.

The organization reflects Du You's understanding of the dynamics and patterns of historical growth. In the preface he explains that he began his book with economic life because it is the foundation of society. With a sound economic foundation, the government can implement educative policies to advance and transform culture (*jiaohua*). Du contended that the acculturation and civilization of the people depended on rituals and music, which he considered the bedrock of the state and society. Not surprisingly then, he devoted almost half of his work to tracing their development. Rituals and music, however, had to be complemented by laws and punishments. In addition, an army must exist for the defense of the country's borders. Yet all these designs of government would not come to pass without talented and capable officials; hence the civil examinations were of the utmost importance in guaranteeing the quality of the officialdom.

Government, staffed by able men, served two main functions. One was to promote a civilized social order through rituals and music; the other was to prevent perversion of this order through laws and punishments, and to protect it with adequate military force (*Tongdian* 1988, 1).

Du You's functional and structural understanding of the evolution of culture and government in history was no doubt inspired by the sort of political discourse in the Sui and Tang eras that centered on the idea of the efficacy of government, the so-called "discourses on the rule of the country" (*zhiguo lun*) (Qu 1999b, 370ff). These discussions were firmly anchored in history because it was the past that furnished the concrete lessons of good government and misrule that explained the fortunes and misfortunes of the rulers and their states. As political exigency came to be associated with a utilitarian past, there arose great enthusiasm for historical learning. The numerous ephemeral regimes in the Age of Disunity constituted a cautionary tale, inspiring many Tang officials, including the official historians, incumbent or retired, to write books through which they exchanged views on the "rise and fall" (*xingwang*) of states so that the Tang would not repeat the same sad fate. Wu Jing's (670–749) *Essentials of Government in the Zhenguan Period* (*Zhenguan zhengyao*) is a good example. Written as a political guide for the ruler, Wu's book drew on the exemplary experience of the so-called Zhenguan (627–649) period in Taizong's reign and offered a quantity of advice on good government: selection and appointment of officials, military defense, choice and education of the heir-apparent, penal law, taxation, and moral cultivation. According to Wu, a court historian who used court diaries of various kinds in writing the book, the stability and longevity of a regime depended primarily on the ruler's attention to agriculture and his judiciousness in avoiding costly military campaigns.

Du You's affirmation of the central role of the bureaucracy and government institutions also represented a pragmatic turn to statecraft in Tang historiography, and his *Comprehensive Compendium* was a paradigmatic illustration (W. Du 1998, 326–331). Although his heavy emphasis on rites and music unquestionably reflected the Confucian ideal of a civilized government, Du's goal was not to promote Confucian moral-ethical tenets but to offer practical methods of government. Historical references notwithstanding, Du did not endorse blind emulation of ancient examples, nor did he regard them as constant and immutable. As one preface remarked, effective government included both harking back to the past and changing with the times: "In order to help the government, one must set up examples. In setting up the examples, one must learn from the past. Yet in learning from the past, one must learn how to adapt to the times" (*Tongdian* 1988, 1–2; Li Han's preface).

But some of Du You's contemporaries deemed his evolutionary view of government too radical. They proposed a conventional, conservative approach to Tang political history and governance. The *Gathering of Essentials of the Tang* (*Tang huiyao*), also a voluminous compendium, is a case in point (McMullen 1988, 201–205). Like Du's *Comprehensive Compendium*, the

Gathering of Essentials was written privately. The authors were two brothers, Su Mian (?–805) and Su Bian (fl. 760–805), who were famed for their erudition in Confucian learning. If Du You sought to propagate the fact of evolution and the need for change, the Su brothers wished to advance a moralistic interpretation of Tang institutional history. Although they shared with Du the central idea that bureaucracy was essential to government, they showed a far greater interest in the education of the bureaucrats, an area in which Confucianism could play a most useful role. The *Gathering of Essentials* therefore paid much attention to scholarly organizations and societies, the system of schools, the institution of canonization, academic controversies, and important literary works presented to the court, displaying an apparent bias for "the civil scholarly tradition in the bureaucracy" (ibid., 202). In contrast to Du You's critical attitude toward past examples, the Su brothers sang the praises of Tang institutions, implying that drastic change and broad reforms were not only unnecessary but would also likely be detrimental.

In spite of its conservative bias, the *Gathering of Essentials* did act as an informative general reference to the Tang bureaucracy. The Su brothers amassed a rich body of material and arranged it in a way that it is easily accessible to readers. Unlike Du You, who freely inserted his views into the *Comprehensive Compendium,* the Su brothers mainly confined their comments to explaining and critiquing their sources. In addition, they limited their work to the Tang period. If Du was praised for pioneering the genre of institutional history, the Su brothers were credited for producing "a true administrative encyclopedia" (Twitchett 1992, 109).

In 804, when the Su brothers presented their work to the throne, it had forty fascicles, covering the reigns of the first nine Tang emperors. As it was very well received by the court and the scholarly community, the History Bureau was ordered to compile a sequel, which was completed in 853 and extended the coverage to the current reign. The version available today was compiled by Wang Pu (922–982), a Song dynasty scholar who continued the two earlier versions by adding coverage of the last years of the Tang. With Wang's elaborations and additions, the *Gathering of Essentials* became a truly comprehensive survey of the Tang institutional structure and development, a complement to the *Old History of the Tang.* The *Old History* centered on the lives and deeds of individuals, but the *Gathering of Essentials* focused on events. They reinforce each other to furnish invaluable sources on the history of the Tang (Qu 1999b, 367). In addition, the *Gathering of Essentials* established a precedent. In the post-Tang dynasties, compiling a *Gathering of Essentials* was one of the important routine tasks of official historians at court.

It is worth recalling when the Su brothers' *Gathering of Essentials* appeared in the mid-Tang, it was a purely individual and private endeavor. Some modern scholars have argued that the Su brothers were able to embark on the project because a prior privately written volume—*Stories of Our Dynasty* (*Guochao gushi*)—was still extant in the early eleventh century

(Twitchett 1992, 110). In other words, they capitalized on one example of the thriving private historiography at the time. Such private endeavors burgeoned even as the Tang rulers established the History Bureau in order to censure and control the writing of history. Official attempts at oversight were not very successful, especially after the An Lushan rebellion. Many major histories produced thereafter were written by private scholars, the *Comprehensive Compendium* and the *Gathering of Essentials* being prime examples. But these two were the tip of the iceberg. The Tang intellectual elite's interest in writing "private histories" (*sishi*) and "historical anecdotes" (*lishi biji*) had certainly existed before the rebellion, but afterward the writing of private histories became more widespread. If the rebellion marked a watershed in Tang history, ushering in the decline of the Tang imperium, it also heralded the loosening of the Tang official grip on historical practices (W. Du 1998, 331ff).

Two important factors drew Tang intellectuals away from court sponsorship and toward private historical enterprises. The literati were dissatisfied with the quality of the official histories compiled by the History Bureau, a degeneration that became especially apparent in the period after the rebellion. The Bureau seemed unable to recover quickly from the huge loss of archives and records that resulted from rebel attacks on the palace. The other factor was growing literati concern about the decline of Tang power. They increasingly turned to history for guidance and inspiration. Their predilection for pragmatic and institutional historiography grew out of their conviction in the usefulness of historical knowledge for statecraft and governance. If the History Bureau no longer produced usable history, then the literati themselves must take up the challenge.

The most outspoken critic of official historiography was Liu Zhiji, but many others echoed his sentiments. Wu Jing, Liu's contemporary and author of the *Essentials of Government,* explained that he had been prompted to write precisely because he found so many faults with the practices of the History Bureau (Inaba 1999, 217–218). Their criticism focused on the biographies written by official historians, which had been the staple of dynastic historiography before Du You and others attempted compilations of institutional history. The problem bedeviling these biographies was that many were written "as laudatory commemorative tributes" to the officials, designed for "the perpetuation of their names and therefore a form of immortality" (McMullen 1988, 191–192). After the An Lushan rebellion, official history came to be plagued by widespread cynicism and rampant distortions. By writing unofficial histories, many authors felt that they were serving the needs of the government by keeping the record straight. At the same time they wanted to express their independent views. Some wrote biographies of those figures whom they deemed meritorious but who were excluded or slighted by official historians. Others, such as Du You and the Su brothers, pioneered the new form of institutional history.

Given the degeneration of biographical historiography into fawning hagiography, the annals-biographic form lost some of its appeal and authority, while the chronicle form associated with the *Spring and Autumn Annals* gained popularity among the Tang scholars and was once again considered history par excellence. Xun Yue's *Han Records* achieved prominence and was often preferred over Ban Gu's *Han History* (Twitchett 1992, 64). The *Spring and Autumn* and the *Han Records* came to be favored because they offered viable alternatives to official history written in the annals-biography style. Moreover, they were seen as exemplary didactic historiography, for in reworking earlier works, Confucius and Xun Yue had imbued their texts with high moral values. Many private historians in the Tang aspired to do the same.

But many of these private scholars did not enjoy full access to archives and often had to rely on unofficial records. Consequently, their writings usually could not compete with official histories in terms of resources. But private historians offset this disadvantage by their relative freedom to voice their independent, and sometimes more truthful, views of history. They avoided court interference, official censorship, and political pressure. In the postrebellion period, as the History Bureau withered under imperial oversight and lost its vitality, private histories flowered. In addition to correcting the distortions and mistakes in official historiography, these private histories censured the disloyal behavior and regicidal acts that had become all too common as Tang power declined.

Political concerns alone did not account for the craze of private and unofficial historiography. Many wrote history simply because they loved studying the past. While many followed Confucius' or Xun Yue's examples, there were others who adopted alternative forms and even invented new ones. In these writings—many belonged to the genre of *A New Account of Tales of the World*—there is valuable information about the lives of both distinguished and ordinary people who were left out in official Tang histories. Quite a number of these unofficial histories, particularly the so-called "historical anecdotes," were written for entertainment purposes, and they bordered on literary writing in style. To a great extent the proliferation of historical anecdotes coincided with, if it did not pave the way for, the emergence of fiction (*xiaoshuo*) in the Tang (S. Lu 1994). Nonetheless, they should be regarded as histories because for the most part their contents were trustworthy as historical materials. Indeed, many of them were utilized later by such skillful historians as Sima Guang, author of *The Comprehensive Mirror for Aid in Government* (Qu 1999b, 361). Most of these private histories are no longer extant, and we know only their titles, but all the same, they testify to the diversity of the Tang historical world. The Tang bequeathed a valuable legacy to the Song, stimulating a tremendous burst of intellectual energy and creativity that accounted for a spectacular growth in historiography.

CHAPTER 5

The Song

Cultural Flourishing and the Blooming of Historiography

It is a historical cliché as well as truism that while the Song paled in comparison with the Tang imperium in terms of military accomplishments and territorial gains, it surpassed its predecessor in intellectual vitality and scholarly output, including the production of history. If it is correct to assert that the modern sense of history began with the European Renaissance, when three crucial intellectual perspectives emerged—a sense of anachronism, an awareness of evidence, and an interest in causation (Burke 1969, 1)—we may contend that such notions for remembering and ordering the past had already been amply evident in the Song.

We are not suggesting that the Song had a "modern" historical outlook in the same sense that Renaissance Europe was later supposed to have had. The examples of historical "modernity" in Song China did not amass sufficient ideational density to yield a coherent and consistent new consciousness about the past. Our making such a comparative observation is not to show the backwardness and ultimate futility of Chinese historical thinking vis-à-vis that of Renaissance Europe, whose path of development has been accepted as the norm of modernity; nor is it meant to anachronistically suggest that the Song scholars were mindfully forging a "modern" way of looking at their past. Rather, we want to highlight Song accomplishments in the pursuit of history not only in comparison with the antecedent Tang, but also in cross-cultural terms. As we explore Song historical production and thought by focusing on key personages and pivotal works, the three concerns—anachronism, evidence, and causation—serve as convenient narrative themes, evaluative criteria, and interpretive devices. Our data on the Song will, of course, demand the addition of others in order to paint an accurate and nuanced picture of historical learning in China from the tenth through the thirteenth century. Thomas Lee has shown that in addition to a sense of anachronism, Song historiography displayed other notable characteristics: a belief in a connection between literary style and the presentation of historical truths; a flourishing of historical criticism; and a perception of the nexus between disparate facts (Lee 2002, 59–60; Cf. Lee 2004b, xi–xxvii).

Ouyang Xiu and the Maturation of the Song Historiography

A strategic point of entry to historical learning in the Song is Ouyang Xiu (1007–1072). Ouyang was a towering political and intellectual figure with an enormous influence on the scholastic developments in the eleventh century. His contributions were pivotal in forging what historians call the "learning of the Qingli reign," which in many ways began the assertion of independence from the Tang and ushered in Song learning itself (Shibaki 1979, 637–650; James Liu 1967, 88). But lest we appear to subscribe uncritically to the Carlylean view that individual geniuses are the sole engine of history, we should place Ouyang's achievements in their proper context. It is noteworthy that even during the frequent regime changes and social upheaval of the so-called period of the Five Dynasties and Ten Kingdoms, the compilation of histories continued unabated. The *Gathering of Essentials of the Five Dynasties* (*Wudai huiyao*) compiled by Wang Pu and presented to the first Song emperor, Taizu, referred to five major veritable records produced in that tumultuous period (F. Tao 1987, 276; Balazs & Hervouet 1978, 177). And quite a few other veritable records appeared during the Five Dynasties, apart from those Wang listed (J. Jin 1976, 114).

Once the Song dynasty was established, historical compilations under the aegis of the court began to flourish. Following the conventions of the Tang, the Song court required production of the veritable records of the various reigns, based on the voluminous primary materials the court kept in the *qijuzhu* (diary of activity and repose), *shizheng ji* (records of current administration), and *rili* (daily records). The fourteen Song reigns, from Taizu (960–968) to Lizong (1225–1264), invariably produced veritable records, although none have survived except those of the Taizong reign, of which twenty fascicles (out of the original eighty) are extant (Balazs & Hervouet 1978, 84; Yin 1985, 199–200).

Besides these copious official annals, the Song periodically compiled a *guoshi* (national history) in the composite or annals-biography (*jizhuan*) style, which covered the important events of several reigns (L. Yang 1961, 45). These national histories were full-scale histories that quite resemble the standard dynastic histories in their organization; they contain basic annals (*benji*), monographs (*zhi*), and biographies (*zhuan*) (Hargett 1996, 426; Yin 1985, 200–201). Altogether, the Song compiled six national histories, the first of which, the *Taizu ji* (Records of [the reign of] Taizu) had only ten fascicles. Later compilations ballooned in size and details. The national history completed in 1030, for instance, covering the first three emperors' reigns, consisted of 150 fascicles (F. Tao 1987, 277–278).

Complementing these were the various "gathering of essentials" (*huiyao*), which detailed governmental institutions and administrative structures and regulations. Wang Pu's *Gathering of Essentials of the Five Dynasties,* is a good example. Two years earlier, in 961, Wang had produced another work of a hundred fascicles in a similar vein on the Tang, *Gathering of Essentials of the Tang* (*Tang huiyao*). These two *Gathering of Essentials* set the pattern for similar works in subsequent dynasties (F. Tao 1987, 278–279; W. Du 2004, 5–28). The early Song also showed keen interest in regions and localities, which resulted in a proliferation of local gazetteers (*difang zhi*), a key Song intellectual accomplishment. We will discuss this further below, but here it is sufficient to note the completion of the seminal and monumental 200-fascicle *Taiping huanyu ji* (Gazette of the territories in the Taiping era) in 980 by Yue Shi (930–1007), on which the eighteenth-century Qing dynasty compilers of the *Siku quanshu* (Encyclopedia of the four treasuries [of writings]) lavished this accolade: "This work is prolific and abundant in its gathering and collecting [of materials], and this is precisely because it seeks to be all-embracing and comprehensive" (Hargett 1996, 417). According to the Qing scholars, this work set the standard for thorough coverage and detail recording, guiding and informing later works of similar nature (ibid.).

Clearly official historiography was already in full swing by the time of Ouyang Xiu. Ouyang worked both in an official capacity at the History Bureau and as a private independent scholar. As an official historian, he played a crucial role in the compilation of the *New History of the Tang* (*Xin Tangshu*), a project that began under the editorial leadership of Song Qi (998–1061) in 1045. Ouyang became the chief editing official in 1055, and the 225-fascicle work was finally completed in 1060. Ouyang took charge of the historical narratives on the various reigns, creating tables and composing monographs on the various institutions. In private, Ouyang wrote the 74-fascicle *Historical Records of the Five Dynasties* (*Wudai shiji*), also commonly known as the *New History of the Five Dynasties* (*Xin Wudai shi*). Both works are generally characterized by terse, concise narratives, rendered in eloquent language. While they are undoubtedly examples of literary elegance, their content and qualities as histories warrant a close look. Both have been criticized for their threadbare descriptions of events, and therefore, despite the evident flaws of the *Old History of the Tang* and the *Old History of the Five Dynasties*, Ouyang's intended replacements of these old works do not quite do the job (James Liu 1967, 105–107; F. Tao 1987, 282–283; D. Wang 1997, 164–173; W. Du 2004, 42–51).

The *New History of the Tang* was unquestionably a more sophisticated history than the old version, in that the compilers, at the very least, had better access to source materials. The new work made far more effective use of tables (*biao*) and monographs (*zhi*). The tables, for instance, include military governors, prime ministers and their familiar pedigrees, and imperial genealogical charts. Those on the military governors (*fangzhen*) are especially useful in outlining the chaotic political configuration of institutions best characterized as military satrapies. The *New History* also has more and better monographs on specialized topics and added three valuable ones on rituals, the civil service examinations, and the military system. The monographs on geography, economy, and scholarship are more comprehensive than those in the *Old History*. In the *Old History*'s "Monograph on the Classics and Literature," for instance, one cannot find works by such masterful poets as Li Bo and Du Fu, or cultural giants like Han Yu and Liu Zongyuan, oversights that the *New History* appropriately remedied (Y. Song et al. 1987, 328–330; F. Tao 1987, 285).

Simply stated, while the *Old History* rested content with direct inclusion and literal restatement of Tang documents and primary sources, the *New History* aimed at forging a historical narrative with elegant language. Moreover, it strove for narrative concision and broad descriptions. The resulting work is highly readable and was praised by contemporaries and later scholars. However, what the *New History* gained in easy readability, it lost in detailed information. The work often failed to fully utilize the voluminous data available in the Tang veritable records. The biographies, unlike those in other standard histories, often do not include details on family background. There are glaring omissions, such as the exclusion of the famous seventh-century Buddhist pilgrim and scholar Xuanzang (596–664). The basic annals of the emperors (*benji*), to which the *Old History* devotes some 300,000 words, is whittled down by the *New History* to a scant 90,000 words. Zealously exercising his authorly prerogative, Ouyang radically altered and sometimes simply expunged Tang documents written in a florid style he disliked. Worse still, although Ouyang and his colleagues used much data ignored by or unavailable to the older work, they did not always carefully check the veracity of the new information. Already in the Song, the *New History* had its critics. Wu Zhen's *Corrected Errors in the New History of the Tang* (*Xin Tangshu jiumiu*), completed in 1089, lists some 460 problems. Wu boldly declared it to be one of the worst official standard histories. But his bilious attack may have been motivated by personal humiliation, for Ouyang had refused Wu's request to work on the Tang history project (F. Tao 1987, 284–286; Y. Song et al. 1987, 330; J. Jin 1976, 123; Balazs & Hervouet 1978, 67). Of greater significance, when Sima Guang, Ouyang's junior contemporary, worked on his own magnum opus, the *Comprehensive Mirror of Aid in Government,* he referred to and incorporated sources from the *Old Tang History* because the earlier history had done a better job of preserving original Tang materials (James Liu 1967, 107–108; J. Jin 1976, 121–124; W. Du 2004, 51–62).

While the *New History of the Tang* was a collective effort under official auspices, Ouyang Xiu wrote *Historical Records of the Five Dynasties* as a private endeavor. He began the work in 1036, when he suffered demotion and was banished to the subprefecture of Yiling just south of the Yangzi, after he had fallen from grace for his vociferous support of the outspoken reformer Fan Zhongyan (989–1052). In the long run this bureaucratic setback actually enhanced Ouyang's reputation as a courageous man of principle (James Liu 1967, 32–35, 108–109; Davis 2004, xlix–l). Ouyang's association with Fan and his reformist cause merits our attention to the extent that it sheds light on the way he approached the history of the Five Dynasties.

Fan Zhongyan had risen to prominence in 1025, when in a letter to the empress dowager and the emperor he forcefully proposed a grand vision for saving "this culture of ours." Fan and many other Song literati (*shi*) such as Ouyang had developed a clear notion of what they thought Chinese culture was and ought to be. This culture (*siwen*) was the cumulative tradition stemming from antiquity that accorded with the natural order of things. Embodied in this culture was the Way (*dao*) of the ancient sages, the normative tradition of China, access to which and realization of which was possible through the use of proper language and literature, especially works in the ancient style (*guwen*), individual moral cultivation, and institutional revival of a sociopolitical order run by talented, upright men. Within this grand vision, however, tension abounded; different literati placed different emphases on the relative importance of the various strands of thought. In the words of Peter Bol, Ouyang Xiu was "a pivotal figure in the eleventh century . . . because he gave full expression to this tension both by harkening back to Fan Chung-yen's call for the transformation of the sociopolitical order through institutional activism and by maintaining a view of culture and morality as the products of individual creativity" (1992, 5). While this is not the place to explore Ouyang's conception of culture—Bol has already done a marvelous job of it (1992, 178–185)—his valuation of Chinese culture did influence his historical view and how he wrote about the Five Dynasties.

Some historical background is germane here. The dynastic decline that began with the An Lushan Rebellion (755–763) in the mid-Tang stimulated the growth and consolidation of a system of military governorship (*jiedu shi*) that progressively dislodged the civil governance of the early Tang. By the time of the Huang Chao rebellion (875–884), military governors dominated China and openly flouted the authority of the Tang court. In 907 Zhu Wen (r. 907–912), the military governor of Henan, destroyed the Tang dynasty and ushered in the period of the Five Dynasties (907–960), a fifty-three-year span during which military governance was the norm (Y. Chen 1974, 1–49; Pulleyblank 1979, 32–60; C. Peterson 1979, 464–560).

Restoration of civil governance was the foremost goal of the early Northern Song rulers and literati. By the reigns of emperors Renzong (r. 1024–1063) and Shenzong (r. 1068–1085), a civil culture had finally become firmly entrenched. Wang Anshi (1021–1086) and Sima Guang, each with his own vision of a Confucian body politic and culture, advocated changes and reforms. The Learning of the Way (*daoxue*), forged by innovative scholars and thinkers such as Zhou Dunyi (1017–1073), Zhang Zai (1020–1077), Cheng Hao (1032–1085), and Cheng Yi (1033–1107), offered another conception of culture as it was supposedly embodied in the Way of the ancient sages. In literature we witness the accomplishments of Su Shi (1037–1101), and in arts, those of Guo Xi (ca. 1020–1090) (Hon 1999, 86–87). In other words Ouyang Xiu lived in a time when military predominance in the state and society appeared to have been safely consigned to the realm of memory. How, then, should the immediate past of the Five Dynasties be remembered? How should history process, represent, assimilate, and domesticate those unhappy and unsavory memories of military dominance?

Very early in the Northern Song, in 974, Xue Juzheng (912–981) had completed an account of the Five Dynasties called *The Old History of the Five Dynasties* (*Jiu Wudai shi*) (Shangjun Chen 1999, 98–117). But Ouyang Xiu thought that this text failed to properly censure the period; the work fell short of offering a correct historical view and understanding, and hence a better account was needed. In fact, this new account was not so much a historical recounting as contemporary reflecting. With the ascendance of civilian rule, Ouyang and the mid-Northern Song literati sought to employ history as a way to clarify and advance their Confucian visions, in the process defining themselves as conscientious *shi* who strove to realize their conceptions of the Confucian culture through practicing their learning. Refracted through Ouyang, the Five Dynasties was a distinctly un-Confucian period whose flaws must be identified and censured so that moral lessons could be drawn. Ouyang's goal, in a word, was unabashedly didactic. He saw himself as following the venerable example of the *Records of the Historian,* using history to reveal the profound principles of governing the state and society and of moral self-cultivation. But as a historian, he was also much inspired by Sima's critical attitude towards sources and had a strong preference for rational explanations of past events, as opposed to the belief in suprahuman intervention (Davis 2004, xlvii–lv).

Therefore, Ouyang's own *Records of the Historian* of the Five Dynasties — popularly known as the *New History of the Five Dynasties* — self-consciously set itself apart from the *Old History* by Xue Juzheng. Although the first complete draft was probably completed in 1053, the work was published posthumously, in 1077. Ouyang, in his *New History,* regarded the Five Dynasties as exemplars of political failure and moral turpitude, while the *Old History* had respected them as independent regimes that soberly came to grips with the particular problems of the time. Their divergent assumptions and conclusions about the fundamental nature of the Five Dynasties period greatly influenced the organization of each work. Ouyang's *New History* treats the Five Dynasties as one degenerate epoch, distinguished by political disintegration and social tumult, not to mention moral anomie and spiritual bankruptcy. His negative conception of the entire period denied the various dynasties any independent status, and therefore Ouyang did not give them separate treatment. Moreover, Ouyang's work does not bother to include monographs (*zhi*), principally because the author regarded the institutions of the Five Dynasties as unworthy of historical examination. Xue's *Old History,* which regarded the Five Dynasties as legitimate, their brevity notwithstanding, allotted each a separate book (*shu*), or history. It also includes twelve monographs on the institutions and implements of the period. The *New History,* ideologically driven by Ouyang's views of Confucian culture, adopts a narrative style that features elegant language and exquisite prose. It aims at succinct descriptions and highly synthesized accounts, seeking to instruct and thus lift up the minds and hearts of readers morally. It is a sophisticated amalgam of history and literature, melding moralism with empiricism (Davis 2004 xlv–xlvii). But the narrative terseness often deprives readers of factual details, while in contrast, the *Old History* delivers many more detailed narratives, albeit in drier prose, frequently simply quoting contemporary primary sources. Xue's work is quite valuable in terms of preserving the raw historical materials, but his indiscriminate reiteration of them takes their veracity for granted and repeats many of their false claims, such as Zhu Wen's claim that he was descended from Zhu Fu, an official who worked for the ancient sage-ruler Shun. Many of Xue's accounts, although lengthier and fuller with facts, are not coherent stories with a beginning, middle and end, whereas Ouyang's laconic narratives are cohesive. Ouyang, who used original sources more critically and consulted more materials, was also able to correct many of the older work's errors (F. Tao 1987, 286–287; Hon 1999, 88–89; Gungwu Wang 1973, 53–63). It is noteworthy that Ouyang's history was a private endeavor, not subject to the usual constraints on court-sponsored compilations. It was, moreover, written generations after the Five Dynasties and aimed not at the imperial readership—the court and the ministers—but at other scholars interested in history. This conception of a broad, historical audience gave Ouyang an authorial freedom that encouraged stylistic innovations and substantive richness (Davis 2004, lvi–lvii; W. Du 2004, 42–51).

The authors' personal histories also affected their historical verdicts on the period between the Tang and Song. Xue Juzheng served as an official in four of the short-lived dynasties. Whether motivated by self-justification or dispassionate historical judgment, Xue believed that the Five Dynasties had developed a workable logic for government and political succession, in which expediency demanded that civil officials of one regime readily switch loyalty and serve another. He did not criticize military rule but accepted it as a necessity (Gungwu Wang 1957, 22–40). Ouyang lived some two generations later, when the civilian psychology had permeated the court and officialdom. As a literatus who viewed his own time and state with satisfaction, confident in the glorious nature of the culture of the day, the Five Dynasties could only appear inferior and brutish. The authors' contemporary situations figured prominently in their historical reconstructions, where they disagreed specifically on four major issues, as Tze-ki Hon (1999, 89–99) points out: the Mandate of Heaven, the Sino-Khitan relationship, kinship based upon adoption, and the moral mission of a Confucian scholar.

Every dynasty maintained its claim to power and political legitimacy by virtue of its putative reception of the Mandate of Heaven, so both Xue and Ouyang had to wrestle with the question of why there were repeated regime changes in the period of the Five Dynasties. Xue held that Heaven's intentions were beyond the understanding and prediction of humanity, whose only sure knowledge of Heaven's intent came through portents and omens. Zhu Wen, who brought Tang rule to an end, was able to do so because he responded to the signs from heaven.

Ouyang Xiu, by contrast, stressed human agency. A degeneration in human affairs explained dynastic decline and collapse, while the flourishing of culture meant dynastic prosperity. This principle was the Mandate of Heaven, according to which the people had the right to dislodge an immoral and corrupt government. To Ouyang, the rapid succession of the regimes in the period of the Five Dynasties revealed the simple fact that there was no Mandate from Heaven whatsoever, as none of the rulers upheld the Confucian Way by consolidating and securing the Five Relationships (emperor-minister, father-son, husband-wife, older brother-younger brother, and friend-friend). Rejecting Xue's political theory predicated on cosmological imperative, Ouyang argued for an activist moral agency operative within the bounds of civil governance based on Confucian mores and ethics. The Five Dynasties were illegitimate precisely because they "brought chaos to" or "confused" (*luan*) the Confucian moral order (Hon 1999, 89–92; Davis 2004, l–lii).

Another paramount issue that no historian at the time could ignore was the role of the Khitan Liao, a menacing force in the north. Shi Jingtang (r. 937–942), founder of the Later Jin dynasty, had ceded them sixteen prefectures in Hebei in 937. Military endeavors by the Northern Song to recover the lost territories were to no avail, and finally, in 1004, the Treaty of Shanyuan accepted the existing boundary (Franke & Twitchett 1995, 108–111). Xue's *Old History* justified Shi's action, arguing that Shi, a Shatuo Turk, could not have toppled the Later Tang without the prompt assistance given him by the Khitan ruler, who personally led his forces to fight on behalf of Shi. It was therefore understandable that Shi, in his gratitude, yielded land to, and pledged to be a son of, the Khitan ruler. Xue gives ample examples of such forged familial relationships, the so-called practice of "uniting hearts by sharing the same family name" (*xixing yi jie qi xin*), which dated back to early Tang times when the dynasty bestowed the royal family name of Li on many Shatuo Turks. Xue essentially saw China as a multiethnic entity, held together not by ancestry but by diplomacy that included such stabilizing practices as pledging to be a ruler's son. But of course Xue did serve in three Shatuo dynasties—the Later Tang, the Later Jin, and the Later Han.

Ouyang Xiu, on the other hand, was highly conscious of the division between China and the barbarians (*yidi*). In his era the Song dynasty faced a host of threatening forces in the north, and Ouyang worried about the survival of China not just as a political unit but also as a cultural entity. Shi Jingtang's intermingling with the Khitan amounted to the destruction of the time-honored rites and rituals of China by subverting the cardinal Confucian values of the Three Bonds (*sangang*) and Five Constancies (*wuchang*), and ignoring normal human relationships and familial ties based on blood. Small wonder, according to Ouyang, that virtuous figures in the Five Dynasties were few and far between (Hon 1999, 92–95).

The practice of "uniting hearts by sharing the same family name" often meant that the adopted son would treat his adopted father as his real father and forsake ties with his natal father. This practice of forging kinship by mutual consent had also enabled the generals in the late Tang and the Five Dynasties to build an elite army known as the "Army of the Adopted Sons" (*yi'er jun*), and many emperors in the Five Dynasties were adopted sons and stepbrothers. Although these men did not inherit the throne by virtue of ancestry and blood relations, Xue Juzheng maintained that they had every right to become ruler because kinship was not solely the product of birth. An adopted son, by dint of loyalty, ability, and hard work, was perfectly qualified to continue a dynastic line.

Ouyang saw such indiscriminate adoption as usurpation of the bloodline, which threatened the very core of the Confucian familial value-system. Artificial kinship based upon mutual consent was motivated by profit and gain and devoid of love and affection. In an attempt to reinforce traditional notions of kinship based on blood ties, Ouyang made a point to include in his *New History* a separate chapter on the family system in the Five Dynasties, the "Chapter on Kinfolk" (Jiaren juan) (Hon 1999, 95–97; Davis 2004 lxvii–lxxiii).

Xue and Ouyang also differed in their conception of the mission of a scholar-official, a disagreement well encapsulated in their judgment of the official Feng Dao (882–954). Feng served as a civil official in four of the Five Dynasties. A skillful negotiator and able politician, he worked under the military leaders, acting as their liaison with the civil officialdom (Gungwu Wang 1962, 123–145). Xue found Feng to be an appealing character, who delicately bridged the chasm between the military and the civil. Moreover, he fulfilled the role of a Confucian scholar to the extent that dutifully playing the role of a minister (*chen*) to an emperor (*jun*) fulfilled the first of the Five Relationships. As one who himself served four different dynasties, Xue saw nothing improper in Feng Dao's tenure under four rulers. A change in regime was the will of Heaven, and to faithfully serve a new ruler was to submit to the Mandate of Heaven.

In Ouyang's depiction, we see a very different Feng Dao, one deserving the most severe moral censure. Ouyang provides scant details on Feng's life but focuses on exposing Feng as an unprincipled official cloaked in Confucian garb. By fulsomely serving any military strong man who happened to be in power, Feng personified the moral degeneration of the Five Dynasties. Ouyang's project to define Confucian culture and the mid-Northern Song's enterprise to consolidate civil governance could not have permitted a generous account of Feng Dao. Ouyang's condemnation of Feng was not merely a condemnation of one person but of an entire age during which weak-kneed civil officialdom cowered before the military state. The ephemeral loyalty of the literati was on full display. They were readily seduced by and succumbed to immediate personal gains (Hon 1999, 97–99; Davis 2004 lxxiii–lxxvi, 430–443).

Comparing the two histories allows us to witness how shifting contemporary situations colored historical perspectives and views. Xue, living in an age dominated by martial institutions and values, took for granted the importance of expediency and compromise so that civil officials might play a meaningful role in the state and society. Ouyang, on the other hand, sought to expunge the last remnants of military governance and un-Confucian practices. He wanted to revivify what he considered the Confucian way of living that depended on absolute moral values and civil governance safeguarded by virtuous men of talents, the *shi*.

The two works, especially Ouyang's history, also amply illustrate the time-honored didactic historical practice of praise and blame established in Confucius' *Spring and Autumn Annals*. Indeed, it was in Song times that this principle came to be used in a highly pervasive, deliberate, and systematic fashion. Ouyang's excoriation of Feng Dao was a perfect example of condemnation through historical judgment. At the same time, Ouyang also distinguished those personages he deemed virtuous and loyal by placing them in biographical narratives entitled "Martyrs to Political Integrity" and "Martyrs to Duty," thereby creating a sort of taxonomy of virtues. Praise and blame were sometimes accorded in a more subtle manner. When describing a man whom Ouyang considered virtuous and righteous, he would focus only on his most notable accomplishments and admirable work, and gloss over his flaws and mistakes which he judged ultimately irrelevant since they did not detract from the man's general worth (Davis 2004, 439–443). Interestingly enough, Ouyang did not claim authorship of the commentaries in the *New History of the Five Dynasties*, where many such commendations and censures appeared. His kinsman and pupil, Xu Wudang, was indicated to be the author. Ouyang may have done this because he realized the potency of such historical judgments in the fractious politics that engulfed the court and officialdom of his time. It was, in the end, advisable to attribute such evaluations to Xu, who, not being part of the political center, was above the fray of factionalism (James Liu 1967, 109–111; Gardner 1938, 12–13; L. Yang 1961, 52).

That Ouyang had presentist concerns and didactic proclivities does not mean that he was an unprincipled, slipshod historian. Ouyang had very specific views about how accurate, factual history should be written and could be produced. He was keenly aware of the shortcomings of court-sponsored official histories, for instance, because individual views and judgments were often submerged, and authors had to toe the official lines of interpretation. But private historical observations and compilations were not so constrained. Thus, apart from writing the history of the Five Dynasties on his own, which eventually received the official imprimatur as a standard history, Ouyang produced *Notes on Returning to the Farm (Guitian lu)*, a collection of notes on events that had escaped the attention of official histories (James Liu 1967, 105). What Ouyang did reflected a common scholarly penchant in the Song, when many literati took to keeping such notes. Eventually they would produce collections of these notes, and *biji* (miscellaneous notes), as these were called, became a popular genre. Although some of these writings fall into the category of literature and fiction, they also yield information of undeniable historical import and value (Lee 2002, 67–68).

Ouyang, like many other Song scholars, was most attentive to the marshaling of information. It is not surprising that, owing to the lack of reliable sources, Ouyang treated the history of antiquity with great caution. He admired the classics, especially the *Spring and Autumn Annals,* with its terse language but apt arguments that said exactly what was valuable in government and everyday practice. If the narrative was skimpy, Ouyang reasoned, it was because Confucius only wrote about what could be corroborated by evidence. For this reason Ouyang regarded with healthy skepticism the elaborations found in the three commentaries to the *Annals.* What troubled him the most was the inclusion of details whose veracity had not been established, a bad practice he thought Han scholars often committed. Even Sima Qian's magnificent *Records of the Historian* did not escape Ouyang's critique for being indiscriminate in its collection and use of information and for failing to excise the bizarre and curious (James Liu 1967, 100–101).

This rage for evidence explains why Ouyang developed a tremendous interest in many related branches of learning. He was actively involved in creating the *Chongwen zongmu,* a catalog of the imperial library. It was a bibliographic innovation in that each of 3,445 titles was annotated, and Ouyang explained how the annotations were and should be done. As a result of the Song's general preoccupation with collecting texts and documents, there existed a fair number of personal libraries that held 25,000 to 50,000 volumes (Davis, 1988, 73; James Liu 1967, 102). Ouyang was also drawn to archaeology, including the study of bronzes, stones, and other artifacts that contributed valuable raw data from the past. From 1045 to 1062 Ouyang collected, catalogued, and annotated inscriptions found on bronze vessels and implements and on stone steles, producing a work of ten fascicles entitled *Jigu lu* (Records of collecting antiques), in which there were more than four hundred colophons. He employed the primary material harvested from such physical artifacts to investigate the accuracy of earlier historical accounts. He not only initiated the technical, antiquarian study of epigraphy, but he also devoted considerable energy to preserving contemporary sources. He argued that the successive drafts of the national history, compiled as raw data for the production of the standard history by the succeeding dynasty, should be conscientiously preserved for future reference. Moreover, he boldly contended that the completed history should not be presented to the emperor so that compilers would not have to worry about incurring royal displeasure, thereby ensuring their independence and impartiality (James Liu 1967, 102–103; W. Du 2004, 63–66).

This attention to evidence nourished Ouyang's skepticism about the veracity of ancient history and texts. Even the classics were not safe from his scrutiny. Ouyang wrote critical works on the *Classic of Changes,* in which he questioned the generally accepted view that Confucius was the author of "Ten Wings," the appended philosophical elaborations. Likewise, he took issue with the standard Mao and Zheng commentaries to the *Classic of Poetry,* faulting their uncritical incorporation of the supernatural from the apocrypha of the Qin-Han period (F. Tao 1987, 288–294). Most notably, Ouyang found the traditional interpretations of *zhengtong* (legitimate political and dynastic succession) at best problematic and at worst untenable. In traditional Confucian historiography the succession of dynasties was explicated in terms of the legitimate continuation of power by a "proper" (*zheng*) ruler who forged "unity" (*tong*). Because of its virtue and moral excellence the new dynasty received the Mandate of Heaven and properly assumed political power by legitimately succeeding the defunct dynasty. The moral assumptions were buttressed by metaphysical beliefs that political change coincided with cosmological transformations. Celestial omens such as eclipses and falling stars signaled the end of a moribund dynasty and heralded the beginning of a new vital one. Just as the five phases or agents of earth, metal, water, wood, and fire succeeded one another and generated in the process movements and phenomena in the natural world, so too in the human world of politics and government, one dynasty followed another in a highly teleological manner. Such was the ideal, holistic integration of Heaven, earth, and humanity (Shigezawa 1972, 395–406; Davis 1988, 68–69; Rao 1977, 1–27; H. Chan 1984, 19–48).

Ouyang placed little store in correlations between celestial portents and human affairs. In the *New History* he argued that in the *Spring and Autumn Annals*, Confucius had merely recorded the strange and catastrophic without matching them with events in the human world. It was only in Han times that prognosticatory excesses and speculative fancies came to dominate observation and study of the extraterrestrial realm, to the point where the theories of the Five Phases acquired much occultist influence in the interpretations of human events.

Ouyang also disparaged the easy juxtaposition of morality with politics in dynastic succession. While he lavishly praised the ancient Three Dynasties of the Xia, the Shang, and the Zhou, and the later empires of the Han and the Tang as classic examples of legitimate succession and governance —they all admirably forged the happy union of moral imperatives with political prerogatives—he pointedly accepted the legitimacy of the short-lived Qin and Siu dynasties that were generally regarded as morally degenerate. Ouyang endorsed their legitimate status because they had succeeded in establishing political mastery over the entire domain of China. To Ouyang, *zheng* could not always be realized in the context of *tong*. A regime's initial lack of moral virtues could be rectified by its continued ability to wield effective power. By bringing about stability and peace, it acquired legitimacy. Unlike the *Old History of the Tang*, Ouyang's *New History* accorded separate annals to the reign of the notorious usurper, Empress Wu, and thus affirmed the legitimacy of her rule, even though his judgments on this female ruler were far from lenient. But for Ouyang, faithful recording of what actually occurred in the past claimed priority over moral judgment. He further averred that the line of legitimate succession, in actual history, could not be continuous since political disruptions perforce meant inevitable lapses. He faulted historians for artificially constructing a pattern of continuous succession where none existed (Davis 1988, 69–73; James Liu 1967, 111–112).

Sima Guang and the High Point of Song Historiography

In Song historiography few matched Ouyang's stature as a great historian distinguished for interpretive astuteness, empirical precision, methodological innovation, and stylistic elegance—with the exception of Sima Guang. In fact, Sima is arguably a more accomplished historian, and is often compared with the great Sima Qian of the Han. His major claim to fame was his authorship of the voluminous *Comprehensive Mirror for Aid in Government*, a work of 294 fascicles. It was nineteen years in the making and covered more than 1,300 years from 403 B.C.E. to C.E. 959. It was the first general history written in the chronicle or annalistic style.

Sima began his project by creating a chronological table, the *Li'nian tu* (Chart of successive years), which he presented to the court in 1064. Two years later, he submitted a historical account of the Warring States period from 403 to 206 B.C.E., entitled the *Tongzhi* (Comprehensive records), which, in revised form, became the first eight fascicles of the *Comprehensive Mirror*. Emperor Yingzong (r.1063–1067) was so impressed that he granted the project imperial patronage, supplying Sima with personal assistance, historical resources, and financial remuneration. The memorial that Sima submitted enunciated the objectives of his ambitious enterprise.

> Since I was a child I have ranged through all the histories. It has appeared to me that in the annals-biography form the words are diffuse and numerous so that even an erudite specialist who reads them again and again cannot comprehend and sort them out; how much the more, though a prince amid his ten thousand daily concerns must wish to know comprehensively the merits and demerits of former ages, will it be difficult for him to accomplish his desire. Disregarding my inadequacy I have constantly wished to write a chronological history roughly in accordance with the form of the *Zuo Commentary*, starting with the Warring States and going down to the Five Dynasties, drawing on other books besides the Official Histories and taking in all that a prince ought to know—everything pertaining to the rise and fall of dynasties and the good and ill fortune of the common people, all good and bad examples that can furnish models and warnings. (Pulleyblank 1961, 153–154, modified transliteration)

Dissatisfied with the composite style of the standard histories—which often truncated the life stories of individuals and the development of events and interspersed related information in the four sections of basic annals, monographs, tables, and biographies—and inspired by the *Zuo Commentary*, Sima adopted the annalistic style of presenting events in an effort to minimize narrative redundancy and reveal historical continuities. Undoubtedly, he compiled this vast history also because he was convinced of history's didactic function. By constructing a history from antiquity to the present, he would expose the dynamic patterns and underlying causes of peace and disorder. And by studying the past and learning its lessons, rulers and the scholar-officials might design the best ways of governance.

In 1067, when Sima recited his *Tongzhi* in the presence of Emperor Shenzong (r. 1067–1085), he won the admiration of the new ruler, who gave the work the much grander title of *Comprehensive Mirror for Aid in Government*, together with a preface. He also received from the emperor the gift of a library collection. With imperial blessings, Sima set up his own history office with his own collaborators, first Liu Bin[1] (1023–1089) and Liu Shu (1032–1078), and later Fan Zuyu (1041–1098). Imperial aegis notwithstanding, his office was independent and autonomous, fully under his oversight and management, and so his work was in essence a private history (Pulleyblank 1961, 151–154; F. Tao 1987, 296–297).

Soon after his project started, Sima, a conservative statesman, became embroiled in factional politics engendered by contending cultural visions and state policies. He found himself pitted against Wang Anshi, who had gained imperial favor for his planned radical reforms. Sima, with his firm conceptions of sound learning and a healthy polity, was adamantly opposed to the obtrusive New Policies Wang proposed and then implemented (Bol 1992, 212–253; James Liu 1959, 105–108). As Wang and his partisans held sway, Sima withdrew from active politics to a sinecure position. What he lost in political clout, he gained in historical productivity. His fifteen-year (1071–1085) withdrawal meant time and energy to complete his grand compilation. Sima's correspondence with his assistant Fan Zuyu provides revealing glimpses into his methodology in organizing his research and writing.

The process began with a chronologically ordered outline. For each chronological segment, pertinent sources of all sorts were amassed and consulted, including the veritable records, standard histories, literary collections, geographical works, biographies, inscriptions, and others, references to which were placed in the proper places in the outline. Additional headings were added as they became necessary. Then came the writing of the "long draft" (*changbian*) that utilized the sources included in the outline. It was a laborious and meticulous process of examining the primary materials, choosing the best accounts, determining the reasons for discrepancies between sources, and ensuring that the versions chosen were the best. Notes were actually made in the draft to explain the inclusion or excision of sources. They were in some ways akin to the modern bibliographical references that provided detailed information on the sources on which the *Comprehensive Mirror* was based. Estimates of the number of works Sima and his collaborators examined range from 220 to 322. The

---

1. The transliteration "Liu Bin" appears in Balazs and Hervouet's *Sung Bibliography*. But the character for "Bin" is commonly pronounced "Ban," so the glossary lists "Liu Ban," with "Liu Bin" noted afterward.

overarching principle was that a lengthy draft was better than a short one, so that important sources would not be inadvertently omitted. Finally, the long draft was distilled to a proper narrative containing the most important points. The draft on the Tang dynasty, which amounted to more than 600 fascicles, was ultimately condensed into an account of some 100 fascicles. When the *Comprehensive Mirror* was completed in 1084, Sima presented it to the court, together with an "Outline" (Mulu) and an "Examination of Discrepancies" (Kaoyi), each in thirty fascicles. The "Examination of Discrepancies" is particularly significant, for it discusses, in a highly objective fashion, the inconsistencies and tensions among the sources and delineates the careful ways in which Sima and his associates arrived at their final narrative. Sima argued that as far as possible historical accounts should be constructed on the basis of direct evidence. In cases where direct evidence was unavailable, critical judgment had to be used to choose the account that "seems to be closest to the truth" (Pulleyblank 1961, 157). By scrutinizing and marshaling objective evidence, and by carefully exercising subjective but judicious historical imagination—considering the motives of historical actors, examining the circumstances surrounding events, and probing the probable causes of actions—the historian arrived at the best account that was closest to the truth (Liu & Song 1986, 1–5; W. Du 2004, 73–78).

As with Ouyang Xiu, Sima did not let his moral revulsion from certain historical personages compromise his empirical dedication to facts. In the case of Empress Wu, commonly regarded as a perfidious and hence immoral usurper, the *Comprehensive Mirror* duly recorded her reign titles. With respect to the Warring States period, it noted and recognized the assumption of the royal title of *wang* (king) by the feudal states of Qin, Chu, and Wei, even though, as we shall see, Sima was much devoted to a hierarchical polity governed by proper rituals and designations (Davis 1988, 70). Just as Ouyang had evaluated political legitimacy and orthodox succession in terms of actual political accomplishments and not the metaphysical schema of the Five Phases, so Sima declared that the effort to establish extraterrestrial correlation with human affairs was merely one technique rulers used to justify their authority. A ruler might grandiloquently proclaim that he had received Heaven's blessings, but if he failed to assert firm control over his domain, he in fact had no legitimacy. Sima submitted that he, as a historian, did "not presume to understand the transitions of political legitimacy, but simply [talked] about them in terms of their [i.e., the regimes'] actual efforts and accomplishments" (Zhuang 2001, 107). In other words he wanted to shift the basis for discussions about the rise and fall of powers from a moral-cosmological one to a historical one. Sima did not have patience for histories that gave credibility to the supernatural. Mortality was part of life and the Daoist occultist and esoteric teachings that sought to overcome this fundamental existential fact were simply nonsense, to which no authentic history should lend credence (F. Tao 1987, 310–314; Tillman 2004, 63–69; W. Du 2004, 79–87).

Read in light of modern historiographical standards, the *Comprehensive Mirror* does, however, leave something to be desired. In spite of its elegant narrative flow and rigorous use of evidence, the work is not, in the end, a history. It is a chronicle that treats events in isolation without contextual interconnection with related and circumstantial happenings. It views the past through the narrow political lens of the rise and fall of dynasties, giving very short shrift to institutional, intellectual, economic, and social developments. Sometimes it takes evidence for granted and does not subject the sources to sufficient interrogation with regard to their provenance and interrelations. Nevertheless, within the format of a chronicle and guided by his conception of authentic history, Sima strove to shape the past with impartiality and arrive at truth on objective grounds (F. Tao 1987, 297–301; Pulleyblank 1961, 155–158; K. Hsu 1983; Song et al. 1987, 336–339).

Sima produced other historical works, most notably the *Jigu lu* (Records of examining the past), in twenty fascicles, and the *Baiguan tu* (Tables of the hundred offices). The former was presented to the court in 1086 as a sort of enlarged version of the *Li'nian tu*, the blueprint of the *Comprehensive Mirror*. It opened with the reign of the legendary sage-ruler of Fuxi and closed with the Song history up to the year 1067. Four fascicles were devoted to the first five Song reigns. The *Tables of the Hundred Offices*, commissioned by the court and completed in 1081, was a study of the Song officialdom. Sima also composed two collections of miscellaneous notes. The first, the *Sushui jiwen* (Records of what the man of the Su river heard) recorded events of the Song. The second, the *Shiyan* (Discerning history), was a historical critique of the legends about the ancient rulers of Yao, Shun, and Yu, especially those conveyed and discussed by Mencius (Bol 1992, 233–234; F. Tao 1987, 296; Balazs & Hervouet 1978, 100–101, 393).

In various works Sima left us clear clues to his very specific view of history and the past. First and foremost, he argued that insofar as the causes of political and dynastic prosperity, degeneration, and demise had remained the same throughout the ages, we may use the past as exemplars; it provided lessons for the rectification of present problems. Such was the didactic function of history. For Sima, there were the immutable Way (*dao*) and Pattern (*ti*) of order and chaos, and they linked the present and the past as a single thread (*yiguan*). To write histories was to illuminate universal principles by bringing into sharp relief particular circumstances. But timeless principles notwithstanding, human action and agency manifested in individual events constituted the dynamics of history and demonstrated the workings of the consistent principles. According to Sima these principles were manifested in terms of imperial statecraft, that is, what the ruler and the state ought to do. One of the most important things was to uphold the ritual order (*li*) which distinguished the roles (*fen*) of the ruler, ministers, and all others in the commonweal, each of whom had their proper names (*ming*). The ritual order forged a stable hierarchy of superiors and inferiors. This human world of ritualistic ordering cohered with the natural order of Heaven-and-earth, where the Great Ultimate (*taiji*) gave rise to the cosmic numbers of two, four, and eight, *ad infinitum.* Preserving the structure of authority based on *li* ensured enduring fortune and lasting peace (Xiao-bin Ji 2004, 5–21; Bol 1992, 233–246).

Sima placed tremendous moral responsibility on the ruler. History told him that the one central *dao* or Way of rulership was the ability to effectively employ talented and trustworthy men from whom the ruler must accept remonstrance. Mistakes were an unavoidable fact of the human condition. A good ruler was not one who did not err, but one who promptly rectified his errors by listening to advice. At the same time the ruler must use his human resources effectively by dispensing proper rewards and punishments (Xiao-bin Ji 2004, 21–26). Realization of the Way of rulership further depended on the possession three virtues: *ren* (benevolence), *ming* (sagacity), and *wu* (strength). Sima explained that benevolence did not mean tenderhearted tolerance of mistakes and negligence, but the effort to teach and morally transform the polity, nurture the people, and better the state and society. Sagacity did not refer to cunning intelligence that was used for relentless and unscrupulous scrutiny. Rather, it was the knowledge of the righteous principles, that is, the recognition of what was safe and what was perilous, and the capacity to discriminate right from wrong. Strength was not oppression, but the firmness to remain steadfastly committed to the correct *dao* in face of treachery and flattery. Studying the past, Sima thought, we can realize this historically demonstrated universal rule: "When the three things [i. e., virtues] are all there, the state has a strong rule. When one is missing, [the state] is weak. When two are missing [the state] is in jeopardy. When not even one is present, [the state] perishes" (F. Tao 1987, 305). Clearly Sima used particular historical data to construct universal principles, according to which the ruler might be guided and cautioned.

That history served as the moral exemplar and ethical arbiter was a notion broadly accepted in Song China. Zeng Gong's (1019–1083) proclamation, when describing how he chose materials for the *Official History of the First Five Reigns of the Song Dynasty,* was typical: "[I]f there is good and evil, which may be used to encourage or warn, and right and wrong, which could be contemplated by later generations, then it will be recorded in detail. Accounts of normal conduct will not be prepared" (Hartwell 1971, 692).

Didactic and Analogical Uses of the Past: History as Contemporary Guide

The past was not only deemed useful, but to Ouyang, Sima, and many other literati in the Song, history provided apt analogies to illustrate and illuminate the social, political, and economic conditions of the present. In short, history was construed in terms of what we may label two ideal types: "historical didacticism" and "historical analogism." While historical didacticism provided moral edification through the lives of individuals, historical analogism, as Robert Hartwell argues, focused on social institutions, with the idea that juxtaposition of similar phenomena in the past and present would yield invaluable comparative insights that would guide contemporary policies. While historical didacticism tended to slip over what was considered morally unsavory, such as dynastic devolution, political disintegration, and foreign incursions and conquests, historical analogism confronted all records and events head-on, convinced that through meticulous study of all events, good and bad, understanding of the current state and society could be established.

Small wonder that in the Song, reading and discoursing on history before the throne became an entrenched system. Rulers were given continuous education via the institutionalized imperial lectures and seminars. Sima Guang's compilation of the *Comprehensive Mirror* was closely involved with this practice of supplying the throne with historical education, and it became one of the histories often read, studied, and discussed in the imperial disquisitions. This system of imperial seminars or lectures, or *jing-yan,* persisted over the next nine centuries. The perceived importance of history in statecraft made it requisite knowledge to be tested in the civil service examinations, where candidates were expected to use historical examples and models to substantiate their views on current practical problems in state and society. History was much taught and highly valued in the schools that had to prepare the candidates for the civil service examinations (Hartwell 1971, 694–699, 703–709).

The study of histories perforce included study of the classics, but the abiding belief was that the past repeated itself and thus history, whether ancient or recent, provided models for contemporary policies. Because of the Song's temporal proximity to the Tang, there was a rage for study of recent history (Lee 2002, 62–63). Zhang Fangping (1007–1091), who initiated the project of revising the *Tang History,* the completion of which owed much to Ouyang Xiu's participation, declared: "Therefore, from the point of view of the contemporary political system, the T'ang is the closest. . . . I desire to have permission to have outlines composed of matters recorded in the biographies and annals of T'ang history, which may be incorporated into present policy and benefit the way of good administration. . . . This was also the intention of Chia I and Ch'ao Ts'o in borrowing Ch'in as analogous to Han" (Hartwell 1971, 695). Fan Zuyu (1041–1098), upon completing his famous *Tang Jian* (Tang mirror), memorialized the throne by saying "[w]hat we can now best hope to use as a mirror is appropriately the T'ang" (Lee 2002, 62).

Arguably, this preference for the history of the Tang adumbrates an incipient awareness that the passage of time meant differences between one time segment and another. It mitigated the time-nullifying classicism that looked back to antiquity as the principal source of inspiration. There was a gradually emergent sense of anachronism. Ouyang Xiu, in the *New History of the Tang,* while celebrating the admirable unity of morals and politics in antiquity and lamenting its dissolution in later times, did not call for the return to antiquity. That, as he indicated, was impossible because the present was different. Ouyang contended that antiquity had come to an end when the Qin established new institutions because politics had been severed from the morals embedded in the rites. It would be futile to ape ancient institutions, although we ought to appreciate and revive the ancient spirit of integrating the moral and the political (Mittag 2004, 204–208; Bol 1992, 195–201). Similarly, even though Sima Guang sought to distill universal, and therefore timeless, principles from history, especially those recorded in the *Spring and Autumn Annals,* he drew attention to the particularities of events, time and again stressing the fact that human actions in specific circumstances were sui generis (Bol 1992, 237). Su Xun (1009–1066) also argued that the classics could be fully understood only in terms of and in conjunction with history, as changes were integrally a part of time, where human agency and surrounding circumstances intersected (Lee 2002, 63–64).

This growing trend of seeking knowledge and insight from the dynamic flow of history did not end appeals to the ancient classics as storehouses of perennial values and blueprints for institutions. To many, the classics and the antiquity they described furnished the timeless cultural standards against which present policies and affairs should be measured. It is, however, important to note that this identification with antiquity did not necessarily mean an uncritical, ahistorical urge to repeat the pristine past. Harking back to the ancient past was a form of historical-mindedness. Wang Anshi's classicism is a case in point. It is well known that Wang's New Policies were much inspired by the classics, specifically *The Institutions of the Zhou (Zhouli)*, which painted an idealized, utopian picture of the antique culture and polity (James Liu 1959, 30–52). But Wang sought no literal return to the past. He pointed out that the ancients themselves created institutions that were in accord with change. To follow antiquity was not to borrow its institutions, but to establish a ritual and normative order in a coherent, organized, and systematic fashion. Thus, the classics were valuable not because they offered specific, individual models for particular institutions and rites but because they suggested the general way to transform the policy wholesale by creating the most appropriate, efficacious ritual order. To Wang, the classics recorded change while simultaneously prescribing a holistic architectonics of mores, rites, and institutions (Bol 1992, 224–233).

Whether it was to tap classical inspiration, perform didactic functions, or establish analogical models, the Song literati, encouraged by the practical reward of success in the civil service examinations, produced history and related works in great quantity and quality. Since history had come to be viewed as the basis of contemporary statecraft, it became highly desirable to compile historical works that classified events and documents so that they might be readily consulted and called into the service by scholars and bureaucrats. Sima Qian had, in the Han, established the monograph, a format which was copied by the standard histories of the various later dynasties. Each monograph covered a specific subject such as geography, finance, astronomy, government apparatuses, or military organization. They were very useful for any exercise requiring historical analogies, but these topically oriented chapters tended to deal with only one dynasty. Liu Zhi, son of the great Tang historical critic Liu Zhiji, produced the first encyclopedic compilation, entitled *The Administrative Compendium* (*Zhengdian*), that systematically recorded historical phenomena for the expressed purpose of providing aid for statecraft. This work, no longer extant, established the template for later compilations, such as Du You's influential *The Comprehensive Compendium* [*on Institutions*] (*Tongdian*). Now, in Song times, there arose a genre known as the *shengzheng lu* (imperial policy chronicle), which in format may be seen as a sort of amalgamation of Sima's *Comprehensive Mirror* and Du's *Comprehensive Compendium*. Written in the annalistic style, materials were ordered chronologically and commentaries were inserted at various places. These commentaries often offered interesting elaborations and analyses. To make the topics under discussion readily apparent, subject headings were listed on the upper margin of every page, and these in turn were entered in a categorized table of topics (Hartwell 1971, 710–711).

In addition, facilitated by the development of printing technology and stimulated by the expansion of geographic knowledge as a result of two centuries of southward thrust and migration, the Song witnessed a proliferation of encyclopedias, or *leishu* (literally, books with classifications). Although these encyclopedic works often included fictional sources, they were rich repositories of historical materials and records (Haeger 1968, 401–409; Lee 2002, 73; Z. Huang 2001, 21). An outstanding example of the *leishu* is the *Archival Palace as the Great Oracle* (*Cefu yuangui*) in 1,000 fascicles, compiled by imperial fiat under Wang Qinruo's (962–1025) directorship. Unlike many other encyclopedic works, the *Archival Palace as the Great Oracle* was truly a historical encyclopedia whose initial working title was *Records of the Lives and Deeds of Rulers and Officials of the Successive Dynasties*. It was renamed by the Emperor Zhenzong in 1013, when the anthology was completed. The new name clearly alluded to the didactic function of history. Just as the ancients used the turtle shell (*yuangui*) as the oracle of divination, so the copious historical and archival records of the lives of the rulers would serve as a sagacious guide to current governance. The emperor himself declared, "It is my desire that this work, through illuminating the events of the successive dynasties, will provide the institutional exemplars and models for the future" (Z. Huang 2001, 25).

The work comprises thirty-one sections, each dealing with a category of the Song polity, ranging from the emperors and princes to the vassals of tributary territories. It offers information on personages and offices, establishing in the process a value system and normative world view via historical judgment. The section entitled "National Histories" (*guoshi*), consisting of thirteen subsections, is particularly interesting for our purposes because it displays the historiographical principles by which the past should be ordered and assessed. For example, the second subsection, entitled "Impartiality" (Gongzheng), records, and thereby praises, instances of historians' unyielding insistence of conveying truths and facts even in the face of the threat of death. The fifth subsection, entitled "Disquisitions" (Lunyi), proffers examples of how historians debated and discussed the merits or disadvantages of the various ways of recording in terms of the historiographical principle of praise and blame. The tenth subsection, entitled "Prefaces by Authors," collects exemplary prefaces important historians wrote for their works, through which we may readily learn of their approaches to writing history. The twelfth section, entitled "Lack of Veracity" (Bushi), castigates those historians who are unwilling to be or incapable of being truthful as moral failures (Z. Huang 2001, 34–43; Qu 1999a, 82–83).

The *Archival Palace* was an important complement to the standard histories. It testified to a sharper sense of what history actually was, duly recognizing the chasm between the past and the way it was recorded by historians. The compilers demonstrated a critical attitude toward evidence, keenly aware that this was how the authenticity of the past could be safeguarded. However, in the final analysis, the goal of this encyclopedic work was to conflate the past and present through analogy and didacticism. Its appeal to history was premised on the conviction that the events and deeds of the past were directly and functionally relevant to the molding of present conduct. The present was essentially the same as the past.

The Vitality of Historical Scholarship in the Southern Song (1127–1279)

The loss of Northern China to the invading armies of the Jurchens, who established the Jin dynasty, meant shrinkage of the dynasty's political domain, but these traumatic developments by no means diminished intellectual vitality. In the Southern Song period, historical output remained impressive, and the paramount notion of history as a mirror reflecting enduring truths continued to inspire statesmen and literati. An important work written in the tradition of Sima Guang's *Comprehensive Mirror* was Yuan Shu's (1131–1205) *Narratives from Beginning to End from the Comprehensive Mirror for Aid in Government* (*Tongjian jishi benmo*).

Although Yuan's historical sources and materials, together with his view of history, came from Sima's work, he did introduce a new format, as the title suggests. His goal was to offer historical descriptions of events from the very beginning to end. Sima's *Comprehensive Mirror* is a chronicle whose organizing principle is chronology, and it is often difficult to follow contiguous details of one event. There is inevitably the obtrusion of other information that may not be relevant, because under one date, several unrelated events may be recorded. Yuan Shu sought to rectify this problem. First he identified 239 important historical episodes or topics recorded in the *Comprehensive Mirror*, such as the An Lushan Rebellion, the campaigns that led to the establishment of the Tang, and the abuse of power by the eunuchs in the Han. Then he gathered all information pertaining to each identified event and constructed a self-contained historical narrative of that event. While his work can be said to be a mere rearrangement of Sima's original, it turned out to be quite influential. Yuan's event-centered and topic-oriented compilation became the template for many later works, initiating a particular style of history called "narratives from beginning to end" (*jishi benmo,* literally, "the roots and branches of recorded events"). Yuan's contribution to traditional Chinese historiography lay in the fact that he highlighted the central importance of continuity, plot, and cohesion in the retelling of historical events, and gave a beginning, middle, and end to each episode. His insight into and reorganization of Sima's original constituted a significant advancement in the Song conception of history. Even though Yuan repeated the words of the *Comprehensive Mirror,* he did offer his own historical judgments at times. Regarding the military confrontations in the period of the Southern and Northern dynasties, for example, during which northern China was ruled by a series of conquest dynasties of barbarian origin, Yuan invariably chose the word "*kou,*" meaning a rampage of banditry, to describe the North's attack on the South. When the South campaigned against the North, however, he always used the word "*fa,*" which denoted the military punishing of a dependent state that restored the proper hierarchical political order. The former term obviously connoted illegitimacy, with the Northern rulers depicted as marauding thieves; the latter indicated the righteous efforts on the part of the Southern rulers to rid the world of chaos and reclaim what was legitimately theirs. Embedded in such verbal conventions were Yuan's historical judgments, shaped by his earnest wish that the legitimate Southern Song would recover the lost northern territories from the illegitimate barbarians (Lee 2002, 68–69; J. Jin 1976, 229–231; Pulleyblank 1961, 158–159; F. Tao 1987, 320–323).

Another important historical work in the Southern Song was the *Comprehensive Treatises* (*Tongzhi*) by Zheng Qiao (1104–1162). It is a general history of 200 fascicles, covering history from antiquity to the Tang dynasty, ambitiously modeled after Sima Qian's *Records of the Grand Historian.* For the most part it adopted the annals-biography (*jizhuan*), or composite style of the standard histories. Zheng did modify the organization somewhat, however. While he preserved the annals and biographies, he used "charts" (*pu*) in place of the customary tables (*biao*), and he composed what were called "summaries" (*lüe*) that replaced the conventional monographs (*zhi*). Zheng's major claim to fame rests on the twenty summaries, several of which blazed new trails, as we will discuss below (Lin 1995, 61–95). Otherwise, Zheng's multidynastic history was largely a culling and assemblage of materials from existing dynastic histories. In that sense, his historiographical contributions were bibliographic and encyclopedic in nature, and reflected the prevailing Song valuation of erudition (Lee 2004a, 163–171; Pulleyblank 1961, 150–151; Mann 1972, 23–57; J. Jin 1976, 194–197; W. Du 2004, 99–102). But Zheng displayed his own significant understanding of history and was unquestionably influenced by the critical spirit of the Tang philosopher of history, Liu Zhiji. His view of history merits a closer look.

Zheng's historical conception was premised on the idea of "synthetic comprehension" (*hui tong*), the idea that history was the distillation, synthesis, and integration of the principles of the world, through which the pervasive Way was comprehended in time, from antiquity to the present. Accordingly, he privileged the writing of general histories, exalting the virtues of Sima Qian's *Records* while disparaging Ban Gu's *History of the Han*. Sima Qian showed "causal relations" (*xiangyin*) and continuities among developments in successive dynasties and periods, while Ban Gu, myopically focused on one dynasty, could not see the seamless web and dynamic flow of history. Zheng's famous twenty summaries (*lüe*) stemmed precisely from his desire to synthesize existing knowledge on an array of subjects by highlighting their main themes and pinpointing their salient features. As Zheng noted, five of the summaries discussed subjects commonly dealt with by scholars in the Han and Tang—rites and rituals, laws and punishments, the civil service, recruitment of talents, agriculture and trade—and he admitted to borrowing quite heavily from Du You's *Comprehensive Compendium*. The remaining fifteen examined topics seldom treated as historical subjects in the customary monographs or treatises in the standard histories: genealogies of the illustrious clans, the six categories of ideograms, the seven phonetic sounds, astronomy, geography, cities and towns, posthumous titles, ceremonial costumes, music, literature and writings, the comparison and verification of documents, diagrams and illustrations, bronzes and stones, cosmological portents of catastrophes and auspiciousness, and fauna and flora. Zheng self-consciously pointed to their novelty, and in some respects he did succeed in providing new perspectives and forging novel approaches. His discussions on the origins and pedigrees of the illustrious clans and magnates were noticeably more detailed than those in earlier works; in the summary on literature and writings, he established new subcategories. Instead of using the four conventional categories—classics, histories, philosophies, and belles-lettres—he set up ones such as rites, music, and elementary learning under the category of classics. His summary on cosmological portents of catastrophes and auspiciousness was a bold attack on the occult theories of Yin-Yang and the Five Phases as superstitions. Zheng repudiated the elaborate cosmological conception of a correlative universe, calling this "learning that betrays Heaven." To Zheng, the Five Phases referred solely to patterns of physical movements and changes that had little to say about human affairs. On the whole, however, the summaries offered little that was appreciably new; they consisted of citations, encapsulations, and recapitulations of information from existing sources. Zheng's accomplishment lay not so much in providing new material as in expanding the domain of history to include subjects hitherto considered to be outside its purview (Lee 2004a, 172–179; Lin 1995, 61–87; Lin 1997, 63–66, 138–144; F. Tao 1987, 330–332, 335–337; Jin 1976, 195–196; T. Wu 1989, 27–28; W. Du 2004, 102–104).

Zheng's encyclopedic approach to the past was a function of his deep appreciation for what he called "solid learning" (*shixue*) that was concretely based on facts and evidence, as opposed to the learning of meanings and principles (*yili*), and the study of prose and verse (*cizhang*), which were merely speculations and ornamentations. History, as solid learning based on material evidence and empirical knowledge, should supply factual information first and foremost. Zheng deemed the "comments" (*lunzan*) that had become customary in the standard histories to be superfluous. The convention of rendering moral judgments on past personages and events was, as we have shown, inspired by the putative goal of the *Spring and Autumn Annals* to praise the good and condemn the wicked. But Zheng contended that the emphasis of this classical text was on institutions, not praise and blame. History, as long as it was properly recorded and supported by evidence, was self-explanatory as far as the good and the evil were concerned. To Zheng, historical narrative itself was the all-revealing mirror (Lee 2004a, 179–187; Lin 1997, 83–88; T. Wu 1989, 27; F. Tao 1987, 334–335).

Zheng Qiao was particularly interested in the phenomena and processes of development and change. Playing the role of a nascent anthropologist, as it were, Zheng speculated that human beings had evolved out of their kin in the animal kingdom. Humans, according to him, belonged to the same category of beings as worms, fish, and other beasts. But human beings were the most intelligent among the myriad creatures. As bipeds, they distinguished themselves from quadrupeds, whose movements forced them to stay close to the ground, by walking upright. Zheng then shifted his speculation from physical to cultural anthropology. He pointed to the evolutionary nature of civilization, from the stage of primitive livings in caves to the highly cultured stage of social and political institutions. The latter stage witnessed the formation of names, kin groups, families, lineages, and the state, together with the invention of writing, use of the calendar, and growth of trade. He posited that the developments and changes in institutions during the Three Dynasties (*sandai*, that is, the Xia, Shang, and Zhou) displayed great adaptiveness and flexibility, in that they were all "in accord with time" (*shishi*). Therefore, ancient implements and institutions could not be replicated today. As time flowed, institutions underwent change. The point of writing history was to sketch both continuities and changes. This recognition of inexorably evolutionary movements in time induced in Zheng a certain sense of anachronism (Lin 1997, 136–138). In short, Zheng Qiao introduced certain novel elements into the Southern Song world of historiography. His encyclopedic approach to the past, supported by his faith in erudition and guided by his broad learning, conjured up a view of history as an interconnected web of multifarious realities undergoing change (W. Du 2004, 105–109). It may perhaps be said that with the appearance of Zheng Qiao's *Comprehensive Treatises*, the Song tradition of *leishu* such as the *Archival Palace* reached an apogee (Lee 2004a, 166–170).

Zhu Xi and the Learning of the Way:
The Moral Conception of History

In the Southern Song, one truly momentous intellectual development was the rise and consolidation of a new form of Confucianism, that is, the Learning of the Way (*daoxue*). Partisans of this new Confucianism issued urgent calls for cultural regeneration by redefining and reinvigorating the Way (*dao*) of the ancient sages; they increasingly harked back to the classics in which the sages' *dao* was supposedly embodied. Although the Daoxue scholars sought classical authorities, they, like the Northern Song literati, demonstrated a penchant for analogical reasoning based on knowledge of the past, and they certainly perpetuated the didactic use of history. But to them the past that mattered was antiquity, which, because of its universal goodness and timeless excellence, could not be rendered into a mere temporal segment (de Bary 1959, 25–49). Zhu Xi (1130–1200) was a Daoxue scholar and thinker who built an architectonic metaphysical system in which ethics consistently connected and cohered with cosmology. He was not primarily concerned with history or the writing of history as such, although arguably his notion of the lineage and transmission of the Way, the universal principle, was a form of historicism. It may be seen as a philosophical-historical schema: the Way begins and flourishes in antiquity and was exemplified by the deeds of the sages from Yao through the Duke of Zhou; it is continued by Confucius and Mencius until the death of Confucius' grandson Zisi; it suffers a long eclipse from Han times because of Buddhism; and then it is finally revived, thanks to the sagacious work of great scholars such as Zhou Dunyi and the Cheng brothers, from whom Zhu himself received the wisdom of the Way (Tillman 1992, 178–186).

However, to Zhu Xi, the philosophical universalism of the Way was meaningless, or at least remained hidden, if actual events in history did not give concrete, tangible, and intelligible manifestation to its timeless idealism. It is not difficult to discern how Zhu viewed and valued history, even though he did say that "learning must have the classics as the basis, followed by the studying of history" (F. Tao 1987, 346), which he described as the "outer skin," as opposed to the classics, which formed the inner core (Schirokauer 1993, 198). Notwithstanding the fact that Zhu judged history to be secondary to the classics, he embraced both, regarding them as the two textual and disciplinary poles of the cultural continuum that constituted the Chinese *tianxia*, the Chinese world of culture. History was the timebound record of the mundane goings-on on the human level that constituted civilization; the classics conveyed the immutably valid messages from the ancient sages blessed with wisdom and sagacity. It may also be argued that for Zhu, history—the study and knowledge of the words and deeds of the ancient sages, the loss and gains from antiquity to the present, the institutions of rites and music, the origins and developments of finance and trade, and the systems and rules of the military organizations—performed the indispensable narrative function of embodying and conveying his philosophical speculations and moral values by revealing the all-pervading and connecting (*yiguan*) principle (*li*). After all, Zhu placed history before the ancient "Six Arts" of rites, music, archery, charioteering, calligraphy, and mathematics (F. Tao 1987, 346; Chun-chieh Huang 1999, 60–62; Schirokauer 1993, 220; cf. Schirokauer 2004, 121–153).

Zhu Xi wrote three historical works. The first, *Outline and Details of the Comprehensive Mirror* (*Zizhi tongjian gangmu*), was a reworking of Sima Guang's *Comprehensive Mirror*. Its purpose was to highlight the good and bad in history in an explicit and systematic manner, praising the good and condemning the bad. The annalistic and chronological outline (*gang*) clearly delineated the main events, which were fleshed out by elaborating details (*mu*) so that "the rule and chaos of the state, and the virtues and inadequacies of rulers and ministers, are well recognized, just as the fingers know the palm" (Q. Tang 1998a, 45–50; Gaoxin Wang 1998, 44; Y. Zhang 1975, 87–119). The second work, *Records of the Origins of the School of the Cheng Brothers* (*Yiluo yuanyuan lu*), was an intellectual history of sorts, which constructed a lineage of learning—that is, the Learning of the Way—that featured the central importance of the philosophies of the two Cheng brothers. The third history, *Words and Deeds of Eminent Ministers of Eight Reigns* (*Bachao mingchen yanxing lu*), provided information on the lives of many officials in the Northern Song (Schirokauer 1993, 195–200). These works, together with Zhu's frequent references to history and history writing, yielded a fairly coherent picture of his historical views.

In his preface to the *Outline and Details,* Zhu clearly filtered his view of history through his philosophical understanding. He posited that history was the intellectual pursuit of investigating things in order to extend knowledge to the utmost, *gewu zhizhi,* his famous epistemological dictum. The outline and elaboration of historical happenings served the ultimate purpose of "illuminating the way of heaven and securing the way of humanity" (F. Tao 1987, 346). Historical learning and study were no mean undertakings—they revealed Principle and the Way, and contributed to moral cultivation. While the Six Classics of the ancient sages had already established the essential and subtle principles and meanings, history—the dynamic flow of time and the substantive occurrences of events—corroborated the ancient sagely teachings. To pursue history was to seek and apprehend the "mind–heart of the sages," the universal *dao.* Just as there was no meaningful history without due attention to the classics, so too the messages of the sages and the ultimate reality of Principle could only find manifestation in the actual affairs that occurred in history (Chun-chieh Huang 1999, 60–73). Hence Zhu disagreed and debated with his contemporary Chen Liang (1143–94), a utilitarian Confucian who sought principles exclusively in the diachronic universe of historical events, and who asserted that values were relative and contingent upon changing contexts. Zhu complained that Chen "abandoned the classics while studying history, neglecting the way of the true ruler and honoring the technique of the hegemons, and going to extremes in discussing the rise and fall of dynasties past and present without investigating the origins of life and demise within the mind-heart" (Q. Tang 1998b, 130; Tillman 1982, 191–193). He faulted people like Chen for their self-deception, that is, for thinking that their narrow study of Confucius' *Spring and Autumn Annals* and Sima Qian's *Records of the Historian* brought them thorough knowledge of the causes of dynastic prosperity and declension. All such historical learning brought them was awareness of what had happened after the Warring States, but not a fundamental understanding of the meanings and principles of the classics. Zhu thus reiterated that "to study the books of history is to seek the principles that inhere in the corresponding things and affairs" (Q. Tang 1998a, 131; Q. Tang 1999, 75–78).

However, studying history was not an introspective affair. As Zhu pointed out, it was a highly practical matter of "scrutinizing the affairs of the world, broadly surveying the surroundings of mountains and rivers, and discerning the causes and courses of rise and fall, peace and chaos, and losses and gains through the ages." History strove to arrive at a comprehensive understanding of the Principle, which required knowing "calendar, laws, astronomy, geography, military matters and governmental structures" (Q. Tang 1998b, 129–130). Such knowledge of Principle equipped one to use historical examples critically as suitable contemporary analogies; it also enabled one to realize the moral, didactic function of history. Through the concrete examples of history, it was possible to juxtapose the past and present, censuring the bad (such as the domination of the court by imperial relatives and eunuchs) and commending the good (such as the virtuous deeds of ministers). In so doing, one learned from the lessons of history, and thus Zhu turned past history into current statecraft. In evaluating the Song problem of a bloated military, for example, Zhu referred to similar mistakes committed by the Han and Tang, and in assessing current inequities in landholding, he recalled the Spring and Autumn period and the Han. Historical analogies offered the most reliable guides to present sociopolitical issues. History was also a way in which judgments were rendered; one praised the good and chastised the bad by recording the past in the proper way. Reminding readers of the "law of the pen" (*bifa*) of the *Spring and Autumn Annals*, Zhu propounded as many as fifteen rules for recording military campaigns so as to register their nature and lessons. History was a mirror. With respect to history's primary function, both Sima Guang and Zhu Xi were indeed birds of a feather (Q. Tang 1998b, 131–134; Schirokauer 1989, 82–83; Schirokauer 1993, 204–206; Qu 1999a, 87; L. Yang 1961, 52).

Although Zhu Xi embraced a time-negating philosophical universalism based on perennial classical truths, he could be quite sensitive to temporal change and the qualitative alteration that followed. In the *Outline and Details* Zhu diverged from Sima's verdict on the legitimacy of political succession (*zhengtong*) with regard to the Three Kingdoms (Wei, Shu, and Wu) that emerged after the fall the of the Han. Sima accorded legitimacy to the Wei because it toppled the Han, albeit through usurpation, and established the largest domain. Sima, as we have seen, based legitimacy on merit. Zhu awarded legitimacy to the Shu state because its founder could claim descent from the old Han imperial line. But when he was in his sixties, Zhu changed his view of *zhengtong* by insisting that political success be the criterion of legitimacy. Legitimate succession meant the ability to forge a regime that unified all of China, a feat accomplished only by the Zhou, Qin, Han, Jin, Siu, and Tang dynasties. Zhu Xi now regarded the Shu kingdom as possessing only a "remnant of *zhengtong*," meaning that although the kingdom possessed the beginnings of legitimacy, it eventually failed to acquire genuine legitimacy because it failed to unify China. In his old age, Zhu Xi developed a view quite close to Sima's. It is important to point out that this shift in Zhu's conception of political legitimacy had much to do with the circumstances of his day. Zhu lived in the Southern Song, when northern China was under the rule of the Jurchen Qin dynasty. Restoration of Song rule over all of China was his earnest wish and urgent goal. Since the Southern Song was linked genealogically to the Northern Song, it had the beginnings of legitimacy, whereas the barbarian Jin could have no such claim. Yet until the South reunited China by driving out the Jurchen, there could be no genuine legitimacy. Here we have yet another example of how the past, or a conception of the past, was made usable for the present (Tillman 1982, 171–172; Gaoxin Wang 1998, 49–50).

Zhu Xi expressed his appreciation for the particularity of events in changing contexts through his philosophic notion of *quan*, which has been variously and appropriately translated as contingency, expediency, exigency, moral discretion, and situational weighing. All of these iterations convey the importance and necessity of practical wisdom and common sense that should be judiciously applied in individual cases, as opposed to the conviction in the notion of *jing*, that is, constant principle, universal standard, and invariant norm. However, by *quan* Zhu did not mean arbitrariness or relativism. Rather, it referred to the astute handling of affairs in accord with the needs of the time. The ability to do so came from the proper cultivation of the self. While there was the constant Way, such as the Five Relationships of ruler-minister, father-son, husband-wife, brother-brother, and friend-friend, specific situations at different times and places often required extraordinary but prudent measures. Thus Zhu took issue with Hu Yin (1098–1156), whose *Dushi guanjian* (Observations from studying history) actually provided Zhu with a good deal of inspiration when he compiled the *Outline and Details*. Hu was a champion of constant principles at all times in all circumstances. He insisted on unwavering adherence to the moral standards of the Three Dynasties and paying unquestioned homage to the sages from Confucius to Mencius. In rendering historical judgment on Empress Wu, Hu argued that she should have been demoted to the status of commoner and ordered to commit suicide so as to restore the dignity of the Tang dynasty. But Zhu claimed that dynastic imperative was one thing; the feelings and responsibilities of her successor, her son Zhongzong, were quite another. It would have been unreasonable for officials to execute the mother and then proclaim loyalty to the son. Zhu also disagreed with his close friend Zhang Shi (1133–1180), who thought that because Emperor Zhongzong was inept, the throne should have been transferred to a prince in a cognate imperial line. Zhu saw this sort of historical evaluation as anachronistic. In hindsight one can know that the emperor will turn out to be weak and ineffective, but given the circumstances at the time there was no compelling reason to remove him.

Zhu Xi did not see the restoration of antique institutions and ritual order as feasible, even though he admired and praised the accomplishments and values of the ancient sages. Zhu's conception of history may be described as degenerative. This in turn was related to his cosmological view that the material force of the universe (*qi*) was qualitatively inferior to what it had been in the distant days of antiquity. But the lesser quality of the present did not render helpless and hapless those living in the present, insofar as human nature and principle remained good. Although history had its inevitable vicissitudes, sagehood always remained a possibility, and it was up to the good men to bring about order and achieve stability. Therefore Zhu was by no means opposed to reforms, which he deemed to be an absolutely necessary way to respond to changing times and needs. His criticisms of Wang Anshi's New Policies, for example, addressed the flaws in the individual measures, not the idea of change per se, which he considered highly laudable (Schirokauer 1993, 207–220).

Not only did Zhu develop a sense of historical change, but he also embraced the historian's sensitivity to the veridicality of evidence and sources. Despite his faith in the classics, he doubted the authenticity of the *Classic of Documents* of the Old Script tradition as a result of his philological analysis of the text. He also expressed his disagreement with the *Zuo Commentary*'s recordings of ancient events, positing that this commentary to the *Spring and Autumn Annals* was composed much later. He even cast doubt on the ancient accounts of the conquest of the disastrous floods by Yu, the founder of the Xia dynasty. Zhu was a prolific and meticulous exegete who carefully examined the words and parsed the phrases of the classical texts. He earnestly believed that their reliability must be ascertained before they could possibly be authoritative guides to the study of ancient history. Zhu did not hesitate to criticize flaws in the *Records of the Historian;* using information he gathered from the ancient *Bamboo Annals,* he took issue with Sima Qian's account of the royal succession in the state of Wei in the Warring States period. Nor did Zhu spare contemporary works. While he lavishly praised Sima Guang's *Comprehensive Mirror,* he faulted it for omitting references to and accounts of moral impropriety and unscrupulous political machinations. Zhu contended that because Sima focused on individual personages in order to make his work morally didactic, he ignored much historical evidence, including information on the customs and mores of society, thereby rendering an incomplete and distorted picture of the past. Zhu's own *Outline and Details* was beset, of course, with the same historical sin of gross omissions and distortions. Nevertheless Zhu asserted that the histories produced by the History Bureau under imperial aegis lacked fidelity to what had actually happened in the past because the process of compilation was often too constrained by political concerns and imperial oversight (Gaoxin Wang 1998, 45–48).

All in all, in his creative synthesis of philosophy and history, Zhu Xi displays a historical view that is sensitive to changes as concrete particular phenomena, whose description requires the use of rigorous historical techniques so that their significance in terms of the universal and pervading Principle may be appropriately brought into the sharpest relief (Huang 1999, 5–6; Chun-chieh Huang 2004, 116–117).

Growth of the Historical Genre of Local Gazetteers

No account of the Song achievements in historiography is complete without reference to the emergence and maturation of a major historical genre, the local gazetteer or local history (*difang zhi* or *fangzhi*), each of which focused on a specific administrative locality. Versions of local histories had been compiled from the Han to the Tang, but most were highly specialized in content and narrowly focused on such subjects as geography, topography, and famous places. They did not, as a rule, provide truly historical information and coverage. Local gazetteers probably originated from the "histories" that were the "treatises with maps and illustrations" (*tujing, tuzhi,* or *tuji*). These treatises became widespread in the Tang. They were compiled by the regional administrative units and submitted every three years to the court for the expressed purpose of furnishing the central government with cartographic, geographic, economic, social, and historical information on the various areas. In the Song, the compilation of such treatises burgeoned both in quantity and quality, no doubt a result of the imperial government's desire to establish tighter control over the regions. These texts became the blueprint of the local gazetteers, whose contents included a wide array of subjects: history of administrative boundaries, schools, populations, local products, local customs, local personages, celebrated places and sites, temples and shrines, geography, water management, and chronicles of significant events. While the *tujing* treatises were compiled primarily for administrative purposes, the gazetteers were increasingly historical in their coverage and intent. Song administrative imperatives, together with the Song intellectual penchant for details, comprehensiveness, and information, and the encyclopedic impulse to gather and present what could be known, fostered a kind of history that dug deeply into the past of individual locales. Yue Shi's (930–1007) *Taiping huanyu ji* (Universal geography of the Taiping reign) in 200 fascicles, for instance, is renowned for its thoroughness and copiousness and set the standard for local geographic-historical works (Hargett 2004, 287–291; Hargett 1996, 407–417; Gan 1998, 86–88; Alitto 1985, 59–63; Fu 1988, 33–37).

By the Southern Song period, every administrative locality had produced its own gazetteer. Altogether about 304 were produced, compared with the roughly 172 that had appeared in the Northern Song. Advances in printing technology may have had something to do with this proliferation, or it may have resulted from the Song court's desire for local and regional information. Perhaps the increased interest in local monuments and artifacts—another reflection of the Song proclivity toward broad learning and antiquarian pursuits—contributed to the development. Or it may have been a function of the fact that the Southern Song elite had developed a much stronger local outlook (Bol 2004, 309–321). Whatever the reasons, gazetteers not only multiplied in quantity but they also exhibited more sophisticated and rigorous techniques of compilation. Many local gazetteers now assumed the form of a scholarly historical monograph, with citations of all sorts of sources. The compilers were most interested in the authenticity of their source materials and the facts they proffered, which led to revision of earlier editions deemed wanting in accuracy and comprehensiveness. Significantly, the local gazetteers were increasingly viewed as any other kind of history, such as the national histories and standard histories, which therefore had to assume a similarly didactic function. Eminent meritorious local personages became moral exemplars for the young in that locality to emulate. Local gazetteers were also seen as repositories of past precedents that could serve as worthy guides for the present. Gradually but surely, they gained respectability among a wide readership. They no longer simply appealed to the imperial administrators, but were read as edifying and informative histories with both moral and administrative import. By the twelfth century most of the gazetteers no longer emphasized geographic and bureaucratic information but human affairs, with ample references to and detailed information on virtuous behavior and ethical norms. One may surmise that the growth of the Learning of the Way, Daoxue, the new Confucianism promoted by people like Zhu Xi, may have spurred orientation of these works toward the moral domain of human affairs (Bol 2004, 309–317; Hargett 1996, 418–436; X. Song 1988, 3–4).

In sum, there is no question that the overall scholarly productivity of the Song was fecund and considerable. The eighteenth-century *Siku quanshu* (Complete works from the four treasuries), a mammoth encyclopedic collection of works published from antiquity to the mid-Qing, provides the evidence. Of the entries under history, 189 titles out of a total of 564 (roughly one-third), or 5,644 fascicles in the total of 21,950 (approximately one-fourth), are from the Song period (Davis 1988, 73). Historical compilations figured prominently in the prolific and vital Song intellectual universe. Both official and private historiographies flourished, spurred on by the compulsion for erudition. They were also fueled by an indiscriminant curiosity about facts and artifacts, which contributed to the proliferation of the encyclopedic *leishu*, the miscellaneous collectanea, and the local gazetteers. The Song court patronized and supported the compilation of historical works, and the standards governing the official compilation of the veritable records and national histories unquestionably became more rigorous. For instance, colored inks were employed to distinguish the different texts that constituted these enormously useful sources: initial texts were written in black ink, excised ones in yellow, and added ones in red. Similarly, the master works by Ouyang Xiu and Sima Guang, not to mention those by Yuan Shu and Zheng Qiao, represented innovations in form and substance. As we have seen, Sima Guang, in deference to the sources and the arduous process of creating the ultimate readable narrative, introduced the "long draft," the original skeleton on which the *Comprehensive Mirror* was eventually fleshed out. The draft was intended as a detailed record of the making of a history. Sima's "Examination of Discrepancies" (Kaoyi) was another notable innovation, revealing the rationale behind his choices of evidence and accounts, and demonstrating his fidelity to accuracy (L. Yang 1961, 57–59; K. Hsu 1983). Even Zhu Xi saw fit to assess the evidence and accounts of the past in a critical manner, even though the universal Principle, revealed in the timeless classics, anchored his intellectual world.

Suffused throughout the Song historians' universalistic claim of history's moral didactic power and analogical revelation was their sensitivity to the dynamic flow of time that had to be illustrated by the use of good evidence; it had to be properly recorded and represented by accurate historical narratives. Haltingly and not always consistently, Song historiography sought to interrogate evidence critically, to construct narratives that highlighted the causes and particularities of past events, and to define the past in terms of its otherness to the present. If we may be permitted a measure of anachronism in identifying certain "modern" historiographical tendencies and elements in the Song, we do catch glimpses of them. Yet in the final analysis Song historiography is best evaluated and appreciated on its own terms and within the context of the long tradition of history writing in imperial China. In this Chinese intellectual soil, the Song produced historiographical fruits that were delectably sweet.

CHAPTER 6

The Jin and the Yuan

History and Legitimation in the Dynasties of Conquest

In 1115 the partially Sinicized Jurchen people, a very loose conglomeration of tribes who had risen to power in northeastern Manchuria, established the Jin dynasty. They rebelled against and in 1125 overthrew their Khitan overlord, the Liao dynasty (947–1125), the nemesis of the Song dynasty. The Liao had never been able to capture substantial Chinese territory, taking only land on the border, but the Jin, from 1127 onward, succeeded in imposing direct control over the northern portion of China proper. The Song withdrew to central and southern China. Before long, however, the Jin themselves faced the recurrent problem that native Chinese dynasties had—pressure from the north, exerted this time by the Mongols. Simultaneously the Jin had to contend with military challenges from the Southern Song. In 1234, after decades of dynastic decline, the Jin dynasty was destroyed by the Mongols, who shortly thereafter also gobbled up the south. In 1271 the Mongol Yuan dynasty was established, a conquest dynasty that for the first time achieved direct dominion over all of China (H. Chan 1984, 51–72).

How did the enterprise of history fare under the Jurchen Jin and Mongol Yuan dynasties? Although both the Jin and the Yuan made deliberate efforts to maintain their cultural and political distinction, they had no choice but to employ Chinese institutions and personnel. As a consequence, the time-honored dynastic endeavor of compiling history, both a cultural practice and a political ritual, continued. The Yuan, for instance, readily sponsored compilations of the histories of the preceding regimes of the Liao, the Jin, and the Song. But as they were ethnically alien to the vast population of Chinese subjects, and having asserted political rule after military conquest, how did they create a usable past for themselves? What particular problems arose in the sensitive process of reconciling their alien origins with their claim to a Chinese throne and territory? What role did history play in the regimes' inescapable engagement with the urgent ideological question of political legitimacy? (Tillman 1995b, 23–38; H. Chan 1970, vi–vii; M. Wang 1989, 15–16; W. Du 2004, 113–117)

Jin Continuation of Traditional Official Historiography

It is fitting to begin with a very brief look at the Khitan Liao. Although not a full-fledged conquest dynasty, it was a Chinese-style regime whose southern regions lay well within China proper and enveloped today's Beijing. The Liao dynasty borrowed a considerable number of Chinese administrative and institutional elements, employed Chinese advisors, used the Chinese language as the lingua franca, and even honored Confucius as the sage. In the early days of the Liao, they had, no doubt under the guidance of Chinese scholars, created offices responsible for compiling historical sources such as the diary of activity and repose (*qijuzhu*). In 941 an imperial edict decreed the writing of the early history of the Khitan. Records are scant, but it can be ascertained that a History Bureau did exist as an integral part of Liao officialdom. Insofar as the Liao saw itself as a dynasty in the Chinese mold, official sponsorship of history was integral to the court's mandate (M. Wang 1989, 17–18).

In 1128 the Jin dynasty formally decreed a compilation of its national history, and produced veritable records for the first ten rulers, beginning with the founder. Subsequently, by imperial fiat, there were compilations of the veritable records of the various reigns, yielding a total of ten sets. There were other compilations, such as the imperial genealogies of the Jin and imperial injunctions from the various reigns. Various units of the institutional organization took charge of recording, assembling, and compiling the primary sources. The Office of Records (*jizhu yuan*) took charge of the diaries of activity and repose, of which they were altogether four sets. The Bureau of Compilation (*zhuzuo ju*) was responsible for the daily records (*rili*), the chronological reordering of the diaries, and the daily recordings (*rilu*) consisted of conversations between the emperors and ministers. The National History Office (*guoshi yuan*), utilizing the resources gathered by the prior two offices, produced both the national histories and the veritable records. It is noteworthy that the office in charge of the diaries of activity and repose stood on its own, independent of other government agencies, so that it might record everything about the emperors and their courts without undue interference (H. Chan 1970, 3–4; M. Wang 1988, 47–51; M. Wang 1989, 19–28). One Jin minister trenchantly declared to the emperor that "[t]he history officials of old recorded without failure the words and deeds of the son of heaven, so that rulers might be properly admonished and warned, knowing what to fear. . . . From this we realize that the words and deeds of rulers must be fully recorded by the history officials without any avoidance" (M. Wang 1989, 21).

In addition the Jin dynasty established a special apparatus that was solely responsible for compilation of the history of the Liao. There were two imperially mandated efforts to compile Liao history. The first was completed in 1148, after eight years, and the second in 1207, after eighteen. Neither version survived, but we do know that they served as the blueprints for the later Yuan compilation (W. He 1998, 60). Many later commenta-

tors praised the quality of the *History of the Jin* compiled at the end of the
Yuan, and one reason this history stood out was that its compilers relied on
the fine primary materials meticulously assembled and preserved during
the Jin dynasty (M. Wang 1988, 47). By all accounts the Jin was a conquest
dynasty that placed great store in history and historical compilations.

The Jin Literati's Conception of History and the Way

This emphasis on history was part and parcel of the Jin's deliberate assimilation of Chinese culture, although it is also important to point out that the
cultural pursuits actively promoted during the reign of Emperor Shizong
(1161–1189) indicated a concerted effort on the part of the Jin ruler to consolidate Jurchen identity. The goal was to assimilate high Chinese culture
without being totally absorbed by it. There was an active attempt to incul-
cate Chinese values made possible by translating the Chinese classics and
histories into the Jurchen language. Moreover, education was promoted
among the Jurchen princes and aristocrats, preparing them to attend the
imperial university. A special examination was created for the Jurchen at
the highest level (the level of "presented scholars" or *jinshi*) of the system of civil service examinations, the curriculum of which included the
Six Classics and the seventeen standard histories (W. He 1998, 59; H. Chan
1984, 68–72). At the same time the Han Chinese literati strove to renew
Chinese learning and values encapsulated in the twin ideals of the Way
(*dao*) — the universal normative order of values and behavior — and Culture
(*wen*) — the cumulative tradition of learning expressed through refined literary abilities and sensibilities. Just as their Song counterparts did, the Jin
Chinese literati pondered the deep philosophic questions of the Learning of the Way (*daoxue*) of Zhu Xi and his colleagues. Simultaneously they
culled examples of utility and morality from history, inspired by the didactic and analogical historiography of Sima Guang and others. Contrary to
the traditional view that Jin scholars were inadequate interpreters of the
Way and Culture, recent scholarship has shown there was vibrant intellectual growth at this time. There was, after all, no iron curtain separating the
Jin in the north from the Song in the south so far as culture was concerned
(Tillman 1995b, 71–73; Bol 1992, 115–117).

Emperor Shizong, whose reign was identified with cultural and intellectual vigor, deeply appreciated the value of history and avidly studied
historical texts. He admitted that while the classics contained sagely messages that were profound, he could not always apprehend their meanings,
whereas every time he opened a history, he never failed to benefit from
it. He had a special fondness for Sima Guang's *Comprehensive Mirror.* He
thought this work illustrated in a most systematic way the rise and fall of dynasties and in doing so offered indispensable practical political and moral
lessons for posterity. In so extravagantly celebrating history, the emperor
was not thinking about antiquarian study of the past, he was promoting a
pragmatic cause because past precedents were unerring guides to present

actions, both political and moral. When Emperor Xizong (1135–1148) initiated governmental reforms to centralize authority, curtail the power of
the traditional Jurchen aristocracy, curb the feudal rivalries among the
Jurchen warlords, and bureaucratize the regime along Chinese lines, he
claimed inspiration from history. History revealed to him the fundamental
fact that the "enlightened and illustrious rulers" (*mingjun*) throughout the
past, such as the much-respected founders of the Tang and the Zhou dynasties, ruled with the aid of able and loyal officials. The emperor proclaimed,
therefore, that the recruitment of talent would be the basis of the Jin polity,
elaborated into a well-defined officialdom consisting of the Six Ministries,
the Censorate, and the civil service examinations. Significantly, Aguda, the
dynastic progenitor, was for the first time credited with transmitting the
legitimate political order (*zhengtong*) to later generations. Thus the Jin developed a clear sense of the legitimate historical succession and continuity.
Ironically, Xizong was by no means a beneficent ruler, but a tyrannical one
ready to use force on his officials and imperial kin. His reign ended with a
coup d'état and his assassination (W. He 1998, 61–62; H. Chan 1984, 60–
63). Despite this contradiction between ideal and reality, the proclamation
poignantly underscores the imperial desire to manipulate history to serve
present exigency.

Unlike Xizong, Emperor Shizong, whom Zhu Xi endearingly called
the "lesser Yao Shun" (*xiao* Yao Shun), was by all accounts a conscientious,
benevolent ruler who apparently did seek to realize the moral-political lessons he learned from studying history (H. Chan 1984, 70–71). History informed him that "without the profoundly stabilizing rule of benevolence,
nothing is adequate in consolidating the establishments of the past." By
saying so, he was commenting on the brutish rule of his predecessor, Emperor Liang (1149–1160), who had ended the equally despotic reign of Emperor Xizong. Using history, Shizong formulated a conception of benevolent rule that embodied several key elements. Benevolent rule began with
a ready and humble acceptance of remonstrance and advice from officials.
Second, only the talented should be recruited and employed in the court.
The emperor specifically had in mind the upright, incorruptible literati
who adhered to and propagated the rituals and norms. Finally, to rule be-
nevolently was to ensure the livelihood of the people (W. He 1998, 62–63).

That the past served as a mirror and guide to the present was a basic
conviction in the historical writings of the Jin literati, many of whom were
particularly interested in why dynasties rose and fell. Zhao Bingwen (1159–
1232), generally regarded as the leading cultural figure in the Jin, saw history in cyclical terms. Just as the moon waxed and waned and the sun rose
and set, so the classics that had been destroyed in the Qin were revived
in the Han; the Way of rulership was eclipsed in the long period after
the demise of the Han but was reinvigorated in the Tang. To Zhao, peace
and chaos naturally ebbed and flowed over time, but they did so in accordance with specific historical circumstances. Even though Zhao likened

cyclical historical developments to, as he put it, "the principle of nature" (*ziran zhi li*), there were factors that contributed to such developments. Good fortune and disasters had specific causes. Zhao identified morals and virtues as the crucial fulcrum on which history balanced. Realization of the cardinal virtues of humaneness (*ren*) and integrity (*yi*) had a direct bearing on whether a regime would survive and endure. In sociopolitical terms the realization of virtues meant rectification and proper implementation of the "great bonds" (*dagang*): first, the enactment and maintenance of moral customs; second, the use of talents; and third, the appropriate application of military force and support of the economy. The foundation of a peaceful, stable rule was simplicity in customs, while the genesis of disorder was the growth of extravagance that corroded society's moral conventions and values. Zhao described a dynastic cycle in which a new dynasty's initial simple, unspoiled customs gave way to indulgent elaboration, resulting in gradual decline. When customs became moribund, the moral order collapsed, and chaos inevitably set in, precipitating the fall of the dynasty. Order and disorder were linked to those who served the dynasty. It was of the utmost importance that the moral and the talented should surround the throne, for the decline and end of a dynasty owed much to corruption at court brought about by flattery and prevarication among feckless, treacherous officials. No regime could exist without military force and economic production, but its prosperity and survival depended on the judicious application of force and a restrained use of economic resources. An infatuation with military force or a profligate taxing of economic resources spelt doom for any power. Zhao concluded that no regime could endure for many generations in the absence of humaneness (M. Wang 2000, 14–15).

As a literatus loyal to the Jin, Zhao had very definite views of the position of his dynasty in history. He affirmed its status as the legitimate successor of the Song, which received the Mandate of Heaven to rule the "central plains," that is, the traditional domain of China. According to Zhao, Emperor Zhangzong (1190–1208) did the correct thing in assuming Earth as the official element, succeeding the Song official element of Fire. Not surprisingly he heartily endorsed Ouyang Xiu's castigation of officials who served more than one dynasty. He denounced such behavior as divided loyalty at best and betrayal at worst. For this reason, when he looked at the period of the Three Kingdoms, he praised the state of Shu as the true successor to the Han because of its blood ties, a view at odds with Sima Guang's, which accorded legitimacy to the state of Wei. Zhao's conception of history was didactically moralistic and focused on the question of legitimacy. Little wonder that he exalted the *Spring and Autumn Annals* as the Ur text in history, whose principle of praise and blame established the highest historiographical standard. He faulted the standard histories for often misjudging and miscategorizing historical personages, and hence failing to bring out the moral significance of their words and deeds. Zhao employed the "rectification of names" (*zhengming*) as the way to bring praise and blame to bear on historical recording. In history, everyone deserved and received one's due (Tillman 1995b, 88–92; M. Wang 2000, 5–6).

But for Zhao Bingwen, history was more than a source of moral exemplars; it was also a storehouse of precedents that shed light on present events. Nothing provided better guidance to current policies than analogues from the past. Thus in the reign of Emperor Xuanzong (1213–1224), when Zhao participated in urgent discussions on the advisability of moving the Jin capital to elude Mongol threats, he sought inspiration from the past. He began his arguments by disagreeing with the judgment of the great Song literary scholar, Su Shi (1037–1101) concerning the relocation of the capital of the ancient Zhou dynasty. Su believed that the decline of the Zhou was set off when it moved its capital to the east. Zhao defended the move, which he considered an action necessary to preserve the dynasty and its culture in the face of barbarian pressure. In fact, Zhao considered it the responsibility of every regime to guard against danger, even in times of peace. When the circumstances called for changes, however drastic, they must be made. Moreover, when the ancient Zhou had relocated its capital, the dynasty not only survived but also endured. Zhao, therefore, favored moving the capital. The Jin did in fact relocate the capital southward from Beijing to Kaifeng in 1215.

Zhao also used this opportunity to discourse on the need to revive the feudal system in order to buttress Jin rule. When he looked back at the past, he discovered that "circumstance" or "expediency" (*shi*) dictated implementation of either the feudal system or the prefectural system, depending on circumstances. Now, he asserted, circumstances required adoption of the former. As with the ancient Three Dynasties, he argued, the Jin faced the encroachment of barbarians. If hereditary fiefdoms were set up, they would act as a barrier defending the Jin house. The feudal lords would fight hard against barbarians, knowing that they were thus protecting their own domains (M. Wang 2000, 5).

Zhao Bingwen's approach to the past found resonant echoes in the historical and historiographical ponderings of other eminent Jin literati, most notably Wang Ruoxu (1174–1243), Yuan Haowen (1190–1257), and Liu Qi (1203–1250). Wang in particular insisted that historical recordings must be complete, including both the morally uplifting and the repulsive. It was better to adopt a plain style that exhaustively accommodated facts rather than to employ an elegant narrative that lacked solid details. Furthermore, it was preferable to be redundant rather than sparing in information. Such thoroughness served one purpose, which was to demonstrate that human relationships founded on the cardinal virtues of humaneness and integrity constituted the stuff of history. Moral meanings and principles took precedent over politics, in that politics was circumscribed and guided by the illuminating teachings of names (*mingjiao*), that is, proper recognition of the ethical code and normative order. History functioned as the constant renewal and reinforcement of lasting moral principles that suffused time. This moral world view governed his evaluation of historical individuals. Wang harshly criticized Liu Bei, the founder of the state of Shu, who had traditionally been regarded as a virtuous, courageous character. Wang faulted him for killing Zhang Yu under the pretext of his disloyalty, when Zhang's only crime was his imprudent prediction, made in private, that the Liu family's mandate to rule was about to end. Wang also condemned Emperor Wu of the Han, who, when he was near death, ordered the execution of the heir apparent's mother so that the new ruler would not be dominated by an influential empress dowager who might endanger the imperial Han line. While many historians had praised, or at least justified, this action in the name of *Realpolitik,* Wang rebuked the emperor for violating Heaven's principle and destroying human feelings. He concluded that the Han ruler did not merit consideration as a historical model. "If one seeks to rule all-under-Heaven with mere laws and regulations," Wang stated, "without the reinforcement of ethics, morals and the virtues of humaneness and integrity in order to exterminate the treacherous strongmen and forestall chaos, one would find it extremely difficult!" (M. Wang 2000, 6–7, quote 20; Tillman 1995a, 99–101).

Yuan Haowen, another Jin scholar of great repute, survived the dynastic change but refused to serve the Yuan out of devotion to the Jin. Fearing that the records of the Jin might not be properly preserved, he dedicated himself to the task of compiling the regime's history. He made a great contribution to the *Jin History* inasmuch as it was his writings that provided the organizational basis and much of the raw material. Because of him, of the three official standard histories of the Jin, the Song, and the Yuan, that on the Jin has been the most highly regarded, renowned for its comprehensive and systematic use of sources. The Yuan compilers openly acknowledged their debt to his work. Yuan Haowen's fervid desire to preserve Jin history stemmed from his conviction that the past was a trustworthy mirror for the present, and that there were many enlightened rulers and upright officials in the Jin dynasty whose deeds must be recorded for the edification of posterity (Meng 1989, 46–48; H. Chan 1970, 5–10). Like Zhao Bingwen and Wang Ruoxu, Yuan also propounded a moral interpretation of governance and the rise and fall of dynasties. But at times, without much elaboration, he seemed to construe the success of a dynasty in terms not only of human efforts but also of cosmological propitiation, hence attributing a substantial role to the blessings of Heaven. The achievement of a grand political enterprise meant the auspicious convergence of great deeds by the able and sagacious, and bountiful production in the natural world. Yuan also viewed happy cooperation between a ruler and his ministers as tantamount to integration between Heaven and humanity (M. Wang 2000, 16).

Liu Qi shared Wang's conception that the macrohistorical process was under the influence of Heaven. Unlike Wang, however, Liu provided concrete substantiation where the will of Heaven had been divined in the realm of human affairs. The Shang dynasty's toppling of the Xia and the Zhou dynasty's destruction of the Shang were acts that corresponded with Heaven's intention. Liu further declared that to be attuned to Heaven's will was merely to follow the minds and hearts of the people. In addition, the cyclical movement of history, as evidenced by the prosperity or decline of dynastic fortunes, was driven by the way the literati were treated. When a regime failed to honor scholars and capitalize on their talents, it weakened; the reverse was also true. Liu contended that a dynasty's life span and fortune were directly related to the "spirit of the literati" (*shifeng*). Reviewing historical developments from the past to present, Liu came to the conclusion that when the literati and scholars valued the traditions embodied in the classics, culture, and learning, they embraced and realized virtues. The result was peace enjoyed by the entire world. But when they pursued power, profits, and crafty arts, the world fell into disarray. Liu applied this universal macrohistorical law to the Jin, and discerned a correlation between the spirit of the literati and sociopolitical circumstances. When the literati were appropriately employed and their talents properly tapped, the state flourished. When the court ignored the literati and became trapped in self-indulgence, the state suffered. Liu claimed that the Jin had lasted for a hundred years because it had wisely utilized the literati, employing even those who had served the Liao and Song. But in the end, it did not endure because the Jin ultimately became preoccupied with the distinction between the ethnic Jin elite and the Han literati, thereby failing to entirely capture the minds and hearts of the literati (M. Wang 2000, 16–18).

It is clear that the Jurchen Jin treated history in the same way as the native Chinese Southern Song did, moralistically, didactically, analogically, and ideologically. The Jin established legitimacy by appealing to the traditional Chinese political-cosmological notion of orthodox transmission, claiming direct descent from the Song. Although Liu Qi attributed the Jin decline to its clinging to Jurchen nativist roots, the regime obviously embraced the traditional Chinese view of history that was in fact part and parcel of a highly deliberate policy of Sinicization (H. Chan 1981, 60–62; M. Wang 2000, 1–24; F. Tao 1987, 375–379).

Yuan Historiography and the Problem of Legitimacy

In 1234 the Jin dynasty was swept away by the Mongols, who in 1276 captured the capital of the Southern Song, and three years later had subjugated all of China to alien rule for the first time in its history. The Mongol Yuan dynasty (1260–1368), once it assumed the mantle of Chinese rule, had no choice but to come to grips with the problem of situating its past in that of the Chinese whom they had conquered and now ruled. To the extent that the Yuan claimed to be a legitimate dynasty, it had to assume the traditional responsibility of compiling the histories of the preceding Song, Jin, and even Liao dynasty. All three histories were closely interrelated, especially during the period when China was divided into the Jurchen north and Chinese south. When the first Yuan emperor, Khubilai (or Shizu, r. 1260–1294), ascended the throne, he acknowledged that the

recording and compilation of history should be part of a dynasty's bureaucratic routine, and he ordered histories produced of the preceding dynasties. But vociferous ideological polemics concerning the legitimacy, or the
lack thereof, of those dynasties soon erupted and bedeviled the project for
decades. Finally, in three short years from 1343 through 1345, the Yuan
historians sidestepped the issue of legitimacy and completed arguably the
single most voluminous (nearly 750 fascicles) historiographical project in
Chinese history, the standard histories of the Liao, the Jin, and the Song
(H. Chan 1981, 56–58; Davis, 1983, 33; H. Franke 1974, 15–19; H. Franke
1978, passim; Naitō 1949, 321–334).

An examination of the protracted process of this compilation reveals
several salient points about the Chinese political and historiographical tradition in the context of alien rule—the interpenetration of academic historiography and political hagiography, the utilitarian bond between writing
about past and justifying the present, the cross-fertilization of the ideology
of legitimation and the historiography of dynastic changes, the tension between acculturation to Sinitic values and preservation of Mongol identity,
and the creative opposition between cultural fealty to Chinese culture and
political loyalty to a conquest dynasty.

To win the support of the Chinese literati, the Mongol rulers quickly
accepted the expediency of supporting Chinese historiographical practices as an integral part of the imperial bureaucratic edifice. At the recommendation of Wang E (1190–1273), a former Jin official who now served the
Yuan as a high-ranking academician in the Hanlin Academy, the scholarly
arm of the officialdom, the National History Office was established within
the Academy. Khubilai was apparently impressed and persuaded by Wang's
arguments that it was a crucial dynastic responsibility to compile histories
of the preceding regimes without bias and prejudice so that the lessons of
the past would be textually embalmed in perpetuity. Appealing to Khubilai's pride, Wang also cleverly argued for the need to write the history of
Chinggis Khan (1167–1227) so as to reveal to the world and retain for posterity the reasons for his greatness and successes in subjugating vast areas
and numerous peoples, including the Khitan Liu and Jurchen Jin. Most
likely, it was a combination of ulterior and practical motives—enhancing
the glory of the dynasty by enshrining the early history of the Mongols,
enriching the new dynasty's knowledge of the conquered, enticing the support of the newly subordinated, and elevating the Yuan vis-à-vis the preceding dynasties—that convinced Khubilai to honor traditional Chinese
historiographical conventions. But the significant fact remains that as a result of his endorsement, the Mongols, whose culture had hitherto been
largely nonliterate, began to construct a historical tradition and initiated
a process of acculturation.

In Khubilai's reign, the official goal was to compile the early Mongol
chronicles, together with the histories of the Liao, the Jin, and the Song,
but progress was slow, largely because there was no consensus on the principles of compilation. To compile separate histories for the three regimes

implied that all three had equal legitimacy, a proposal that displeased the Chinese literati, who felt distinctions should be made. But making such distinctions was a task fraught with ideological and political implications, requiring proper criteria of discrimination. Since no agreement was reached regarding such criteria, the effort languished. However, the Yuan did make steady progress in compiling the veritable records. In 1303 the records of the first four pre-Yuan reigns were completed, followed by those of Khubilai's reign in 1304. By the end of the Yuan, the dynasty succeeded in producing veritable records for all the reigns (H. Chan 1981, 64–67; Ichimura 1929, Appendix; F. Tao 1987, 381–382; J. Jin 1976, 116, 119; Davis 1983, 42–44).

From 1312 to 1332 there were renewed calls for the completion of the histories of the Liao, the Jin, and the Song. But again the issue of *zhengtong* reared its implacable head. The question of the orthodox transmission of the political order from one dynasty to another continued to haunt the Yuan literati, frustrating the endeavor of historical compilation (H. Chan 1981, 68–72; Davis 1983, 33–42). The burning issue of the day was to formulate the correct principles for composing the histories, based in turn on the proper conceptualization of their relative status. Legitimacy was particularly thorny because alien conquest dynasties were involved. The Yuan court was obviously aware that they, like the Jin and the Liao, were of alien origin, to say nothing of the fact that they had toppled the Song, whose legitimate dynastic succession was unimpeachable.

In the welter of ideas concerning political legitimacy, two main lines of thinking emerged. The first called for emulation of the *History of the Jin Dynasty* (the dynasty that lasted from 265–420, not to be confused with the Jurchen Jin dynasty), compiled during the Tang dynasty. This history deals with a period in Chinese history when barbarian invasions and conquests were commonplace, and it discriminates between the alien kingdoms and the Han Chinese imperial house of the Jin dynasty. The annals of the aliens appear in an independent section called the *zaiji* (contemporaneous records) that is separate from the customary *benji* (basic annals) of the Jin (Song et al. 1987, 261–262). The rationale for suggesting this approach was that the Southern Song had continued the legitimate line of succession of the Northern Song. Even though the Jin had ended Song rule in northern China, the Song dynasty itself persisted. Just as barbarian regimes cropped up in China while the early Jin dynasty maintained its legitimate rule, so both the Jurchen Jin and Khitan Liao existed while China was very much under the sovereign rule of the Song. It was therefore logically sound and historically accurate to accord the Song basic annals, and consign the histories of the Liao and the Jin to contemporaneous records.

The opposing argument appealed to the precedent furnished by the *History of the Southern Dynasties* and the *History of the Northern Dynasties* (Song et al. 1987, 267–268). These were Tang dynasty compilations that did not distinguish the foreign regimes from the Chinese ones. All were simply regarded as political entities occupying certain territories. This school of thought saw the Liao as a sovereign state that appeared during the late Tang period and grew into a powerful force that rivaled the authority of the Northern Song. As such, it deserved recognition as a legitimate state. As for the Jurchen Jin, because it had brought an end to the Liao and coexisted with the Southern Song, it also warranted orthodox status. Therefore the best way to handle the histories was to adopt a tripartite format—the Liao and the Jin would constitute a "history of the north" and the Southern Song, a "history of the south," while the Northern Song would be accorded a separate "history of the Song."

Both stances left something to be desired. The first privileged the Song, and correspondingly accorded the Liao and Song of foreign origins inferior status. This, in turn, cast doubt on the legitimacy of the Yuan, who were also aliens who had risen to power as invaders and then conquerors. The second position, by legitimizing the authorities of the Liao and the Jin, also affirmed the legitimate status of the Yuan. But it also did fundamental violence to the sense that the Song should enjoy an elevated status as the legitimate successor to the Tang, not to mention the Song claim of unparalleled cultural and scholarly achievements. No one was entirely satisfied, while everyone became entrapped in the effort of trying to balance two incompatible positions, and the project stalled (H. Chan 1981, 72–74; F. Chen 1972, 16–23; Davis 1983, 43–44).

Finally, between 1343 and 1345, the compilation received new impetus. Emperor Shundi (r. 1333–1368) was known for his major push toward adopting and adapting to Chinese institutions and cultural values, and Chancellor Toghto (1314–1355) and his associates were also strongly in favor of Confucianizing the Yuan state and court (Dardess 1973, 75–118). The emperor wanted the histories completed, for he saw them as a way to rally the support of the Chinese literati while buttressing the Yuan claim to political legitimacy. He placed Toghto in charge of the history project, decreed the recruitment of proper personnel, and pledged the necessary financial support. Although the time was auspicious for relaunching the long-delayed enterprise, given the generally pro-Chinese atmosphere in the court, the question of *zhengtong* stubbornly persisted as the major impediment.

It was at this time that yet another line of thinking emerged regarding orthodox succession. This posited that none of the three dynasties was entirely legitimate, but each had some claim to legitimate rule by virtue of their ability to maintain their dominion for a substantial period of time. Proponents of this view sought credibility from historical analogy to the political situation that emerged after the fall of the Han in the third century, when the Three Kingdoms arose and coexisted in contention. By conquering the Liao, the Jin, and the Song, the Mongol Yuan dynasty achieved legitimacy. Needless to say, this position failed to quell the polemics over legitimate succession and elicited objections from the opposing camps of thought. One of the most vocal critics was Yang Weizhen (1296–1370).

Yang Weizhen's case is interesting and sheds light on the deeply felt experience of divided loyalty in a period when China was under the rule of a conquest dynasty. When Yang was born, the Yuan was already firmly established, so he never experienced the spiritual anguish of a loyalist. He was a renowned scholar and literatus with the highest examination degree. In short, he was a member of the literate elite valued by an increasingly Confucianized Yuan state. Yet when he was summoned to the capital to participate in the history project, he was ambivalent. On the one hand, he was indisputably loyal to the Yuan as a subject of a political order and regime of which he was proud. Toghto's preference for a highly ambiguous principle of legitimacy, which gave none of the three legitimacy, injured his cultural sense of loyalty to the cumulative Chinese tradition. To put the Liao and the Jin on a par with the Song, or even worse, to say that the Song had only partial legitimacy, was totally at odds with his Chinese sense of orthodoxy. Yang contended that the Southern Song had inherited *zhengtong* from the Northern Song, whose orthodox position was then assumed by the Yuan. The Liao and the Jin were marginal powers that had no share of legitimacy. Yang used two principal arguments to justify the legitimate status of the Southern Song. First, he held that a regime need not occupy the "central plains," that is, all of China proper, in order to stake the claim that it was continuing the line of political transmission and succession. Rather, the Southern Song's blood ties and lineage relations to the Northern Song more than offset the fact that the Southern Song had not established dominion over all of China.

Second, he conflated the political notion of *zhengtong* with the cultural-intellectual notion of *daotong* much celebrated by Zhu Xi and his colleagues. Just as the political order was transmitted, so the cultural order of China, embodied in the *dao*, or Way of the ancient sages, was passed down from generation to generation. Zhu Xi had argued that the ancient Way was transmitted from the ancient sages to Mencius, after whom it went into eclipse, but was revived in the Northern Song, thanks to the teachings of a succession of scholars, from Zhou Dunyi through the Cheng brothers to Zhu himself. Yang Weizhen extended Zhu's notion of the lineage of the Way by asserting that the true Way had been inherited and continued by the Yuan Confucian Xu Heng (1209–1281), the great scholar intimately associated with the court of Khubilai. To the extent that the Yuan was in possession of the authentic Way, the cumulative tradition of China, it also claimed political legitimacy, following the Southern Song. As Yang stated, "where there is 'Succession of the *Dao*' there is [also] 'political succession' (*zhitung*)" (Davis 1983, 48–49). Conversely, since the Liao and the Jin never attained the orthodox Way in any shape or form, they lay outside the realm of political orthodoxy.

Although Yang's scheme did grant the Yuan stature as holder of the Way and inheritor of China's grand philosophical tradition, it still cast a huge shadow on Mongol legitimacy because they, like the Khitan Liao and the Jurchen Jin, were conquerors of undeniably non-Chinese stock.

Moreover, by directly linking Yuan legitimacy to the Southern Song, the nature of the Mongol dominion before 1279 when the Song was finally subjugated became nebulous. As a consequence, Toghto deemed Yang's interpretations highly undesirable and in fact unacceptable. Aggrieved that his deeply sincere views had fallen on deaf ears, Yang left the History Bureau in protest (Davis 1983, 42–51; H. Chan 1981, 89–90; Shaochuan Zhou 2001, 93–97).

Fearing further dissension and ideological polemics generated by well-known scholars like Yang Weizhen, and troubled by the specter that the historiographical project might once again fall into a state of limbo, Toghto decided to ignore opposing views and forge ahead. He unilaterally embraced the following line of argument: the Liao, the Jin, and the Song could claim no complete legitimacy, while the Yuan, having vanquished the three powers, naturally assumed orthodox political status. Under Toghto's forceful leadership, composition of the histories finally got off the ground and was soon moving at full speed. Toghto did not quite see the project through to completion, however. In 1344 he resigned his directorship when he stepped down from his chancellorship. Nonetheless, the histories were completed with unprecedented speed—the Liao history was finished in April 1343, the Jin in November 1344, and the Song in December 1345 (H. Chan 1970, 16–21).

The three histories follow the standard histories in format; they consist of imperial annals, monographs, tables, and biographies. The compilers struggled to be objective, giving, for instance, Jin and Song loyalists their proper places, and they tried to accommodate accounts that were not necessarily consistent with those offered from the Yuan perspective. Inevitably, however, biases crept in. Rulers and personages in the last days of the Jin and the Song were treated harshly because it was necessary to show that the Mongol Yuan were justified in removing the wicked and undesirable on behalf of China. The early dealings of the Mongols with the three powers were also recorded in such a way that only positive aspects of the Yuan progenitors would be highlighted (W. Du 2004, 117–123). A revealing case is how the *Song History* treats the end of the Southern Song dynasty and the loyalists' resistance.

The Song loyalists themselves, of course, testified to their own experiences and recorded their responses to the crisis of foreign invasion and the fall of all China to foreign rule. While many Chinese literati submitted to the Yuan regime and worked loyally for their new lord, quite a few remained loyal to the memory of the defunct Song and constructed their own accounts. How did each group perceive and describe loyalism? How did they interpret the sociopolitical tumult and psychological agony? How did they express their bitter feelings and melancholy views of the present? The most famous and influential of the loyalist accounts was that by Wen Tianxiang (1236–1283). In the writings that made up his collected works (*Wenshan xiansheng quanji*), Wen described his experience of resistance, imprisonment, and finally, impending execution. It was resistance literature couched in intimate biographical terms, a first-person account in which the conscious goal was to bequeath to posterity a morally edifying record. Using himself as the example and mirror, Wen extolled the virtue of loyalty to one's dynastic master and cultural heritage, and celebrated the value of sacrifice for the right cause. While descriptions of the past could be emotionally compelling, psychologically uplifting, and spiritually inspiring, as historical accounts they were also incomplete, fragmentary, one-sided, myopic, self-serving, and self-righteous. Wen did not hesitate to criticize many of his fellow loyalists, not to mention the defectors, in an effort to enhance the nobility of his own views and actions (Jay 1990, 589–596).

On the other hand, the *Song History* had its own biases. Although it did grant the Song loyalists their biographies—many were duly categorized as martyrs, loyal and righteous men, indicating that the compilers did consult the Song loyalist accounts—the events surrounding the fall of the Southern Song were largely recorded from the perspective of the Yuan generals involved in the grand enterprise of invasion and drew almost exclusively from Yuan sources. There is no question that the compilers muted the scathing criticisms and modified unsavory incidents in telling of the Mongol invaders and conquerors. In addition, the *Song History* underscored the magnanimity and clemency of Khubilai's policies. Even as it praised the devotion of the loyalists to their dynastic lord, it took great pains to convey the moral distinction of the Mongol generals entrusted with the task of destroying the Southern Song. In this moral calculus, the Mongols more than measured up to the Chinese loyalists and martyrs. The Mongol conquerors, by performing rituals to honor and propitiate the loyalists, were shown to have displayed sympathy for their plight and admiration for their steadfastness. But significantly, the *Song History* was most explicit in pointing out that the actions of the loyalists were futile and ultimately wrong, for they were at odds with Heaven's intent. Brutal executions, sometimes by gruesome mutilation that induced protracted pain and slow death, were deliberately glossed with laconic rhetoric such as "unyielding, they perished." The *Song History* also amplified the Mongol claim to legitimacy by referring to it as "the Great Yuan" in the annals for the year 1232, even though the Mongols did not actually declare establishment of the Yuan dynasty until 1271 (Jay 1990, 596–598).

In the Yuan rendering of events we see once again the past being brought into service on behalf of the present. Notwithstanding the officially declared historiographical policy of truthful and complete recording without fear of censure and censorship from above, the Yuan official historians constructed a version of history palatable to the ruling regime, whose legitimacy and beneficence were at once affirmed.

The three histories do, however, exhibit innovative features. In the Liao and the Jin histories, for instance, the monographs and the tables record the interactions and communications between various states and peoples, conveying the complex geopolitical landscape of twelfth- and thirteenth-century northeast Asia. Khitan and Jurchen terminology was also included, reflecting the compilers' awareness of the multiethnic and multilingual nature of that particular time and place in Chinese history. However, there are also clear signs of strain as a result of the great haste of their compilation. Inconsistencies and redundancies abound—historical figures are wrongly identified; names are confused, especially non-Chinese ones; statements contradict one another in the same text; and so on. Important events are also omitted. The language and narrative are often unrefined and unfinished, especially in the *Liao History*. The *Song History*, on the other hand, suffers from plodding, stodgy language, not to mention a choppy narrative, the direct result, it would appear, of the compilers' inability to digest the voluminous sources available to them. The *Jin History*, by comparison, has been commended for its concision and readability, largely because of the high quality of its sources and the work of both Yuan Haowen and Liu Qi, which went a long way toward organizing and preserving the Jin materials (H. Chan 1981, 91–93; H. Chan 1970, 39–41; Shaochuan Zhou 2001, 103–109). In view of their enormous contributions to Yuan historiography, it is worthwhile to look at Yuan and Liu more closely.

The Historiographical Contributions of Private Scholars

After the fall of the Jin, Yuan Haowen, who refused to serve the new Yuan regime, dedicated himself to the task of collecting and preserving the dynasty's records. This included pursuing what we call oral history, for he interviewed people involved in critical events. His most complete extant work is the *Zhongzhou ji* (Records of the central plains). The title itself connotes the legitimacy of the Jin dynasty. Zhongzhou—literally, the "middle territories," and by extension, the "middle kingdom"—was the ancient name for Henan, which represented the traditional center of Chinese civilization; it was also the domain of the Jurchen Jin. Primarily a collection of Jin poetry, the *Zhongzhou ji* nevertheless furnishes valuable historical information. By avocation a poet and a historian, Yuan produced what may be called historical poems (West 1995, 281–303; Suzuki 1955, 36–54). His anthology included poems not just by literary figures, but also by the Jin emperors, officials, and other personalities. Works by the Liao and Song authors who served in the Jin court were included. Most important, Yuan included valuable biographical details of the authors. Most of the biographical entries pertain to individuals, but some are composite in nature. In keeping with the traditional historiographical principle of moral adjudication, Yao bestowed accolades and imposed censure on personages and events. His conscientious effort did much to preserve the literary culture and other aspects of the Jin past (H. Chan 1970, 68–94).

Liu Qi's most notable contribution to Jin historiography lay in his *Guiqian zhi* (Memoirs from retirement). Although this work consists largely of anecdotes, episodic narratives, and miscellaneous reflections—it has therefore usually been classified as belonging to the genre of fictive writings (*xiaoshuo*)—the information in it has enormous historical value. Liu, as a major literary figure well connected to the Jin literati, was in a position to observe closely the important people and events of his day. His goal was to record the great tumult in the waning days of the Jin so that posterity might come to know the reasons for the dynasty's decline and fall. As we have seen in our earlier discussion on Jin historiography, Liu teased out the moral meanings of the past and reached broad conclusions about the ups and downs of political fortunes in history. His reflections were firmly based on his knowledge of ancient and recent history. In particular, his *Memoirs* provide detailed information on the institutions of the Jin, together with Liu's sober diagnoses of their problems, such as the pervasive apathy of the ruling elite, the systematic corruption and declining morale in the officialdom, the lack of testing on practical matters in the civil service examinations, and the inflation of the paper currency. He vividly portrays emperors and princes, civil and military officials, literary figures and works, and the Mongol invasion (H. Chan 1970, 121–166). He tells us in no uncertain terms the aims of his *Memoir:* "Moreover, what I have seen and heard, that which could serve as admonition and warning, I should not let perish without being transmitted. Therefore I must muse upon these events during my leisure, write down what I have got, and call my records the *Guiqian zhi.* . . . I hope that in future times when people came to write history, they might find my memoir worth consulting" (ibid., 131–132). His graphic, candid first-hand accounts are among the best sources on the Jin dynasty, especially its last days.

Another scholar who made an indelible mark in the world of Yuan historiography was Su Tianjue (1294–1352), especially known as the author of two important works, the *Guochao mingchen shilue* (Brief records of eminent officials of our dynasty) and *Guochao wenlei* (Literature of our dynasty classified by genre). Unlike Yuan Haowen and Liu Qi, he served the Yuan and in fact established a very prosperous career in various official capacities, including being a compiler of the veritable records of several reigns. In an effort to complement the annalistic veritable records with biographically oriented narratives, he started compiling the *Brief Records of Eminent Officials* when he was only twenty years old and completed it in 1329. His main aim was to record the deeds and misdeeds of both the rulers and officials as lessons for posterity. He knew that it had its limitations. It was, after all, a private compilation of only fifteen fascicles composed from insufficient sources, and hence his title *Brief Records.* He hoped that more detailed and full-fledged works of a similar nature could be produced with the backing of official resources, and thus recommended to the History Bureau the ways of producing the needed comprehensive compilations. The first step was to establish a complete list of officials to be studied, followed by the diligent culling of all pertinent sources and documents related to these subjects. For his own private compilation, which covered the lives of forty-seven officials, Su employed no less than 120 sources, including official documents, private writings, epitaphs, inscriptions on stones and steles, and memoirs. It is a testimonial to the caliber of his work that the official *Yuan History*, in its rendition of the biographies of Yuan personages, relied a good deal on Su's materials. Su further warned against leaving out individuals who failed to achieve high official positions, since talents and morals did not always translate into bureaucratic success. The ethical accomplishments of such people must be properly recorded so as to serve as the "guide for subsequent generations" and "edification for the future." But it was equally important to duly record evil actions and wicked deeds as cautionary tales (H. Franke 1961, 119; Shaochuan Zhou 2001, 190–194, 196–201).

Su's other work, *Literature of Our Dynasty* completed in 1334 in seventy fascicles, is an indispensable source for the study of Yuan literary accomplishments. Interestingly enough, even though Su collected odes, poems, eulogies, dirges, prefaces, and memorials, his main criterion for inclusion was not literary elegance but practical utility. He selected only those writings that "are pertinent to politics and add to the moral teachings of the world." Their literary sophistication and beauty are significant only to the extent that they "remedy the vulgarity of customs." Most important, the texts must complement and reinforce existing historical records and writings. The result was that his work clearly privileged treatises and prose that directly shed light on politics and institutions. Of the seventy fascicles, poetry and the like comprise only nine. Clearly Su's conception of historiography was heavily informed by the traditional ideal of the direct utility of the past (Shaochuan Zhou 2001, 194–196).

Institutional Histories

The Yuan, like other dynasties, also compiled works on the administrative structure, statutes, and precedents of the Yuan officialdom. The *Dynastic Statutes and Regulations of the Sagely Administration of the Great Yuan* (*Da Yuan shengzheng guochao dianzhang*) contains two parts. The first has sixty fascicles, while the second is a running text not divided into fascicles. It offers information on the general structure of the Yuan government, together with detailed descriptions of the Six Ministries of Personnel, Finance, Rites, War, Punishments, and Public Works, covering the period from the reign of Khubilai to 1322 (F. Tao 1987, 382–383). Another notable compilation in the same vein was the *Huangchao jingshi dadian* (The imperial dynasty's grand institutions for managing the world) in 880 fascicles, which provides coverage up to the year 1330. It is no longer extant in its original form, but huge portions were used in the composition of the *Yuan History*. Parts of it were also incorporated into the famous Ming dynasty encyclopedia, *Yongle dadian* (The grand compendium of the Yongle reign). This compilation was mandated and closely monitored by Emperor Wenzong (1328–1332), who attached to it great symbolic meaning. Through this textual production, the emperor proclaimed his reign as a new beginning, which took stock of the administrative practices and rules of the past and looked forward to a fresh chapter in Yuan dynastic governance. Here we have a clear example of how the writing of history was simultaneously the making of a political statement (Lam 1992, 77–80; W. Du 2004, 131).

To be sure, this huge administrative history was more than a statement to inaugurate one reign. It was meant as a celebration and summation of the dynasty's accomplishments by affirming and asserting the multiethnic nature of the Yuan dynasty, a vast domain that encompassed an unprecedented number of peoples and cultures. It delineated the highly complex and well-organized administrative structure and underscored the Yuan's numerous projects to improve transportation, build roads and canals, and construct irrigation and flood-control projects. It advertised the regime's patronage of learning and cultural activities. It declared, in grand Confucian fashion, the principle of Yuan governance, which was to safeguard the livelihood of the people—the root and basis of the country. It extolled Yuan efforts to promote agriculture, lessen taxes, curtail acquisition of land and tax evasion by local magnate, and curb spending. It emphasized that the dynasty had bolstered educational institutions so as to strengthen the social fabric by reinforcing the Three Bonds and Five Relationships. In a nutshell, it revealed how the "Way of the ruler" (*wangdao*) with its "virtuous governance" (*dezheng*) was realized in the administration, legislation, and institutions of the Yuan. This was another perfect example of history being used to serve current purposes—the provision of policy guidelines and glorification of the reigning dynasty's achievements (Shaochuan Zhou 2001, 178–187; Langlois 1978, 99–116; Langlois 1982, 125–135).

As part of the Mongol Eurasian empire, the Yuan dynasty ruled over a large domain. It had to collect geographic and administrative information on regions and localities in order to institute and maintain effective administration. As early as 1285, Khubilai ordered compilation of a general compendium that would assemble the disparate locally oriented geographic and administrative gazetteers into one work of nationwide coverage. In 1324 the *Da Yuan yitongzhi* (The general compendium of the unity of the great Yuan) in 1,300 fascicles was completed. Earlier forms of such compendia had already been produced in the Sui dynasty, and they became more commonplace in the Song, when it became customary to collect regional gazetteers to form a larger text. But the Yuan product was truly spectacular, several times more detailed than its later counterparts in the Ming and Qing dynasties. Each prefecture received one fascicle's worth of coverage, and each fascicle included information on the origins and developments of the prefecture, descriptions of its major towns and cities, topography, produce and products, local customs and personages, and so on. Although no longer extant, its many parts were absorbed into similar compendia of the Ming and Qing periods (F. Tao 1987, 382; Hargett 1996, 410).

Historiographical Innovation in Ma Duanlin's Private History

Of private histories, the *Wenxian tongkao* (Comprehensive investigation of the literary traditions) by Ma Duanlin (1254–1324/5?) was indubitably the most celebrated. Greatly pained by the fall of the Song, Ma refused to serve the Yuan but instead dedicated himself to preserving, understanding, and explicating the cultural heritage of China, especially that bequeathed by the Song. He plunged himself headlong into the composition of a universal history with a particular emphasis on the origins and evolution of institutions, statecraft, and governance. The 348-fascicle *Comprehensive Investigation,* completed in 1307, was a voluminous work twenty years in the making. Together with two important antecedent works, Du You's *Tongdian* (Comprehensive compendium [on institutions]) and Zheng Qiao's *Tongzhi* (Comprehensive treatises), the three texts are generally known as the Three Compendia (*santong*). Indeed, they display many commonalities in terms of purpose, subject matter, and focus. All three works emulated Sima Qian's and Sima Guang's efforts to provide a comprehensive history from antiquity to the recent past, the goal of which was to reveal broadly the twists and turns of institutional development over time and place. The central belief was that through panoramic surveys of vast historical landscapes, one would comprehend the universal principles and laws that underlay historical change. Second, as opposed to the focus on political and biographic portrayals in the standard histories, the Three Compendia emphasized the crucial importance of institutional and bureaucratic change. Third, they all sought to be thorough, using a wide variety of sources, sometimes quoting them extensively, but at other times abridging them, and often commenting on them. Fourth, the three authors distinguished their works by carefully categorizing and classifying the topics they examined. Such taxonomical organization permitted systematic exploration of a vast array of subjects. Fifth, they approached historical records with a healthy dose of skepticism, especially those involving supranatural explanations based on the esoteric cosmological theories of Yin-Yang and the Five Phases. Sixth, perhaps because of their wariness about any neat integration of human deeds with natural happenings in moral terms, the trio were diffident about assigning history the moral function of praising the good and censuring the bad. As we have seen, Zheng Qiao was especially emphatic that historians not read too much into the way Confucius composed the *Spring and Autumn Annals.* They should refrain from concluding with sweeping certitude that moral judgments lay embedded in every word and phrase. Last, Du, Zheng, and Ma were inspired by the practical function of history. They saw their works as storehouses of historical precedents, the analogical analyses of which would yield practical insights for the understanding of the present circumstances and the formulation of current policies (H. Chan 1982, 27–32, 40–48; J. Jin 1976, 235–239; W. Du 2004, 132–133).

Of the three, Ma's work was arguably the most comprehensive in terms of topics and chronology, not to mention his more critical and extensive employment of sources. Whereas Du dealt with eight categories of subjects, and Zheng with twenty, Ma's *Comprehensive Investigation* systematically examined twenty-four subjects in as many sections: land taxation; coinage and currency; population and census; corvée and duties; customs and tolls; markets and trades; local tributes; national expenditure; examinations and recruitments; schools; government offices; imperial and auxiliary sacrifices; imperial ancestral temples; court rituals; music; the military; punishments; books and bibliographies; imperial genealogy; system of enfeoffment; numerological and astrological configurations; prodigies of nature; geography; and foreign peoples. It is, in other words, a superior work in many ways. Ma intended to comprehensively (*tong*) investigate (*kao*) the cumulative literary traditions constituted by the reliable and trustworthy classics, histories, government records and the miscellaneous writings of individual scholars (*wen*), and all other worthy and corroborating commentaries and cognate writings (*xian*). In so doing, he sought to expose the nexus between laws and institutions, and reveal the interlocking patterns of growth and development of bureaucratic apparatuses and governmental offices. Ma believed that while the political histories of dynasties and periods were unrelated and demonstrated no generalizable patterns, institutions displayed organic unity and historical continuity that demanded comparative study across time (H. Chan 1982, 36–39; Song et al. 1987, 351–352; F. Tao 1987, 352–354; W. Du 2004, 134–136).

To put it another way, Ma placed the relatively new wine of institutional studies into the old bottle of historical analogism, based on his conviction that in this arena, too, past precedents served as efficacious present guides. History, especially institutional history, was a revealing mirror that reflected both correct and erroneous ways of government. By interrogating the history of laws, statutes, and regulations in both politics and economics, Ma repudiated the role of extrahuman forces, reduced the mechanistic practice of levying praise and blame, and chose to probe causation (*gu*) in the changes that occurred in the past. In delineating specific causes of specific institutional changes throughout history, Ma sought to make the larger point that the passage of time meant the alteration of circumstances. Obdurate adherence to old practices, or worse still, idealistic revival of ancient ways, went against the flow of time and was thus anachronistic. Commenting on the abandonment of the well-field system in the Warring States period, which had encouraged communal agriculture, and the end of the Tang tax system based on payment in kind and service, Ma concluded that the changes might not be as egalitarian and equitable in design and intent, but they were more responsive to and more appropriate for the existing circumstances (H. Chan 1982, 48–51; Shaochuan Zhou 2001, 163–169).

Ma's sensitivity to change gave him a keen sense of epochal shifts. To him, Chinese history had witnessed two major periods of transformation, from antiquity to the Qin period, and from the Han to the end of the Song. Within these two broad segments of time, Ma identified smaller stages of notable developments. His periodization was animated by and explicated in terms of the dynamic interplay between two opposing pairs of phenomena, *gong* (public-mindedness or impartiality) versus *si* (private interest or self-centeredness), and *guang* (brightness or Heaven) versus *yue* (darkness or earth). The first pair contained a prescriptive and normative moral-political concept—devotion to public welfare and the corresponding curtailing of selfish interests—as the fundamental way to foster and maintain a prosperous state and society. Indulgence in selfish desires and individual interests spelt inevitable doom for any commonwealth. The behavior and culture of the ruling elite and literati determined the fortune, good or ill, of the larger community. The second pair, brightness and darkness, derived from the cosmogonic notion that before things came into being and before time (and therefore also before history), brightness and darkness did not exist, and there was no differentiation between Heaven and earth. But with the emergence of the myriad things, the realms of Heaven and earth separated, and a distinction appeared between brightness and darkness. Ma correlated this cosmological development with historical evolution. As there were light and dark, and Heaven and earth, so too there were heavenly affairs and human occurrences, religious values and secular undertakings. These polarities provided Ma with a theoretical framework through which he elucidated changes in history, as the diffused social, political, and economic institutions in ancient times gave way to the centralized imperial bureaucracy of later periods.

Ma took great pains to first dissect the development of the "feudal system" (*fengjian*), the system of enfeoffment that defined the political order of ancient China. That this system worked perfectly well at one time owed much to the fact that the kings and lords did not view their territories as private possessions. It was a time when a sense of territoriality was not firmly entrenched, and the body politic was enlivened by a communal sense of public good and sharing. But with the rise of the Qin dynasty, the creation of the "prefectural system" (*junxian*) altered the basis of power; the ruler claimed ownership of all the territories under his rule, and hence there also emerged a concept of the value of individual interests. According to Ma, this was not simply a matter of change of the minds and hearts of the rulers; the conditions of the time had become different. Although the prefectural system might be inferior as it embodied and reflected the self-oriented values of both the state and the rulers, it fitted the needs of the time. The enfeoffment system could not have worked effectively when the political picture had become so much more complex and elaborate. Ma asserted that the sages themselves told us "not to be at odds with the times" (*weishi*), and so they acceded to the replacement of the old system by the new prefectural system (H. Chan 1982, 51–55; F. Tao 1987, 354–355; W. Du 2004, 136–139).

Similarly, informed by his sense of anachronism, when Ma analyzed the evolution of government offices and population changes in ancient

China, he constructed a history marked by different stages of development. Ancient history could be divided into three periods: the first covered the period from the very beginnings of Chinese civilization to the times of Yao and Shun; the second was the Three Dynasties of the Xia, the Shang, and the Zhou; and the third came with the Qin creation of a universal empire. These epochs denoted the change from public-mindedness to self-centeredness and reflected the cosmological shift from a state of integration of Heaven/brightness with earth/darkness to one of the differentiation between the two. Differentiation meant diversification of all government functions and a growing complexity of the imperial bureaucracy, which in turn meant that the uncorrupted sagely rule based on righteousness no longer could suffice. The result was the increasing use of coercive measures to sustain law and order. In addition, as the population grew, human capacities and talents also became highly varied and the specialization of labor and professionalization of duties produced a more elaborate network of human relationships. Such historical dynamics also weakened a lofty sense of the common good, but that could be rectified by the conscious renewal and restoration of public-mindedness aimed at communal betterment.

This institutional history expressed in a language of values went hand in hand with Ma's political theory of the rise and growth of highly centralized imperial power. In his various surveys of institutional development, such as those pertaining to the transition from the feudal to the prefectural system, the evolution of the examination and recruitment systems, and the unfolding of the taxation system, Ma focused on the less-than-desirable, albeit unstoppable, growth of imperial authority through successive phases of history. Concentration of power at the top was a symptom of the self-centered quest for individual interests by the ruler and the ruling elite, which resulted in exploitation of the people. Ma linked an understanding of past phenomena with comprehension of present problems and saw that similar problems beset the Song, especially the Southern Song. His *Comprehensive Investigation* contained detailed descriptions of recent Song institutional history and offered his diagnoses of the problems he discerned. This historical exposition was also very likely a veiled attempt to reveal the similar governmental maladies that also afflicted the Yuan (H. Chan 1982, 59–68).

Ma focused on four major weaknesses in the Song regime. First was exorbitant taxation necessitated by heavy national expenditure. Second was malfeasance and corruption in the Song officialdom, where sinecures predominated. Third was a bloated military that mistook quantity for quality and was expensive to maintain but ineffective in warding off foreign incursions. Fourth was the weak-kneed appeasement policy toward the ever-threatening barbarian forces (Shaochuan Zhou 2001, 165–174). In short, Ma Duanlin, with his evolutionary and dynamic understanding of the flow of time, distilled from his panoramic survey of China's institutional history the laws and patterns of change, which in turn furnished the most reliable guide for tackling current problems.

History and the Learning of the Way (Daoxue)

As we have seen in the Song, the enduring instinct to establish the architectonics of change was not a monopoly of historiography. Zhu Xi and the Confucian proponents of the Learning of the Way, Daoxue — the new Confucianism that sought to integrate human affairs (and their moral-ethical iterations) with metaphysical first principles — had also been much inspired by the complex interconnections between past and present and had, accordingly, propounded their own notion of change. The Mongol Yuan, after some initial hesitancy, faced the daunting fact of ruling a vast Chinese majority whose cultural elite remained firmly committed to the traditional values of Confucianism. They had little choice but to adapt. While conserving their power through a hybrid political order that grafted a Chinese-style civil officialdom onto the traditional Mongol military apparatus, the Yuan, between 1313 and 1315, during the reign of Emperor Renzong (r. 1311–1320), established a Confucian orthodoxy. It was based on the teachings of Zhu Xi and the Learning of the Way, whose institutional expression and consequence was the newly constituted civil service examination system (de Bary 1982, 1–4). A host of Chinese scholars followed the footsteps of Zhu as self-conscious keepers of the flame of Daoxue. Inspired by the master's teachings and his mission of moral self-cultivation as the basis of the Confucian Way, they reflected on the cultural and symbolic capital of China, including its past (de Bary 1981, 21–24, 91–126). It is therefore germane to conclude our consideration of Yuan historiography by taking a brief look at the conception of history as it was filtered through the philosophy and metaphysics of Daoxue, Learning of the Way.

One of the most influential Confucian scholars in the Yuan was Xu Heng. Apart from being a teacher of great reputation, Xu served first as an educational intendant and then the chancellor of the Imperial College. He actively and effectively propagated Zhu Xi's teachings and consolidated the canonical status of the Four Books — Analects (*Lunyu*), *The Great Learning* (*Daxue*), *The Doctrine of the Mean* (*Zhongyong*), and *Mencius* (*Mengzi*) — which Zhu had promoted as the quintessential textual embodiment of the sages' teachings. In keeping with the Daoxue metaphysical interpretation of the workings of the universe, Xu affirmed the Way as the Great Ultimate (*taiji*) — that is, ultimate reality that was also *li*, Principle, whose multiple manifestations could be seen in the myriad things (H. Chan 1982, 209, 211–218). Guided by this overarching ultimate reality, the flow of time followed a certain universal pattern. This pattern was by no means abstract and obscure, for the why's and how's of all things could be seen most concretely in the rise and fall of political fortunes. Xu posited that there was neither uninterrupted peace nor perpetual disorder. Within peace were always seeds of chaos, and in the midst of disorder, there were already opportunities for regeneration. Prosperity bred senescence, while deterioration did not preclude movement toward regeneration.

In highly philosophical terms Xu further theorized that the successions of peace and disorder resulted from the tug of war between Heaven's forces and human ones. When the former were in ascendancy, culture, the state, and society were guided by the ideals and values of simplicity (*zhi*); but when the latter held sway, there was the pervasive tendency toward refinement (*wen*) that readily degenerated into indulgence in extravagance and an obsession with outward forms as opposed to inner substance. As we have seen, both Sima Qian and Han New Script thinkers such as Dong Zhongshu had employed the notions of simplicity and refinement to characterize two different stages of civilizational development in their cultural ethos. Xu used a similar historicist language and schema to propound his own dialectical alternation of peace and disorder. Such a conception of history was heavily tinged with fatalism, and Xu himself ascribed the interchange of the two phenomena to the force of destiny (*ming*). Yet he also infused a healthy dose of human agency to mitigate this fatalism—by destiny he meant that which had to happen at a certain time, and a certain time *in* history meant specific circumstances. When looking at peace or disorder, one had to penetrate beneath the phenomena to probe the long-terms forces in history. If a dynasty collapsed, it was because forces of destruction had been at work. When the process of decline continued unabated, a dynasty would reach the point where the actual objective circumstances were such that it could no longer be saved. For Xu, the truly sagacious historical figures were those who had the ability to recognize the trends of the times and the dictates of the circumstances.

But making change, according to Xu, did not mean pursuing and adopting any actions whatsoever in the name of expediency. In history, positive changes were always those that conformed to the Way of the ruler (*wangdao*), namely, statecraft and governance based on virtues and moral suasion. In contradistinction was the Way of the hegemon (*badao*), which was motivated by the pursuit of profits and backed by coercion. To forge a stable state required winning the hearts and minds of all-under-Heaven (*tianxia*). As with Ma Duanlin, Xu stressed the importance of public-mindedness and impartiality on the part of the ruler, for this was instrumental in securing the willing submission of the people. But whereas Ma saw public-mindedness as an institutional requirement for the proper operation of the laws, statutes, and imperial bureaucracy, Xu regarded it essentially as a moral force, although it was no less potent in the political domain. To be attentive and devoted to the public interest was to be compassionate and loving (*ai*) toward the people, and this compassion or love was in turn the realization of the cardinal virtue of humanity (*ren*). In short, humanity is the very principle (*li*) of compassion. The flux of history and the pattern of change were guided by the overarching principle, the quotidian expression of which were the virtues that enlivened and defined good government. In the final analysis, Xu, a Daoxue Confucian, interpreted history in meta-ethical terms as the exemplification of the moral forces inherent in the universe (Shaochuan Zhou 2001, 4–7, 15–16, 24–26).

As Xu Heng and the other Daoxue literati sought to define, promote, and consolidate what they regarded as the orthodox lineage of the Confucian Way, the *daotong*, they were simultaneously redefining and reinforcing what it meant to be Chinese. Put simply, to be Chinese was to be Confucian. This assertion had direct implications for any effort to determine the historical legitimacy of the Yuan dynasty with reference to *zhengtong*, the orthodox transmission of the political order. To the Confucians who served the Mongol rulers, the Yuan dynasty was Chinese insofar as it adopted the Confucian Way. Insofar as it did so, it deserved to be the legitimate ruler of China. From their arguments concerning the regime of the Yuan, they generalized about the interrelationship between China and cultural others, expounding in the process some broad historical views on the nature of Sino-barbarian interaction. Here they diverged significantly from Zhu Xi, whose *Outline and Details of the Comprehensive Mirror* stressed the difference between the Chinese and the barbarians. To Zhu, revival and preservation of the orthodox Way was one crucial way to defend Chinese culture in face of ever-imminent barbarian incursions. To the Yuan Confucians, the Way was the universal system of values to which everyone, including Mongols, could aspire. By virtue of embracing the Chinese dynastic order and the Chinese way of rule, the Yuan had attained the Confucian Way (W. Chan 1982, 197–208; H. Franke 1982, 162–178).

Xu likened conflicts between the Chinese and their neighbors to squabbles within a family. All-under-Heaven constituted one family; both the Han Chinese and the barbarians were members of humankind. A ruler was legitimate as long as he ruled with the cardinal virtue of humanity (*ren*). To rule humanely specifically meant adopting the Han Chinese ways of governance. In his memorials to Khubilai, Xu explicitly pointed to the causal relationship between Sinicization and political longevity by referring to historical examples. The Northern Wei dynasty (386–534) established by the Toba, the Liao by the Khitan, and the Jin by the Jurchen, were all enduring regimes, thanks to their submission and subscription to Chinese values and institutions. Those numerous kingdoms established by conquest which failed to Sinicize themselves simply came and went. But Xu took pains to say that such cultural and institutional assimilation was necessarily a gradual process of no fewer than thirty years, for he feared igniting revulsion and resistance among the traditional Mongol elite. Nonetheless, his main thesis was that historical records provided crystal-clear indications that Chinese ways of governance and cultural values encompassed and accommodated all those who adopted them (H. Franke 1982, 214–218).

Hao Jing (1223–1275), another Yuan Confucian master who studied under the great scholar Yuan Haowen, also strove to collapse the demarcation between the Chinese and the so-called barbarians. He forcefully proclaimed that to the extent that the Yuan employed the talents of the literati and followed Chinese ways, the dynasty was the legitimate ruler of China. The Mandate of Heaven was not bestowed only on certain domains or peoples; rather, it was given to those morally distinguished leaders who followed the *dao*, the Way. This, as Hao further clarified, was the moral-ethical tradition of China, together with its age-old institutions, implements, and learning. As with Xu Heng, Hao buttressed his contention with historical examples, pointing to the accomplishments of the Tuoba Wei dynasty. He also praised the achievements of the Jin dynasty for "using the Chinese [ways] and thereby transforming [their] barbarity" (*yongxia bianyi*) (Shaochuan Zhou 2001, 74–88).

Hao Jing and Xu Heng both culled evidence from history that lent credence to their supraethnic argument of political legitimacy, based on universalistic assumptions of an overarching Way. Yuan Confucianism—the appeal to a time-nullifying, totalizing, and transcendent order of values—ultimately had to embody a sort of historicism, a resort to actual examples in the past to construct a pattern of how things worked. History not only supplied precedents, played didactic roles, and exemplified good and evil, but also in the ultimate sense, it constituted the very Way that sought to transcend it.

CHAPTER 7

The Ming

The Flowering of Private Historiography and Its Innovations

The establishment of the Ming (1368–1644) meant the revival of a native Chinese dynasty, a regime of considerable longevity and accomplishment. Yet compared with those of the Song, Ming achievements in historiography seem to pale. The Ming could rival neither the quantitative fecundity nor qualitative innovation of the Song. By Ming times, many historiographical conventions had become well entrenched and were taken for granted as authoritative models. But the Ming spanned almost three centuries, and it would be grossly reductive and simply wrong to posit that all historical writings merely followed old ruts. The writing of history in the Ming did experience dynamic growth, and there were in fact ample examples of creativity, both in form and substance.

The Ming was a period of vibrant intellectual and cultural change. Literacy burgeoned, spurred on by economic expansion and urban development, especially in the lower Yangzi area. In addition, the growth of the civil service examinations stimulated the production of reading materials, including those on history, which was an important subject in the examinations. A corollary to the growth of readership was an increased demand for books and writings. The technology that supported both writing and reading made great strides, developing simultaneously with increased literacy. No longer was the reading public a relatively small literati group. Many more segments of society had easy access to reading material and appreciated cultural achievements. Commercial enterprises reprinted works produced by the court so that cultured people would have ready access to great books—the Confucian canon, the standard histories, the Ming law code and administrative statutes, and the like. The building of personal libraries became popular, and scholars began to acquire in earnest books that they would preserve in their own collections (W. Franke 1988, 726–727; Brook 1998a, 129–133; K. Wu 1942–1943, 203–260).

The monograph "Bibliography of [Ming] works" (Yiwen zhi), in the standard history of the Ming compiled in the Qing, gives a good indication of the variety and volume of historical works produced in the Ming. According to this source, there were ten categories of works of history—

official histories (*zhengshi*) such as the standard histories and the veritable records, miscellaneous histories (*zashi*), sundry historical recordings (*shichao*), anecdotes (*gushi*), geography (*dili*), genealogies (*pudie*), biographies (*zhuanzhi*), together with works on the imperial bureaucracy (*zhiguan*), rites and ceremonies (*yizhu*), and penal codes (*xingfa*) — organized around 1,378 subcategories that amounted to some 27,547 fascicles. Clearly in sheer size Ming historical production was by no means insignificant, especially given the unfortunate fact that vigorous Qing censorship resulted in the purging and destruction of many Ming works (F. Tao 1987, 389–390).

Official Historiography and the Production of Encyclopedic Anthologies

One noteworthy accomplishment during the Ming was the official compilation of many massive encyclopedic works. Imperial editions of the Confucian classics appeared that included the commentaries and interpretations of Zhu Xi and his Song followers, as the Ming court actively promoted Confucian worship and a Confucian orthodoxy (Chu 1999, 495–524; Wilson 1996, 563–571). Moreover, in accordance with convention the new dynasty embarked on the composition of the *Yuan History,* together with the compilation of its own veritable and other court records. The mammoth *Yongle Encyclopedia* (*Yongle dadian*) comprises 12,000 volumes (*ce*). Compiled during the reign of the Yongle emperor (1403–1424), it was at the time the largest compilation ever undertaken in Chinese history. Subsequently, massive official geographic works were compiled, and the sixteenth century saw the publication of the voluminous *Gathering of Essentials of the August Ming* (*Da Ming huidian*) and the *Collected Ceremonies of the August Ming* (*Da Ming ji li*), produced under the supervision of the Directorate of Ceremonial (*sili jian*), which stored the printing blocks in its Storehouse of Classics (*jingchang*). As a consequence these collections were also known as "Volumes of the Storehouse of Classics" (*jingchang ben*). They were distinguished by their high quality, a testimonial to the advances in printing technology. These works served as prototypes for the later encyclopedic compilations during the Qing (W. Franke 1988, 728–729; K. Wu 1942– 1943, 228–229).

A brief look at the process of compiling some of these impressive historical anthologies is in order. To the extent that history was construed as an appropriate expression of imperial power, the Ming, like all prior dynasties, accorded central importance to the ordering of the past. The institutional home of these historiographical undertakings was the Bureau of National History (*guoshi guan*), situated in the Hanlin Academy. The top graduates of the metropolitan examinations were recruited as compilers, but their appointments depended on specific projects at hand, as there was no fixed number of posts. Other officials were also responsible for compiling the national history. Especially important was the recording of the imperial audiences (the diary of activity and repose) that furnished the initial raw materials for the veritable records. This practice, however, was abandoned in the early 1390s and imperial audience proceedings were not again recorded until 1575 as a result of a plea by Zhang Juzheng (1525–1582) (X. Li 1999, 91–92). The memorial Zhang submitted reveals how the Bureau of Historiography was supposed to have worked. First, the document stressed the utmost significance of maintaining detailed records of the deliberations that took place in the imperial audiences. Those officials who lectured on the classics, being in close proximity to the emperor, were charged with the duty of recording all the imperial edicts, proclamations, commands, patents, as well as the memorials from the grand secretaries, the top officials in the bureaucracy. Other recorders took charge of the memorials from the six ministries, which constituted the records of current government (*shizheng ji*). Second, the historiography officials should be stationed as closely as possible to the emperor so that they might capture the entire picture of what was happening. In case of a secret meeting involving only the emperor and his top officials, the latter should promptly convey to the Bureau what had transpired. Third, documents should be properly and conscientiously transferred to the Bureau. Fourth, whatever was said should be recorded in its entirety without embellishment, stylistic or substantive, in order to ensure fidelity to the original utterances. Fifth, every month the recordings should be bound into seven volumes—one consisted of materials from the imperial audiences, and the other six from the six ministries. After inspection by the Grand Secretariat, they should be sealed, safely locked up, and not opened again until the compilation of the history of the dynasty.

There were also the daily records (*rili*) that usually covered only a span of several years. In 1373, for instance, a group of officials recruited from the Hanlin Academy was entrusted with the task of compiling the *Daily Records of the Great Ming* (*Da Ming rili*). These compilers were sequestered in a designated space within the palace for some nine months and completed their job in 1374. But when the diary of activity and repose was abolished in the early 1390s, that also ended compilation of the daily records. In a ripple effect, the national history, which depended on these raw materials, could also not be composed. This glaring omission in the official historiography of the Ming was lamented by quite a few of Ming scholars, such as the eminent Wang Shizhen and Shen Defu, whom we shall again meet below. Wang openly chastised the dynasty for being derelict. He said that no other dynasty was as remiss as the Ming, and that such utter failure to detail what took place in imperial audiences made the task of writing authentic history immensely difficult, if not impossible. Shen perceptively observed that the veritable records were already secondary sources, and that the absence of primary sources in the form of the national history was a serious lacuna in the Ming's archival collection (X. Li 1999, 91–92). Notwithstanding these obvious omissions, Taizu, the founder of the Ming, did order compilation of a vast variety of records of his reign relating to administrative statutes, law codes, and rites and rituals (W. Franke 1988, 736–741; Imanishi 1963, 597–615; Y. Tao 1944, 54–56; H. Chan 1975, 688–689).

These raw materials laid the groundwork for the compilation of the all-important veritable records, which involved high-ranking officials other than those working in the Historiography Bureau. In fact, the grand secretaries were the directors, aided by Hanlin academicians, all of whom were appointed by the throne. To add further prestige to the project, a member of the most distinguished nobility was named the inspector, although his role was largely honorary. Compilation of the records of each reign typically involved close to a hundred officials and consumed between three to five years. These compilations were not meant to be published. Upon completion of the final version, the drafts were burnt. One good copy was presented to the throne with much solemn ceremonial fanfare and it was then sealed. The veritable records were not supposed to be opened again, until the next dynasty assumed responsibility for compiling the Ming's standard history. However, a duplicate copy was also kept at the Grand Secretariat for use at the discretion of the emperor and the grand secretaries. In the 1530s, for added security, it was decided that because of their immense value all existing veritable records would be copied and placed in a newly constructed building specifically designed for their safe storage. The subsequent Qing dynasty continued to use that building, which underwent major repairs in the early nineteenth century.

The veritable records adopted the annalistic style of presentation with a chronological structuring. They relied heavily on edicts and memorials, and focused on the actions the emperors had taken in response to exigencies and crises. Primarily they reflected the viewpoints of the throne and officials involved. Complicating matters somewhat, events were often not recorded under the dates they took place but under those when they were reported and deliberated in imperial audiences. Predictably, there were entries pertaining to matters such as bureaucratic appointments, campaigns, and unusual natural phenomena like eclipses and earthquakes. But the information in the veritable records could be quite varied. For instance, mention of the death of a high-ranking official might be followed by a brief biography. In addition, other sorts of information were provided at the end of each year, including population figures, taxation levies, and foreign envoys.

Imperial Manipulation of Official Historiography

Despite the announced goal of objectivity, it was not difficult for the supervising grand secretaries to influence the contents of the veritable records and cast events in lights favorable to them (W. Du 2004, 149–158). On two infamous occasions, sealed records were broken open and rewritten. The first case concerned the veritable records of the reign of the founding emperor, Taizu (r. 1368–1398). These had been completed during the reign of his successor, the Jianwen emperor (r. 1399–1402), who was eventually deposed by his uncle, the prince of Yan, the fourth son of Taizu. Since the new emperor, the Yongle emperor or Chengzu (r.1403–1424), had usurped the throne, he for obvious political reasons wanted to rewrite history. Because the existing records affirmed the legitimacy of the deposed Jianwen emperor, the Yongle emperor ordered them to be recompiled. To play it safe, he had the old version burned. Still he was not quite satisfied with the new records because they had been composed hastily in a few months. After several years he ordered the sealed records opened again and demanded yet another revision, which was completed in 1418. Needless to say, rewriting meant the insertion of manufactured events and statements that served to explain and justify the emperor's usurpation (H. Franke 1961, 60–76; W. Franke 1988, 741–753; Mano 1963, 6–69; F. Tao 1987, 397–400; H. Chan 1975, 689–691).

Quite apart from the Yongle emperor's blatant distortion and concealment of events, compilation of the veritable records of the reign of Taizu revealed another problem endemic to traditional Chinese historiography—the perceived need to glorify, and indeed mythologize, the life and deeds of the founding emperor. Compilers resorted to using quasi-historical accounts, employing sources of dubious authenticity, not to mention deliberate fabrication. The story of Taizu, the Ming founder, whose personal name was Zhu Yuanzhang, was particularly prone to historiographical manipulation and hagiographic burnishing, for he rose dramatically from poverty and lowly station to greatness. An orphan once reduced to the abject life of a mendicant monk, Taizu had managed, through sheer gumption, dogged determination, and no small measure of dumb luck, to join the rebel army, rise to command, and finally subdue the Mongols after a seventeen-year campaign. One compelling task for historiographers was to reconcile the emperor's humble beginnings with his accomplishments as the Son of Heaven. Moreover, exaggerating Taizu's achievements by inference celebrated the Yongle emperor and made him the rightful occupant of the throne because he was the son who supposedly most took after his father.

Consequently, the veritable records included a fanciful account that Taizu's mother dreamed, on the eve of giving birth to the future emperor, of ingesting a magic pill offered by a Daoist priest. When the emperor was born, the room was filled with crimson brightness; light emanated from the house, visible to neighbors who mistook it as fire. There was also the story of a Daoist priest telling the emperor's father that one day he would become a noble, hinting at the fact that his son was to become ruler and bestow numerous honors on his father. After Taizu had entered a monastery as a novice, he was said to have had to take a journey, on which he encountered a venerable scholar. In return for carrying a heavy load of books, the old man examined Taizu's physiognomy and foretold his future as a great leader. When Taizu returned to the monastery, the room in which he stayed was illuminated by brilliant light. Finally, divine forces revealed to him that it was his destiny to join the rebelling forces, indicating that his ultimate overthrow of the Yuan was prompted not just by his own personal desire, but by the will of Heaven. In other words he had received the Mandate of Heaven. Other mysterious events illustrating his suprahuman qualities occurred while Taizu was campaigning against the Yuan. A locality suffering a severe drought was relieved by the timely arrival of rain, thanks to Taizu's earnest prayer to Heaven. A snake with legs, resembling a dragon, the symbol of imperial authority, was reported to have visited the future emperor. Such fictive embellishments surrounding the actually remarkable life of Taizu had precedent in many previous accounts of the rise of prior emperors, where prodigious happenings underscored the extraordinariness of the leaders in question. An encounter with Daoist immortals seems to be a recurring motif, as is a fortuitous meeting with sagacious scholars. The divining of imperial destiny is also commonplace, as well as dreams predicting future greatness.

The provenance of these tales is hard to determine, and their retelling by historiographers nearly always meant their elaboration, for it was standard practice to celebrate the extrahuman qualities of a dynasty's founder. The Son of Heaven was no ordinary mortal. In both official and unofficial histories the imperial sire was purposefully depicted as an archetype, an ideal, righteous being blessed with miraculous capabilities. However, the early real-life struggles and sufferings of Zhu Yuanzhang afforded especially colorful dyes with which to color these dramatic yarns. Moreover, the circumstances under which the veritable records of his reign were compiled also contributed to exaggerated portrayals of his image. When history is so infused with hyperbolic imaging and imagining, it functions as official propaganda. Thus a kind of fictive realism complemented, as we have seen, the other dominant ideological forms of historical expression in traditional China, historical analogism and moral didacticism (H. Chan 1975, 691–711).

Not only did imperial imperatives and prerogatives impinge directly on how the veritable records were compiled, but the intense factional strife that bedeviled the late Ming court also played an interfering role. The most notorious example occurred in the making of the veritable records for the reign of Guangzong, who was emperor for only one month in 1620. When the succeeding Emperor Xizong (r. 1620–1627) ordered the compilation of Guangzong's records, partisan struggles were rife at court, and history readily became the arena for hostile polemics. The Donglin party, having established ascendancy over its main opposition, the Zhe party, used the opportunity to present their interpretations of what had happened in the recent past. In particular they consolidated their version of the so-called "Three Cases" (san'an) —a cause célèbre that involved political partisans in a life-and-death struggle.

The Three Cases stemmed from the controversial action, or inaction, of the Wanli emperor (r. 1573–1620), and are, in fact, a fascinating illustration of the dynamics of the imperial Chinese court. Ming imperial house law decreed that the reigning emperor's oldest son should be named the heir apparent. But the Wanli emperor kept delaying the announcement that his oldest son, Zhu Changluo, would be his successor. This unusual delay sparked off tremendous debates about the emperor's real intentions.

The matter was seen to be of such gravity that the debates were known as the "struggle for the basis of the country" (*zheng guoben*). In 1601, in face of such uproar, the emperor, notwithstanding his great reluctance and displeasure, proclaimed Zhu Changluo as his successor. Yet rumors continued to fly that the ruler was scheming to dislodge him in favor of Zhu Changxun, a younger son of the emperor's beloved imperial concubine Lady Zheng. To quell protests and suspicions, the Wanli emperor built Zhu Changxun an extravagant residence in the province of Henan and sent him away from the Forbidden City in 1614, whereupon the first case, the so-called "Stick Case," occurred. In May 1615 a man named Zhang Cha, armed with a stick, somehow found his way into the Forbidden City where the heir apparent lived and was promptly arrested. At first Zhang was judged to be a mentally disturbed loner. But as the legal examinations proceeded, the Donglin partisans suspected an assassination plot and demanded a broader investigation. As accusations flew and the officialdom was engulfed in uproar, the Wanli emperor had little choice but to intervene. In an imperial audience he proclaimed his love for Zhu Changluo, now thirty-two years old, and chided the officials for stirring up controversy where there was none. His son in turn castigated the assembled officials for casting doubt on the loving relationship between himself and his father. He also claimed that there was no need for any large-scale investigation because Zhang Cha was clearly an insane man acting on his own. This ended the case temporarily. The Donglin partisans who had raised the specter of a planned assassination were dismissed, although in 1620, after the Wanli emperor passed away, they were recalled to office. Soon the controversy revived and was given a new lease on life.

Zhu Changluo, who succeeded Wanli as Emperor Guangzong, occupied the throne for just a month, dying under mysterious circumstances in September 1620. This precipitated the second case, the so-called "Red Pill Case." The central question was whether the emperor, who had apparently been in perfectly good health, had been poisoned by a medication that he took. The death of Guangzong, the emperor who had recalled many of the dismissed Donglin partisans, renewed the conspiracy theory that had first been broached in the Stick Case. The Donglin sectarians spread the story that while the pills directly caused the monarch's demise, there had also been other deliberate acts to undermine his health. First, he had been fed a debilitating purgative, but prior to that, the notorious Lady Zheng, Wanli's favorite concubine, had presented him with eight singing girls, whose purpose was to exhaust him with sexual indulgence. The main faction opposing the Donglin, the Zhe party, saw these accusations as fabrications produced out of paranoia. So once again factional conflicts roiled.

The Red Pill Case was closely linked to the third case, the "Moving Out of the Palace Case." The Donglin partisans argued that Lady Zheng, Wanli's favorite concubine, and Lady Li, Guangzong's beloved concubine (who was also guardian and stepmother of the heir apparent, Zhu Youxiao, the future Emperor Xizong, because his birth mother had died), had conspired to control the court as the reigning emperor languished in ill health in the Qianqing palace. When the emperor died in late September 1620, there was the urgent matter of securing the Ming throne because the heir apparent was barely fifteen years of age. While some saw merit in having Lady Li serve as the regent, many objected, especially the Donglin partisans. A group of the officials decided that they should fetch the emperor-to-be from the Qianqing palace and escort him to the Ciqing palace, the proper official residence for the heir apparent. This they did. They also maintained that Lady Li, being neither the birth mother of the heir apparent nor the empress, must move out of the Qianqing palace. The eviction of Lady Li was accomplished, but it ignited another round of fierce factional debates, in the course of which the young emperor, who was under the influence of the Donglin partisans, issued a number of remarkable edicts that revealed the abuse he suffered from the woman, who was now portrayed as aggressive and ambitious.

To the Donglin partisans, the Three Cases threw into sharp relief the malevolent forces that imperiled the dynasty—first, botched assassination, then successful murder, finally *lèse-majesté*. To their opponents the Donglin group manufactured conspiracies and self-righteously flaunted their moral rectitude. The newly enthroned Xizong, however, following his father's earlier move, continued to reinstall the Donglin elements at court, at least for the moment (Dardess 2002, 9–30).

When Xizong decreed the compilation of the veritable records of his father's reign in 1621, the Donglin were in ascendancy. It is therefore hardly surprising that the events of the Guangzong reign, together with the related ones of the Wanli reign, were filtered through the Donglin perceptions. To be fair to the compilers, no blatant partisan accusations appear in the records themselves. They are relatively short, only eight fascicles, but it took the compilers three long years, possibly a result of their struggle to produce a narrative that both represented their views and minimized overt bias. In other words, there appears to have been some effort to maintain impartiality. While the chief compiler, Ye Xianggao, acknowledged that events had occurred that could not be explicitly recorded without violating the convention of honoring the deceased emperor's memory—he may have been thinking of Wanli's infatuation with Lady Zheng—he insisted that it was the compilers' duty to be as faithful to the facts as possible, since their task was to bequeath truthful historical records to posterity. Emperor Xizong himself may have injected some sense of moderation and judiciousness into the project. He was intent on halting the seemingly endless polemics stemming from the Three Cases. To that end he issued edicts that called for a stop to extreme accusations and farfetched innuendoes (Yanqiu Yang 1998, 49–51).

By 1624 it had become clear that Xizong was tired of the moral strictures of the Donglin faction, and he increasingly placed his trust in the eunuch Wei Zhongxian, around whom the anti-Donglin forces rallied. Between 1625 and 1627 Donglin members were purged, often in a cruel and bloody manner. But what also needed to be expunged was the Donglin version of the past. Hence the emperor ordered the compilation of the *Main Documents of Three Reigns* (*Sanchao yaodian*), that is, the three reigns of Wanli, Guangzong, and Xizong. This new work, completed in four short months in 1626, was supposed to have set the record straight in accordance with the views of the anti-Donglin faction. It reopened the Three Cases and offered these conclusions: the assailant in the Stick Case was indeed a deranged loner who acted on his own; Emperor Guangzong got seriously ill and died an untimely death because of his grief over his father's demise; and the Moving out of the Palace Case was nothing but proof of the Donglin party's political ambitions and aggrandizement. The *Main Documents* included memorials from officials concerning the Three Cases, together with official judgments on their contents. Needless to say, memorials submitted by Donglin members were severely criticized. This official history became the vehicle for political persecution and propaganda, and copies made by the Ministry of Rites were distributed to officials.

Meanwhile, the *Veritable Records of the Guangzong Reign*, compiled by officials in or associated with the Donglin group and completed in 1623, was removed from the Imperial Historical Archives and unsealed, a fate that had also befallen the veritable records of the Ming dynastic founder, Taizu. The Guangzong records were revised in such a way that they would correspond with those of the *Main Documents of Three Reigns*. Xizong died three months prior to completion of the revisions in 1628. With the accession of the new emperor, Chongzhen (r. 1628–1644), and the reemergence of Donglin power, the *Veritable Records of the Guangzong reign* was rewritten yet again, and the preceding version, along with the *Main Documents of Three Reigns*, were burned (W. Franke 1988, 749–750; Yanqiu Yang 1998, 51; Asano 1944, 254–285). It should also be noted that even as the court strove to recast recent events in lights acceptable to the emperor and the dominant faction in power, efforts were also being made to curtail publication of private histories that offered their own interpretations. When compilation of the *Main Documents* was about to begin, the emperor issued an edict that banned private accounts of the Three Cases. A series of preexisting works on the proscribed subjects were to be destroyed, and those who violated the ban were to be punished for the crime of "deceiving the masses with demonic words" (Yanqiu Yang 1998, 51–52).

The other most important dynastic historiographical responsibility was the history of the previous dynasty, in this case the history of the Yuan. The Ming Bureau of History failed, however, to do an exemplary job. The *Yuan History*, in 212 fascicles, was hastily put together in less than a year in 1369–1370, and it has generally been regarded as the most shoddily produced and poorly edited of the standard histories (W. Franke 1988, 753; Mote 1962, 162–165). Already in the Ming many private works were devoted to remedying its flaws, and attempts at redaction, revision, and improvement continued well into the Qing period. It behooves anyone who consults the Ming work today to peruse the twentieth-century supplementary work, the *New Yuan History* (*Xin Yuanshi*), in 257 fascicles, by Ke Shaomin. Several possible reasons account for the less-than-sterling performance of the Ming compilers. The erudite chief compilers, Song Lian (1310–1381) and Wang Yi (1321–1372) were not knowledgeable about the Mongols. Moreover, those who participated in the project may not have put forth their best effort because they were compiling the history of a conquest dynasty that they despised. But perhaps most important, the founder of the Ming, Taizu, was a merciless tyrant capable of severe cruelty toward his ministers and officials. The compilers feared that delays might rouse the wrath of the emperor. Moreover, wary of their ruler's caprice and unpredictability, they refrained from rendering historical judgments and expressing critical views. The inferior quality of the *Yuan History* is very likely the result of the inhibition and trepidation on the part of the compilers, who labored in an oppressive environment. When they were not under direct imperial oversight, both Song Lian and Wang Yi, for instance, produced historical works of far higher caliber (F. Tao 1987, 391–392).

Privately, Song Lian wrote the *Records of the Sagely Rule of Hongwu* (*Hongwu shengzheng ji*). Even though on the surface it is a straightforward record of the policies and achievements of the Hongwu reign, it is also quite critical of the severity and harshness of Taizu's rule. While Song likened Hongwu to the much-eulogized founder of the Han dynasty, Gaozu, who also rose from a humble commoner background, he faulted the Ming ruler for lack of compassion as his reign progressed, and for destroying the beneficent government that he had instituted when he first ascended the throne. Song also penned a local history, *Records of Personages from Fuyang* (*Fuyang renwu ji*), that celebrated the accomplishments of notable past personalities. In it he affirmed the Confucian moral conception of the body politic, whose well-being depended on the rectitude and integrity of the people in charge. With highly colorful language that verged on the melodramatic, Song voiced his moral lessons in terms of a universal historical norm—upright men forged peaceful rule, whereas wicked ones induced rebellion.

> It is indeed to a great extent that politics is reliant on [upright] individuals, who control the illumination of the yin forces and shading of the yang ones, assume the power to reward the good and punish the bad, and control the ins and outs of life-and-death situations. When they serve in the court, the four seas enjoy benefits. When they serve in one district, the district enjoys good fortune. As long as there are the right people [in charge], there will be enlightenment above and peaceful obedience below. Paeans will be sung in the name of universal peace. If the situation is reversed, then poison will flow through the four borders. The gods will be wrathful and the people will grumble, thereby causing disloyalty and disorder. When disloyalty and disorder reign supreme, there is the calamity of rebellion. (F. Tao 1987, 394)

Song's rumination on the grand pattern of history served as a warning to the ruler that the longevity of the regime depended on his moral excellence (W. Du 2004, 158–162).

Similarly, Wang Yi, writing as a private historian, placed great store in the role of personalities in his conception of dynastic rise and fall. In addition to moral uprightness, he made a point of stressing practical knowledge and singling out the pivotal roles of those superior men (*junzi*) who "are erudite and possess special insights," and who "comprehensively know the learning concerning Heaven and humanity, clearly revealing the practical matters of utility such as mathematics and bureaucratic techniques . . ." (F. Tao 1987, 395–396). Wang asserted that it was the historian's responsibility to discern the laws of history so as to illustrate the essential "way" (*dao*), "substance" (*ti*), and "principle" (*li*) of the myriad things as they evolved in the dynamic flux of time from antiquity to the present. An accomplished history was one that told stories according to concrete facts with proper language, establishing the laws of change and providing precedents from past records as guides to the present. A historian and his history, as with Sima Qian and Ban Gu and their histories, could then appropriately render judgments in accordance with the time-honored principle of praise and blame (F. Tao 1987, 395–396; W. Du 2004, 163–165).

We should note that under imperial auspices, the Ming published a variety of historical documents. The Bureau of History produced a sequel to Zhu Xi's *Outline and Details of the Comprehensive Mirror* that covered the period from 960 to 1367; it was an unremarkable imitation of the original. By special imperial fiat, other compilations were undertaken outside the purview of the Bureau. There was, for example, the *Ancestral Instructions of the Imperial Ming* (*Huang Ming zuxun lu*), which contained imperial guidelines for dynastic policies, coupled with edifying maxims defining the conduct of the princes. There was also the *Great Proclamations* (*Da gao*), composed of pronouncements by the founder of the dynasty. Its overt purpose was to address both commoners and officials, promoting proper conduct and actions while warning against transgressions. Some didactic and propagandistic morality books targeted the rural masses, such as *Words for the Education of the People* (*Jiaomin bangwen*). The Ming also compiled and published administrative statutes and the regulations of the Ming officialdom, including the Ming legal code. The *Gathering of Essentials of the August Ming*, for example, detailed the structures and workings of the entire bureaucracy. All these compilations were periodically updated and revised (W. Franke 1988, 753–755). However, despite the scale and variety of production, Ming official historiography boasted neither stylistic innovation nor substantive creativity. In fact, it can be argued that from the Yuan on, most official works were undistinguished. This ossification of government-sponsored historiography may well have reflected a strengthening of an authoritarian Confucian orthodoxy (L. Yang 1961, 53). Yet in the domain of private historiography, the picture was much more varied and dynamic.

Private Historiography

Already in the late Ming and early Qing, scholars were struck by the fact that an unprecedented number of private histories had been produced from the mid-Ming onward. In the Ming-Qing transitional period, for example, Tan Qian, whose work we shall examine later, remarked that "there were so many private unauthorized histories and family chronicles that the oxen bearing them perspired and that they filled the house to the rafters, unaccountably numerous" (X. Li 1999, 94). This immense interest in compiling history may have been connected with a concurrent literary movement to revive the ancient style of prose and poetry. Not only did the Ming literati write their own historical accounts, but they also reprinted many old works, an endeavor facilitated by the advances in printing technology (Maowei Qian 2001, 27). Many were popular histories that catered to the masses—epic narratives based on historical documents but much embellished and expanded with the authors' fictive additions, and hence they may be better described as historical romances or sagas. One of the most elegant and influential examples is Luo Guanzhong's *Romance of the Three Kingdoms* (*San'guo yanyi*), written in the early Ming. From the mid-Ming on, inspired by Luo's popular masterpiece, many similar works on different historical periods appeared. Yuan Hongdao (1568–1610), a famous late Ming literary figure, observed that there seemed to be a craze for such fictionalized history, which nonetheless served to imprint on the minds of the masses some of the most significant myths, events, and personages in history. Thanks to the popularity of historical romances, everyone seemed to be versed in the signature events of the Han dynasty, such as the founder's rise to power from humble commoner background, his contention with General Xiang Yu for the control of China, usurpation of the dynasty by Wang Mang, and dynastic reinvigoration during the reign of Guangwu. According to Yuan's vivid description of this obsession with historical tales, "everywhere under Heaven, from the gentry to the village men and townswomen, and from the seventy-year-old seniors to three-foot-tall infants, . . . none are unable to recite the stories from beginning to end, detailing the names and places. From morning till evening and from dusk till late night, they tirelessly tell tales, forgetting to eat and sleep" (X. Li 1999, 96).

As with official historiography, many private works focused on contemporary events. According to the bibliographies in the standard *Ming History*, of the 110 officially sanctioned compilations, sixty-nine dwelt on contemporary history. With regard to private compositions, 201 of the 217 items identified dealt with Ming events. While such works undeniably furnished valuable information, much of it based on first-hand observations, their quality varied. As an eminent Ming historian, Wang Shizhen, commented, many of such writings, unregulated by the conventional standards in official compilations, were often partial; they were prone to include the unsubstantiated and the strange and in the end merely represented the authors' narrow viewpoints, idiosyncrasies, and grievances (Xiaoshu Li 1999, 93–94; H. Xu 1997, 17–22).

Although it is important to point out that what was putatively private cannot be easily distinguished from the official — many authors were either former officials or aspiring ones — nonetheless, the flourishing of private historiography in the Ming was an important intellectual phenomenon. Historians working in private, even if they were or wished to be government officials, were free from direct government supervision and the protocols of court-mandated compilations. They certainly had more room for creativity and innovation, and after the mid-Ming there was no doubt a gradual increase in private historical production (W. Franke 1988, 756–760; Ng 1984, 46).

One fifteenth-century historian of note was Qiu Jun (1421–1495). As a career official who served in many high-ranking capacities, Qiu participated in several court-mandated compilations, such as the veritable records of the reigns of Yingzong (1457–1464) and Xianxong (1464–1487). Under imperial order he was also involved in the writing of the sequel to Zhu Xi's *Outline and Details of the Comprehensive Mirror,* admittedly a work of no great historical merit. Yet as a private historian, Qiu penned an innovative volume, *The Correct Bonds in Universal History* (*Shishi zhenggang*) that was avowedly inspired by Zhu's work. Outside the straitjacket of official conventions, Qiu was able to stretch his imagination and exercise his ingenuity to write a history that honored Zhu's spirit without parroting the master's form and format. As Zhu had, Qiu perceived history to be a storehouse of lessons with which to prod the flaccid moral conscience of the present state and society. His book, as Qiu proclaimed, was devoted to "making manifest the changes in the world, and recording the geneses of events" (Zhuoran Li 1984, 172). He began his history with the Qin dynasty precisely because it signaled in a major turning point by bringing an end to the antique Three Dynasties of the Xia, the Shang, and the Zhou and laying the imperial foundation for the bureaucratic empires of the Han, the Tang, and the Song. In the process of recording the significant events, Qiu sought to reveal their meanings in terms of preservation of the three universally correct bonds under Heaven: strict demarcation of the Chinese from the barbarians, establishment of the meaning of the relation between a ruler and his ministers, and preservation of the spirit of the relation between father and son. To study and write about the past was to illustrate the workings of these perennial relations (Zhuoran Li 1984, 169–175; W. Du 2004, 165–168).

Qiu, following Zhu Xi, applied the historiographical principle of praise and blame. He was especially concerned with determining the political legitimacy (*zhengtong*) of every dynasty in history. In order to indicate clearly their legitimacy, or lack thereof, he devised a graphic system that allowed readers to see his judgment at a glance. In the text the names of those dynasties that inherited the orthodox line of succession are placed within a circle; the dynasties of the Qin, the Han, the Tang, and the Song are all circled. Qiu further subdivided this group in two: dynasties that were fully orthodox and those that were partially orthodox. The fully orthodox names appeared in vermillion, the partially orthodox in black. The Qin, for instance, was given incomplete orthodox status because of the dynasty's relentlessly repressive rule, despite its enormous accomplishments in unifying China. The name "Qin" was therefore printed in black. The names of dynasties considered illegitimate were not placed within a circle; instead what appeared in the text was simply an empty circle. The Northern and Southern dynasties that eventually emerged after the collapse of the Han were all indicated by empty circles. The regime that Qiu Jun deemed the most illegitimate was the Mongol Yuan dynasty; it was marked with a dark solid circle. As Qiu explained, the Mongol conquest and rule of China represented an epoch that was entirely suffused with the dark, miasmic *yin* forces. It was a time when the order and hierarchy of Heaven and earth were in such complete disarray that Qiu depicted it as an ominous, darkened circle, an unprecedented calamity since the creation of the world. Using this innovative format with alacrity and clarity, Qiu meted out judgments on the various dynasties (Zhuoran Li 1984, 76–189).

Qiu's historical view was very much integrated into his cosmological conception of the dialectic movements of all things in the universe. Just as the way of Heaven consisted of the *yin* and *yang* forces, so the way of the world consisted of peace and disorder. These polar forces and phenomena interacted. Qiu identified China and the morally superior men with *yang*, which was the manifestation of Heaven's principle. Barbarians and mean people Qiu associated with *yin*, an expression of pernicious human desires. When the bright *yang* forces pervaded, China was respected and safe, and morally profound men became leaders, Heaven's principle held sway, and an era of peace came into being. But when the turbid *yin* forces predominated, barbarians grew powerful, and mean people reigned supreme, human desires ran rampant, and the result was an epoch of disorder. Qiu placed much importance on moral leadership and rulership, which he interpreted in terms of his cosmological views. The masses, with their private desires, had to be properly guided by a ruler on whom order and peace depended. This was the rule of history, and Qiu's own work aimed to provide the evidence for this universal pattern of human flourishing and degeneration (Zhuoran Li 1984, 190).

There is little question that Qiu was much animated by a strong sense of the otherness and odiousness of barbarians, to the extent that he insisted they should be excluded from China. His view reflected the historical and geopolitical circumstances in which he lived. The Ming was a native Chinese dynasty that had overturned the first complete dominion over China by a barbarian people, the Mongols. To affirm the distinction between China and the surrounding barbarous people was to celebrate the restorative effort of the Ming. Qiu also lived in a time when the Ming faced tremendous pressures from the barbarians. In 1449 Emperor Yingzong amassed an army of half a million and personally led a campaign against the Mongols, with results nothing short of catastrophic. Instead of overwhelming the Mongol forces, the Ming army was routed, the emperor captured, and the Mongols attacked Beijing, the capital. Qiu's work was born in this period of grave national crisis; its preoccupation with the question of warding off the barbarian as a historical principle was a perfect example of the appropriation of the past to serve the needs of the present, explicating contemporary foreign relations and military affairs with history (Zhuoran Li 1984, 196–198).

The late fifteenth and early sixteenth centuries witnessed further proliferation of private historiography (W. Du 2004, 175–179). Lu Shen (1477–1544), an admirer of Liu Zhiji, produced a new and carefully edited version of Liu's *Comprehensive Perspectives on Historiography*. He also penned the *Essentials of the Comprehensive Perspectives on Historiography* (*Shitong huiyao*), which inspired the writing of similar works devoted to explicating the value of the Tang masterwork. Liang Menglong (1527–1602) compiled the *Anthology of the Essentials of Histories*, which brought together the prefaces, forewords, postscripts, and other prefatory summaries from existing historical works. Writers like Qu Jingchun (1507–1569) and Bu Dayou (1512–c. 1602) were distinguished for their achievements in historical criticism and historiographical analysis. Qu wrote the *On the Merits and Deficiencies of Historical Learning from Past to Present* (*Gujin shixue deshi*) in which he critiqued various standard histories and other influential works, such as Zhu Xi's *Outline and Details of the Comprehensive Mirror*. He minced no words, for example, in pointing out the shortcomings of the *Song History*. He claimed that the imperial annals failed to capture the great deeds of the court, often recording trivial matters related to ministers; the biographies of the officials similarly failed to highlight the significant and therefore often appeared no different from myopic family chronicles; the presentation was on the whole repetitive and redundant, and the language stodgy and cumbersome. On the other hand, Qu praises Zhu's *Outline and Details* for faithfully conveying the messages of the classics and assimilating the best of all the histories. To Qu, the organization of Zhu's text was exemplary for its clarity, thanks to the chronological ordering. Moreover, following the example of the *Spring and Autumn Annals*, Zhu properly condemned the wicked and commended the good, revealing the great human bonds while issuing warnings against moral transgressions.

Qu systematically outlined the goals and methods of writing history, a sacred act mandated by Heaven. He listed the "four responsibilities" (*sishi*) of a historian: developing a proper sense of focus on the task at hand and refusing to be distracted by other pursuits; cultivating patience and perseverance and knowing that haste will result in omissions; nurturing a sense of professional devotion and abandoning thoughts of taking other jobs; and conscientiously collecting sources such that all published sources will be consulted. Qu then discoursed on the "five purposes" (*wuzhi*) of historical composition: arriving at the moral Way and its meanings; announcing the laws against transgressions; comprehending the connections between past and present; illuminating achievements and sacrifices; and making manifest the upright and talented. Third, Qu pinpointed the "three rules" (*sanke*) governing historical cogitation: narrating the development of events from beginning to end; illuminating evil deeds; and making manifest the meanings of calamities and prodigies.

Bu Dayou compiled the *Essential Meanings of Historical Learning (Shixue yaoyi)*, a general history of historiography. Fascicle one describes the official institutions of history writing and the general conventions and guidelines for the compilation of official history, including critiques of classic works such as *Records of the Historian, the Han History,* and the *Later Han History*. Fascicle two consists of comments on the standard histories from the *History of the Three Kingdoms* to the *Yuan History*. Fascicle three focuses on Sima Guang's *Comprehensive Mirror* and cognate works such as Zhu Xi's *Outline and Details of the Comprehensive Mirror*. Fascicle four examines a variety of historical works such as Ma Duanlin's *Comprehensive Investigation of the Literary Traditions,* Du You's *Comprehensive Compendium,* and Zheng Qiao's *Comprehensive Treatises*. Fascicle five is a collection of some two hundred miscellaneous pieces that seek to fill the lacunae in the previous four fascicles. Both Bu and Qu demonstrated an astute consciousness of history as a discipline, a distinct intellectual endeavor that required focused analysis and specialized study. Instead of confusing past events with the historical effort to record and describe them, the two authors, like Liu Zhiji, pondered the meaning and method of producing historical narratives (Maowei Qian 2001, 26–35).

The prevailing trend of private composition of history continued unabated in the late Ming period, from the Wanli reign that began in 1573 to the end of the dynasty in 1644. Arguably, historical writing displayed an increasingly higher level of sophistication as many writers demonstrated a more critical use of sources. The fact that the veritable records were no longer kept as secret archives but were open to public circulation aided the growth of private historiography, especially with regard to the history of the Ming itself. It is therefore useful to take a closer look at several major private compilations that have roughly the same chronological coverage of the standard *Ming History* so that we may make some meaningful comparisons between the unofficial compositions and the official one.

One notable unofficial history that covers a large portion of the Ming (approximately from 1368 to 1572) is the *Hidden Treasures in the Celebrated Mountains (Mingshan cang)*, a book with the more conventional and self-explanatory title of *Forgotten History of the Thirteen Reigns of the Ming (Ming shishan chao yishi)*. It consists of 100 fascicles although only the first forty-five are numbered. Written by He Qiaoyuan (1558–1632), it has a preface by Qian Qianyi (1582–1644) dated 1640 (Goodrich & Fang 1976, 507–509). The format, with some modifications, resembles that of the standard histories. Instead of using the typical four sections of imperial annals, biographies, monographs, and tables, He subsumed his information under thirty-five "records" (*ji*), although these records clearly do include annals, biographies, and monographs. There are no tables, but these did not appear in all the standard histories either. The *Records of Model Design* (*Dianmo ji*) is very like the imperial annals. Other records pertain to the deeds of the empresses, princes, and nobles, and events related to them. There are biographies of important ministers and officials, accomplished scholars and virtuous women, together with those of trivial personages like Daoist priests and merchants. "Separate Records" are the equivalents of the monographs found in the standard histories, with each devoted to various institutions such as laws, river navigation, military affairs, salt administration, grain transport, foreign affairs, coinage, and music. Some records contain "comments" (*lunzan*), which are also found in the official histories.

While the format of the *Hidden Treasures* resembles that of the standard *Ming History*, there are some noteworthy differences. All the biographies in the *Hidden Treasures* are categorized, placed in specific *ji*. For example, the biographies of Guo Zixing (d. 1355) and Han Lin'er (d. 1367), one-time comrades of the Ming founder, Taizu, are placed within the "Records of the Origins of the Heavenly Dynasty." By situating their biographies in the *ji* that deals with the founding of the dynasty, their roles as crucial contributors to the establishment of the regime are clearly acknowledged. The *Ming History*, in contrast, while reserving separate fascicles for their biographies, placed neither Guo nor Han in categorized sections such as those entitled "The Loyal and the Righteous" (Zhongyi) and "The Filial and the Righteous" (Xiaoyi). The *Hidden Treasures* also subtly denigrated the foes of the dynastic founder by placing their biographies in specific records. To reveal their unsavory roles in the Yuan-Ming transition, for instance, the lives of Chen Youliang (1319/20–1363), Zhang Shicheng (1321–1367), and Fang Guozhen (1319/20–1374), all rivals of Taizu, are consigned to the *ji* entitled "Records of the Expulsions by the Heavenly Dynasty," suggesting that they were banished to the dustbin of history. The *Ming History* biographies of these figures do not clearly inform the reader whether they belong to the group of the praised or that of the blamed. In the parts on eunuchs and other officials, the *Hidden Treasures* also makes a point to discriminate the good from the wicked. Thus, He Qiaoyuan effectively used the format of his work as a means to apply the historiographical principle of praise and blame.

The *Hidden Treasures,* unlike the *Ming History,* which was written under Manchu Qing rule, did not handle the issue of foreign affairs with the same degree of caution and sensitivity. The *Ming History* simply avoided covering the history of the northeast, the homeland of the Manchus, but the *Hidden Treasures* provided good coverage of the genesis and rise of Manchu power. The title of the record in question — "Records of Imperial Enjoyment" — suggests that the Ming's dealings with foreigners were a sort of dynastic fortune. It classifies foreigners into different groups: the Jurchen Manchus, who originated in the areas of Xihai and Jianzhou northeast of China proper, are classified as the "northeastern barbarians." Then there is the group called the "southeastern barbarians," featuring Korea and Japan, both of which are discussed in detail. Countries such as Ryukyu, Vietnam, and Siam constitute a subdivision that receives more laconic treatment. Another subdivision includes places like Malacca, Sumatra, and Luzon. Portugal is not listed, although it is mentioned in the narratives of contact with other states. It appears that He Qiaoyuan followed the roster of barbarians in the *Gathering of Essentials of the August Ming*. The division of "northern barbarians" deals with the Tartars, while that of "western barbarians" lists more or less the same countries included in the section on "western region" in the *Ming History*. In general, the *Hidden Treasures* followed the traditional Chinese designation of foreigners in accordance with the four cardinal directions of north, south, east, and west. Significantly, in this record on foreign countries, He pointedly referred to threats from the north and argued for the strengthening of defenses along the northern frontiers. He mentioned the menace in the south posed by Japanese pirates, pejoratively called "dwarf bandits" (*wokou*), but dismissed them as temporary disturbances, even though he was impressed by their martial prowess.

Another record that merits mention is the "Additional Records of the Various Officials." This contains only the biographies of officials who stayed steadfastly loyal to the Jianwen emperor, the victim of usurpation by his uncle, the Hongwu emperor. These officials maintained their loyalty in face of persecution, and thus earned He's accolades as righteous officials in a separate record devoted only to them. By the same token, He placed evil eunuchs in a separate record, for the purpose of bringing their wicked deeds into sharp relief. As a private historian untrammeled by official protocols, He was free to adopt any format congenial for his conveyance of historical information and judgments.

He Qiaoyuan was conscious of the inherent impediments to writing a history of the contemporary dynasty. First, the historian needed to avoid tabooed things and any reference or even hint of sacred names (*jihui*) hampered a historian's ability to record faithfully and truthfully. Second was the more intractable problem of reliable, substantive sources, although release of the veritable records from the imperial archives in the Ming times did help. In a preface to the *Hidden Treasures* written by Li Jiantai (*jinshi* 1625), Li promptly exposed the flaws and inadequacies of the veritable records which, as far as he was concerned, tended to be uncritical, recording commendations rather than criticisms. They concentrated on the official matters of the court and as a result simply ignored much of what was happening in society. In fact, it could be argued that the perceived insufficiencies of the veritable records spurred private historiography that might produce a better, more comprehensive account of the recent past (Ng 1984, 47–50).

Another important private history on the events of the Ming was *Evaluations of the Events of Our Dynasty (Guoque)* by Tan Qian (1594–1658). Written in the annalistic style, it contained 104 fascicles, with 4 additional introductory fascicles. The first draft was completed in 1627 but stolen in 1647. Tan rewrote the work and completed it in 1653, adding the history of the last reign, that of the Chongzhen emperor (1628–1644), together with a narrative of the first reign of the exiled Southern Ming dynasty—the Hongguan reign of 1645 (Goodrich & Fang 1976, 1239–1242; Z. Jin 1989, 43–46; F. Tao 1987, 411–413). The added portion, covering the period from 1628 to 1645, was written during the early Qing, but Tan did not avoid reference to the names of the early Qing emperors; nor did he refrain from referring to the Manchus, who originated in Jianzhou, as the "slavish subjects of Jianzhou" (Jianlu). Tan almost surely saw himself as a surviving subject of the Ming, and we may regard his history as a Ming work.

Tan was prompted to write his massive history because he was very dissatisfied with the existing works on the Ming, including the veritable records. To him they only scratched the surface and failed to penetrate the inner core of important matters. He also discerned much bias in the texts, especially pervasive partisan views in the veritable records of the reigns of the emperors Shenzong and Xixong. As Tan pointed out, official compilers were often creatures of the throne and those in power, such that they had to contend with political pressure and the emperor's oversight. Citing the instance of the compilation of the veritable records of Taizu, when many officials suffered persecution, Tan complained that the "authority of history" (shiquan) was gravely compromised and circumscribed by political demands, as could be seen in the many deliberate evasions and distortions in the accounts of the Jianwen reign. Tan also believed that joint and commissioned histories tended to stifle creativity and induce incoherence. He praised, for instance, Ouyang Xiu's *New History of the Five Dynasties*, a private work, but criticized the *New History of the Tang*, an official work, even though it was compiled under the general editorship of Ouyang (Z. Jin 1989, 46; Ng 1984, 51–52).

However, the work that really convinced Tan of the need to produce an alternative comprehensive dynastic history was the *Comprehensive Annals of the Imperial Ming* (Huang Ming tongji) by Chen Jian (1497–1567), which Tan examined in 1621. Supposedly a thorough history of the dynasty, it missed or neglected much that was significant, and the entire text was filled with errors and inaccuracies. Tan decided that a truly comprehensive history of the dynasty had to be compiled, one that marshaled sufficient and better sources. The true basis of Tan's dissatisfaction was his fundamental conviction that even though "a regime may be destroyed, its history must not be destroyed." So driven by his belief that the past must be preserved regardless of political vicissitudes and changes, and troubled by the lack of acceptable accounts of the recent past, Tan embarked on a truthful and thorough history in the annalistic style. He followed, but improved upon, both the veritable records and Chen's *Comprehensive Annals*. To collect materials, Tan traveled far and wide, even spending two years in Beijing. From the veritable records, he selected only the most salient accounts, which he complemented and supplemented with a vast array of sources—local gazetteers, collected statutes, inscriptions on stones and steles, and so on. All these he carefully examined for errors and other deficiencies before using them in his work. Altogether Tan spent thirty-six years on his masterpiece, using some 270 different sources, while rewriting and revising it six times (Ng 1984, 49–51; Z. Jin 1989, 46–47; F. Tao 1987, 413–415).

By adopting the annalistic format, Tan's *Evaluations* obviously differs from the *Ming History* with its composite style, but Tan's four introductory fascicles consist of tables similar to those in the standard history, although they are not as detailed. Tan included more tables, however, thirteen, as opposed to five in the *Ming History*. Tan introduced one entitled "Paying Tribute," which lists the foreign states that presented tribute to the Ming, information that is not found in the late official history. When used effectively, the tables saved space while revealing important facts. Minor events and personages could also be placed in tables, thereby freeing the narrative from encumbering details.

Following the example of Sima Guang's *Comprehensive Mirror* and other standard histories, Tan inserted and appended comments on events and personalities. Notably, these comments are not always placed at the end of a fascicle. They are interspersed throughout the text so that evaluations are interlarded with narratives. Tan not only tendered his own comments, which number over 900, but also included 1,200 others by different writers (Z. Jin 1989, 48–49; Ng 1984, 50). Although based on the veritable records, Tan's work differs from them considerably. For example, the Ming government compiled no separate veritable records for the problematic reign of Jianwen. The records of this reign constituted the first nine fascicles of the veritable records of the Yongle reign, and they bore the telling title of "Records of the Events of the Removal of Troubles by Order of Heaven," which clearly indicated the legitimacy of the Yongle emperor's actions insofar as they were mandated by Heaven. Moreover, the next eight fascicles continued to use the reign title of Hongwu inasmuch as the Yongle emperor, the usurper, had abolished the reign name of Jianwen. It should also be noted that in the veritable records of the founder, Taizu, the reign title of Hongwu was used until the thirty-fifth year, although in reality the reign lasted only thirty-one years (W. Franke 1968, 16; W. Franke 1988, 748). Tan's *Evaluations* rejected periodization that had resulted from political manipulation and expediency. His account restored the reign of Jianwen and accorded it the same status as the other reigns, thereby affirming its rightful place in history. As Tan remarked, just as the Han dynasty did not destroy the imperial annals because of the illegitimate domination of Empress Lü, and the Tang dynasty did not excise parts of the veritable records as a consequence of the usurpation of Empress Wu, so too the records of the Jianwen reign in the present dynasty must be preserved. At the same time, however, he vigorously applied the principle of praise and blame. He commended those persecuted officials loyal to the Jianwen emperor and celebrated them as models of virtues (Ng 1984, 50–53).

Another private history that deserves our attention is *A Special An-*

thology from the Yanshan Studio (*Yanshantang beiji*) by Wang Shizhen (1526–1590). Composed of 100 fascicles, it is a collection of treatises on a host of subjects covering the period roughly from the beginning of the dynasty in 1368 to the 1580s, with a preface dated 1590 (Goodrich & Fang 1976, 1399–1405). Wang produced a history on the contemporary dynasty because he was not one who immersed himself in antiquarian studies. Erudition in ancient and past matters was commendable, he remarked, but if one failed to connect and relate such knowledge to the present, it was all for naught. Wang lived in a time of obvious dynastic decline, and he wanted to write a history of the Ming dynasty that would reveal the causes of many pressing problems so as to provide clues and guides to their rectification. In addition, as with Tan Qian, he was quite disappointed with both the official veritable records and also the myriad private writings on the Ming. His own work would set the record straight (C. Gu 1983, 337–339; W. Du 2004, 179–183).

Unlike He Qiaoyuan's *Hidden Treasures*, which adopts a modified composite style, and Tan Qian's *Evaluations*, which follows the annalistic format, Wang's *A Special Anthology* features no definite organization. Some of the treatises (*kao*, or investigations) resemble sections in the *Ming History*. The "Treatise on the Court Eunuchs," for instance, resembles the biographic sections in the official history devoted to eunuchs. However, Wang's treatise made a point to include lengthy discussion on the institution of eunuchs in an effort to provide a better sense of context. Wang's work also includes genealogical tables and brief biographies of the imperial princes and hereditary nobles, which are not that different from those in the *Ming History*. Other treatises are quite like the monographs found in the standard histories, in that they deal with institutions such as the examination system, schools, and military affairs (Ng 1984, 53).

For our purposes the treatise of greatest interest and significance is "A Critical Treatise on the Errors in Historical Works" (Shisheng kaowu). As the title suggests, it is dedicated to exposing the mistakes and problems found in all kinds of histories, including inscriptions, biographies, and family chronicles. Wang began with a denunciation of Ming official historiography: "The national historiography never failed in its task to such an extreme degree as under our dynasty." It was distinctly lacking in objectivity since everything came second to political need. The veritable records, for example, were compiled only after the death of the emperor, for fear of recording events that might antagonize the emperor when he was alive. Wang also criticized the use of paltry sources. Compilation of the records depended on memorials from the Censorate that supervised the Six Ministries, and these were supplemented by files from the Bureau of Remonstrance. In the Ming, however, there was neither a national history nor a diary of activity and repose to serve as corroborating materials. "As to national disgraces and imperial faults," Wang continued, "there was reason for evasiveness and they [i.e., the official compilers of the veritable records] did not dare to write. But the worst of all was that those in charge of writing had their private sympathies and aversions therein; thus even if there was material to rely upon and nothing to evade, they did not wish to write; and therefore if they wrote, it did not correspond to the facts" (W. Franke 1968, 19).

Wang was quick to point out that private historical works had their own flaws and shortcomings. Many authors bore grudges and utilized their works to make accusations against enemies and those they disliked. Also, as private citizens remote from the actions of the court and government, many relied on hearsay and fell prey to rumors. In addition, most unofficial works appealed to the sensational, embracing bizarre and extraordinary happenings as a device to engage their readers (Ng 1984, 54). Yet in spite of the obvious pitfalls of both official and unofficial historiography, Wang argued for judicious appropriation of their information. Their faults notwithstanding, all had something valuable to offer:

> The official historians are unrestrained and are skilful at concealing the truth; but the memorials and laws they record and the documents they copy cannot be discarded. The unofficial historians express their opinions and are skilful at missing the truth; but their verification of right and wrong and their abolition of taboo of names and things cannot be discarded. The family historians flatter and are skilful in exceeding the truth; but their praise of the merits of [the] ancestors and their manifestations of their achievements as officials cannot be discarded. (H. Franke 1961, 67–68)

"Those family histories which contain truthful accounts and are worth commendation," Wang continued, "I dare not discard; those private histories which contain false accounts and should be destroyed, I dare not salvage. In the case of an unclear [historical event] which can be explained by two sets of evidence, I preserve both of them" (Ng 1984, 55).

Wang echoed Tan Qian's preference for individual compilation, as opposed to commissioned collective enterprises. For him, joint effort often resulted in inconsistencies as regards facts and incoherence with respect to prose. Although individual endeavor was difficult since one's energy and knowledge were limited, the advantage was coherent presentation and stylistic uniformity. He substantiated his argument with historical examples. The individual efforts of Zuo Qiuming, Sima Qian, and Ban Gu were far superior to those of the many standard histories, all joint efforts. Like Tan Qian, Wang also praised Ouyang Xiu's *New History of the Five Dynasties,* a work he composed on his own, but thought much less of the *New History of the Tang,* the collective work he edited. Wang explained his preference tautologically: "There is no other reason than that it is the difference between joint and individual effort" (Bao 1965, no page). It may be surmised that the flourishing of private historiography in the late Ming owed much to a prevailing feeling that individual compilations, being free of official strictures and the interference of collaborators, were superior.

Wang Shizhen was an independent thinker who sought escape from the constraints of rote orthodox learning. Using as an example a recent history of the Song, he claimed that the late Song was mired in cultural malaise because of its uncritical adherence to received learning based on wholesale acceptance of the classics and their presumed universality. As a historian, Wang urged reference to actual events in history and not the ideals encased in the classics. History was everywhere in evidence. To the extent that everything, every person and every event, would inexorably recede into the past and constitute the domain of history, "within and between Heaven and earth, there is nothing that is not history." The classics were in fact merely a special kind of history that focused on principles (Yanqiu Yang 2001, 40–41).

The three private histories reviewed above consciously aimed at providing complete and systematic narratives of historical events. There were other works, however, that were essentially assemblages of notes and observations. Their haphazard presentation of material does not necessarily detract from their value as historical sources, and some are treasure troves of information on the Ming. A good example is *Private Gleanings* (*Yehuo bian*) by Shen Defu (1578–1642). The version that is now extant has thirty fascicles, together with four supplementary ones written by a descendant of the author's, Shen Zhen, in 1713. Shen Defu wrote two prefaces, dated 1606 and 1619 (Goodrich & Fang 1976, 1190–1191). Except for those that pertain to literature, prodigies of nature, strange occurrences, and other trivia, the notes deal essentially with the political and institutional history of the Ming from the establishment of the dynasty to the Wanli period. Taken as a whole, the text functions as a kind of comprehensive general Ming history up to roughly 1619. The first two fascicles, entitled "The Successive Reigns," resemble the imperial annals of the standard histories, in that they are accounts of the main events of the various reigns, ordered chronologically. But there are discontinuities and gaps, as Shen recorded only those events that he considered significant. This purposeful selectivity in coverage is also evident in his treatment of the institutions such as the civil service examinations, the Six Ministries, and other governmental apparatuses. In general, his notes are not as detailed as the descriptions found in the topical monographs of the standard *Ming History*.

Notwithstanding its random form and the fact that the *Private Gleanings* may not be a systematic history, Shen was a careful writer who was often critical and discriminating in his use of sources. He produced a work that contains much useful information on and insight into Ming events and personages. As with the other authors we have examined, Shen was quite dismayed by the quality of the official Ming historiography:

> The present dynasty has no National History. The Veritable Records of the successive emperors are taken as history. [This fact alone] already indicates inadequacy. Furthermore, the Veritable Records of Taizu went through three compilations. Officials who helped establish the dynasty were initially portrayed as great men. However, those who did not meet the approval of the

Jingnan compilers [that is, those who served under the Yongle emperor]
were expunged [from the later versions of the Veritable Records]. The four
years of the reign of Jianwen completely disappeared. Later historians can
only recover one or two out of hundreds and thousands [of facts]. Although
events about Jingdi [that is, Daizong, r. 1449–1457] are appended to the
Veritable Records of the Yingzong reign [1457–1464], and the administration [of the Jingdi reign] can still be investigated, there has been too much
tampering with facts. (Ng 1984, 56)

Awareness of the shortcomings of official Ming historiography goaded
many scholars into private ventures. Shen therefore did not find it at all surprising that private histories had multiplied and commanded great popularity. Yet referring to ideas that Wang Shizhen had voiced in his celebrated
"A Critical Treatise on the Errors in Historical Works," Shen decried the
falsehoods perpetrated by many private writers who used their works to
express personal grievances, and in doing so distorted the past and confused right and wrong. Shen cited the example of a scholar who, having
repeatedly failed the civil service examinations, vented his frustrations by
writing a venom-filled history of the examination system. Shen cautioned
readers to be aware of the ulterior motives of many authors and alerted
them to other inadequacies in the world of privately written history (Ng
1984, 56–57).

Similar to Shen's *Private Gleanings* is Zhang Xuan's *Records of Things
Heard and Seen by Xiyuan* (*Xiyuan wenjian lu*), a copious work in 107 fascicles,
covering the period from the beginning of the dynasty to the early 1620s.
It contains two prefaces, dated 1627 and 1632 (Goodrich & Fang 1976, 78–
80). This work explores some 260 topics, organized under three sections.
The first includes subjects concerning moral-ethical and scholarly cultivation, where questions and examples of filiality, loyalty, social relations, and
learning are discussed. The second examines the structures and workings
of governmental institutions such as the Six Ministries, together with accounts of the notable deeds and actions of officials. Here the most detailed
topic discusses the Ministry of War and comprises thirty-one fascicles. It
is quite understandable that Zhang devoted much effort to the history of
military organization and war, given the worsening defense situation as the
late Ming faced constantly encroaching forces from the north. The third
section consists of miscellaneous notes and observations on a wide variety
of subjects such as religion, medicine, unusual occurrences, folklore, and
so on.

Discussions on each topic are divided into two parts, the "past statements" (*qianyan*) and "past deeds" (*wangxing*). The former consists of quotations from Ming works, with occasional citation of memorials and im-
perials edicts. These statements serve as illustrations, substantiations, and
corroborations of the topic in question. Regrettably, Zhang did not specify his sources, although the authors' names were given. The "past statements" are often lengthier than the "past deeds," which include general

discussions and descriptions that are at times supplemented by biographical information. On the topic of the History Bureau, for example, more space is allotted to quoting relevant statements—views of past writers on the writing of history—than to description of the actual operation of the Bureau itself.

This section on the ways of doing history provides a sampling of the Ming views on the subject. Many of the writers quoted insisted on writing histories that were faithful to the truth, and all of them regarded historical undertakings as endeavors charged with moral responsibility. Zhang himself had been prompted to write his work precisely because neither the official veritable records nor the many private works impressed him. Although he embraced the lofty aim of providing posterity with a more accurate account of the major events of the Ming, he did not at all regard his work as a complete history. Expressing a certain measure of pessimism when facing the solemn task of telling truth about the past, Zhang exclaimed, "Writing a truthful history is so difficult!" (Ng 1984, 59). Writers whom he quoted voiced their critical views on the writing of history. Wang Zudi (1531–1592), for instance, maintained that just as every family had its genealogies and records, a country had its history. But while recording the past was a given, Wang was clearly wary that such an act was fraught with problems, especially that of arriving at the truth. He urged historians to be dispassionate and refrain from "altering the portrayal of an event because of one's own likes and dislikes." In compiling a chronicle, "one cannot gloss over the truth according to one's predilections and aversions." Xue Xuan (1389–1464), dismayed by the fact that there were many writers who "have been influenced by their likes and dislikes," thereby "failing to render the truth," asked readers to be discriminating with texts and materials from the past. He quoted Mencius: "It is just as well that we do away with books if we were to believe in them entirely" (Ng 1984, 57).

Ye Sheng (1420–1474) discussed the general problems that beset the writing of history more broadly. The first problem was selectivity. Histories were often incomplete, not only because of space constraints, but also because of pressure from the court and other sources. He quoted Ouyang Xiu's lament: "One cannot write down what one wishes; one dare not write down what one wishes." Second was the legal requirement that historians avoid things tabooed, a problem very much related to the first. Third was the expectation and tendency to follow conventions and protocols, which choked innovation and creativity. Fourth was the inability to be impartial and fair. Fifth was the lack of historical talents and acumen (Ng 1984, 57–58).

Many of the writers that Zhang quoted specifically targeted the inadequacies of Ming official historiography. Wang Zudi explained the popularity of private historiography in terms of the perceived shortcomings of official works, which all too frequently failed to produce comprehensive accounts for fear of censure from the court. Many of the fawning official compilers were bent on flattery rather than truth. Wang specifically protested the suppression of the events of the Jianwen reign. He feared that those events would be obliterated from historical memory, since the scores of works that purported to report what had happened during that reign were full of errors and inconsistencies that had been repeated and perpetuated. He lamented this sad state of affairs and warned of its gravity, asserting once again that the truth of history could not be assailed: "How can this in any way be a small matter? . . . Under heaven, only history is incorruptible" (Ng 1984, 59).

Wang Ao (1450–1524) pointedly noted that in the olden days, the left historian recorded the utterances of the imperial audiences while the right historian recorded the deeds. He praised the works of Sima Qian and Ban Gu, who came from families of historians and therefore knew their sources. Because of their profound historical knowledge and unflinching honesty in recording what they knew and saw, reading the accounts of these historians, gushed Wang, was "like actually witnessing events as they occurred in those times." By contrast, the Hanlin academicians were official historians. Even though their official rank brought them close to the court, they were still too distant from the throne to be effective recorders of what took place in imperial audiences. In any event the Ming no longer kept detailed records of occurrences at court and during audiences, and consequently the throne had lost touch with the historian-officials. Wang went on to describe the highly unsatisfactory process of contemporary recording:

> When a history is compiled, the memorials and correspondence of the various Boards are gathered. The [records of the Six] Ministries . . . are separately placed under ten Commissions. The Ministries with bulkier records are each managed by two Commissions. The Commission allots appropriate personnel to compile the various records in a chronological form, producing an integrated history. The Vice-Directors [of a Commission] then edit it. The final touches are added by the Director, that is, the Grand Secretary. Only officials of the third rank and above are given a biography [in these histories]. Moreover, only their official ranks and promotions are recorded. Occasionally, there are comments with regard to their merits and deficiencies, but not all those are entirely fair.

Wang Ao summed up his criticism with a scathing rhetorical question: "What will the later ages choose as creditable and believable?" (Ng 1984, 58).

This feeling that official Ming historiography lacked credibility was shared by Huang Shengzeng (1490–1540), who pointed to its early degeneration after the compilation of the veritable records of Taizu's reign. Things quickly went downhill when the Yongle emperor decided to rewrite the sealed records. The records of the Yongle reign were also full of problems because they deliberately omitted events and personages that might have reflected poorly on the perceived legitimacy of the usurper. Such practices set a bad example, but were repeated time and again in later compilations. Huang concluded, "Consequently, throughout the successive reigns, the good who have upheld tradition and law are not given lavish praise; and the evil are not severely blamed. The spirit of admonition and caution has indeed perished. . . . If history is done in such a way, it is not a blessing to the country at all" (Ng 1984, 58–59).

These scholars expressed their deep regret at the evident decline in the official historiography of their own dynasty and did not hesitate to criticize it. They feared the loss of the country's collective cultural memory that only history could preserve. Because this was so, the writing of history was an incorruptible, sacred, and time-honored task tied to the well-being of the dynasty. If official historiography was not to be trusted, then there must be better private histories. And in the Ming, it was the many private works that exhibited historiographical innovation and creativity. Especially in the latter part of the dynasty, many scholars consciously let go of orthodox interpretations of history. For instance, in 1522 Zhu Yunming (1461–1527) completed a work of historical criticism with the provocative title *Master Zhu's Records of Wrongful Knowledge* (*Zhuzi zuiyan lu*). The work was devoted to challenging established views of many historical events and figures. An example was Zhu's attempt to demythologize the motivations and actions of the founders of the Shang and Zhou dynasties, King Tang and King Wu, traditionally regarded as noble and righteous rulers who destroyed tyranny and received the Mandate of Heaven. Zhu boldly contended that on the contrary, both rose to power through brute force, overwhelming the preexisting dynasty with sheer power. They had not received a mandate to rule. Rather, they had established their regimes by exterminating the previous rulers. Their conquest was the result of violent, bloody campaigns. Zhu Yunming also challenged the orthodoxy of Zhu Xi, claiming that even though Zhu Xi could be credited as a grand synthesizer of learning, he should not be viewed as a perfect sagely scholar after whom could come no capable successors. History, Zhu Yunming reminded us, changed, and so should the world's reception of Zhu Xi's learning. Wang Shizhen had high praise for Zhu Yunming's critical reevaluation, calling it a "model work distinguishing right from wrong" (Yanqiu Yang 2001, 36–37).

Perhaps the best-known iconoclastic interpreter of history and tradition was Li Zhi (1527–1602), who was eventually thrown into prison for "daring to propagate a disorderly way, deceiving the world and defrauding the masses" (Peng & Li 2001, 36). One of his most famous works, *A Book to be Concealed* (*Cangshu*), in sixty-eight fascicles, Li completed toward the end of his life, and it is a summation of his final views on history and the world. This work was essentially organized in the composite style of the standard histories, complete with imperial annals and biographies, but it has no tables or monographs. It covers the period from the Warring States period (403–221 B.C.E.) to the end of the Yuan in 1368, and contains more than 800 biographical entries, many of which cannot be found in the official histories. There is a sequel in twenty-seven fascicles, comprising some 400 entries on Ming biographies. Another work of Li's with significant historical import is the *Commentary on the Essentials of the "Outline of History"* (*Shigang pingyao*). It was intended as a supplement to *A Book to be Concealed*. Inspired by and following the example of Sima Guang's *Comprehensive Mirror*, this work comprises twenty-five chronologically ordered "annals," covering a period from the very distant past of the mythical emperor Yao to the demise of the Yuan dynasty. Another notable work is *A Book to be Burned* (*Fenshu*). It also has a sequel, but there is some question as to who wrote it. Although *A Book to be Burned* is primarily a collection of Li's letters, miscellaneous essays, and poems, it does contain some of his comments on historical events and thoughts on the writing of history (Peng & Li 2001, 36–37; H. Chan 1980, 3–5, 20–25, 155–156, 163, 164, 167–168; X. Lin 1998, 61–62; de Bary 1970, 201–203).

Li Zhi was a bold contrarian who played the role of a gadfly, challenging accepted wisdom and authority. One opening statement in *A Book to be Concealed* may be taken as the bedrock of his philosophy of history: "Human judgments are not fixed quantities; in passing judgments, men do not hold settled views" (Goodrich & Fang 1976, 811). In other words, that human conceptions change is a natural corollary of the inexorable flux of time. Admittedly a natural-born provocateur skeptical of inherited interpretations—"It is fortunate that I was naturally endowed with guts. What people in the past have joyfully appreciated as the upright I mostly treat as untrue. [I] mostly regard them as stale and dull [ideas] that have no practical use. What they have disdained, rejected, spitted on and castigated I treat as useful for the support of individuals, families and the state" (Peng & Li 2001, 39)—he pleaded for the recognition of anachronism in make judgments about the past. Li likened debates on right and wrong to the succession of night and day. What was right yesterday could well be wrong today. Even if Confucius were alive today, he would not know how to determine what was right and what was wrong (Peng & Li 2001, 39; Yanqiu Yang 2001, 37). Reinterpreting the past began with the demolition of orthodox views. In Li's time, orthodoxy was much determined by the teachings of the Learning of the Way identified with Zhu Xi. Just as Confucius' views could not be held up as universally valid norms, so too the Four Books and Six Classics, the textual canon of authority, could not be embraced as perennial guides to action. Li criticized historians and scholars for adhering without thinking to ancient words. It was doubtful that all of those words actually came from the mouths of the sages, but even if they did, they were medicine dispensed for a specific ailment; they were not a timeless panacea for all illnesses.

To Li, Daoxue was to blame for constantly talking about the classics as though they were ultimate ideas fit for eternity. Such teaching served as a refuge for deception. Li was particularly repelled by Daoxue's practice of creating archetypes of virtue of historical figures to glorify the ideals of loyalty, filiality, and righteousness, because the nuances and actualities of history did not permit such easy generalizations about people and events. The historiographical principle of praise and blame established by the *Spring*

and Autumn Annals could not be embraced as a timeless norm. It was, as Li
described it, "the history of one specific time-period." Li, echoing Wang
Shizhen, argued for using both the classics and histories. In fact, he asserted that all Six Classics were actually histories; they revealed not eternal
norms but that "the [W]ay is repeatedly moving, changing and transforming without being static, and so it is not possible to seize upon [it] as the one
definite handle." It was through the particularities and realities of history
that the authority and value of the classics could be seen and appreciated.
By the same token, Li did not subscribe to the idea of legitimate political
succession (*zhengtong*) that so dominated the writing of the standard histories precisely because such a generalized ideal flattened the complexities
of history. Each dynasty had to be examined in terms of its actual achievements, not its supposed place in some preordained pattern of succession
(Maowei Qian 1999, 82–83; Yanqiu Yang 2001, 41).

In Li Zhi's historical judgments and evaluations, praise was always bestowed in accordance with actual accomplishments, not in conformity with
norms of accepted behavior. An effective ruler was perforce in accord with
the demands and exigencies of his time, and his policies and visions were
those that fit the circumstances. Learning and scholarship were, in the last
analysis, statecraft, useful for the "ordering and management of the world"
(*jingshi*). Li had no patience for pedants, pretenders who hid behind the
Way and spoke loudly in the name of Daoxue, when their real intention
was merely to establish their reputation and seek short-term benefits. Many
scholar-officials excelled in empty talk about the Way and virtuous ideals,
but failed miserably when it came to "ruling the world and the country."
Thus Li refused to condemn rulers and ministers who were blamed in conventional historiography for their alleged contravention of Heaven's principle and for pursuing benefits. He accepted them as long as they effected
necessary changes and brought betterment to the state and society. The
first emperor of the Qin was a perfect case in point. While duly noting the
severity of his rule, Li called him "one unique emperor throughout past
and present" for his great accomplishments of unifying China and establishing a centralized bureaucratic state. Li also generously accorded accolades to those in history who advocated and implemented polices that enriched the state. He took strong issue with the traditional Confucian view
that statecraft was not anchored on the search for wealth and profits. He
argued that those "who could not manage wealth cannot rule the world"
(Maowei Qian 1999, 85). In fact, to the extent that everyone had desires
and desires constituted the necessary motivations for action, profits were
legitimate desires, as it was only reasonable for people to expect benefits
for their labor. Without salaries, there would be no officials; without the
prospect of harvest, there would be no farming. Utility was a fact in life, as
borne out by the facts of history (ibid., 84–88).

Li used history to praise and blame, but his central criterion was not
conventional. He regarded practical success and failure as the measure.
For instance, he rehabilitated the much-criticized figure of Feng Dao,

whom Ouyang Xiu had reviled as a fickle minister with no sense of loyalty. Li argued that by serving successive lords, Feng had succeeded in facilitating a smooth, relatively bloodless transition from one regime to another, minimizing the amount of brutal fighting. On the other hand, Li lambasted the Tang general Zhang Xun, who, in the name of loyalty and honor, refused to surrender a city that had been long under siege and who resorted to cannibalism—killing the weak and the old in order to feed his soldiers. Expediency and good reason, according to Li, demanded that Zhang surrender and preserve human lives, not adhere to some lofty principles. Li's historiography sought emancipation from the so-called "established principles" (*dingli*) and immutable "Three Bonds and Five Constant Relations" (*sangang wuchang*) ensconced in the Confucian didactic and moral conceptions of the past. Li assessed personages and events in terms of historical context—the dynamic succession of particular events *in* time—and expediency of utility—the pursuit of efficacious sociopolitical policies as opposed to blind faith in implacably held ideals (Maowei Qian 1999, 86; Peng & Li 2001, 43; cf. Zhuoran Li 1982, 33–46).

Looking at the Ming world of historiography, one may be impressed by many of the massive official compilations such as the *Yongle Encyclopedia* and the many collections of statutes, not to mention the many gazetteers and geographies, both local and national (W. Franke 1988, 777–781). But innovations appeared few and far between in official historiography. Nor were there impressive historians such as Liu Zhiji or Sima Guang in the Ming. But in the realm of private historiography, the picture was more varied and vital. Breaking loose from the constrictions of official format and spurred on by dissatisfaction with both historiographical and philosophical orthodoxy, a good number of writers undertook the task of ordering the past rigorously but also imaginatively.

CHAPTER 8

The Qing

Histories and the Classics

In 1644 China came under the rule of the Manchus, and another dynasty of conquest, the Qing, was established, despite residual resistance from remnant Ming forces on the periphery. While consciously retaining their ethnic identity by a variety of institutional and cultural means, the Manchu rulers sought to build and consolidate a highly Confucianized regime. Historiography, as the cultural and political manifestation of the Confucian vision of polity and society, took center stage in the intellectual world supported by the court. At the same time, in the domain of private historiography, the Qing was a fecund period of creativity and productivity.

Private Historiography and the Emergence of Historicist Views

From the period of the Ming-Qing transition in the seventeenth century through the High Qing era of the eighteenth, scores of scholars developed views of the past that were astutely aware of the anachronistic differences between different segments of time. As they sharpened the distinction between the past and the present—and thereby historicized the passage of time—they also honed their investigative skills, exercising punctilious care in treating texts as evidence in their effort to arrive at the truths of the past. Although it may well be argued that examples of such a sense of anachronism and preoccupation with textual evidence can be found in the Song, Qing ideas of the past—that is, the past as temporally and substantively other than the present—were so extensive as to constitute a special intellectual accomplishment of late imperial China. If we may generalize, there was a unique Qing climate of thought, of which the conceptions and treatments of the past were an integral part.

One feature of the intellectual climate of the Ming-Qing transitional period was the aversion, or at least indifference, to speculative metaphysics and spiritual introspection. The constructive side of this revulsion against the abstract was the preference for concrete learning with practical, utilitarian implications that might help order the world by rectifying social, political, and economic problems. In this quest for solid learning, the classics—the words of the sages—were read in new light and reexamined as the storehouse of values and lessons. But history also figured prominently as the Qing scholars sought to understand present problems by interrogating the past—not an idealized past that was universalized as a grand metaphysical order of reified ideas, but one made up of actual events, pulsating with the deeds and thoughts of historical personages (H. Chang 1974, 46–61; Ng 1995, 239–240, 254–257; Ji 2001, 96–105). Several innovative thinkers who lived through the Ming-Qing transition personified this intellectual orientation. Each in his own way embraced history as a means to understand the world, a world enlivened not by introspective values and quintessential substance, but one defined by the state and society, governed by workaday utility and quotidian practicality. One such pivotal thinker was Huang Zongxi (1619–1695).

As with many of his contemporaries, Huang Zongxi was particularly interested in the history of the Ming. His family owned copies of the veritable records of the dynasty's various reigns, which he studied diligently. To complement such official sources he collected and canvassed all sorts of materials, including biographies, geographies, and astronomical studies. Huang was convinced that good histories could be built only on thorough research. He lambasted his contemporaries for hastily writing histories that were inadequately based on limited sources. Furthermore, many of them imitated Sima Qian and Ban Gu, and improperly ignored the many other styles of history. Huang cautioned against rigidly privileging one particular format, pointing to the merits of different historical approaches. He explained that in the case of annals, the past was framed in an orderly manner by using chronology as the principle of organization; the composite style prominently featured biographies and provided focused information on people's lives; the narrative style, weaving together isolated particulars, offered a coherent account of events from beginning to end. Guided by the imperative of thoroughness in source-gathering and flexibility in format, he penned the *Case Studies of Ming History* (*Ming shi'an*) in 240 fascicles, which unfortunately is no longer extant. In writing this massive work, Huang eclectically employed different styles and incorporated materials found in both official and private historiographies (F. Tao 1987, 424–425; Deng 1999, 89; W. Du 2004, 231–243).

His greatest historical work was undoubtedly the *Intellectual Lineages of Ming Confucians* (*Mingru xue'an*) in sixty-two fascicles, an intellectual history of the Ming period. In terms of the provenance and salient features of the teachings of some 308 Ming scholars, Huang categorized them into nineteen intellectual lineages. Since he recognized the dynamic changes that had taken place over the lengthy Ming period (about 270 years), Huang also divided the dynasty's intellectual developments into three major periods (Wilson 1995, 184–192). His goal was to reconstruct in detail the characteristic accomplishments of the various schools. Although Huang saw himself as a follower of the school of Wang Yangming, he sought to transcend any sectarian loyalty. He criticized earlier works similar to his, such as Zhou Rudeng's *Orthodox Transmissions of Sagely Learning* (*Shengxue zongchuan*) and Sun Qifeng's *Orthodox Transmissions of the Learn-*

ing of Principle (*Lixue zongchuan*), for distorting the picture of intellectual development in the name of partisanship—Zhou's work leaned toward the teachings of Wang Yangming, while Sun's toward those of Zhu Xi. Because they were devoted to celebrating the learning of their own academic sect, they included only those with whom they identified, excluding all outsiders (Wilson 1995, 167–184). Moreover, Huang insisted that his explication of the scholars' ideas and achievements be based on firsthand reading of the primary sources. He was loath to rely on secondary discussions of the materials he chose to include in his massive history. About each intellectual lineage, Huang wrote a succinct description of its origins and main tenets, followed by individual entries of the selected scholars. These consisted of a biography, excerpts of representative writings, and Huang's own comments. Conspicuously absent was the traditional prefatory contrivance of making separate references to the sages' tenets as the authoritative fountainhead of the various schools of learning. Huang's approach suggested that any individual dynasty with its own laws and institutions was a legitimate unit worthy of serious study (de Bary, 1975 197–198; Ching 1987, 12–20; W. Du 1988, 191–199). In taking this approach, Huang forged the first true intellectual history in China, one that remains enormously useful for present-day study of the Ming world of learning. Upon the completion of this masterwork in 1676, Huang began a similar history of the Song and Yuan dynasties, but he managed to finish only the preface and seventeen fascicles before his death. His children and disciples continued his work, and Quan Zuwang (1705–1755) finally completed the entire text of a hundred fascicles (F. Tao 1987, 421–423; Yi 1987, 316–318; Deng 1999, 89–90; W. Du 2004, 244–248).

Another famous work by Huang that deserves scrutiny is *Waiting for the Dawn: A Plan for the Prince* (*Mingyi daifang lu*). Although it is a treatise on political theory and practice rather than a history, it could not have been written without a deep understanding and rich knowledge of Chinese history. As a political testament that offered a master plan for substantive reforms, the work not only revealed the fundamental principles of good government, summed up the essence of Chinese civilization, and recounted the workings of the institutions of imperial China, but it also articulated a sharp sense of historical change. We can, as a consequence, distill from it a distinct historicism, a clear conception of the past. As Huang pointed out, despite Mencius' dictum that history was marked by cyclical alternation between periods of peace and disorder, China had not lifted itself out of the phase of disorder since the time of antiquity and the establishment of the Qin. What Huang saw in the long span of Chinese history was continuous oppression of the people. If peace and chaos were determined by whether the people were happy or in distress, Huang rejected the rise and fall of dynasties as a significant factor in history. What counted was the condition of the masses, who had, unfortunately, been mired in a state of unremitting repression since the founding of the oppressive Qin with its flawed institutions. The central problem throughout Chinese history had been an excessive concentration of power at the center that bred a phlegmatic, top-heavy bureaucracy that inhibited local initiative and precluded flexible adjustment to exigencies. The Mongol conquest further aggravated the endemic problem of overcentralization. Throughout the march of time, China had drifted farther away from the pristine civilization of the ancient past when the sages' values had been realized in the practical world of state and society. Thus, on the whole, we may say that Huang viewed Chinese history as a prolonged process of progressive deterioration.

For Huang, the process of devolution could be halted only with a revival of the ancient system of enfeoffment that would loosen the iron grip of power by the top. Idealist though Huang was, he was no naïve utopianist. Far from advocating a simple replication of the ancient institutions, he argued for revival of the spirit and principle of governance embodied in the system of enfeoffment, in which the ruler spurned the monopoly of power and domination of the state. By delegating and sharing power with those below, especially the prime minister, the ruler assumed the responsibility of serving the people. In addition, active cultivation of the moral and the talented in the schools would ensure the creation of a literate, knowledgeable citizenry whose public opinion would provide the yardstick by which to judge right and wrong. In other words, what Huang called for was the realization of the time-honored principle of the primacy of the people (*minben*), according to which governance would be guaranteed by law and the ruler would serve the state as the servant. Huang used the historical realities he had analyzed in *Waiting for the Dawn* to illustrate and corroborate this general principle (F. Tao 1987, 418–420; Yi 1987, 296–297; Struve 1988b, 474–502; de Bary 1993, 5–42). Huang saw the pursuit of history as an integral component of a general quest for knowledge. While plumbing the classics in order to understand and manage the world might constitute the core of learning, he pointedly remarked that history was indispensable. "Without the constant study of history, the changes and transformations of principles cannot be corroborated and verified" (W. Gu 1986, 38).

It is appropriate here to take note of one of Huang's most accomplished disciples, Wan Sitong (1638–1702). Like his teacher, Wan refused to serve the new Qing dynasty, although as an admired and learned scholar, he had been formally invited by the court in 1678. Fiercely loyal to the defunct Ming, Wan involved himself deeply in compiling a private history of the dynasty. In 1679, when the Qing opened a bureau to compile the standard history of the Ming, Wan was again invited and once more he declined. He did, however, agree to go to Beijing and become an informal consultant to one of the directors, but he refused to accept a salary or title. Perhaps he consented to indirect involvement out of the desire to secure access to classified documents for his own work. Indeed, while he was staying in the capital, he gathered many sources that complemented the veritable records for his history of the Ming. Just a few years before his sudden death in 1792, Wan was already planning to return home to focus on its completion. When he died, he probably had already completed a rough draft of as many as 500 fascicles. But it is difficult to ascertain how much he had accomplished because after he died, his personal libraries and manuscripts were dispersed (X. Zhang 1968, 213–226; Struve 1988a, 90–91; F. Tao 1987, 426; Fang 1996, 398–409).

Interesting enough, even before Huang Zongxi completed his peerless intellectual history of the Ming, Wan himself had already penned *Lineages and Academic Schools in the Confucian Forest (Rulin zongpai)* in sixteen fascicles. It is obviously a much shorter work, but its chronological coverage is far broader, as it covers the time from Confucius to the Ming. It is, however, a mere listing of the different schools that Wan identified throughout history, and as such may more appropriately be described as a historical chart or table. But it is not without merit. While many works of this nature were strongly influenced by the authors' personal sectarian loyalties, Wan aimed to be inclusive. He refused to privilege the orthodox Learning of the Way personified by Zhu Xi, for example, and gave other Southern Song scholars their rightful space. He also included scholars from Buddhism and Daoism, although he placed them in appendices. With regard to Ming scholars, Wan's text lists some 470 figures, while Huang's contains only about 200 (Struve 1988a, 92–96; Fang 1996, 60–70).

Wan used history to construct a usable past for his own present position, most notably, his loyalty to the Chinese Ming regime. Because of the obvious political danger of writing directly about the surviving subjects (*yimin*) of the Ming, Wan voiced his opinion by writing about the Song loyalists in the Song-Yuan transition. In *A Broad Record and Correction of Errors Concerning the Surviving Subjects of the Song (Song yimin guanglu dingwu)* and *A Record of the Loyal and Righteous in the Song (Songji zhongyi lu)*, he warmly commended the surviving subjects of the Song for not forgetting their former masters, and he rehabilitated those loyalists described in the official *Yuan History* as "bandits." He also referred to the Zhou-Shang transition in antiquity. The Zhou had naturally characterized the remaining Shang resistance as "recalcitrant subjects," but from the vantage point of the Shang, Wan said, these individuals warranted the label of "righteous stalwarts." Wan established criteria for application of the positive term "surviving subjects" to late Song-early Yuan figures, implying that the same criteria should be used in his own time. According to Wan, the epithet should be conferred only on those who resolutely refused to serve the Yuan. Anyone who participated in the examinations of the new regime would be disqualified, even if that person did not obtain an official position in the government. Wan even excluded scholars who lectured to large crowds in public arenas. His rationale was that in the newly established alien dynasty, all loyal surviving subjects, while continuing their diligent pursuit of scholarship and learning, must discreetly assume a low profile, for they were bereaved and in mourning (Fang 1996, 107–112).

Like Huang Zongxi, Wan saw history as instrumentally useful for the ordering of the world, but unlike his teacher, Wan did not develop the sort of comprehensive, panoramic critique of imperial despotism. He was nonetheless convinced that only through careful study and analysis of institutional development over the long term could "the grand schemes of ordering the state from the past to the present" be understood and effectively appropriated for use in current times. He wrote about systems of agriculture, taxation and revenue, and military structure, revealing their strengths and weaknesses. He explored causal factors in the fall of the Ming: economically it had used silver currency ineffectively and had spent exorbitantly; politically it had engaged in intense factional strife and fractious court politics; and militarily it had allowed the degeneration of the militia system and incurred the enormous costs of conscription. In history Wan discerned the irreducible principles of good government—incorruptibility, frugality, and attention to the needs of the people. An obtrusive, oppressive government that burdened the people could not survive. The rule of history was such that when the sufferings of the people became extreme, the state collapsed. Wan boldly declared that when the people saw government exactions to be worse than the rampages of banditry, they had a right to rebel. Under such circumstance, the rebels acted in a Way (*dao*) that was defensible, even though they appeared superficially to be violating the normal Way of loyalty. Positing benevolent rule as the cornerstone of efficacious statecraft, Wan subjected the Ming rulers to criticism. Of the sixteen Ming emperors, he lambasted half of them as being despotic and uncaring, and consequently failing to tend to the needs of the people (Fang 1996, 116–152, 159–173).

As a practicing historian, Wan systematically outlined his working principles and methods. First was the necessity to establish factual credibility by ensuring the veracity of all the included information. Like many Ming writers, Wan reacted to the fact that the national histories and veritable records of the Ming left much to be desired, and private histories, though abundant, could not always be trusted. The historian had to use official sources, but he should examine them rigorously and complement them with private materials. Second, information should be presented in readable and appealing language. Third, when examining and evaluating the actions of past personages, the historian had to rise above personal preferences and loyalties and strive for impartiality. He must also be broad- and fair-minded, taking into account the circumstances surrounding events and actions. Piecemeal recording and narrow focus on deeds by themselves yielded an incomplete or even distorted picture. The felicity of praise and blame depended heavily on the historian's cautious, judicious assessment. Fourth, it was better to record facts copiously than to risk omitting them, because bequeathing facts and information to posterity was the historian's foremost task. And finally, the historian should embark on private efforts of compilation if possible because collective compilations under imperial auspices faced unavoidable obstacles that inevitably detracted from the quality of the final products, most notably pressure from above and lack of cohesion among authors (Struve 1988a, 96–100; Fang 1996, 201–235).

Another polymath of the Ming-Qing transition who produced works of significant historical import was Gu Yanwu (1613–1682). His two best-known historical compositions are *A Treatise on the Merits and Deficiencies of Territorial Administrations* (*Tianxia junguo libing shu*) and *Records of Knowledge [Acquired] Daily* (*Rizhi lu*). The *Treatise*, in 102 fascicles, is a systematic institutional, social, and economic history of the Ming. Gu not only described the structures and operations of many government institutions but also exposed their decline and corruption in the context of the socioeconomic situation of the Ming. The *Records of Knowledge*, in thirty-two fascicles, which Gu completed late in life, is a random collection of notes and writings on a vast array of subjects, including politics, economics, literature, classical studies, laws, astronomy, geography, and, needless to say, history. In this work Gu evaluated many of the standard histories, from Sima Qian's masterpiece to Sima Guang's. He praised Sima Qian for his ability to seamlessly weave moral judgments into his narratives, but he also corrected scores of factual mistakes. While many commentators faulted Sima Guang's *Comprehensive Mirror* for failing to include literary figures, Gu defended the exclusion because the work was intended as an aid to government and so space was not required for literary matters (Fu 1987, 31–39).

Gu clearly indicated his method of doing history. He deemed broad and thorough gathering of sources to be a matter of the first order. Consultation of primary sources was especially crucial. He criticized his contemporaries for relying on secondary materials and likened such practice to forging new coins by melting down old ones. Conducting serious scholarship was analogous to minting coins by first mining copper in the mountains. The historian must consult original sources instead of rehashing what had been said. In writing biography, it was the author's responsibility to read all the works his subject had composed. In addition, the author must be familiar with the context of the subject's life. If he was an important official in the central government, then the author ought to be thoroughly familiar with the history of court affairs. If the subject was a local official, then the author must acquire knowledge of the local customs, mores, geography, administration, and so forth. Moreover, sources should not be confined to written texts. Oral history was an activity which Gu promoted and in which he engaged. He told of his own indomitable quest for sources. He not only visited celebrated places and large cites, but also explored abandoned lands and ghost towns. He would copy as many texts as possible as they became available in his search. Whenever he found a hitherto unknown or ignored source, he would be "so overjoyed that he could not sleep" (W. Gu 1986, 53–54; W. Du 2004, 210–212). Assembled sources must be rigorously scrutinized. To ensure their believability and veracity, all factual accounts had to be corroborated by both internal and external evidence. Not even the accounts in the canonical *Spring and Autumn Annals* could be accepted without verification. Authenticated facts served as the raw material from which to fashion the historical retelling of events and biographies, and these involved construction of coherent stories, each with a beginning, middle, and end. The meaning of past events could be established only by comprehensively detailing their origin and development; piecemeal, truncated descriptions obscured historical significance.

Furthermore, historical learning required humility, by which Gu meant proper acknowledgment and citation of sources. At the same time that all sources should be viewed with healthy skepticism, they also had to be treated with proper respect. Whenever words were cited, their authors had to be acknowledged. When the historian encountered an author's quotation of another's words, both should be acknowledged. Gu regarded it hubris to appropriate words as one's own without giving their progenitors their due; it was a practice that amounted to obliterating the authors themselves from history. This sense of humility was related to the virtue of impartiality. According to Gu, the historian should not be biased and overly selective in recording events of the past. Even blatantly partisan views must be recorded for posterity's information and reference. Gu therefore disagreed with the customary practice of manipulating the imperial annals in order to show orthodox, legitimate transmission of political authority. Often the annals of allegedly illegitimate reigns were expunged or else subsumed under the dynastic calendar of the dynasty deemed to be orthodox. Gu argued for a contrary practice. He maintained that the histories of the much-maligned Northern and Southern dynasties after the fall of the Han, the Five Kingdoms following the Tang, and the Liao and Jin dynasties of conquest, should all be recorded in accordance with their own dynastic calendars. By the same token, historical personages not included in the standard histories should not be altogether ignored. If they made contributions to state and society, their biographies should be written even though they might not be regarded as illustrious personages in traditional accounts. (F. Tao 1987, 438–442; Fu 1987, 39–42; W. Du 2004, 212–224).

Most important, an individual's historical knowledge ought to be realized in everyday living. To pursue knowledge for knowledge's sake rendered one a pedant and dilettante. Because "historical books are composed to mirror what happened in the past so as to provide lessons for the present" (W. Gu 1986, 54), Gu stressed the importance of broad learning that was of practical use and benefit to the state and society. Writings and literature (*wen*) were more than words of purely academic, intellectual significance; they should be dedicated to "illuminating the Way." Illumination of the Way did not mean recondite discourse on the essence of ultimate reality but "the recording of the affairs of the state, revelation of the concealed [sufferings] of the people, and the joyful disquisition on the goodness of humanity." Any learning that claimed to have shed light on the Way ought to be "of benefit to the world . . . and the future" (F. Tao 1987, 433–434). History was, in brief, statecraft. "To refer to the past," as Gu said, "in deliberations about the present is scholars' practice of statecraft to order the world" (W. Gu 1986, 54). Studying the past, one came to know the universal principles of management of the world. One central principle was the absolute requirement that the ruler and state promote and guarantee the welfare of the people. The rise and fall of dynasties and the succession of regimes brought about changes of all sorts: reign titles, costumes, implements, units of measurement, and so on. But one principle remained unchanged: the world could not be truly won without benevolence, the noblest expression of which was the preservation and protection of the people (*baomin*). Rulers benevolent to their people were truly invincible, and their regimes endured. History revealed two kinds of destruction. First was the collapse of a state, whereupon there was merely a change of the dynastic name and replacement of one royal family by another. The second was the demise of all-under-Heaven (*tianxia*, that is, the whole of Chinese culture and civilization), whereupon the ritual order with its virtues and morals was destroyed. Peace and disorder coincided not simply with dynastic change but were directly related to the state of the minds and hearts of the people; they were results of how people thought and acted. When customs and mores were vulgar, the minds and hearts of the people were debased and coarsened, resulting in the death of culture. It was the ruler's responsibility to preserve the people in such a way as to uphold, strengthen, and realize moral bonds and virtuous mores (F. Tao 1987, 435; Fu 1987, 39).

Small wonder that Gu advocated institutional reforms for the amelioration of people's lives. He declared that "under Heaven, there are no prevailing customs that cannot be altered." Laws and institutions (*fa*) had to be changed when the times and circumstances changed: "If *fa* are not changed, there can be no salvation [of culture]. The present circumstance is such that changes are inevitable. If we go against the reality that changes are in order and obdurately stick to the principle that there should be no change, there will surely be great calamities!" (F. Tao 1987, 435–443) Like Huang Zongxi, Gu had great faith in the ancient system of enfeoffment which, he argued, gave the people a sense of belonging to their own localities under their own control. By delegating authority and distributing lands and responsibilities under this system, the ruler no longer treated the regime as his private property but as a true commonwealth. People's voices—public opinions—were duly heard and accommodated, their livelihood bettered, and wealth equalized. Gu's ideal political system was one in which the spirit of feudalism suffused the imperial bureaucratic system of prefectures and districts (Ono 1967, 221–222; F. Tao 1987, 436–437; Struve 1988b, 474–479; Vermeer 1995, 204–215). By identifying among the brambles and briars of historical details the universal principles of governance, Gu imbued the past with present meaning.

More prolific in output and more systematic in historical views than either Gu Yanwu or Huang Zongxi, Wang Fuzhi (1619–1692) was another intellectual giant of the Ming-Qing transition. Like Gu and Huang, Wang was not so much a historian as a thinker who pondered the meaning of the past by commenting on existing historical works. Nonetheless, he wrote several much-admired and well-known historical texts. *On the Comprehensive Mirror* (*Du Tongjian lun*) is a critical reflection on Sima Guang's *Com-*

prehensive Mirror; the *Song lun* (On the Song), though on the surface an analysis and criticism of sectarian Song politics, was a veiled attack on the debilitating factional strife of the late Ming; and the *Veritable Records of the Yongli Reign [1651–61]* (*Yongli shilu*), which Wang compiled while serving in the resistance government of the Southern Ming dynasty. As ardently as Huang and Gu, Wang ascribed to history the supreme functional and instrumental value of providing guidance for the present and future. Those who did bad history would never be able to reveal the causes of success and failure in statecraft and government, which is to say that only those who comprehended the past through history could aid in the grand enterprise of ordering the world. In *On the Comprehensive Mirror,* Wang emphasized that when Sima Guang used the metaphor of a mirror to represent history, he was not saying that history simply reflected what happened. Rather, what was mirrored in words required our deep reflection—our thinking about how success and failure came about. This, in turn, should stimulate thought as to how such success could be emulated, and such failure remedied or avoided. Historical knowledge should lead to action, or else it remained mere words on paper, indulgent academic exercises that ultimately destroyed the will to initiate beneficial changes (Teng 1968, 118, 120, 122; F. Tao 1987, 446–447; W. Du 1988, 21–50).

Wang Fuzhi's historical views were intertwined with his metaphysical and philosophical theories, which were animated by a fundamental notion of the inevitability of change. The substance (*zhi*) of all things inexorably underwent change even when outward forms appeared constant. Things that appeared to be similar across time were in reality different. In addition, Wang conceived the world as one constituted primarily of concrete things (*qi*), that is, implements, instruments, institutions, and so on. Reality was not some abstract, ineffable, and transcendent essence; it was defined by the very things of everyday life. Applied to history, Wang's metaphysical and philosophical notions demanded that the histories and institutions of every dynasty and period be treated as sui generis. Owing to the passage of time, the ways of the Han and Tang, for instance, could not be the same as those of today. Time was not some passive indicator of the flux of reality. As the *Classic of Changes* stated, time referred to the changes that inexorably occurred as one came to grips with the problems and demands posed by reality (*biantong*) (Teng 1968, 113–115; McMorran 1975, 447–458; F. Tao 1987, 453–455). This bred in Wang an evolutionary view of history.

Wang theorized that humanity's progenitors were animals who were bipeds and walked upright and that the Chinese, even in the times of Yao and Shun, were barbarians. Civilization, and therefore history, grew and progressed over time, a product of cultural accretion and accumulation. As time changed, so did circumstances and conditions (*shi*). Thus the institutions and implements of one dynasty or a period could not be readily adopted wholesale in another. Unlike Gu Yanwu and Huang Zongxi, Wang rejected the possibility of reviving the ancient feudal system of enfeoffment. The bureaucratized system of prefectures and districts had come into being and endured because it was appropriate for the circumstances and served the needs of the times. The feudal system had worked well in antiquity because it was in tune with the natural tendencies and circumstances then. But the sages of the olden days could not have established it as an immutable system for all ages. They did not have the prescience to foretell the most efficacious measures for posterity thousands of years hence. Things and affairs changed with altered circumstances; so too did laws and institutions. Principles (*li*) were not eternal. The only perpetual principles were those that accorded with the tendencies of the time. Whenever principle corresponded with circumstance, the will of Heaven was manifested (W. Du 2004, 259–276).

Wang thus demythologized Heaven, which had been construed as some mysterious transcendent reality. Heaven, in his historical and historicized explication, was the natural order of things wherein implements effectively addressed timebound problems. Following Mencius, Wang further asserted that Heaven's will was identified with the minds and hearts of the people. Sagacious rulers anticipated needed changes as time progressed so as to satisfy the yearnings of the people; inept rulers adopted policies that were at odds with time and thwarted the hopes of their subjects. As a consequence Wang, like Gu Yanwu and Huang Zongxi, fervently criticized excessive concentration of power in the hands of rulers, even though he doubted that one could revive ancient institutions such as the feudal system. Highly concentrated imperial authority often resulted in the neglect of people's material well-being and social justice, since rulers tended to view the domain as their own private properties. Wang insisted that cultural progress and political success meant safeguarding and improving people's livelihood. History time and again told stories of dynastic success when rulers tended to the needs of the people. Significantly, as Wang affirmed the circumstantial and temporal particularities of each dynasty—he famously claimed that what constituted justice was different in specific time periods—he pointed to the comprehensive universal justice that bridged the chasm of past and present. From the crowded events of history, he distilled one universal principle: the primary responsibility of the ruler was to guarantee the welfare of the people through benevolent and public-minded government (Teng 1968, 115–117; McMorran 1975, 447–458; F. Tao 1987, 450–455, 458–459; W. Du 2004, 253–259).

In Wang's conception of Heaven and his view of history as the interaction between time, circumstance, and principle, there was no room for the traditional historiographical assumption that dynastic change was the cosmological displacement of one cosmic agent by another. The notion of legitimate political succession—*zhengtong*—had often been coupled with an esoteric belief in the movement of the Yin-Yang forces and the corresponding five phases/agents/powers/virtues of earth, wood, metal, fire, and water. Wang delinked any such connection between political fortunes and cosmological activities. No supernatural forces affected human deeds or the course of history. Even when the notion of *zhengtong* was divorced

from fanciful cosmological moorings, Wang did not find it justified or valid.
To begin with, there were no legitimate successions to speak of, even during the much-admired antiquity. Leaders became rulers often by brute
force. *Zhengtong* was an after-the-fact justification of a regime's rise to
power and subjugation of the defeated. Moreover, history clearly showed
that there were scores of occasions when China disintegrated as a unified
entity, and dynasties succeeded one another without any clear lines of succession. When a dynasty finally did succeed in reuniting China, such as the
Sui after the period of the Northern and Southern dynasties, it did so without following any recognizable line of succession. Whatever continuity of
legitimacy the Sui claimed was fabricated. The situation was the same with
the Song when it unified China after the period of the Five Dynasties and
Ten Kingdoms, a time when there had been many successions with no apparent orthodox lines. The case of the Qing was no exception. It was no
inheritor of any legitimate order.

Wang's rejection of this historiographical convention owed much to
his views on the relationship between China and its barbarian neighbors.
To Wang, there were two "great defensive embankments" (*dafang*) that
served as demarcations and barriers between two groups of human beings.
First was the distinction between profound persons of moral superiority
and mean folk of inferior moral constitution. Second was that between the
Chinese and barbarians. Wang regarded barbarians as creatures of another
species, to whom the normal rules of interhuman relations did not apply.
He went so far as to say that it would be perfectly acceptable for the Chinese to defraud, attack, and even kill them. There is little doubt that Wang's
characterization of barbarians stemmed from his anger at the destruction
of the Ming dynasty and his pain at the devastation the Manchu conquest
had caused. Wang rejected Qing legitimacy, and he begrudged their using
the notion of *zhengtong* to manipulate history. Previous dynasties of conquest, such as the Jin and the Yuan, had certainly endeavored to assert
their legitimacy with historiographical legerdemain. To deprive the Qing
of any legitimate claim to authority, Wang declared the notion of *zhengtong* to be completely without meaning as historical fact. It was a purely
political construction. To eschew altogether the problem of manufactured
and historically baseless notions of *zhengtong*, Wang chose not to recognize dynasties as the most useful temporal units for investigation of China's
past. Instead, he broke the long span of Chinese history into epochs, the
number of which varied, depending on what he wanted to illustrate. In
On the Comprehensive Mirror, for instance, Wang offered a scheme of periodization that began with the Shang and Zhou dynasties and ended with
the beginning of the Ming that contained seven epochs. But elsewhere he
constructed another that consisted of only three (Teng 1968, 115, 117–118;
F. Tao 1987, 455–458).

Wang insisted on history's practicality. History not only supplied moral
lessons, but also established precedents that served as reliable guides in
the worlds of socioeconomic and political affairs and policies. As a con-

sequence, one principal concern of history was to investigate and explain the factors involved in the success or failure of rulership and government. Wang was aware that such exploration would not always yield tidy answers. There would be divergences, variations, and exceptions in the midst of general patterns. Why were some regimes successful only in a limited way, and why were some failures more spectacular than others? In the process of historical examination, the investigator had to imaginatively enter the minds of those in the past and fathom how one might act if placed in a similar situation, taking into account the surrounding circumstances. Judgment — praising and blaming — were integral parts of a historian's task. It required meticulous care to ensure sound, balanced, and fair criticisms, and they depended not only on erudition but also self-reflection and self-questioning. Neither hyperbole nor understatement was appropriate. When one was unsure, one's statements and judgments should be tempered with qualifications, and even if one was confident of what had happened, it was preferable not to propound one's views as incontrovertible conclusions. A terse style and laconic language, as opposed to florid and flowery verbiage, best suited historical discourse. The goal was to piece facts and interpretations into a coherent narrative. When examining well-known events, there was no need to recapitulate their details. Rather, the focus ought to be placed on determining their origins and causes and ascertaining their historical veracity. In this process the historian uncovered the engine of history: the interpenetration and correspondence of time and circumstance, on which success and failure rested (Teng 1968, 118–119; G. Luo 1972, 18–26; F. Tao 1987, 449–450; W. Du 2004, 250–276).

In the seventeenth century — a time of great changes — history was increasingly seen as a practical way to comprehend the world, while introspective, metaphysically orientated learning seemed increasingly obtuse and irrelevant. Instead of focusing on the pursuit of "honoring the virtuous moral nature" (*zun dexing*), scholars like Huang Zongxi, Wan Sitong, Gu Yanwu, and Wang Fuzhi embraced the "intellectualism" of pursuing inquiry and learning (*dao wenxue*). Knowledge through solid study of history and the classics appeared to have claimed priority over spiritual enlightenment through inward moral cultivation (Yü 1975, 105–146). As the goal of achieving moral purism of the mind gave way to technical betterment of the world, the quest for the essential and subtle was dislodged by the search for the practical and concrete. The burgeoning concern with ordering the world (*jingshi*) and a conviction concerning the efficacy of institutional management demanded and strengthened the study of history, which furnished the guide to statecraft and governance (Yamanoi 1954, 135–150; H. Chang 1974, 36–61). In looking to the past for lessons, many early Qing scholars came to appreciate the particularistic, multivalent, dynamic nature of things as presented in history more keenly than immutable universals and unchanging principles embedded in the mind (W. Peterson 1979, 12).

While we may reasonably argue that a prevalent "historicism" or "historical-mindedness"—the appreciation of changing particulars and the contingency of specific events and values—informed the thoughts and writings of many early Qing intellectuals, the notion of timeboundness was quite at odds with the dominant assumptions of the Confucian Learning of the Way. Daoxue was based on a fundamental notion of ultimate reality—the Way (*dao*), Principle (*li*), the Great Ultimate (*taiji*)—that inhered in humanity's Heaven-endowed virtuous nature (*dexing*). This orientation toward ultimacy and universality meant that proponents of Daoxue saw history primarily as a demonstration of the Way/Principle, which prescribed universally valid values external to time and whose significance did not diminish even with a change of context. The overarching Way/Principle rendered the particularities of historical events incidental, blurring the lines between ontological-moral perfection and technical-practical improvement (Metzger 1977, 197–205; Ng 1993b, 564–565).

Despite Zhu Xi's enthusiasm for the study of history, his world view was essentially constructed out of a conception of the universe as temporally and spatially integrated; there was one Principle, the myriad manifestations of which constituted the world. The classics, the textual embodiment of principles, were superior to history, which he described as "matters and affairs of the outer skin." This world view nurtured two conceptions of the past. The first was the conviction that there was an essentially permanent, universal natural order of things, making the past and the present substantively and substantially the same. The second was that time was degenerative—the past was qualitatively better than, and therefore, different from the present (cf. Logan 1977, 18). Note that the second conception did not contradict the first, in that it merely addressed the degeneration in form. The present, purged of its defects, could return to and retrieve the essential substance of the past. Zhu Xi certainly saw the Way as constant: the Way of the antique Three Dynasties was the same as the Way of the Han, the Tang, and the Song. This perspective of a timeless exalted antiquity meant that the ancient past was the warehouse of universal values that shed light on present problems, to the extent that they were directly applicable to the present. But Zhu also claimed that the Han and the Tang were qualitatively inferior to the Three Dynasties, after which the Way had been beclouded by selfish human desires. The Way was immutable, but it was unrealized in later times. As there was an eternal unity, events in history were necessarily merely its partial representations. History, being repetitions in a universe that was essentially static, could not be an agent that remade anything or forged new values (Ng 1993b, 564–567).

Clearly seventeenth-century thinkers did not abandon altogether the ideal of antiquity as the norm, inspiration, and guide. But their classicist regard for the ancient past was tempered by their historical appreciation for the particularities of different dynasties or periods. Huang Zongxi offered a metaphysics that was quite accommodating of changes. In his opening lines of *Intellectual Lineages of the Ming Confucians*, he says, "Through-

out Heaven and earth is the mind-heart, whose changes are unpredictable. It is inexorably manifested in myriad different forms. The mind-heart
has no fundamental substance. Fundamental substance is that which is
achieved by its efficacious effort. Therefore, to plumb the principle is to
probe the myriad different forms of this Mind, not the myriad different
forms of the myriad things" (Mu Qian 1964, 1:2). In metaphysical language Huang hammered out messages that were sensitive to change in
the concrete world of experience and effort. Reference to the mind-heart
notwithstanding, Huang affirmed the multiplicity and complexity of phenomena. The mind-heart itself was dynamic in nature, and having no fundamental substance, it was defined by efforts and hence established the
primacy of the external world (Ching 1987, 12–20). Consequently, Huang
propounded a dynamic view of institutional growth. Revival of the ancient
institutions of the classics was impractical. No wonder he proclaimed that
"under heaven . . . there have not been laws and institutions that could not
be overthrown." As his *Waiting for the Dawn* made clear, Huang saw his own
time as one dynamically bound to the past. There was antiquity with sagely
rule, followed by two thousand years of disorder as a result of growing despotism. Now the time had come for institutional change.

Wang Fuzhi also formulated a historicist metaphysics that explicated
the idea of principle in terms of circumstances, tendencies, and conditions. Principle was not some mysterious transcendent force. It was simply
the immanent pattern of all things and affairs—that which was certain
and necessary, that which was self-evident and natural, and the why and
the wherefore of individual things. Principle could not be discussed in
the absence of circumstances. Because circumstances changed in time, so
did Principle, and such changes cried out for the intervention of human
agency. "When one accords with the times, one complies with that which
the time makes inevitable in order to save oneself, and so escape from dis-
aster" (McMorran 1975, 457). To Wang, the unique circumstances governing the institutions of each age were what constituted the Way of that age,
to which human agency responded. Every dynasty should rule in accord
with its time and establish the institutions particular to that epoch, because
the classics and antiquity supplied no perennial models. "As to setting up
schemes or arranging for details, neither the *Book of History* nor Confucius said anything about them. . . . [B]ecause the ancient institutions were
meant to govern the ancient world and cannot be followed today, the superior man does not base his activities on them, and because what is suitable today can govern the world of today but will not necessarily for the
future, the superior man does not hand it down to posterity as a model"
(W. Chan 1963, 701).

Gu Yanwu, on the other hand, tended to avoid metaphysical pondering. His sense of history was manifested in his evaluation of institutions based on his knowledge about their development and context. He
regarded periodic reforms as necessary to forestall calamities, so he advo-

cated modifying the preexisting prefectural system: "If we understand that the feudal system changed into the prefectural system, we will also understand that as the prefectural system has in turn fallen into decay, it too must change. Does it mean that there will be a return to feudalism? No, it is impossible. But if some sage who could invest the prefectural system with the essential meaning of feudalism were to appear, then the world would attain order. . . . Now, the defects of the prefectural [system] have developed to their utmost. . . . But still, it was followed in all its details. That is why the livelihood of people is diminishing daily; that is why China is growing weaker daily." Gu's diagnosis of problems coalesced around a keen sense of anachronism that recognized the considerable gulf between the present and the past; he was aware of the impossibility of directly applying the classics to current problems. "Just as today we cannot write [as though we were writing] the Two Han histories, so too the two Han histories could not have been written as the *Classic of Documents* and the *Zuo Commentary*" (Ng 1993b, 570).

We should remember, however, that Huang, Wang, and Gu never lost faith in the classics as the repository of universal values. Huang embraced the enduring principles bequeathed by the ancient Three Dynasties even as he trenchantly critiqued the despotic imperial institutions. He affirmed the constant ancient principle of governance — unswerving devotion to the people — that had been ignored since the Qin. He talked at length of the necessity to revive at least the spirit behind the antique institutions. Wang Fuzhi, perhaps the most articulate on the notion of change, also measured the particularities of the dynasties against the universals found in the classics. "For the best way of government, there is nothing better than to examine the *Classic of Documents* and modify it with the words of Confucius. But the central point is whether the ruler's heart is serious or dissolute. . . . The great function of government is to make use of worthy men and promote education. In dealing with people, it should bestow humanity and love to the highest degree. Whether in the government of Yao and Shun, in the Three Dynasties, or [in the period] from the Qin and Han down to the present, in no case can these principles not be extended and applied" (W. Chan 1963, 701; modified transliteration). Similarly, Gu Yanwu enjoined rulers to uphold the timeless Four Bonds (*siwei*): the cardinal virtues of propriety (*li*), rightness (*yi*), integrity (*lian*), and the sense of shame (*chi*). History was full of changes, but the pattern of the rise and full of dynasties revealed perennial values; expedient sociopolitical reformulations perforce unfolded within the constant Confucian moral order (Ng 1993b, 572).

The early Qing scholars did not radically historicize and thereby relativize values; it was not their avowed goal to do so. Nonetheless, their appeal to the universal and the transhistorical was soberly counterbalanced by their earnest desire to implement timely measures relevant to current needs, and these they identified through their deep knowledge of the contingent changes in history.

Official Historiography and the Confucianized Manchu Monarchs

While the literati in their private historiography conceived of the past in terms of the dynamic growth of cultures and institutions, the Manchu rulers assumed the time-honored tasks of compiling the history of their own dynasty and that of the preceding one. Through these enterprises they would, like other dynasties, try to acquire the imprimatur of political legitimacy. But the projects would prove to be fraught with complications and delays.

Compilation of the *Ming History* was a protracted affair, taking a total of ninety years. One year after the conquest of China, in the second year of the reign of the Shunzhi emperor (r. 1644–1661), it was decreed that the official history of the Ming be compiled, but the final work was not completed until 1735, and it was not presented at court until 1739, during the reign of Qianlong (1736–1795). No other dynasty had ordered compilation of the official history of the predecessor so soon after the establishment of the new regime, and no other standard history took so long to complete (Tang, Wang, & Fu 1983, 320–327; Lai 1984, 51–56). Interestingly enough, as early as 1653 a brief version was finished, but it was a threadbare chronicle based almost exclusively on the Ming veritable records, lacking the customary treatises and tables. Since it satisfied neither in coverage nor in substance, it was never formally presented to the court, although the Shunzhi emperor did read it. Around 1665 a number of officials memorialized the throne, pressing for production of a proper history written in the conventional composite style and informed by a much wider array of sources. But the work languished and the process of compilation was in limbo. One major reason was that the Shunzhi court was preoccupied with constructing the early history of their own Qing dynasty, which came into being in 1616. The Shunzhi emperor ordered compilation of several major works: the imperial injunctions and maxims of the first two Qing emperors, the administrative statutes of the Shunzhi reign, and an encyclopedic work that would include the *Comprehensive Mirror* and related works such as Zhu Xi's synopsis (Ho 1999b, 49–56).

Work on the *Ming History* resumed in 1665 in the early years of the Kangxi reign (1662–1722), but the process continued haltingly. Now the problem probably resulted from the emperor's interference, for he had expressed overt interest in the compilation and therefore exerted deliberate control. It is useful here to consider more closely the Qing court's attitude toward the whole project, particularly the history of the Ming-Qing transitional period. The Shunzhi emperor himself, having endorsed the compilation of the *Ming History,* seemed not to have meddled with the process. In addition, his court encouraged the gathering of materials from private sources to ensure comprehensiveness, even though the early Qing did suppress and destroy records relating to the often bloody and brutal Manchu conquest. Certainly there was systematic obliteration of the records of the remnant Southern Ming dynasty. In addition, there were cases of persecution, most notably the literary inquisition against an anti-Manchu work by Zhuang Tinglong (d. 1660), *Brief Records of Ming History (Mingshi jilue)*. This resulted in the death of some seventy people, although the whole tragic affair might not have occurred had the work not been seized by an official hostile to the Zhuang family who used this opportunity to harm them. Nevertheless, the official proclamations of the Shunzhi reign called explicitly for diligent culling of materials on the last years of the Ming, especially since there were no veritable records for the last reign.

After 1644, if writings avoided language that might suggest or allude to the illegitimacy of the Qing, the court apparently saw no need to proscribe them. Surviving subjects of the Ming no longer in contention with the Qing were apparently able to compile accounts on the fall of the dynasty without persecution (Xie 1999, 58–61). Even when a work was formally censored, the author might not face punishment. A case in point was Gu Yingtai, who supervised the compilation of the famous *Records of Events from Beginning to End in Ming History (Mingshi jishi benmo)* (H. Xu 1997, 18–22). He was indicted by a censor in 1661 because the work he had overseen indicated in one place that the powerful rebel Li Zicheng, who threatened to topple the Ming and nearly established his own kingdom, was destroyed by a Ming force and not by the righteous Manchu-Qing who delivered China from the evil grip of this bandit-rebel. But the Shunzhi court let the matter rest and did not levy punishment (Struve 1989, 5–7; Wilson 1994, 62; Ho 1994, 123–151; Ho 1998b, 156–158).

This policy of accommodating different accounts of the Ming-Qing transition apparently continued under the Kangxi emperor. In 1665 an edict encouraged the submission of private materials to the Ming History Bureau, including even those that might contain tabooed words. The compilers, desperate for sources on the final years of the Ming, offered to expunge dangerous verbiage from submitted works while preserving the substance and spirit of the original documents. It was decided, furthermore, that the *Ming History* would emulate the inclusive spirit of the *Song History* compiled under the Mongol dynasty, where records of the Song princes' resistance against Yuan rule were integrated into the annals of the Southern Song emperors. And following the examples of the *Song History* and the *Yuan History*, which included biographies of Song and Yuan loyalists, the *Ming History* would likewise acknowledge Ming loyalists. Indeed, by the mid-Kangxi period, works on the Qing conquest had proliferated, some of which even used the imperial reign titles of the Southern Ming. Perhaps by then the Qing regime had become sufficiently confident of its legitimate claim to have embraced and represented the great cultural tradition of China, in which dynastic successions were merely incidental changes. As custodian and protector of this great tradition, where virtuous, righteous behavior was duly praised, and perfidious, wicked deeds condemned, loyalists of all stripes in different periods must be properly honored for their faithfulness, trustworthiness, and valor. The passage of time and consolidation of Qing rule blunted any political sting from the unsavory fact that the Manchus had once encountered fierce resistance. The very acts of resistance could now be co-opted as illustrations of profound ideals that deserved their enshrinement in history (Struve 1989, 8–11; Ōtani 1978, 1–37).

In such ostensibly clement circumstances, we might expect the timely completion of the *Ming History*, but that was not the case. The main reason was the Kangxi emperor's constant interference. Since he proudly considered himself an erudite scholar of the classics and history, he also held himself responsible for any mistakes. As a consequence he took an active interest not only in the *Ming History* but also in the veritable records. When Kangxi reactivated the History Bureau, the established practice was to submit only completed works to the emperor for his approval. In 1684, however, Kangxi ordered that drafts in progress be submitted to him to ensure that his editorial and substantive changes were incorporated. Knowing that the emperor would examine their work closely, many of the compilers approached their work with extreme caution. The invasive imperial presence cast a thick pall over the History Bureau, discouraging initiative and inducing diffidence. Worse still, in the name of forestalling errors, Kangxi abolished the office responsible for compiling the diary of activity and repose. Instead, he used Hanlin academicians, five at one time on a rotating basis, to do the recording under his supervision. When there were important matters to be deliberated in the imperial audience, the emperor even assigned the task of recording to the Inner Secretariat (*neige*) that was directly under his control. To advance his own views on history, Kangxi personally produced an edition of Zhu Xi's *Outline and Details of the Comprehensive Mirror* and two related works, which he distributed widely throughout the government. He entitled his own work *The Complete Edition of the Comprehensive Mirror for Aid in Government with Imperial Comments,* and in it included some one hundred of his own interpretations and ideas on the events and personages found in the original works (Ho 1998a, 107–123). Such energetic promotion of the imperial view of history meant that compilers were consequently more than content not to press ahead with the completion of the *Ming History* (Ho 1998b, 158–167; Ho 1996, 1–27).

The succeeding Yongzheng emperor (r. 1722–1735) restored the office responsible for compiling the diary of activity and repose. He also appointed editors to continue compiling the *Ming History.* Moreover, he mandated biographies of those illustrious and loyal officials who had served in the first four reigns of the Qing dynasty. For these compilations the throne ordered a thorough gathering of sources and their submission to the History Bureau. However, the Yongzheng emperor was quite suspicious of the value and credibility of private sources. In 1726 he severely criticized two private histories on the reign of Kangxi, claiming that such works detracted from the authority of the official records. Yongzheng justified his doubts on two grounds. First, few possessed the talents to write good, reliable histories. Private compilations, which were not subject to any scrutiny or required to meet any standard, often distorted the past. The History Bureau, on the other hand, was staffed by learned, capable officials who were carefully chosen to shoulder the grave responsibility of writing a "trustworthy history" (*xinshi*) of an age. Second, there was the endemic problem of faulty recording. Yongzheng said that he had been present in many audiences held by the Kangxi emperor, and personally knew what went on and what was said on those occasions. But when he read the official records, he discovered many discrepancies. What was recorded simply did not match what he himself saw and heard. He devised an experiment to test his suspicion by inviting officials from various offices to record the edicts that he delivered orally. When the various written versions reached him, he found many inconsistencies, mistakes, and imprecise language. In order to prevent errors, he henceforth required that the drafts of imperial proclamations be first submitted to him for approval before their declaration and enactment. The emperor reasoned that if official efforts were laden with mistakes, private enterprises were even more prone to errors, since petty scholars, eager to cater to popular tastes, were more likely to purvey sensational tall tales. For all intents and purposes, Yongzheng dismissed private, unauthorized compilations altogether. Like his father, he played an active role in official historiography, which contributed to the sluggish compilation of the *Ming History*. Compounding the problem was that literary inquisitions had again become commonplace in the Yongzheng period, making writing a dangerous affair. Improper or careless words could be construed as treason (Mou 1982, 62; Ho 199b, 167–171).

Institutional problems endemic within the History Bureau also contributed to the tortuous process of compilation. The Bureau was poorly organized and run. Topics were divided among compilers by the random process of drawing lots, so compilers often had to write on topics about which they had scant knowledge or little enthusiasm. Many editors held their titles without doing much, although their inaction may well have stemmed at least in part from fear induced by the emperor's intrusions. Although the emperors did not oversee day-to-day affairs at the Bureau, they seem to have interfered freely. They did not, however, apparently press the History Bureau to expedite the completion of the *Mingshi*. Completed drafts were often not treated with care. When one team took over the task from the prior one, frequently manuscripts were missing or misplaced. Since personnel turned over frequently, those who participated in the project viewed their assignment as temporary and were unwilling to expend much effort. As the process dragged on, it became more difficult to avoid tabooed names. The customary practice was not to use any words, phrases, or language that could be associated with the imperial names and titles, such as the reign names for "Kangxi" and "Qianlong." It could not have been easy to make sure that the text in no way contained references or allusions to the tabooed words or subjects of the four reigns of Shunzhi, Kangxi, Yongzheng and Qianlong (Tang, Wang, & Fu 1983, 307–310; Lai 1984, 84–88).

The *Ming History* was finally completed in 1735, in the last year of the Yongzheng reign, and was presented to and approved by the succeeding

Qianlong emperor four years later. The Qianlong emperor also played an active role in the production of official historical works, often prescribing the general rules and principles of compilation. He was always ready to edit, often making changes to drafts and even revising finished works. To him, it was imperial prerogative to render historical judgments on the past so that the enduring principles of right and wrong be distinguished. He regarded praise and blame as the highest duty of history and to fulfill this noble obligation, he compiled the *Edited Views of the Comprehensive Mirrors of the Successive Ages with Imperial Critiques* (*Yupi lidai Tongjian jilan*), an encyclopedic anthology of works written in the style of Sima Guang's *Comprehensive Mirror*. In it the emperor included several thousand of his own interpretations and opinions. Subsequently, he selected 798 of them to form a separate work. It was his explicit intention that his works serve as guides to reading and studying the long history of China (Ho 1999a, 671–694; Ho 2000, 132–167). In 1765 the emperor reopened the bureau specializing in compilation of the national history of the Qing, and made as its foremost goal the biographies of all important officials since the establishment of the dynasty. Given the activist role that the Qianlong emperor assumed in the writing of history and the importance he attached to official compositions, it is not surprising that he had little appreciation for private historiography. According to him, it was prone to mistakes and distortions, easily influenced by personal likes and dislikes, and not subject to any standard of accuracy (Ho 1998b, 171–175).

The Methodology of Evidential Research and Historical Learning

The fact that the throne actively engaged in the task of historical production, coupled with its highly negative attitude toward private compilation, seemed to have exerted a direct impact on the way the literati viewed the pursuit of history. Given the tight rein that the emperor held over history, many scholars turned away from complete histories to focus on exposing errors in existing works and verifying the accuracy of historical information. A rigorous quest for factual certitude appeared to have overshadowed board discourse. Instead of writing histories, the Qing historians increasingly excelled in rewriting them (W. Du 2004, 311–325). Shao Jinhan's (1743–1796) meticulous and thorough effort to revise the official *Song History* was a case in point. Taking advantage of his editorial membership in the imperial project of compiling the *Complete Works of the Four Treasuries* (*Siku quanshu*)—the gargantuan bibliographic effort to assemble every worthy work composed in all of Chinese history—Shao was able to comb through the sources available in the imperial libraries. He painstakingly collected material and examined it closely for its veracity. In the process Shao developed and systematized a system for conducting research and rectifying errors in the *Song History*. He began by comparing the standard history with historical works on the Song, including inscriptions and private biographies. He sought to purge the Song standard history of internal contradictions and inconsistencies by carefully comparing the evidence in the imperial annals, biographies, and monographs. In addition, Shao restored the *Old History of the Five Dynasties* and made invaluable contributions to the compilation of *A Continuation of the Comprehensive Mirror*. This work extended the original Song text by Sima Guang to include the history of the Yuan and made improvements on the original (Nivison 1966, 51–52, 196, 206; B. Luo 1999c, 104–108; W. Du 2004, 387–411).

Examples of the scholarly penchant to correct errors and corroborate facts in preexisting historical works abounded in the mid-Qing, for it was a time when evidential research, or *kaozheng*, became a dominant intellectual trend. Scholars channeled their intellectual energy into exegetical and philological investigations of the classics, the textual embodiment of the past. While the main targets of investigation were the classics, the critical attitude toward evidence, the broad gathering of sources, and the discriminating employment of investigative methods spilled over into history (Zeng 1999, 62–69). The *kaozheng* spirit and approach were well exemplified, for instance, by the historical endeavors of Wang Mingsheng (1722–1797), renowned for his substantial *Critical Studies of Seventeen Standard Histories* (*Shiqishi shangque*) in 100 fascicles, and of Qian Daxin (1728–1804), famous for his monumental *Critical Notes on the Twenty-two Histories* (*Ershi'ershi kaoyi*) and for his rewriting of the *Yuan History* (W. Du 1983, 280–313; Z. Huang 1996, 121–136; W. Du 2004, 352–355). Wang proclaimed that truthful recording and recounting of facts was the foundation for the practice of praise and blame. Only when truth and the facts were ascertained, and all doubts dispelled, might one undertake the task of bestowing accolades and levying criticisms (W. Du 2004, 325–329). Qian declared that praise and blame would be properly dispensed if historical facts were told without concealment and adornment. Truly judicious praise and blame emerged out of evidence undistorted by biases such as personal selfishness and political expediency (Elman 2002, 129–130).

Qian Daxin was especially systematic and demanding in the application of methods he deemed necessary for restoring truth to history. According to Qian, sound method began with the right perspective—to pursue knowledge was to seek truth in actual facts and real events (*shishi qiushi*), and as a consequence he wrote *Critical Notes on the Twenty-two Histories*, which was devoted to disposing of inaccurate historical facts by replacing them with authentic ones. To do this successfully, Qian insisted that one must use the best editions of existing historical works and complement this with myriad other materials, such as writings on topography, rituals, astronomy, phonetics, and linguistics, including inscriptions on bronze and stones (Zeng 1998, 64–69; W. Du 2004, 331–346). To arrive at a comprehensive view of the past, Qian called for the study of genealogies and biographies, geography, and the origin and evolution of institutions. The goal of all this was to shed light on what was right and wrong, so that posterity might use history as a guide to action. History was morally didactic, clearly showing that virtue began with benevolent rule for the benefit of the people. From this vantage point Qian made the pronouncement that histories and classics were no different, to the extent that both contained practical teachings and edifying lessons on moral cultivation. Thus Qian's historiography, while often astute in its analysis and austere in its call for exactitude, was dedicated to the ultimate goal of social and political amelioration in moral terms, as opposed to instrumental and institutional ones (W. Du 1983, 289–313; Q. Huang 1991, 29–37; Q. Huang 1994, 3–26; Wei 1998, 53–60; B. Luo 1999a, 90–94; W. Du 2004, 347–351).

In this regard Qian differed from Zhao Yi (1727–1814), another historian inspired by the *kaozheng* spirit, whose goal was to transcend the seemingly disparate and unconnected details in order to arrive at generalized patterns of social and institutional development. Zhao's best-known work was his *Nian'ershi zhaji* (Notes on the twenty-two standard histories). Although praise and blame were unavoidable and necessary, Zhao warned against turning history entirely into the service of moral adjudication. He used Ouyang Xiu's *New History of the Tang* as the typical negative example. It performed its avowed task of revealing the good and the bad, the right and the wrong, often in the name of the ideological principle of legitimate transmission of dynastic authority, and to do this, facts were simplified, distorted, or simply omitted. Zhao sought to investigate problems and issues in the dynastic histories by first outlining all germane evidence, followed by systematically studying the pertinent facts. Only then did Zhao inductively construct his hypotheses. Zhao was particularly interested in institutional history. The study of the past must be useful and utilitarian in the sense that it would be at the service of statecraft. Unlike Huang Zongxi and Gu Yanwu in the early Qing, whose understanding of history led them to advocate a relatively decentralized system of local enfeoffment, Zhao's historical research convinced him that the bureaucratic centralism of the prefectural system under the strong rule of the emperor was crucial for maintaining national strength and forging communal unity (Priest 1986, 29–43; X. Bai 1999, 48–54; W. Du 2004, 485–502).

Thus the mid-Qing saw the production of few full-fledged histories—the reconstruction of coherent historical narratives. But a considerable number of remarkable works on historical criticism and sleuthing appeared, guided and inspired by the prevailing *kaozheng* evidential methodology. While *kaozheng* historiography sought to correct the flaws of old and existing scholarship, it also honored the past, inasmuch as learning was cumulative. Scholars such as Wang Mingsheng, Qian Daxin, and Zhao Yi pointed to new facts and advanced new interpretations only when the evidence allowed them to do so. Truth came from authentic, concrete facts, no more and no less. But in addition, truth must benefit the present. History ought to be practical and utilitarian, proffering moral guidance and providing instrumental direction for institutional betterment. Such was the meaning of *kaozheng* historiography (B. Luo 1999b, 90–94).

Kaozheng learning, although mainly applied to classical studies, was closely related to history as well and the cultivation of a sound sense of anachronism. It is reasonable to suggest that the mid-Qing intellectual project appeared anchored in the fundamentalist—hence ahistorical—goal of retrieving the antique Way enshrined in the classics, and this is true to the extent that *kaozheng* learning sought to describe and understand the cultural order of the sage-rulers embodied in the classics so that universal guiding principles might be found (Yü 1976b, 147–149; Elman 1984, 29–32). Nevertheless, a sober respect for history animated much of *kaozheng* scholarship. Even though the ancient past and the classics were conceived as the repository of universal truths, when they were systematically subjected to meticulous examination, the ancient past became problematized and a host of questions arose. Which were the authentic classics? What part of antiquity was to be restored? How should scholars go about apprehending the past? What began as a philological and theological classicization of antiquity aimed at banishing Daoxue metaphysical mystification ended as partial historicization of the classics themselves. The ancient past and the classics became historical objects to be studied, and the fundamentalist end of ascertaining universal truth was invested with a historicist means. As a result the classics were historicized, and seen as histories (W. Du 1983, 271–279; Z. He 1989, 33–58; B. Luo 1999b, 90–94; Z. Liu 2001, 85–86; Elman 2002, 102–104, 127–134; W. Du 2004, 202–204).

The historicist ethos of the mid-Qing period was well represented by the thoughts of Dai Zhen (1724–1777) and Zhang Xuecheng (1738–1801). Dai Zhen's historicism stemmed from his reformulation of the totalizing and universal notion of Principle (*li*). He posited that everything had its own principle, which varied in accordance with the thing itself. Principle was the "inner texture of things" (*tiaoli*), the organizational pattern and textural configuration of material force (*qi*). The Way (*dao*) was nothing but the aggregate of human relations, consisting of the very ordinary matters of living, drinking, eating, talking, and acting. Through his idea of expedient weighing of circumstances, or *quan*, Dai questioned the notion of an essential principle invariant through time. There was always change, the meaning and significance of which could be revealed only with intelligent observation and exhaustive investigation. There were no constant right and wrong; time-related expediency rendered the important into the insignificant, and vice versa. Dai identified expediency as one of the central characteristics of being good (*shan*) that defined the commonality of humanity. This appreciation for change was reflected in his fervent interest in examining the origin and development of things *in* history—phonetics, costumes, place names, implements, nomenclature and categories of fauna and flora, mathematics, musical instruments, and so on. The principles and meanings of the sages, that is, the Way itself, could be found in the historical records—administrative statutes, penal laws, institutions, and the like (C. Cheng 1970, 14–53; Yü 1982, 386–389; Chin & Freeman 1990, 33–41; Ng 1993b, 573–574).

But Dai's historicism was neither consistent nor full-fledged. Although he claimed that expediency was integrally a part of goodness, he often construed this goodness as the totalizing Way, in which individuality was simply a variation or expression. In grandiose terms Dai described this inherent goodness as the formation and transformation of Heaven and earth, the functions and capacities of nature. Individual nature was the "allotment" (*fen*) that was a part of the "way of Heaven." Heaven's allotment was human destiny, which, to the extent that it produced the human constitution, was also human nature. In this way the mind contained all the virtues of Heaven that provided the pattern of the myriad deeds. It was by perceiving the mind of Heaven-and-earth that the individual mind was realized. By the same token, seeing the mind of the sages allowed apprehension of the mind of Heaven-and-earth. Such a universalizing philosophical view was hardly different from the Daoxue holistic integration of self, Heaven-and-earth, and the sages' mind, even though Dai did maintain that this oneness could be achieved only through the study of actual things *in* time—the classics, institutions, and things of all manner that were the substantiation of the sages' mind.

Such was the ambiguity of Dai's historicism. On the one hand, the ancient past must be studied, not intuited. The mind was not self-referential and demanded the exploration of the facts of ancient historical reality. On the other hand, antiquity was a timeless past, and since the mind encompassed everything, including the universal mind of the sages and Heaven-and-earth, it granted no true autonomy for observable facts in the phenomenal world. Classical studies were pursued not for the sake of knowing facts but for attaining oneness with the universal way of antiquity. Insofar as the Six Classics were the guide to spiritual enlightenment, even though the sages were physically gone, their minds, being one with the mind of Heaven, became the mind of those who followed the Way. The inalienable moral principles bequeathed by the sages constituted a sort of transcendent *a priori* knowledge—a "sagely intelligence" that enlightened the mind and thus comprehended the Way and everything. Inspired by the eternality of the ancient Way, Dai desired a return of the moral system of antiquity, but this required careful, rigorous examination of the historical records. Herein lay the source of Dai's historical sensitivity toward differentness, particularity, individuality, and contingency. Despite the ambiguity, Dai juxtaposed the classics with their perennial Way with history and its expediency. In this way historical learning became complementary with classical studies (C. Cheng 1970, 33–34; Ng 1993b, 574–576; Yü 1976a, 102–110; Chin & Freeman; 60–61; D. Cheng 2002, 20–32).

The most eloquent synthesis of history and the classics came from Zhang Xuecheng, who produced arguably the most thoughtful systematic view on the nature and practice of history. He opened his innovative historiographical treatise *General Principles of Literature and History* (*Wenshi tongyi*) with the proclamation that "the Six Classics are all history." By this he meant that "the ancients never ever talked of principles in separation from affairs. The Six Classics are the statutes and records of the ancient rulers' government" (quoted in S. Lin 1997, 184–185; Shimada 1969, 123–

157). Here we find the cornerstone of Zhang's view of history. History was, first and foremost, the history of institutions and the laws of antiquity. Any talk of principles would be empty talk, unless they were discussed with reference to the actualities of the past and the records of history. If the classics were the records of antiquity, they were timebound. Correspondingly, the Way that resided in them was not universal but temporally circumscribed. Research into the distant past revealed the meanings concealed in the classics and shed light on what had occurred back then. But "as to the development of events which occurred thereafter, the classics could not have anything to say" (Nivison 1966, 201–210). Zhang went so far as to say that Confucius was but one among many illustrious philosophers (Ng 1993b, 576–577; Inoue 1996, 51–55; Elman 2002, 132; W. Du 2004, 415–418). By asserting their immanence in time, Zhang historicized the classics and the antique Way. Zhang proposed a different understanding of the Way, a naturalistic one that lay beneath the flow of history as the "why and wherefore" (*suoyiran*) of occurrences and things, which evolved with changes in material existence. It was some sort of transcendent, normative ideality that prescribed "what things ought to be" (*dangran*) (Nivison 1966, 140–144; Yü 1976a, 45–53).

Instead of regarding the classics as the sacral embodiment of the incorporeal *dao*, Zhang saw them in terms of the corporeal and experiential material force (*qi*). While scholars traditionally used the classics as the point of departure in their exploration and promotion of Confucius' teachings — assuming that the classics were writings that recorded or embodied the Way — Zhang contended that these texts should be considered part of the realm of material force. Even Confucius himself, in transmitting the classics, had pointed to the ancient writings as the material expression of the concrete and tangible Way. Zhang also explained the idea of the Way in terms of another notion of concreteness and tangibility, that of implements (*qi*, a homonym of *qi*-qua-material force), in the absence of which the Way could neither be seen nor explicated. The Way could only be illuminated and revealed by tracking and tracing the evolution of things in history (Nivison 1966, 150–151; S. Lin 1997, 70–72). Hence Zhang made the boldly historicist pronouncement that the classics recorded only the laws and institutions of the ancient rulers. Insofar as they described the material realities of the ancient Way, the classics were histories. According to Zhang, in the period of the Three Dynasties history was recognized as learning that was intimately related to human affairs. History lent corroboration to the lofty discourses and ideas on human nature, revealing in the process Heaven's mandate. In antiquity, when theory was properly substantiated by practice, there was an admirable unity of *zhi* (rulership) and *jiao* (teaching) that effected a coherent and unified Way (Nivison 1966, 60–62; Jiang 1988, 175–182).

Zhang was in fact propounding the view that time was evolutionary in the sense that culture changed. Even in antiquity "the Three Rulers did not imitate one another; the Three Sovereigns and Five Emperors also did not follow one another" (Zhou & Tang 1962, 211). In order to know the Way-in-history, the entire course of history had to be examined. As the Way moved and evolved dynamically, it took on different meanings and displayed different characteristics in different periods—the Way of recent history was not necessarily that of antiquity. The sages of antiquity could not have exhaustively apprehended the meaning and substance of the Way because numerous institutions grew in history as conditions and circumstances changed. If there was an immutable Way, it was the fact that changes defined the human condition. Consequently, one could not ignore the study of current history. Erudition about the ancient past was impractical, if it was not complemented by practical knowledge of the present. Zhang stressed the importance of current institutions, calling for the study of existing institutions that regulated human relations and made possible daily utility. Such was solid learning based on careful documentation of the development of social and political institutions, not only at the central and regional levels of government, but also local administration. Zhang was especially interested in adapting the form of the standard dynastic histories (annals, tables, monographs, and biographies) to local histories (Nivison 1966, 144–150, 216; Yü 1976b, 49–50; Ng 1993b, 576–577; S. Lin 1997, 146–151; Q. Wang 2002, 251–276; W. Du 2004, 426–430). Whether it was the history of antiquity, the history of the present, or documentation of the growth of central or local government, historical scholarship was pursued for the amelioration of state and society. "Historical scholarship," Zhang concluded, "is employed to manage the world. It is certainly no composition and narration of empty words" (S. Lin 1997, 181).

But Zhang did not see the past simply as successive parades of relative spatial forms and temporal segments. Instead of particularizing the ancient past and the classics once and for all, Zhang sought in them the universally normative. There was indeed a dynamic and constantly evolving Way-in-history, and it pertained to the pattern of change of the political, social, and institutional polity—government, schooling, territorial administration, and the economy. These were changing forms of life relative to their own place and time, manifesting their own Way, that is, the specific meaning of their particular pattern of change. But above and beyond these particular Ways was the transhistorical Way of the ancient sages, enshrined in the classics, which Zhang called "the essential Way" (*daoti*). This essential, substantive Way, exhaustively explicated in the classics, left nothing unembodied. This transhistorical Way was in fact the provenance of all learning and philosophy, which in one way or another attained and participated in the understanding of at least some aspects of the essential Way. Zhang also described this Way as the "illustrious moral teachings" (*mingjiao*) of the sages, which had constituted the foundation of peace since ancient times. No regime could truly achieve order and prosperity in the absence of such moral teachings. Moral teachings of the rituals bequeathed by the ancient sages were the very stuff and source of governance, then and now (Chow & Liu 1984, 127–133).

Quite obviously Zhang did not intend to destroy the authority of the ancient texts. Rather, he warned against literal repetition and inflexible emulation of them. He maintained that history had to encapsulate the essence of the principles of the Classics. The narration of events in time served precisely the greater purpose of revealing the profound Way that pervaded history. In history could be seen the manifestations and work-ings of this authoritative Way, the meaning of which had already been thoroughly expounded in the classics. With rhetorical flourish, Zhang pro-claimed that the great meaning of the classics was as brilliant as the sun and moon, and the events of the Three Dynasties could be projected as guides for the ensuing hundred ages. He even claimed that both Confu-cius and the Duke of Zhou established norms and built the Way to such an extent that there could be no subsequent accretions. This note of finality meant foreclosure of the historical process. The absolute normative tradi-tion had come into being once upon a time, providing the most instructive and edifying path for all ages. In this great essential Way of the illustrious moral-ritual teachings of the sages, Zhang's historicism dissolved (Chow & Liu 1984, 128–130; Ng 1993b, 578; Vermeer 1995, 227–230). While Zhang Xuecheng, and Dai Zhen for that matter, often saw the past in temporally and spatially specific terms, they ultimately appealed to the universalist values and enduring principles identified with antiquity.

Historical Epochs and Schemes of Periodization

Neither Zhang Xuecheng nor Dai Zhen developed concepts of periodiza-tion, such that the past would be conceived in terms of successive stages and epochs, that is, identifiable temporal segments with specific character-istics. Other scholars did, however. In the eighteenth century, when philo-logical and evidential studies of the classics predominated, some scholars were drawn to the Western Han New Script classical tradition. Within this commentarial tradition now appeared several highly systematic concep-tions of the past as historical schemas. The New Script classics were called that because they had been written originally in the new script of the West-ern Han dynasty (202 B.C.E.–C.E. 9), rather than the Old Script used in the Zhou dynasty (1122?–256 B.C.E). These were texts that had been recon-stituted and reconstructed in the Western Han period because many of the originals had been destroyed or lost in the Qin dynasty (221–207 B.C.E.) and during the Qin-Han transition. As they were being reconstructed, pri-marily through the memory of the elderly scholars who had studied them prior to the Qin, a new commentarial tradition came into being. Before long, however, the Zhou classical texts began to resurface, written in the old script; and hence both New Script and Old Script classics existed at the same time. Textually and interpretively the two versions could vary sig-nificantly, and controversies raged as to which corpus was authentic. The Old Script classics were attacked by the New Script partisans as forgeries, while the Old Script supporters branded the New Script classics as flawed reproductions based on faulty memories. The New Script texts held sway in the Western Han, but by the Eastern Han dynasty (C.E. 25–220), the Old Script tradition gradually became dominant and remained so until the eighteenth and early nineteenth centuries.

At that point the New Script classics reemerged as an important subject for classical studies, thanks first to the fact that in the late seventeenth century the Old Script *Classic of Documents* was proved to be a forgery. The Old Script-New Script controversy reignited (Elman 1984, 177–180). With the exegetical works of Zhuang Cunyu (1719–1788) and his grandson Liu Fenglu (1776–1829), the New Script tradition established a distinct voice in the Qing intellectual world. In the process of developing their interpretations of the New Script classics, these two scholars advanced conceptions of the past and schemas of history. The New Script classical tradition, which had revolved around the *Gongyang Commentary* of the *Spring and Autumn Annals,* was anchored to the idea of "revealing the profound principles concealed in subtle language" (*weiyan dayi*). Knowledge of these great principles meant practical ability to manage the world. In addition, this exegetical tradition had offered particular historical schemas that ordered the political and dynastic successions in the ancient past (Xia, Shang, and Zhou) as well as methods of historical recording and interpretation.

Zhuang Cunyu accepted the major New Script classical historical notions of "Preserving the Three Systems" (*cun santong*), "Unfolding of the Three Ages" (*zhang sanshi*), and "Instituting a Universal System of Rule" (*da yitong*). On the idea of "Preserving the Three Systems," which affirmed the legitimacy of the dynastic succession from Xia to Shang to Zhou, he wrote that the establishment of each of the Three Dynasties was bestowed by Heaven, and with the alternation of Simplicity (*zhi*) and Refinement (*wen*), the ancient institutions and implements became complete and comprehensive, as evidenced by the fact that the Three Dynasties each developed their own calendar and cosmic color. For Zhuang, to honor the idea of "Preserving the Three Systems" was to acknowledge the legitimacy of dynastic succession and illuminate the fact that the Mandate of Heaven was conferred on many and not just one family. Regarding the notion of "Unfolding the Three Ages," Zhuang adopted the standard New Script meanings. One referred to phraseological manipulations in conveying Confucius' nuanced treatment of historical events and personages from different ages. The three ages were as follows: the period that Confucius learned about through transmitted records; the period he learned about through contemporary accounts by living elders; and the period that he personally witnessed. Confucius, through his subtle use of language, felicitously narrated events belonging to different periods and thereby revealed their significance while at the same time bestowing praise and imposing blame. The other meaning referred to Confucius' view of ancient historical development, which made reference to He Xiu's idea of a historical progression from the "age of disorder," through the "age of approaching peace," to finally arrive at the "age of universal peace."

Although Zhuang subscribed to Han New Script historicism, he re-formulated the idea of "Preserving the Three Systems." In Han times the notion of the "Three Systems" was a teleology of historical succession. The tripartite sequence was a sort of universal model of movement in history. To Zhuang, this pattern of historical replacement ended with the Spring and Autumn period. But the termination of this historical series meant the inauguration of a new one—Confucius and his teachings ushered in a new time frame. Zhuang thus created a historical space for the antiquity of the Three Dynasties. However, if Zhuang subtly historicized antiquity by mitigating the panhistorical implication of the idea of "Three Systems," he affirmed the suprahistorical significance of the teachings of Confucius and the *Annals*, which would persist as guides to ethics and government "for ten thousand ages." His belief typified the traditional Chinese view of the ancient past, in which the constancy of history provided a firm basis for sustaining moral values. Nevertheless, Zhuang's conception was informed by a sense of historical change. When laws and institutions became mori-bund, they had to be changed, even though those making the changes should seek guidance from the principles of the *Spring and Autumn Annals.* The *Annals*, as Zhuang pointed out, wrote about extraordinary develop-ments and events so as to indicate the arrival of changes (S. Zhang 1979, 3–4; Z. Tang 1980, 145–147; Ng 1994, 10–18; Q. Chen 1997, 64–68).

Liu Fenglu advanced his own historicism within the New Script clas-sical tradition. He accepted the central Gongyang notion of "Linking the Three Systems," together with the related idea of the alternation of Sim-plicity and Refinement. Discerning the continuity of the Three Systems meant recognizing the evolution of the way of governance. Like Zhuang Cunyu, Liu alluded to the termination of the cycle and regarded the Spring and Autumn period as the start of a different series of historical develop-ments. While ascertaining the classical basis of the "Three Systems," he suggested that its meanings did change in time. To the ancient sages the notion had simply referred to the sequential succession of the ways of the Three Dynasties, but as far as the later Confucians were concerned, link-ing the Three Systems meant "emulating the later king" (*fa houwang*). The "later king" referred to Confucius in particular and the Lu regime in gen-eral, in the sense that Confucius laid down the flawless guidelines for pos-terity. Confucius was the paragon whom the succeeding ages were to follow and emulate. Confucius, in his day, worked in accordance with the pat-tern of dynastic succession of antiquity, that is, within the continuity of the Three Systems, and the hundred ages since his time would follow his au-thority and teachings. In Liu's historical conception, Confucius occupied a pivotal position. Confucius, with his knowledge of antiquity, implemented the practice of "Linking the Three Systems" and in the process defined the enduring principle of rulership and governance. Confucius was the uncrowned king envisioned in the *Spring and Autumn Annals.* Confucius became king by virtue of his creating the institutions that would be imple-mented by the later sages. Although Confucius was not a king, he was a sage and his ideals expressed in the *Spring and Autumn Annals* were just as exalted as those of the sage-kings. The *Annals* embodied the ideals of the "Three Beginnings" (that is, the Three Dynasties) and furnished the values and means that would rectify the problems of the ensuing ages.

As with Zhuang Cunyu, Liu reconceptualized the notion of "Linking the Three Systems" by locating the Three Systems historically *in* antiquity. Confucius and the *Spring and Autumn Annals* ushered in a new beginning and established for posterity the way of governance. Thus Liu created new segments of time—the Three Dynasties of antiquity, Confucius and the *Annals,* and then posterity. Moreover, through the idea of Confucius as the uncrowned king from the state of Lu, Liu also constructed a usable historical model of political and moral ideals. Confucius received the Mandate of Heaven as an uncrowned king, whose words would serve as enduring guides to action. Confucius thus achieved a sort of immortality by virtue of his sagehood. But his immortality and the lasting value of the *Spring and Autumn Annals* did not negate history; they illuminated the typical and recurrent ethical, moral, social, and political problems through the ages. Liu acknowledged that in the historical world, changes were inevitable. Confucius' treatment of the barbarian states in the Spring and Autumn period was a good example. While the ideal age of the *Spring and Autumn* was the age of universal peace when China reigned supreme and the barbarian states submitted to it, the historical reality was that barbarian states such as the Qin, Chu, and Wu became leading powers, effectively overshadowing the Zhou house and other Chinese states. Confucius duly recorded such facts, dispassionately dispensing sound and fair judgments, even praising the Qin as a state with righteous rule and effective administration. Even the sage could not have arrested the decline of Zhou institutions. Liu's conception of the sagely ideal with transhistorical efficacy was sensibly balanced by his acceptance of the human order of successive time and historical changes.

Moreover, in its essentials Liu Fenglu's historicism was animated by the goal of forging a good society and government by harking back to the *Spring and Autumn Annals.* Historical notions of "Linking the Three Systems" and "Unfolding the Three Ages" were normative-political ideals. They pointed to an inescapable fact in a political society—the succession of authorities. They also vouchsafed historically tested certainties for the management of state and society. To Liu, the central purpose of Confucius and the ancient sage-kings was to order the world (*jingshi*). The *Annals* was the source of rituals and norms; it was also a book of laws and punishments. History and the study of history were, in the last analysis, statecraft (S. Zhang 1979, 4–6; Z. Tang 1980, 147–153; Ng 1994, 18–31; Q. Chen 1997, 99–115).

Another scholar inspired by the historicism inherent in the New Script classical tradition was Gong Zizhen (1792–1841), who studied at one time with Liu Fenglu. Gong propounded his own schematic notion of the Three Ages, which he derived from his understanding of the *Spring and Autumn*

Annals. Since the beginning of written records, he claimed, there had been Three Classes (*sandeng*) of ages: an age of orderly rule, an age of disorder, and an age of decay. Each was characterized by its talent (*cai*), or the lack of it. While the Han New Script historicist scheme was one of improvement—from an age of weakness and disorder, through an age of approaching peace, to an age of universal peace—Gong's was regressive, descending from orderly rule to decay. Gong did not fully elaborate his idea, for he paid scant attention to the intermediate age of disorder. He did, however, specify differences between the age of orderly rule and the age of decay, paradoxically by noting their ostensible similarities. In the age of orderly rule, for instance, the dominant color was a great plain color because the ostentation of using the five colors had been abandoned. In the age of decay, black and white were mixed up, since there was the inability to distinguish between colors. The age of decay, Gong noted ironically, therefore resembled that of orderly rule because both had abandoned colors. Similarly, the highest note and lowest note of the pentatonic scale were confused in the age of decay, so that sounds were fused into one great cacophonic mess. It therefore resembled the age of orderly rule when sounds were purposefully rare but uniform. In the age of decay people were confused and thus ignorant of what and how to criticize, and this silencing of critical voices resembled the absence of complaints in the age of orderly rule, when the people were content. Gong concluded that in the age of decay, talents and competence were sorely wanting. Gong counseled self-scrutiny, asking his contemporaries not to delude themselves into thinking that they lived in an age of orderly rule because they mistook superficial prosperity as a sign of fundamental strength and stability. In short, Gong saw his own time as one of disorder and yearned for the age of approaching peace and universal peace envisioned in the *Spring and Autumn Annals.*

After 1819 Gong began to develop a notion of the Three Ages as a progressive historical development—from disorder to universal peace. But his goal was always to universalize the classical historicist schema so as to reveal its contemporary relevance. The notion of the ancient Three Ages became a general principle of historical change. The succession of ages formed a coherent historical series with a beginning and end, in which the flux of time was linked by the Confucian Way (*dao*). Every historical series witnessed this Way in action. However, this Way was not the transcendent one of internal sagehood and spiritual enlightenment. Instead, every age was defined by a specific set of problems, of which there were three categories, each associated with one of the Three Ages. The first category involved the livelihood of people; the second the establishment and implementation of institutions; and the third the knowledge of moral nature and the way of Heaven. Thus the Three Ages indicated more than mere temporality, it also provided significance in pragmatic terms. Every age encountered its own particular problems and had to respond to those challenges. Since problems changed with the age, there was not one universally efficacious method of responding. Gong steadfastly pointed to changes *in* time.

The Three Ages provided a pattern of historical time in which he could illustrate specific problems and responses to them; the thread of historical continuity was spun out of classical yarn (S. Zhang 1979, 16–17; G. Xu 1980, 76–80; Ng 1993b, 245–256).

Gong's historicism was fused with his pragmatism, and both were inspired by the classics. The classics illustrated the changing concerns of government in time as new circumstances arose. In the age of disorder, people's livelihood was the central problem, rectification of which should be the first priority of government. When the people's livelihood was secured, the age of approaching peace arrived, and the regime's responsibilities shifted to other areas, such as establishing the proper rites and rituals. When the people's livelihood had been secured, and institutions and rites had been consolidated, the age of universal peace arrived. In this great age, scholars, who were treated as valued guests and honored as teachers, addressed and resolved the ultimate problems of realizing human nature and the way of Heaven. This was the age of ultimate political and cultural achievement—the institution of a grand universal system of rule—when the barrier between the core and the periphery, the barbarians and the Chinese, no longer existed. There would be unity among all-under-Heaven (S. Zhang 1979, 12–16; G. Xu 1980, 80–84; Q. Chen 1997, 170–179).

But Gong's historicism was laden with ambiguity. Although he moved with confidence from the world of classical ideals to the present world of pragmatic concerns, accepting the reality of antiquity and connecting it to the present, he did not see history in terms of a radical vision of progress in the sense that it represented the ineluctable cumulative growth of humanity. Despite Gong's emphasis on the ever-changing nature of values and norms, he believed that the past embodied in the classics remained the norm, and it was through history that the universal ancient Way could be understood and apprehended. By history, Gong meant ancient history in particular, the perennial relevance of which he ascertained. The idea and practice of "Preserving the Three Systems" was important precisely because knowledge of the past was important. This ancient practice demanded that the ruling regime appropriate the resources of the previous dynasties—their virtuous and talented descendants, their history and experience, and their rites and institutions. Looking at the history of the ancient Three Dynasties, Gong came to the conclusion that the experiences of antiquity provided the original points of reference for contemporary actions. His reformism was thus in many ways fortified by the classics and sanctioned by ancient history (Ng 1993b, 253–256; Zhao 1982, 267–270, 273–276).

Wei Yuan (1794–1856), like Gong Zizhen, was an enormously important intellectual figure in the first half of the nineteenth century. He, too, studied for a while with Liu Fenglu. Wei wrote on a wide variety of subjects, offering remedies for the besetting social, economic, and political problems of his time. He wanted to reveal great meanings concealed in the subtle language of the classics. Inspired by the New Script classical tradition, he forged a historicism based on an alternation between "Simplicity" and "Refinement," and the succession of the "Three Systems." By appealing to these ideas of changing cultural and political imperatives in history, Wei suggested that his own time was on the threshold of a new cycle, ready for change. He sought further support from the notion of the Three Ages, which he believed explained the way Confucius recorded events of the different "ages" with proper language in the *Spring and Autumn Annals*. As we have seen, Confucius was supposed to have used different language to highlight the moral import of the events of different ages. In the *Annals* he established the methods of recording historical events in the "Three Ages" so as to dispense proper moral judgments. In this delicate process of mixing stylistic recording with substantive teaching, he revealed the universal way of governance. Rulers of all ages should thus study his *Spring and Autumn Annals*. Wei explained that the Three Ages also represented three different kinds of worlds. The remote age that Confucius knew through transmitted records was the age of "attained peace." The closer age that he knew through the contemporary accounts of living elders was the age of "arising peace." The age that Confucius experienced himself was the age of "universal peace." This version of New Script historicism furnished the basis for Wei's own conception of historical movement (Ze Wu 1962, 44–50; G. Xu 1980, 72–74, 85–88; Ng 1996, 61–68; Q. Chen 1997, 238–241).

Wei developed a *leitmotif* of the inevitability and necessity of change. He was guided by his ontological conception of ultimate reality as "oneness" (*yi*), by which he meant that nothing existed alone. All beings were dialectically involved, in that they must have their opposites. This dialectic generated dynamism in history. History was no static condition but a process given over to circumstances, constantly in interaction with the particular needs of particular segments of time as they succeeded one another. To Wei, the cosmic-human world was constantly in flux, propelled by the "transformative material force" (*qihua*). Both nature and history bespoke the inexorability of change. The Heaven and earth of old were not the same as their counterparts now. Stars died and were born; rivers altered course; flora and fauna evolved. Likewise, aspects of culture in the human historical world changed: diet, attire, music, dance, punishment, institution, military strategy, and so on. Wei metaphorically likened the universe from antiquity to the present as a great chess game, and history contained the myriad moves. Neither past nor present ways should be promoted or upheld in any inflexible manner. Wei declared that history revealed much progress since the Three Dynasties, when the feudal principle of private (*si*) authority held sway. The abolition of corporal punishments, the consolidation of the imperial administrative system of prefectures and districts, and the rise of examinations to recruit officials expanded the public (*gong*) domain. Even if the ancient sages were resurrected to undertake reforms, they would not undo these changes. Revival of antiquity was wishful thinking. Wei bluntly stated that more benefits would accrue as a result of further changes to the old institutions. There were no methods of perennial usage and eternal practicality. The only historical constant was that as entrenched institutions outlived their usefulness, there should be reforms in accord with the times (Z. Wu 1962, 34–39; G. Xu 1980, 87–94; J. Wang 1993, 166–167).

Nonetheless, it was not Wei's goal to turn history into sheer contingency and circumstantiality. Inherent in his idea of change was a clear sense of constancy. Underlying the flux of transformative material force was the unchanging Way, the fundamental anchor of reality. In chess, the game to which Wei likened history, the moves were always changing. but the rules did not change, and one could learn ways in which to win the game. There were suprahistorical or transhistorical insights, what Wei called "change in the midst of constancy." Changes, after all, grew out of the primal oneness, which was the Way and in which was dissolved the dialectic antinomy of opposites. Wei sometimes went so far as to explain the all-encompassing oneness in terms of the Daoist sense of ultimate universal nothingness, which negated the possibility of time, and therefore history. Thus Wei's inevitability of change was counterbalanced by his conception of reversion, revival, or return. While it was true that even the ancient sage-kings could not reverse the tide of history, it was also true that if the principle of rulership modeled on the sage-kings were pursued, in the natural course of time there would be the return to the origin. Wei argued that the key to effecting such return lay in purging selfish desires by following the Way, so that there would no longer be desires, as taught by Confucius. To battle the body and curb the desires stemming from it, one must appeal inwardly to the mind-heart. As Wei put it, "the mind-heart of humanity is the mind-heart of heaven-earth," and "as the body is within the mind-heart, myriad things are replete within my own self" (Ng 1996, 81–82). With this holistic vision of the ontological plenitude of the self that united Heaven and humanity, Wei's ideas of contingent change were qualified. Even though Simplicity and Refinement alternated, circumstances changed, and the Three Ages followed each other, the constant Way, the pure and simple "mind-heart of high antiquity" persisted. Each historical age, in its own circumstantiality and contingency, as a facet or perspective of the total truth, discovered, realized, and returned to the ultimate truth. Wei lived in a time when symptoms of dynastic decline had become quite evident. In spite of Wei's call for reform, animated by a historicism of change, his vision of renewal of, and return to, the putative greatness of antiquity must have been a comforting ideal. Wei's reformism was unmistakably grounded on both historicism (idea of contingent change) and classicism (ideal of eternal value) (ibid., 80–85).

Wei Yuan produced several notable historical works. He helped compile a voluminous anthology of Qing essays on statecraft, the *Anthology of Essays on Statecraft in the Imperial Dynasty* (*Huangchao jingshi wenbian*), in 508 fascicles. Although it is not a history as such, it is a valuable assemblage of secondary writings on a vast variety of subjects—institutions, agriculture, military affairs, laws, and the like. He also compiled *A Record of the Two Administrations of the Military and Economy in the Ming Period* (*Mingdai bingshi erzheng lu*) in seventy-eight fascicles, a collection of essays on military and economic affairs in the Ming. The objective of this work was to reveal the causes of that dynasty's decline. In addition, Wei was the author of several works on the military campaigns the Qing conducted against the British. As Sino-Western relations became increasingly an important concern of the Qing state, Wei devoted much effort to studying the West, and this led to composition of his most famous work, the *Illustrated Gazetteer of Maritime Nations* (*Haiguo tuzhi*). It was the first systematic Chinese investigation of the history and geography of the European countries. Not only did Wei focus on the southern coastal frontier, but he also penned historical and geographic treatises on the northern borders. In the more traditional historiographical vein, Wei edited and revised the hastily compiled *Yuan History*. Wei was truly a polymath, a historian as well as philosopher of history (Ōtani 1971, 33–75; J. Wang 1993, 155–163; Q. Chen 1997, 254–260).

Thus while the Qing produced no notable monumental history, the Qing world of historiography was varied and vibrant. The *kaozheng* evidential methodology yielded rigorous interrogations of the classics and histories. The classicist impulse to apprehend the universal Way of antiquity was counterbalanced by the historicist tendency to view the past as particular segments of time. If there was enormous veneration of the eternal norms of the ancient sages, there was also palpable celebration of change, especially in the workaday world of sociopolitical and institutional ordering and adjustment, where human agency propelled the dynamism of history. Zhang Xuecheng's masterpiece not only expressed such historical sensibility, but it also offered keen observations and sound approaches to the craft of historical writing. To Qing scholars and historians, the past was at once an alien country and their native land.

Epilogue

Historians often arrogate to themselves the exclusive responsibility and prerogative of interpreting the past, that unmistakably human world that might as well be on another planet as it speaks such an alien language. Commerce and communication with this parallel universe seem best left to historians with their appropriate training and expertise. Yet every now and again the services of the historian may not be needed, when something from the past shines through and pierces the opaqueness that is its temporal otherness, appealing powerfully to our present sensibilities (cf. Schama, 1999). A case in point is the traditional Chinese conception of the enterprise of history as a pragmatic endeavor—the teaching of lessons in political, social, and personal life; the custodianship of collective memories; the stewardship of culture; and the profession of normative values. In imperial China history was the holy owl, ready to pounce on vermin and then soar into the heavenly heights, heralding the good. In this postmodern age of ours, much haunted by *fin de siècle* anomie and understanding—the death of God, the demise of the novel, the silencing of music, the death of the past, and alas, the end of history—the confident Chinese refusal to treat history as the pursuit of knowledge of the past purely for its own sake, and the dogged insistence on decoding and revealing the meanings germane to the conduct of life, are more than comforting; they may be necessary. They may serve to melt the cold impersonality and disinterested ennui that have frozen out and alienated those who are not academic historians.

As we have seen, the Chinese historians appropriated the past with its paradigmatic events and personages for ethical edification. This ethical usage of history included both explication and adjudication. History functioned as the very explanation of the relevance of the past to the present. Its retrospective gaze at the past aimed at identifying the significance and importance of tradition, and significant elements gleaned from the past served as the framework for consideration of present-day ethical and moral action. But history also interrogated the past as the subject matter, and not as the assumed basis and framework of ethical actions. In other words, it was the prospective act of assessing the present situation in light of knowledge of the past (Cua 2002, 487–488). But whether history functioned in its explicatory or adjudicative mode, it focused on the practical, organic relationship between the past and present. Unlike the constant modern historical recall of the slippage between human schemes and historical events, the Chinese historians concentrated on retelling their concordance.

In celebrating the practical import and purport of traditional Chinese historiography, we are not saying that we should do history the way the Chinese did. Overarching and insistent normative imperatives do stand in the way of cool and cognitive understanding of the past. At the same time we should not forget that throughout this book we have drawn attention to the highly discriminating scrutiny and impressively broad use of evidence on the part of the Chinese historians. By any standard of comparison, they did not pale. Sima Qian, as we recall, cited no fewer than eighty-two sources, not including myriad less substantial writings such as short treatises and memorials, not to mention oral testimonies and physical artifacts. Moreover, he examined these sources carefully and informed readers of their merits and drawbacks. The critical tradition based on an uncompromising factuality that the Han established continued to inform and inspire Chinese historians, whose works more often than not displayed a remarkable degree of evidential sophistication and thoroughness. We should also not forget that the history of historiography in imperial China was dynamic. New arguments, insights, and formats emerged and evolved throughout the ages to address the perennial problem of ordering the past through historical narratives.

There were philosophies of history as well as periodizing schemas of history, some of which demonstrated an astute awareness that the past was not an undifferentiated mass, but consisted instead of different temporal segments. In short, there were many instances where Chinese historical thinkers and practitioners showed a sharp sense of anachronism, even though, in the end, they did not quite generate a lasting conception of marking off the present from the past, such as a notion of medievality, for example (Brook 1998b, 154–163).

Our particular reference to the purposeful moral import of Chinese historiography has its own presentist agenda. Would not a serious look at this aspect of history-making in imperial China prod the conscience of, and shed some light on, the contemporary ways of doing history? Our point is that the technical hermeneutics of modern historical science, whose ideal goal is to let the past speak for itself, may end up silencing it, as its voice is already quite muffled in the contemporary world. When an academic historian cringes at meaning and sincerity, he or she may well deprive the historical discipline of its moral seriousness, if not social and cultural relevance. What good is history if it is no longer relevant to actual lived experiences? Why listen to the past if comprehension of what it says is not directly related to the apprehension of the human condition and the purposes of human existence? Contemporary Western historical writings and literature abound with jeremiads lamenting history's loss of relevance and usefulness (Breisach 1983, 404–405; Munz 1977, 1–2, 9–11). Academic history has come to represent, in Hayden White's words, the "repressed sensibility" of European modernity (1966, 115).

By contrast, while the Chinese were developing their exacting and elaborate historical hermeneutics of reading sources and verifying facts, they embraced what we may call a moral aesthetics of history. They saw the past the way a mirror reflects the world; they felt the past deeply and took it for what it concretely was — heroic and praiseworthy figures of virtue and integrity, brutish and damnable personages of vice and perfidy, triumphant creation of dynasties, and tragic fall of regimes. To the Chinese historians, the crumbling of culture — the sum total of accumulated experiences and values accrued in history—meant decay of the idea of the human, and therefore they were never tired of repeating the pieties of the sages. For all the diversity of temper and style in imperial Chinese historiography, the Chinese historians and historiographers were all yea-sayers. In one common voice they affirmed that the present could always be redeemed, and the future always held hope. History, warts and all, though brimming with examples of harm and hurt, never failed to vouchsafe the lessons and values for moral and sociopolitical revivification. Chinese thinkers believed historical memory truly counted because it meaningfully conjoined the imprint of the past and the plan for the future.

Needless to say, such a moral aesthetics of history meant that imperial China did not develop the kind of cognitive history that eventually arose in the modern West. Such history was premised on the sense of anachronism that made a substantive differentiation between *past* and *present;* historical intelligibility came to be established through a relation with the past as the *other.* This very relation, which denoted and affirmed the otherness of the past, gave rise to lineal epochal conceptions, the hallmark of modern historical consciousness. In its essentials this modern Western historicity consists of two elements: a lineal account of sequence and an evaluation of a distinct period in the context of the sequential series (de Certeau 1988, 2–3; Graham 1997, 45–62). As we have seen, despite intermittent examples of relativizing individual time periods and savoring the provisional in different historical contexts, the Chinese did not develop a fully fledged historicism in the Western sense. In the end Chinese historians did not slight the altars of the sages, their temples did not fall into mossy ruins, and tradition was not deauthorized. To the extent that history was not severed from the ultimate grounds on which ethics and morality were based, the past continued to be the enshrinement and embodiment of the universal Way, which remained the ultimate source of norms and values (Ng 2003, 52–54, 57–61).

It is important to realize that introducing a cross-cultural comparative perspective does not suggest a line of inquiry that presumes Western developments as the norm by which other cultures are measured. Nevertheless, by now we are familiar with ubiquitous questions such as these: Why was there no science or scientific culture in traditional China? Why was there no civil space and public sphere? Why was there no military culture and psychology? In indicating that there was no sustained development of modern historicism in the Chinese case—there were, as we recall, instances of brilliant perception of anachronism and causative nexus—we are not in effect posing a tendentious question whose subtext is that there ought to have been the same developments in China as in the West (cf. Brook 1998b, 163–164). Our comparative effort is based on an awareness that the comparisons do not in any direct way inform us of the nature of the things compared. They are, instead, akin to metaphors, offering ways in which things might be conceived and thereby redescribed. They are, to put it another way, disciplined fancies and speculations made in the name of enhancing understanding. The understanding would be this: that the customary way of looking at the past shifted as the underlying cultural grounds—the foundation and fountainhead of norms and values—shifted.

And the ground did indeed shift in China. In Gong Zizhen and Wei Yuan's engagement with history, we get an inkling of the historiographical sea change that was to occur. During their lifetime Gong and Wei witnessed rebellions, political reversals, economic dislocations, social malaise, Western encroachment, and finally war. The stock phrase of *wai'luan nei'huan* (external disorder and internal menace), much used in traditional Chinese historiography, was truly a felicitous depiction of the realities of their world. They viewed their own time as standing in an extraordinary relation to the future, one that would have to reckon with new forces engendered by Western incursion. Gong and Wei projected their sense of crisis and anxiety onto history, and, as we have seen, their historical view became an important element in the call for reform of the state. No longer preoccupied primarily with praise and blame, inspired and guided by the spirit of evidential learning, they stressed in their historical scholarship the seeking of truth from facts. Yet in the end both Gong and Wei appealed to the ancient canon. To them, the perennial value of the classics was still intact and therefore usable; they still regarded the classics as the storehouse of wisdom and inspiration. Although Gong and Wei, with their sense of historical change, might not treat the classics as literally true, they continued to embrace their relevance.

By the last quarter of the nineteenth century, however, a new kind of historical awareness had emerged as the fundamentals of the Confucian world view loosened and became destabilized, and China was drawn into the maelstrom of world history. Especially from Japan, China began to absorb contemporary European historiography, particularly that of the German tradition. Liang Qichao (1873–1929), arguably the leading figure in this new movement, called for a "historiographical revolution" (*shijie geming*) that vociferously clamored for the writing of a "new history." That history, unlike the traditional dynastic histories, should no longer be focused on the country's rulers and officials, concerned primarily with individuals and ethics. History should be a science that examined all aspects of society in the past. Nevertheless, new and scientific though history must become, the desire to confront the present through manipulating and understanding the past remained. The past was still employable, but it would be used in a substantially different way. The new ways of writing history would be part and parcel of the project of nation-building. History would not only be the foundation of scientific learning, but it would also be a mirror of the new citizenry of China, a people galvanized by patriotism. Just as the rise and growth of power and nationalism in the European countries owed much to the study of history, so too in China the embrace of progressive modern Western historiography, which probed the evolution of human history and revealed the common laws and patterns in it, would lay the foundation of a strong Chinese nation-state. Liang and his colleagues also began to construct a new periodization of Chinese history, modeled on the Western tripartite division of the ancient, medieval, and modern (Moloughney 1992, 13–30; Q. Wang 2000a, 43–54).

The historiography of modern China lies outside the purview of this study. But perhaps this all-too-brief reference to the historiographical changes and innovations in the modern era will serve to remind us that while Liang Qichao and his comrades wore their new historicism like a badge of honor, they were in some ways embittered intellectuals who felt let down by the age-old dream of a harmonious society of moral excellence and ethical distinction. Therefore, at the same time that they were radicals destroying the old historiographical temple and laying ground for a new one, they were busy digging up the past in hopes of finding a new present. The historical analogy and classical didacticism of a Sima Qian or a Sima Guang might be blunt, crude instruments working on behalf of political and moral certitude, but historical reference remained the surest way to present an argument and to make a point, as Liang Qichao and others were well aware. How else could they create a new nation and a new people if they did not first recreate a new past?

In so connecting the "new history" and its spokespeople of twentieth-century China with the past, we are by no means diminishing their very real and considerable epistemological changes. Modern Chinese historiography was indeed fundamentally different from its traditional counterpart, as it expanded conceptual horizons, embraced new ideologies, and experimented with alternative narrative styles. Social Darwinist, scientific, liberal, and Marxian thinking all fueled different conceptions of the past and formed the bedrock of varying visions of China as a nation-state in the family of sovereign entities in a transnational world. Yet the fact remains that the new historical and historiographical endeavors forged an intellectual revolution by plumbing the past. Such, of course, is the inevitable Gordian knot of the past and present in the writing of history (Q. Wang 2001, passim, especially 1–2; 208–209).

The historiography of imperial China may be an orphaned mode of expression in our contemporary world of historical learning, but its assertion of the meaning and purpose of history cannot be lightly cast aside. To the extent that history has not ended, the human quest for meaning, short of appealing to religious transcendence, depends a great deal on how the past is written and used. The past must be constantly refashioned to fit our self-image, and the historians and historiographers in imperial China knew this well. There is no other way.

Glossary

ai 愛
aiqi 愛奇
An Lushan 安祿山
ba 霸
Bachao mingchen yanxing lu
　八朝名臣言行錄
badao 霸道
baiguan 百官
Baiguan tu 百官圖
Ban Biao 班彪
Ban Gu 班固
baobian 褒貶
baomin 保民
Bei Qishu 北齊書
Beishi 北史
beng 崩
benji 本紀
biannian/shi 編年/史
biantong 變通
biao 表
bieyi 別異
biezhuan 別傳
biji 筆記
bishi 比事
bo 伯
Boyi 伯夷
Bu Dayou 卜大有
buque 補闕
Bushi 不實
buxiu 不朽
cai 才

Cai Yong 蔡邕
Cangshu 藏書
Cao Cao 曹操
Cefu yuangui 冊府元龜
Chang Qu 常璩
changbian 長編
Changsun Wuji 長孫無忌
chen 臣
Chen Jian 陳建
Chen Liang 陳亮
Chen She 陳涉
Chen Shou 陳壽
Chen Yinke 陳寅恪
Chen Youliang 陳友諒
Cheng Hao 程顥
Cheng Yi 程頤
chengwang 懲妄
Chenshu 陳書
chenyi 臣儀
Chongwen zongmu 崇文總目
chouyin 紬引
Chu Suiliang 褚遂良
ChuHan chunqiu 楚漢春秋
Chunqiu 春秋
cizhang 辭章
congfu 從赴
conggao 從誥
Cui Zhu 崔杼
cun santong 存三統
Da gao 大誥
Da Ming huidian 大明會典

265

Da Ming ji li 大明集禮
Da Ming rili 大明日曆
Da Tang chuangye qijuzhu
    大唐創業起居注
da yitong 大一統
Da Yuan shengzheng guochao
    dianzhang 大元聖政國朝典章
Da Yuan yitongzhi 大元一統志
dafang 大防
dagang 大綱
Dai Zhen 戴震
dangjin 當今
dangran 當然
dao 道
dao wenxue 道問學
daoti 道體
daotong 道統
daoxue 道學
daoyi 島夷
dashi 大史
datong 大同
dazhu 大祝
dexing 德性
dezheng 德政
Dianmo ji 典謨記
difang zhi 地方志
diji 帝紀
dili/zhi 地理/志
dingli 定理
Dong Zhongshu 董仲舒
Dongguan hanji 東觀漢紀
Du Fu 杜甫
Du Tongjian lun 讀通鑑論
Du Weiyun 杜維運
Du You 杜佑
duanlan chaobao 斷瀾朝報
Dushi guanjian 讀書管見
Duxing 獨行
duyi zhi 都邑志
Ershi'ershi kaoyi 二十二史考異
erti 二體
fa (laws and institutions) 法
fa (military actions) 伐
fa houwang 法後王
Fan Ye 范曄
Fan Zhongyan 范仲淹

Fan Zuyu 范祖禹
Fang Guozhen 方國珍
fangshi 方士
fangwu zhi 方物志
fangzhen 方鎮
Fei Guoyu 非國語
feijin shigu 非今是古
fen 分
Feng Dao 馮道
fengjian 封建
Fengjian lun 封建論
fengshan 封禪
Fenshu 焚書
furen 夫人
Fuyang renwu ji 浦陽人物記
gaitian shuo 蓋天說
gang 綱
Gaoseng zhuan 高僧傳
gewu zhizhi 格物致知
gong 公
Gong Zizhen 龔自珍
Gongyang zhuan 公羊傳
Gongzheng 公正
Gu 故
Gu Yanwu 顧炎武
Gu Yingtai 谷應泰
Guan Yu 關羽
guang 光
Guiqian zhi 歸潛志
guirang 貴讓
Gujin renbiao 古今人表
Gujin shixue deshi 古今史學得失
Guliang zhuan 穀梁傳
Guming 顧命
Guo Xi 郭熙
Guo Zixing 郭子興
Guochao gushi 國朝故事
Guochao mingchen shilue
    國朝名臣事略
Guochao wenlei 國朝文類
Guoque 國榷
guoshi 國史
guoshi guan 國史館
guoying qiye 國營企業
Guoyu 國語
gushi (anecdote) 故事

gushi (blind historian) 瞽史

Gushi kao 古史考

guwen 古文

Haiguo tuzhi 海國圖志

Han (dynasty) 漢

Han Fei 韓非

Han Lin'er 韓林兒

Han Yu 韓愈

Hanji 漢紀

Hanjin chunqiu 漢晉春秋

hanmen 寒門

Hanshu 漢書

Hanshu xue 漢書學

Hao Jing 郝經

haozu 豪族

He Chengtian 何承天

He Qiaoyuan 何喬遠

Heyang 河陽

Hongwu shengzheng ji 洪武聖政記

hou 后

Houhan ji 後漢記

Houhan shu 後漢書

houzhu 後主

Houzhuan 後傳

Hu Shi 胡適

Hu Yin 胡寅

Huai'nanzi 淮南子

Huan Tui 桓魋

Huan Wen 桓溫

Huang Chao 黃巢

Huang Ming tongji 皇明通紀

Huang Ming zuxun lu 皇明祖訓錄

Huang Shengzeng 黃省曾

Huang Zongxi 黃宗義

Huangchao jingshi dadian
　　皇朝經世大典

Huangchao jingshi wenbian
　　皇朝經世文編

Huayang guozhi 華陽國志

hui 諱

hui tong 會通

huishi 穢史

huiyao 會要

hujian fa 互見法

Huojing 惑經

ji 集

Jia Yi 賈誼

Jiang Yong 江永

Jianlu 建虜

jianyao 簡要

jiao (teachings) 教

jiaohua 教化

Jiaomin bangwen 教民榜文

jiaoshu lang 校書郎

Jiaren juan 家人卷

jiashi 家史

jiaxun 家訓

jie 節

jiedu shi 節度使

Jigu lu (by Ouyang Xiu) 集古錄

Jigu lu (by Sima Guang) 稽古錄

jihui 忌諱

Jin (dynasty in the post-Han
　　period) 晉

Jin (Jurchen dynasty in the Song
　　period) 金

Jin Yufu 金毓黻

jingchang ben 經廠/本

Jingji zhi 經籍志

jingshi (classics and history) 經史

jingshi (statecraft) 經世

jingu 今古

jingyan 經筵

jinshi 進士

Jinshu 晉書

jinwen 今文

jishi 記事

jishi benmo 記事本末

Jisi zhi 祭祀志

Jiu Tangshu 舊唐書

Jiu Wudai shi 舊五代史

jiupin zhongzheng zhi 九品中正制

jiuzhi 九旨

jiwei 即位

jiyan 記言

jizhu yuan 記注院

jizhuan/ti 紀傳/體

jun 君

Junguo zhi 郡國志

junshu 郡書

junwei 君威

junxian 郡縣

junzi 君子
Kang Youwei 康有為
kao 考
Kaoyi 考異
kaozheng/xue 考證/學
Ke Shaomin 柯劭忞
kezhi 可知
Kong Yingda 孔穎達
kou 寇
langzhong 郎中
lantai lingshi 蘭臺令史
leishu 類書
li (principle) 理
li (rituals) 禮
Li Baiyao 李百藥
Li Bo 李白
Li Dashi 李大師
Li Jiantai 李建泰
Li Shimin 李世民
Li Yanshou 李延壽
Li Yuan 李淵
Li Zhi 李贄
Li Zicheng 李自成
Li'nian tu 歷年圖
lian 廉
Liang Menglong 梁夢龍
Liang Qichao 梁啟超
Liangshu 梁書
Liao (dynasty) 遼
lide 立德
Lienü 列女
liezhuan 列傳
ligong 立功
Liji 禮記
Linghu Defen 令狐德棻
lingshi 令史
lishi biji 歷史筆記
Liu Ban (Liu Bin) 劉攽
Liu Bei 劉備
Liu Fang 柳芳
Liu Fenglu 劉逢祿
Liu Kuang 劉覎
Liu Qi 劉祁
Liu Shipei 劉師培
Liu Shu 劉恕
Liu Xie 劉勰

Liu Xin 劉歆
Liu Yizheng 柳詒徵
Liu Zhi 劉秩
Liu Zhiji 劉知幾
Liu Zongyuan 柳宗元
Liudian 六典
liujia 六家
liujing 六經
Lixue zongchuan 理學宗傳
liyan 立言
Lu (state) 魯
Lü Buwei 呂不韋
Lu Jia 陸賈
Lu Shen 陸深
luan 亂
lüe 略
Lun liujia yaozhi 論六家要旨
lunbian 論辯
lunyi 論議
Luo Guanzhong 羅貫中
Luo Zhenyu 羅振玉
Lüshi chunqiu 呂氏春秋
Ma Duanlin 馬端臨
Ma Rong 馬融
minben 民本
ming (destiny) 命
Ming (dynasty) 明
ming (names) 名
ming (sagacity) 明
Ming shi'an 明史案
Ming shisan chao yishi
　　明十三朝遺史
mingjiao (illustrious moral
　　teachings) 明教
mingjiao (teaching of names) 名教
mingjun 明君
Mingru xue'an 明儒學案
Mingseng zhuan 名僧傳
Mingshan cang 名山藏
Mingshi jilue 明史記略
Mingshi jishi benmo 明史紀事本末
Mingyi daifang lu 明夷待訪錄
mingzu shi 民族史
mishu lang 秘書郎
Mozi 墨子
mu 目

Mulu 目錄
Naitō Konan (Torajirō)
　　内藤湖南(虎次郎)
Nanqi shu 南齊書
Nanshi 南史
nei qizhu zhu 内起居注
Nian'ershi zhaji 廿二史扎記
nüshi 女史
Ouyang Xiu 歐陽修
Pan'geng 盤庚
Pei Songzhi 裴松之
pianji 偏紀
pianwen 胼文
pipan shixue 批判史學
pu 譜
pudie 譜牒
puxi 譜系
qi 氣
Qian Daxin 錢大昕
Qian Qianyi 錢謙益
qianyan 前言
Qiao Zhou 譙周
qihua 氣化
qiju sheren 起居舍人
qijulang 起居郎
qijuzhu 起居注
Qilue 七略
Qing (dynasty) 清
qingtan 清談
Qiu Jun 丘濬
Qu Jingchun 瞿景淳
quan 權
Quan Zuwang 全祖望
Qubi 曲筆
Qunshu zhiyao 群書治要
quqi fanchong 去其繁重
ren 仁
Rikkokushi 六国史
rili 日曆
rilu 日錄
Rizhi lu 日知錄
ru/xue 儒/學
Ruan Xiaoxu 阮孝緒
Rulin zongpai 儒林宗派
san'an 三案
Sanchao yaodian 三朝要典

sangang 三綱
sangang wuchang 三綱五常
San'guo yanyi 三國演義
San'guozhi 三國志
sanke 三科
sanshi (three ages) 三世
sanshi (three histories) 三史
santong (three systems) 三統
sha 殺
Shang (dynasty) 商
shanggu 上古
Shangshu 尚書
Shao Jinhan 邵晉涵
Shao Yong 邵雍
Shen Defu 沈德符
Shen Yue 沈約
Shen Zhen 沈貞
Sheng 乘
Shengxue zongchuan 聖學宗傳
shengzheng lu 聖政錄
shi (circumstances and
　　conditions) 勢
shi (insight) 識
shi (intellectual) 士
Shi Jingtang 石敬塘
shi/xue (historian, scribe/
　　historical study) 史/學
shi (to kill, murder) 弒
Shiben 世本
shichao 史鈔
shifeng 士風
Shigang pingyao 史綱評要
shiguan 史館
Shihuo zhi 食貨志
Shiji 史記
shijia 世家
Shijing 詩經
shilu 實錄
Shiqishi shangque 十七史商榷
shiquan 史權
Shisheng kaowu 史乘考誤
shishi 適時
shishi qiushi 實事求是
Shishi zhenggang 世史正綱
Shishuo xinyu 世說新語
Shitong 史通

Shitong huiyao 史通會要

shixue 實學

Shixue yaoyi 史學要義

Shizheng ji 時政記

Shizhuan 史傳

shizu/zhi 世族/志

Shu (kingdom in the post-Han period) 蜀

shu 書

shuci 屬辭

shuer buzuo 述爾不作

Shun 舜

Shunzong shilu 順宗實錄

Shuowen jiezi 說文解字

Shuqi 叔齊

si 私

si gaizuo guoshi 私改作國史

sifang 四方

Siku quanshu 四庫全書

sili jian 司禮監

Sima Guang 司馬光

Sima Qian 司馬遷

Sima Tan 司馬談

sishi (four responsibilities) 四事

sishi (private history) 私史

siwei 四維

siwen 斯文

Song (dynasty) 宋

Song Lian 宋濂

Song lun 宋論

Song Qi 宋祁

Song Ruoxin 宋若莘

Songshu 宋書

Su Bian 蘇弁

Su Mian 蘇冕

Su Shi 蘇軾

Su Tianjue 蘇天爵

Su Xun 蘇洵

Sui (dynasty) 隋

Suishu 隋書

Sun Qifeng 孫奇逢

Sun Sheng 孫盛

suolu 索虜

suoyiran 所以然

Sushui jiwen 涑水記聞

suwang 素王

Taichu 太初

taiji 太極

Taiping huanyu ji 太平寰宇記

Taishi 泰誓

taishi/ling 太史/令

Taishigong shu 太史公書

Taizu ji 太祖記

Tan Qian 談遷

Tang (dynasty) 唐

Tang huiyao 唐會要

Tang Jian 唐鑑

Tangshi 湯誓

Taowu 檮杌

ti 體

tian 天

tianming 天命

tianren ganying 天人感應

tianren guanxi 天人關係

tianren heyi 天人合一

tianren sance 天人三策

tianxia 天下

Tianxia junguo libing shu 天下郡國利病書

tianyuan difang 天圓地方

tiaoli 條理

tong santong 通三統

tong/shi 通/史

Tongdian 通典

Tongjian jishi benmo 通鑑紀事本末

Tongzhi 通志

tuji 圖紀

tujing 圖經

tuzhi 圖志

Wan Sitong 萬斯同

wang 王

Wang Anshi 王安石

Wang Ao 王鏊

Wang Fuzhi 王夫之

Wang Guowei 王國維

Wang Mang 王莽

Wang Mingsheng 王鳴盛

Wang Pu 王溥

Wang Qinruo 王欽若

Wang Ruoxu 王若虛

Wang Shao 王劭

Wang Shizhen 王世貞

Wang Yangming 王陽明
Wang Yi 王褘
wang zhengyue 王正月
Wang Zudi 王祖嫡
wangdao 王道
wangxing 往行
Wei (kingdom in the post-Han period) 魏
Wei Dan 魏澹
Wei Yuan 魏源
Wei Zheng 魏徵
Wei Zhongxian 魏忠賢
weishi 違時
Weishu 魏書
weiyan dayi 微言大意
wen 文
Wen Daya 溫大雅
Wen Tianxiang 文天祥
wenci 文辭
Wenshan xiansheng quanji 文山先生全集
Wenxian tongkao 文獻通考
Wenxin diaolong 文心雕龍
wokou 倭寇
Wu (kingdom in the post-Han period) 吳
wu (shaman) 巫
wu (strength) 武
Wu Dacheng 吳大澂
Wu Jing 吳兢
Wu Zetian 武則天
Wu Zhen 吳縝
wuchang 五常
Wudai huiyao 五代會要
Wudai shi 五代史
Wudai shiji 五代史記
wuwei 無為
wuxing 五行
wuzhi 五志
Wuzhi 武志
Xi Zuochi 習鑿齒
Xia (dynasty) 夏
Xiang Yu 項羽
xiangyin 相因
xianzhu 先主
xiao Yao Shun 小堯舜

Xiao Zixian 蕭子顯
xiaokang 小康
xiaoshi 小史
xiaoshuo 小說
Xiaoyi 孝義
Xie An 謝安
Xin Tangshu 新唐書
Xin Tangshu jiumiu 新唐書糾繆
Xin Wudai shi 新五代史
Xin Yuanshi 新元史
xingfa 刑法
xingwang 興亡
xinshi 信史
xiuzhuan 修撰
xixing yi jie qi xin 錫姓以結其心
Xiyuan wenjian lu 西園聞見錄
Xu Hanshu 續漢書
Xu Heng 許衡
Xu Shen 許慎
Xu Wudang 徐無黨
xuanxue 玄學
Xuanzang 玄奘
xue 學
Xue Juzheng 薛居正
Xue Xuan 薛瑄
Xun Yue 荀悅
Xunzi 荀子
Yan Hui 顏回
Yan Shigu 顏師古
Yang Weizhen 楊維楨
Yanshantang bieji 弇山堂別集
Yao 堯
Yao Shou 姚壽
Yao Silian 姚思廉
Yaodian 堯典
ye 野
Ye Sheng 葉盛
Ye Shi 葉適
Ye Xianggao 葉向高
Yehuo bian 野獲編
yi (oneness) 一
yi/yifa 義/義法
yi'er jun 義兒軍
yiguan 一貫
Yijing 易經
Yiluo yuanyuan lu 依洛淵源錄

Yimin (recluse) 逸民

yimin (surviving people) 遺民

yishi 逸事

Yiwen zhi 藝文志

yizhi yifa 以制義法

yizhu 儀著

yonghui 用晦

Yongle dadian 永樂大典

Yongli shilu 永歷史錄

yongxia bianyi 用夏變夷

youshi 右史

Yu 禹

yu lunduan yu xushi 寓論斷於敘事

Yuan (dynasty) 元

Yuan Haowen 元好問

Yuan Hong 袁宏

Yuan Hongdao 袁宏道

Yuan Shu 袁樞

yuanding 元鼎

yue 岳

Yue Shi 樂史

Yuejing 樂經

Yueling 刖令

yueqi ciwen 約其詞文

yufu 輿服

Yugong 禹貢

Yunhan 雲漢

Yupi lidai Tongjian jilan
     御批歷代通鑑輯覽

yushi 御史

zaiji 在紀

zan 贊

zashi 雜史

zazhuan 雜傳

Zeng Gong 曾鞏

Zhan'guoce 戰國策

Zhang Cha 張差

Zhang Fangping 張方平

Zhang Fei 張飛

Zhang Juzheng 張居正

zhang sanshi 張三世

Zhang Shi 張拭

Zhang Shicheng 張士誠

Zhang Xuan 張萱

Zhang Xuecheng 章學誠

Zhang Xun 張巡

Zhang Zai 張載

Zhao Bingwen 趙秉文

Zhao Yi 趙翼

zheng guoben 爭國本

Zheng Qiao 鄭樵

Zheng Xuan 鄭玄

Zhengdian 政典

zhengming 正名

zhengshi 正史

zhengtong 正統

Zhenguan zhengyao 貞觀政要

zhengyue 正月

zhi (rulership) 治

zhi (straightforward) 直

zhi (substance, simplicity) 質

zhi (to know; knowledge) 知

zhi (treatise monograph) 志

Zhi Dun 支遁

zhiguan 職官

zhiguo lun 治國論

Zhishu 直書

zhong 忠

zhonggu 中古

Zhongyi 忠義

Zhongzhou ji 中州記

Zhou (dynasty) 周

Zhou Dunyi 周敦頤

Zhou Rudeng 周汝登

Zhouli 周禮

Zhoushu 周書

zhu 祝

Zhu Changluo 朱常洛

Zhu Changxun 朱常洵

Zhu Wen 朱溫

Zhu Xi 朱熹

Zhu Youxiao 朱由校

Zhu Yuanzhang 朱元璋

Zhu Yunming 祝允明

zhuan 傳

Zhuang Cunyu 莊存與

Zhuang Tinglong 莊廷鑨

zhuanshu 撰書

zhuanzhi 傳記

Zhuge Liang 諸葛亮

zhuji 注記

Zhulin qixian 竹林七賢

Zhushu ji'nian 竹書紀年
Zhuzi zuiyan lu 祝子罪言錄
zhuzuo ju 著作局
zhuzuo lang 著作郎
Zi Gong 子貢
ziran 自然
ziran zhi li 自然之理
Zisi 子思
Zizhi tongjian 資治通鑑

Zizhi tongjian gangmu
資治通鑑綱目
Zou Yan 鄒衍
zu 卒
zun dexing 尊德性
zuo (to make) 作
Zuo Qiuming 左丘明
zuoshi 左史
Zuozhuan 左傳

Bibliography

Alitto, Guy. 1985. "Zhongguo fangzhi yu xifangshi de bijiao" (A comparison of the Chinese gazetteers with histories in the West). *Hanxue yanjiu* 3, 2:59–71.

Analects (Lunyu). 1997. *The Analects of Confucius: A Literal Translation with an Introduction and Notes.* Translated by Chichung Huang. New York: Oxford University Press.

Asano, Chūin. 1944. "Min jitsuroku zakkō" (Investigations into the Ming veritable records). *Kita Ajia gakuō* 3:254–85.

Bai, Shouyi. 1999. *Zhongguo shixueshi lunji* (Essays in the history of Chinese historiography). Beijing: Zhonghua shuju.

Bai, Xinghua. 1999. "Zhao Yi de shixue piping" (Zhao Yi's historical criticism). *Shixueshi yanjiu* 3:48–55.

Balazs, Etienne. 1961. "L'histoire comme Guide de la Pratique Bureaucratique." In *Historians of China and Japan,* edited by W. G. Beasley and E. G. Pulleyblank, 78–95. London: Oxford University Press.

———. 1964. *Chinese Civilization and Bureaucracy.* Translated and edited with an introduction by Arthur F. Wright. New Haven: Yale University Press.

Balazs, Etienne, and Yves Hervouet. 1978. *A Sung Bibliography.* Hong Kong: Chinese University.

Bao, Zunpeng. 1965. "Wang Shizhen ji qi shixue" (Wang Shizhen and his historical scholarship). Introductory essay to Wang Shizhen, *Yanshantang beiji* (A special anthology from the Yanshan Studio). Taipei: Xuesheng shuju.

Barrett, T. H. 1998. "China and the Redundancy of the Medieval." *The Medieval History Journal* 1, 1:73–89.

Bauer, Wolfgang. 1976. *China, and the Search for Happiness.* Translated by Michael Shaw. New York: The Seabury Press.

Beasley, W. G., and E. G. Pulleyblank, eds. 1961. *Historians of China and Japan.* London: Oxford University Press.

Bol, Peter K. 1992. *"This Culture of Ours": Intellectual Transitions in T'ang and Sung China.* Stanford: Stanford University Press.

———. 2004. "Local History and Family in Past and Present." In *The New and the*

Multiple: Sung Senses of the Past, edited by Thomas H. C. Lee. Hong Kong: The Chinese University Press.

Breisach, Ernst. 1983. *Historiography: Ancient, Medieval, & Modern.* Chicago: University of Chicago Press.

Brook, Timothy. 1998a. *The Confusions of Pleasure: Commerce and Culture in Ming China.* Berkeley: University of California Press.

———. 1998b. "Medievality and the Chinese Sense of History." *The Medieval History Journal* 1, 1:145–164.

Burke, Peter. 1969. *The Renaissance Sense of the Past.* London: Edward Arnold.

———. 1976. "Tradition and Experience: The Idea of Decline from Bruni to Gibbon." *Daedalus* 105:137–52.

Cang, Xiuliang, and Deliang Wei. 1983. *Zhongguo gudai shixueshi jianbian* (A concise history of Chinese historiography). Haerbin: Heilongjiang renmin chubanshe.

Chan, Hok-lam. 1970. *The Historiography of the Chin Dynasty (1115–1234): Three Studies.* Münchener ostasiastische Studien, no. 4. Wiesbaden: Franz Steiner Verlag.

———. 1975. "The Rise of Ming T'ai-tsu (1368–98): Facts and Fictions in Early Ming Official Historiography." *Journal of the American Oriental Society* 95, 4:679–715.

———. 1980. *Li Chih 1527–1602 in Contemporary Chinese Historiography: New Light on His Life and Works.* New York: M. E. Sharpe, Inc.

———. 1981. "Chinese Official Historiography at the Yüan Court: The Composition of the Liao, Chin, and Sung Histories." In *China under Mongol Rule,* edited by John D. Langlois, Jr. Princeton: Princeton University Press.

———. 1982. " 'Comprehensiveness' (*T'ung*) and 'Change' (*Pien*) in Ma Tuan-lin's Historical Thought." In *Yüan Thought: Chinese Thought and Religion under the Mongols,* edited by Hok-lam Chan and Wm. Theodore de Bary. New York: Columbia University Press.

———. 1984. *Legitimation in Imperial China: Discussions under the Jurchen-Chin Dynasty (1115–1234).* Seattle: University of Washington Press.

Chan, Wing-tsit. 1963. *A Source Book in Chinese Philosophy.* Princeton: Princeton University Press.

———. 1982. "Chu Hsi and Yüan Confucianism." In *Yüan Thought: Chinese Thought and Religion under the Mongols,* edited by Hok-lam Chan and Wm. Theodore de Bary. New York: Columbia University Press.

Chang, Hao. 1974. "On the Ching-shih Ideal in Neo-Confucianism." *Ch'ing-shih wen-t'i,* 3, 1:36–61.

Chang, Kang-i Sun. 2001. "Liu Xie's Idea of Canonicity." In *A Chinese Literary Mind: Culture, Creativity, and Rhetoric in* Wenxin Diaolong, edited by Cai Zhong-qi. Stanford: Stanford University Press.

Chang, Kwang-chih. 1984. *Art, Myth and Ritual: The Path to Political Authority in Ancient China.* Cambridge MA: Harvard University Press.

Chen, Chi-yun. 1975. *Hsün Yüeh (148–209): The Life and Reflections of An Early Medieval Confucian.* Cambridge: Cambridge University Press.

Chen, Fangming. 1972. "Song Liao Jin shi de zuanxiu yu zhengtong zhi zheng"

(The compilation of the histories of the Song, the Liao, and the Jin, and the polemics concerning political legitimacy). *Shihuo yuekan* 2, 8:10–23.

Chen, Jinzhong. 1981. "Zhongguo chuantong shixue gongzuo de neihan yu dezhi qianshuo" (A preliminary discussion of the inner meanings and special characteristics of the traditional Chinese historiographical endeavor). *Donghai daxue lishi xuebao* 4:37–68.

Chen, Qitai. 1997. *Qingdai Gongyangxue* (Gongyang learning in the Qing period). Beijing: Dongfang chubanshe.

———. 1999. *Shixue yu minzu jingshen* (Historiography and the national spirit). Beijing: Xueyuan chubanshe.

Chen, Shangjun. 1999. "Qing ji 'Jiu Wudai shi' pingyi" (A critique of the *Old History of the Five Dynasties* edited in the Qing). *Xueshu yuekan* 9:98–113.

Chen, Shih-hsiang. 1968. "Forward." In *The Chronicle of Fu Chien: A Case of Exemplar History*, translated by Michael Rogers, iii–vii. Berkeley: University of California Press.

Chen, Tongsheng. 1993. *Zhongguo shiguan wenhua yu Shiji* (The *Records of the Historian* and the official historical culture in China). Shantou: Shantou daxue chubanshe.

Chen, Xueliang. 1998. *Sima Qian renge lun* (Sima Qian's character). Shanghai: Shanghai renmin chubanshe.

Chen, Yinke. 1974. *Tangdai zhengzhi shih shulun kao* (A preliminary study of the political institutions in the Tang dynasty). Hong Kong: Zhonghua.

Cheng, Chung-ying. 1970. *Tai Chen's "Inquiry into Goodness."* Honolulu: University of Hawai'i Press.

Cheng, Dennis Chi-hsiung (Zheng, Jixiong). 2002. "Dai Zhen 'fenxian' 'yiti' guannian de sixiangshi kaocha" (An inquiry of Dai Zhen's notions of "particularity" and "oneness" in the history of ideas). Paper presented at the Conference on Hermeneutics and Classical Chinese Exegesis, Shantong University.

Chin, Ann-ping, and Mansfield Freeman. 1990. *Tai Chen on Mencius: Explorations in Words and Meaning, A Translation of the Meng Tzu tzi-I shu-cheng.* New Haven: Yale University Press.

Ching, Julia, ed. 1987. *The Records of Ming Scholars: A Selected Translation from Huang Tsung-hsi's Ming-ju hsueh-an.* Honolulu: University of Hawai'i Press.

———. 1997. *Mysticism and Kingship: The Heart of Chinese Wisdom.* Cambridge: Cambridge University Press.

Chow, Kai-wing (Zhou Qirong), and Kwang-ching Liu (Liu Guangjing). 1984. "Xueshu jingshi: Zhang Xuecheng zhi wenshilun yu jingshi sixiang" (Ordering the world with learning: Zhang Xuecheng's discourse on literature and history and his statecraft thought). In *Jinshi Zhongguo jingshi sixiang yantaohui lunwenji* (Proceedings of the conference on the theory of statecraft of modern China), edited by Zhongyang yanjiuyuan jindaishi yanjiusuo. Taipei: Institute of Modern History, Academia Sinica.

Chow, Kai-wing, On-cho Ng, and John B. Henderson, eds. 1999. *Imagining Boundaries: Changing Confucian Doctrines, Texts, and Hermeneutics.* Albany: State University of New York Press.

Chu, Hung-lam. 1999. "Ming Taizu de Kongzi chongbai" (The Confucian worship of Zhu Yuanzhang). *The Bulletin of the Institute of History and Philology, Academia Sinica* 70, 2: 483–529.

Clark, Hugh R. 2004. "Reinventing the Genealogy: Innovation in Kinship Practice in the Tenth to Eleventh Centuries." In *The New and the Multiple: Sung Senses of the Past,* edited by Thomas H. C. Lee. Hong Kong: The Chinese University Press.

Collingwood, R. G. 1946. *The Idea of History.* Oxford: Clarendon Press.

Crawford, Robert B. 1963. "The Social and Political Philosophy of the *Shih-chi,*" *Journal of Asian Studies,* 22, 4 (August): 401–416.

Creel, Herrlee G. 1937. *The Birth of China.* New York: Frederick Ungar.

Cua, A. S. 2002. "The Ethical and the Religious Dimensions of *Li* (Rites)." *The Review of Metaphysics* 55:471–519.

Cutter, Robert Joe, and William Gordon Crowell, trans. 1999. *Empresses and Consorts: Selections from Chen Shou's* Records of the Three States *with Pei Songzhi's Commentary.* Honolulu: University of Hawaiʻi Press.

Dardess, John W. 1973. *Conquerors and Confucians: Aspects of Political Change in Late Yüan China.* New York: Columbia University Press.

———. 2002. *Blood and History in China: The Donglin Faction and Its Repression, 1620–1627.* Honolulu: University of Hawaiʻi Press.

Davis, Richard L. 1983. "Historiography as Politics in Yang Wei-chen's 'Polemic on Legitimate Succession'." *T'oung Pao* 69, 1–3:33–72.

———. 1988. "Sung Historiography: Empirical Ideals and Didactic Realities." *Chinese Culture* 29, 4:67–80.

———. 2004. "Introduction." In Ouyang Xiu, *Historical Records of the Five Dynasties.* Translated by Richard L. Davis. New York: Columbia University Press.

De Bary, Wm. Theodore. 1959. "Some Common Tendencies in Neo-Confucianism." In *Confucianism in Action,* edited by David Nivison and Arthur Wright. Stanford: Stanford University Press.

———. 1970. "Individualism and Humanitarianism in Late Ming Thought." In *Self and Society in Ming Thought,* edited by Wm. Theodore de Bary. New York: Columbia University Press.

———. 1975. "Enlightenment." In *The Unfolding of Neo-Confucianism,* edited by Wm. Theodore de Bary. New York: Columbia University Press.

———. 1981. "The Rise of Neo-Confucian Orthodoxy in Yüan China." In *Neo-Confucian Orthodoxy and the Learning of the Mind-and-Heart,* edited by Wm. Theodore de Bary. New York: Columbia University Press.

———. 1982. "Introduction." In *Yüan Thought: Chinese Thought and Religion under the Mongols,* edited by Hok-lam Chan and Wm. Theodore de Bary. New York: Columbia University Press.

———, trans. 1993. *Waiting for the Dawn: A Plan for the Prince, Huang Tsung-his's Ming-i tai-fang lu.* New York: Columbia University Press.

De Certeau, Michel. 1988. *The Writing of History.* Translated by Tom Conley. New York: Columbia University Press.

Deng, Lequn. 1999. "Huang Zongxi de shixue tezheng" (The characteristics of Huang Zongxi's historical learning). *Xueshu yuekan* 7:89–92.

Du, Weiyun. 1983. "Qingdai shixue zhi diwei" (The status of Qing historical learning). *Shixue pinglun* 6: 1–13.

———. 1988. *Qingdai shixue yu shijia* (Historiography and historians in the Qing period). Beijing: Zhonghua shuju.

———. 1993. *Zhongguo shixueshi* (History of Chinese historiography). Vol. 1. Taipei: Sanmin shuju.

———. 1998. *Zhongguo shixueshi* (History of Chinese historiography). Vol. 2. Taipei: Sanmin shuju.

———. 2004. *Zhongguo shixueshi* (History of Chinese historiography). Vol. 3. Taipei: Sanmin shuju.

Du, Yu. 1982. "Chunqiu zuoshi zhuan xu" (Preface to the *Zuo Commentary* of the *Spring and Autumn Annals*), *Zhongguo lish yaoji xulunwen xuanzhu* (Prefaces and essays of essential works in Chinese historiography, selected and annotated). Annotated and edited by Lei Gan. Changsha: Yuelu shushe.

Dubs, Homer H., trans. 1938. *The History of the Former Han Dynasty*. With the collaboration of Jen T'ai and P'an Lo-chi. 2 Vols. Baltimore: Waverly Press, Inc.

———. 1946. "The Reliability of Chinese Histories," *The Far Eastern Quarterly* 6, 1 (November): 23–43.

Durrant, Stephen W. 1995. *The Cloudy Mirror: Tension and Conflict in the Writings of Sima Qian*. Albany: State University of New York Press.

Egan, Ronald. 1977. "Narratives in *Tso Chuan*," *Harvard Journal of Asiatic Studies* 37:323–352.

———. 1979. "The Prose Style of Fan Yeh," *Harvard Journal of Asiatic Studies,* 39:2 (December): 339–401.

Elman, Benjamin A. 1984. *From Philosophy to Philology: Intellectual and Social Aspects of Change in Late Imperial China*. Cambridge, MA: Harvard University Press.

———. 1990. *Classicism, Politics, and Kingship: The Ch'ang-chou School of New Text Confucianism in Late Imperial China*. Berkeley: University of California Press.

———. 2002. "The historicization of classical learning in Ming-Ch'ing China." In *Turning Points in Historiography: A Cross-Cultural Perspective,* edited by Q. Edward Wang and Georg G. Iggers. Rochester: The University of Rochester Press.

Eno, Robert. 1990. *The Confucian Creation of Heaven: Philosophy and the Defense of Ritual Mastery*. Albany: State University of New York Press.

Fang, Zuyou. 1996. *Wan Sitong pingzhuan* (A critical biography of Wang Sitong). Nanjing: Nanjing daxue chubanshe.

Feng, Youlan (Fung Yu-lan). 1952. *A History of Chinese Philosophy*. Translated by Derk Bodde. 3 Vols. Princeton: Princeton University Press.

Franke, Herbert. 1961. "Some Aspects of Chinese Private Historiography in the Thirteenth and Fourteenth Centuries." In *Historians of China and Japan,* edited by W. G. Beasley and E. G. Pulleyblank. London: Oxford University Press.

———. 1974. "Chinese Historiography under Mongol Rule: The Role of History in Acculturation." *Mongolian Studies,* 1:15–26.

———. 1978. *From Tribal Chieftain to Universal Emperor and God: The Legitimation of the Yüan Dynasty*. Munich: Bayerische Akademie der Wissenschaften.

———. 1982. "Wang Yün (1227–1304): A Transmitter of Chinese Values." In *Yüan*

Thought: Chinese Thought and Religion under the Mongols, edited by Hok-lam Chan and Wm. Theodore de Bary. New York: Columbia University Press.

Franke, Herbert, and Denis Twitchett, eds. 1995. *The Cambridge History of China*, Vol. 6. London: Cambridge University Press.

Franke, Wolfgang. 1961. "The Veritable Records of the Ming Dynasty (1368–1644)." In *Historians of China and Japan*, edited by W. G. Beasley and E. G. Pulleyblank. London: Oxford University Press.

———. 1968. *An Introduction to the Sources of Ming History*. Kuala Lumpur: University of Malaya Press.

———. 1988. "Historical Writing during the Ming." In *The Cambridge History of China*, Vol. 7, *The Ming Dynasty, 1368–1644*, Part 1, edited by Frederick W. Mote and Denis Twitchett. Cambridge: Cambridge University Press.

Frykenberg, Robert Eric. 1996. *History and Belief: The Foundations of Historical Understanding*. Grand Rapids, MI: Eerdmans Publishing Co.

Fu, Yongke. 1987. "Gu Tinglin zhi shilun"(The historical discourses of Gu Yanwu). *Zhonghua wenhua fuxing yuekan* 20, 6:31–43.

———. 1988. "Fangzhixue yu shixue zhi yanjiu" (The study of the local gazetteers and historical research). *Zhonghua wenhua fuxing yuekan* 21, 2:33–42.

Gan, Hongliu. 1998. "Lun Song Yuan Ming sandai zhishu zhong biaoti de yingyong" (On the use of tables in the gazetteers of the three periods of the Song, the Yuan, and the Ming). *Liaoning daxue xuebao* 1:86–88.

Gardner, Charles S. 1938. *Chinese Traditional Historiography*. Cambridge MA. Harvard University Press.

Gongyang zhuan (Gongyang commentary). 1993. In *Sishu wujing* (Four books and five classics). Annotated by Wu Genyou. Beijing: Zhongguo youyi chuban gongsi.

Goodrich, L. Carrington, and Chaoying Fang, eds. 1976. *Dictionary of Ming Biography, 1364–1644*. New York: Columbia University Press.

Grafflin, Dennis. 1990. "Reinventing China: Pseudobureaucracy in the Early Southern Dynasties." In *State and Society in Early Medieval China*, edited by Albert E. Dien. Stanford: Stanford University Press.

Grafton, Anthony. 2001. *Bring Out Your Dead: The Past as Revelation*. Cambridge, MA: Harvard University Press.

Graham, Gordon. 1997. *The Shape of the Past: A Philosophical Approach to History*. London: Penguin.

Gu, Cheng. 1983. "Wang Shizhen de shixue" (The historical learning of Wang Shizhen). *Mingshi yanjiu luncong* 2:331–346.

Gu, Weiying. 1986. "Zhongguo chuantong zhishi fenzi dui lishi zhishi de taidu—yi Gu Yanwu wei zhongxin" (The attitude of the traditional Chinese intelligentsia toward historical knowledge—using Gu Yanwu as the focus). *Shixue pinglun* 11:35–56.

Guliang zhuan (Guliang commentary). 1993. In *Sishu wujing* (Four books and five classics). Annotated by Wu Genyou. Beijing: Zhongguo youyi chuban gongsi.

Haeger, John W. 1968. "'The Significance of Confusion': The Origins of the *T'ai-p'ing yü-lan*." *Journal of the American Oriental Society* 88:401–410.

Hall, David, and Roger Ames. 1987. *Thinking through Confucius.* Albany: State University of New York Press.

Han, Yu-shan. 1955. *Elements of Chinese Historiography.* Hollywood: W. M. Hawley.

Hanshu. 1962. Ban Gu. *Hanshu (Han History).* Beijing: Zhonghua shuju.

Hardy, Grant. 1999. *Worlds of Bronze and Bamboo: Sima Qian's Conquest of History.* New York: Columbia University Press.

Hargett, James M. 1996. "Song Dynasty Local Gazetteers and Their Place in the History of *Difangzhi* Writing." *Harvard Journal of Asiatic Studies* 56, 2:405–442.

———. 2004. "Historiography in Southern Sung Dynasty Local Gazetteers." In *The New and the Multiple: Sung Senses of the Past,* edited by Thomas H. C. Lee. Hong Kong: The Chinese University Press.

Hartwell, Robert M. 1971. "Historical Analogism, Public Policy, and Social Science in Eleventh- and Twelfth-Century China." *American Historical Review* 76, 3:690–727.

He, Wanying. 1998. "Jindai shixue yu Jindai zhengzhi" (Historical learning in the Jin dynasty era and politics in the Jin dynasty era). *Beijing shifan daixue xuebao* 3:58–64.

He, Zheheng. 1989. "Luelun Jiao Xun zhi shixue" (A brief discussion of Jiao Xun's historical learning). *Wenshizhe xuebao* 37:33–58.

Henderson, John B. 1984. *The Development and Decline of Chinese Cosmology.* New York: Columbia University Press.

———. 1991. *Scripture, Canon, and Commentary: A Comparison of Confucian and Western Exegesis.* Princeton: Princeton University Press.

Henry, Eric. 1992. "Chu-ko Liang in the Eyes of His Contemporaries," *Harvard Journal of Asiatic Studies* 52, 2 (December):589–612.

Ho, Koon Piu (He Guanbiao). 1994. "Should We Die as Martyrs to the Ming Cause? Scholar-officials' Views on Martyrdom during the Ming-Qing Transition." *Oriens Extremus* 3, 2:123–151.

———. 1996. "Qing Gaozong dui Nan Ming lishi diwei de chuli" (The positions of the Southern Ming regimes in Chinese history: views of Emperor Kao-tsung of the Ch'ing dynasty). *Xin shihxue* 7, 1:1–27.

———. 1998a. "Qing chu junzhu yu *Zizhi tongjian* ji *Zizhi tongjian gangmu*" (Early Qing Emperors and the *Zizhi tongjian* and the *Zizhi tongjian gangmu*). *Zhongguo wenhua yanjiusuo xuebao* (new series) 7:103–132.

———. 1998b. "Qingdai qianqi junzhu dui guansi shixue de yingxiang" (The influence of Manchu emperors on official and private historiography in early and high Qing China). *Hanxue yanjiu* 16, 1:155–184.

———. 1999a. "Qing Gaozong 'Yuzuan Zizhi tongjian gangmu sanbian' de bianzuan yu chongxiu" (Emperor Ch'ien-lung's *Yü-chuan Tzu-chih t'ung-chien kang-mu san-pien:* An account of its compilation and revision). *Bulletin of the Institute of History and Philology, Academia Sinica* 70, 3:671–697.

———. 1999b. "Shunzhi chao 'Mingshi' bianzuan kao" (The compilation of the *Ming History* in the reign of Shunzhi). *Dalu zazhi* 2:49–70.

———. 2000. "Qing Gaozong 'Yupi lidai Tongjian jilan' bianzuan kaoshi" (An inquiry and explanation of *An Overview of the Comprehensive Mirrors of the Successive Ages Edited by the court*). *Lingnan xuebao* (new series) 2:131–168.

Holcombe, Charles. 1989. "The Exemplar State: Ideology, Self-Cultivation, and Power in Fourth-Century China," *Harvard Journal of Asiatic Studies* 49, 1: 93–139.

———. 1994. *In the Shadow of the Han: Literati Thought and Society at the Beginning of the Southern Dynasties.* Honolulu: University of Hawai'i Press.

Hon, Tze-ki. 1999. "Military Governance versus Civil Governance: A Comparison of the *Old History* and *New History* of the Five Dynasties." In *Imagining Boundaries: Changing Confucian Doctrines, Texts, and Hermeneutics,* edited by Kai-wing Chow, On-cho Ng, and John Henderson. Albany: State University of New York Press.

Hou Hanshu. 1965. Fan Ye. *Hou Hanshu (Later Han History).* Beijing: Zhonghua shuju.

Hsu, Cho-yun. 1999. "The Spring and Autumn Period." In *The Cambridge History of Ancient China: From the Origins of Civilization to 221 B.C.,* edited by Michael Loewe and Edward Shaughnessy, 545–586. Cambridge: Cambridge University Press.

Hsu, Cho-yun, and Katheryn Linduff. 1988. *Western Chou Civilization,* New Haven: Yale University Press.

Hsu, Kwan-san (Xu Guansan). 1983. "The Chinese Critical Tradition." *The Historical Journal* 26, 2:431–446.

Huang, Chun-chieh. 1995. "Historical Thinking in Classical Confucianism—Historical Argumentation from the Three Dynasties." In *Time and Space in Chinese Culture,* edited by Chun-chieh Huang and Erik Zürcher. Leiden: E. J. Brill.

———. 1999. "The Philosophical Argumentation by Historical Narration in Sung China: The Case of Chu Hsi." *Wenshizhe xuebao* 51:5–23.

———. 2002. "The Ch'in Unification in Chinese Historiography." In *Turning Points in Historiography: A Cross-Cultural Perspective,* edited by Q. Edward Wang and Georg Iggers. Rochester: University of Rochester Press.

———. 2004. "The Philosophical Argumentation by Historical Narration in Sung China: The Case of Chu Hsi." In *The New and the Multiple: Sung Senses of the Past,* edited by Thomas H. C. Lee. Hong Kong: The Chinese University Press.

Huang, Qihua. 1991. "Qian Daxin 'jing shi wu er xue' sixiang ping shu" (Comments and explanations on Qian Daxin's idea that "the classics and histories are not two separate learning"). *Shumu jikan* 25, 2: 28–45.

———. 1994. "Qian Daxin de shixue shulun" (On Qian Daxin's historical learning). *Guoshiguan guankan* (new series) 16:1–35.

Huang, Zhaoqiang. 1996. "Qian Daxin Yuanshi yanjiu dongji tanwei ji xueren dui Qianshi shuping zhi yanjiu" (An inquiry into the motives behind Qian Daxin's research of Yuan history and an investigation of scholars' critiques of Mr. Qian). *Dongwu daxue lishi xuebao* 2:91–140.

———. 2001. "Cefu yuanguei Guoshi bu yanjiu" (A study of the section on historiography in the *Mansion of Documents for Great Divinations*) *Dongwu daxue lishi xuebao* 7:19–52.

Hung, William. 1969. "A T'ang Historiographer's Letter of Resignation," *Harvard Journal of Asiatic Studies* 29:5–52.

Ichimura, Sanjirō. 1929. "Genchō no jitsuroku oyobi Keisei Daiten ni tsuite" (On the Yuan dynasty Veritable Records and the *Grand institutions [wherewith] to Manage the World*). In *Mōkoshi Kenkyū* (Studies on the history of the Mongols), edited by Yanai Watari. Tokyo: Toko Shoin.

Iggers, Georg G., and Q. Edward Wang. 2001. "Western Philosophy of History and Confucianism." *Taida lishi xuebao* 27:21–35.

Imanishi, Shunjū. 1963. "Minki sandai kikyochū kō" (An investigation into the diary of activity and repose of three Ming reigns). In *Mindai Man Mō kenkyū* (Studies of the Manchus in the Ming), edited by Tamura Jitsuzō. Kyoto: Kyōto daigaku bungaku.

Inaba, Ichirō. 1999. *Chūgoku no rekishi shisō* (Historical thought in China). Tokyo: Sōbunsha.

Inoue, Susumu. 1996. "Rikkyō mina shi setsu no keifu" (The genesis of the notion of "the Six Classics are histories"). In *Mimmatsu Shinso no shakai to bunka* (Society and culture in the late Ming and early Qing), edited by Ono Kazuko. Kyoto: Mingwen.

Jardine, L. A., and A. T. Grafton. 1990. "'Studied for Action': How Gabriel Harvey Read his Livy." *Past and Present* 129:30–78.

Jay, Jennifer W. 1990. "Memoirs and Official Accounts: The Historiography of the Song Loyalists." *Harvard Journal of Asiatic Studies* 50, 2:589–612.

Jenner, W. J. F. 1992. *The Tyranny of History: the Roots of China's Crisis*. London: Penguin Books.

Ji, Xiao-bin. 2004. "Mirror for Government: Ssu-ma Kuang's Thought on Politics and Government in *Tzu-chih t'ung-chien.*" In *The New and the Multiple: Sung Senses of the Past*, edited by Thomas H. C. Lee. Hong Kong: The Chinese University Press.

Ji, Xueyuan. 2001. "Jingshi zhiyong: Zhedong xuepai de jingdianxing zhixue yuanze" (Ordering the world and extending utility: the classical nature of the principle of pursuing learning of the Zhedong school of learning). *Zhongguo wenhua yuekan* 256:96–105.

Jiang Yibin. 1988. "Zhang Xucheng 'liujing jieshi' de 'yizhi'" (The intentions and aims of Zhang Xuecheng's [idea that] "the six classics are all history"). *Huagang wenke xuebao* 16:175–187.

Jin, Jing'an (Jin Yufu). 1976. *Zhongguo shixueshi* (Chinese historiography). Taipei: Dingwen.

Jin, Yufu. [1944] 2000. *Zhongguo shixueshi* (History of Chinese historiography). Zhijiazhuang: Hebei jiaoyu chubanshe.

Jin, Zhezhong. 1989. "Tan Qian *Guojue* chutan" (A preliminary inquiry into Tan Qian's *Tolls on the Country*). *Zhonghua wenhua fuxing yuekan* 22, 1:43–53.

Jiu Tangshu. 1975. Liu Xu. *Jiu Tangshu* (Old Tang history). Beijing: Zhonghua shuju.

Kamata, Tadashi. 1993. *Saden no seiritsu to sono tenkai* (The establishment and expansion of the *Zuo Commentary*). Tokyo: Taishūkan.

Kennedy, George A. 1942. "Interpretation of the *Ch'un-ch'iu,*" *Journal of the American Oriental Society* 62:40–48.

Kieschnick, John. 1997. *The Eminent Monk: Buddhist Ideals in Medieval Chinese Hagiography.* Honolulu: University of Hawai'i Press.

Kleeman, Terry F. 1998. *Great Perfection: Religion and Ethnicity in a Chinese Millennial Kingdom*. Honolulu: University of Hawai'i Press.

Lai, Fushun. 1984. "Qing xiu Mingshi tili zhi yanjiu" (An investigation into the organization and format of the *Ming History* compiled under the Qing). *Mingshi yanjiu zhuankan* 7:51–88.

Lam, Yuan-chu. 1992. "A Study of the Compilers of the Yüan *Ching-shih tadian*." *T'oung Pao* 78, 1–3:77–93.

Langlois, John D., Jr. 1978. "Yü Chi and his Mongol Sovereign: The Scholar as Apologist." *Journal of Asian Studies* 38, 1:99–116.

———. 1982. "Law, Statecraft, and the *Spring and Autumn Annals* in Yüan Political Thought." In *Yüan Thought: Chinese Thought and Religion under the Mongols*, edited by Hok-lam Chan and Wm. Theodore de Bary. New York: Columbia University Press.

Lee, Thomas H. C. 2002. "New Directions in Northern Sung Historical Thinking (960–1126)." In *Turning Points in Historiography: A Cross-Cultural Perspective*, edited by Q. Edward Wang and Georg Iggers. Rochester: Rochester University Press.

———. 2004a. "History, Erudition and Good Government: Cheng Ch'iao and Encyclopedic Historical Thinking." In *The New and the Multiple: Sung Senses of the Past*, edited by Thomas H. C. Lee. Hong Kong: The Chinese University Press.

———. 2004b. "Introduction." In *The New and the Multiple: Sung Senses of the Past*, edited by Thomas H. C. Lee. Hong Kong: The Chinese University Press.

———, ed. 2004c. *The New and the Multiple: Sung Senses of the Past*. Hong Kong: The Chinese University Press.

Lei, Jiaji. 1990. *Zhonggu shixue guannian shi* (A history of the ideas of history in medieval China). Taipei: Xuesheng shuju.

Leslie, Donald D., Colin Mackerras, and Wang Gungwu, Eds. 1975. *Essays on the Sources for Chinese History*. Columbia: University of South Carolina Press.

Lewis, Mark Edward. 1999. *Writing and Authority in Early China*. Albany: State University of New York Press.

Li, Wai-yee. 1994. "The Idea of Authority in the *Shih chi* (Records of the Historian)," *Harvard Journal of Asiatic Studies* 54, 2 (December): 345–405.

———. 1999. "Knowledge and Skepticism in Ancient Chinese Historiography," In *The Limits of Historiography: Genre and Narrative in Ancient Historical Texts*, edited by Christina Shuttleworth Kraus, 27–54. Leiden: E. J. Brill.

Li, Xiaoshu. 1999. "Fengjian chuantong shixue de moluo yu tongsu shixue de xingsheng—Mingdai shixue tanlun" (The decline of the traditional feudal historical learning and the rise of popular historical learning) *Beijing shehui kexue* 1:91–96.

Li, Xueqin. 1985. "Shangdai de sifeng yu sishi" (Four winds and four seasons in the Shang). *Zhongzhou xuekan* 5:99–101.

Li, Zhuoran. 1982. "Jiao Hong zhi shixue sixiang" (The historical thinking of Jiao Hong). *Shumu jikan* 15, 4:33–46.

———. 1984. "Qiu Jun zhi shixue" (The historical learning of Qiu Jun). *Mingshi yanjiu zhuankan* 7:163–208.

Li, Zongtong. 1953. *Zhongguo shixueshi* (History of Chinese historiography). Taipei: Zhonghua wenhua chuban shiye weiyuanhui.

Liang, Qichao. [1922] 1980. *Zhongguo lishi yanjiufa* (Methods for the study of Chinese history). In *Liang Qichao shixue lunzhu sanzhong* (Liang Qichao's three historical works), 43–180. Hong Kong: Sanlian shudian.

Liji (Classic of rites). 1993. In *Sishu wujing* (Four books and five classics), 211–342. Annotated by Wu Genyou. Beijing: Zhongguo youyi chuban gongsi.

Lin, Shimin. 1995. "Zheng Qiao de Tongzhi lüe ji qi shixue" (Zheng Qiao's "Summaries" in his *Tongzhi* and his historical study). *Xingda lishi xuebao* 5:61–95.

———. 1997. *Shixue sanshu xinquan: yi shixue lilun wei zhongxi de bijiao yanjiu* (New interpretations of three works on historical learning: a comparative study based on historical theories). Taipei: Xuesheng shuju.

Lin, Xiaoping. 1998. "*Shigang pingyao* de 'pi' yu 'ping' "(Criticisms and Evaluations in the *Shigang pingyao*). *Shixueshi yenjiu* 4:61–62.

Liu, James T. C. 1959. *Reforms in Sung China: Wang An-shih (1021–1086) and his New Policies.* Cambridge, MA: Harvard University Press.

———. 1967. *Ou-yang Hsiu: An Eleventh-Century Neo-Confucianist.* Stanford: Stanford University Press.

Liu, Jie. 1982. *Zhongguo shixueshi gao* (A draft history of Chinese historiography). Zhengzhou: Zhongzhou shuhuashe.

Liu, Naihe, and Song Xianshen, Eds. 1986. *Sima Guang yu Zizhi tongjian.* Jilin: Jilin wenshi.

Liu, Yizheng. 1969. *Guoshi yaoyi* (The principal meanings of [our] nation's history). Taibei: Zhonghua shuju.

Liu, Zhonghua. 2001. "Shixi Qingdai kaojuxue zhong yizi zhengjingshi de fangfa" (An attempt to analyze Qing evidential learning's method of using [pre-Qin] philosophy to corroborate the classics and histories). *Qingshi yanjiu* 1:85–94.

Liu, Zongyuan. 1979. *Liu Zongyuan ji* (*Liu Zongyuan's works*). Beijing: Zhonghua shuju.

Loewe, Michael. 1986. "The Former Han Dynasty." In *The Cambridge History of China*, Vol. 1, edited by Denis Twitchett and Michael Loewe. Cambridge: Cambridge University Press.

Loewe, Michael, and Edward Shaughnessy. 1999. Eds. *The Cambridge History of Ancient China: From the Origins of Civilization to 221 B.C.* Cambridge: Cambridge University Press.

Logan, George, M. 1977. "Substance and Form in Renaissance Humanism." *Journal of Medieval and Renaissance Studies* 7, 1:1–34.

Lu, Sheldon Hsiao-peng. 1994. *From History to Fictionality: The Chinese Poetics of Narrative.* Stanford: Stanford University Press.

Lu, Yaodong. 1998. *Weijin shixue ji qita* (Wei and Jin historiography and other essays). Taipei: Dongda tushu.

Luo, Bingliang. 1999a. "Qian Daxin zhongshishi yu zhong baobian" (Qian Daxin's emphasis on facts, and emphasis on praise and blame) *Shixueshi yanjiu* 4:72–73.

———. 1999b. "Qingdai Qianjia shijia shixue piping fangfalun de jige wenti" (A few questions concerning the theory and method of historical criticism of the historians in the Qianjia period of the Qing era). *Hebei xuekan* 2:90–94.

———. 1999c. "Shao Jinhan dui Songshi yanjiu de zhongyao gongxian" (Shao Tingcai's important contributions to the research of Song history). *Qiushi xuekan* 1:104–108.

Luo, Guang. 1972. "Wang Chuanshan de lishi zhexue" (The philosophy of history of Wang Fuzhi). *Zhexue lunji* 1:9–26.

Mann, Albert. 1972. "Cheng Ch'iao: An Essay in Re-Evaluation." In *Transition and Permanence in Chinese History and Culture: A Festschrift in Honour of Dr. Hsiao Kung-ch'üan,* edited by D. C. Bauxbaum and F. W. Mote. Hong Kong: Cathay Press.

Mano, Senryū. 1963. "Min jitsuroku no kenkyū" (A study of the Ming veritable records). In *Mindai Man Mō kenkyū* (Studies of the Manchus in the Ming), edited by Tamura Jitsuzō. Kyoto: Kyōto daigaku bungaku.

Maspéro, Henri. 1978. *China in Antiquity.* Translated by Frank Kierman, Jr. Amherst: University of Massachusetts Press.

Mather, Richard, B., trans. 2002. *A New Account of Tales of the World* (*Shishuo xinyu*). 2nd edition. Ann Arbor: Center for Chinese Studies, University of Michigan.

McMorran, Ian. 1975. "Wang Fu-chih and Neo-Confucian Tradition." In *The Unfolding of Neo-Confucianism,* edited by Wm. Theodore de Bary. New York: Columbia University Press.

McMullen, David. 1988. *State and Scholars in T'ang China.* Cambridge: Cambridge University Press.

Mencius. 1970. *The Works of Mencius.* Translated by James Legge. New York: Dover Publications, Inc.

Meng, Fanju. 1989. "Yuan Yishan dui Jinyuan shixue de gongxian" (Yuan Yishan's contributions to Jin historiography). *Zhonghua wenhua fuxing yuekan* 22, 9:46–49.

Metzger, Thomas. 1977. *Escape from Predicament: Neo-Confucianism and China's Evolving Political Culture.* New York: University of Columbia Press.

Mittag, Achim. 2004. "History in Sung Classical Learning: The Case of the *Odes* (*Shih-ching*)." In *The New and the Multiple: Sung Senses of the Past,* edited by Thomas H. C. Lee. Hong Kong: The Chinese University Press.

Moloughney, Brian. 1992. "From Biographical History to Historical Biography: A Transformation in Chinese Historical Writing." *East Asian History* 4:1–30.

Momigliano, Arnoldo. 1966. "Time in Ancient Historiography." *History and the Concept of Time, History and Theory: Studies in the Philosophy of History.* Beiheft 6.

Mote, Frederick W. 1962. *The Poet Kao Ch'i, 1336–1374.* Princeton: Princeton University Press.

———. 1976. "The Arts and the 'Theorizing Mode' of the Civilization." In *Artists and Traditions: Uses of the Past in Chinese Culture,* edited by Christian Murck. Princeton: Princeton University Press.

———. 1980. "Foreword." In *Li Chih 1527–1602 in Contemporary Chinese Historiography: New Light on His Life and Works,* edited by Hok-lam Chan. New York: M. E. Sharpe, Inc.

Mou, Runsun, 1982. "Lun Qingdai shixue shuailuo de yuanyin" (On the decline of historical learning in the Qing period). *Mingbao yuekan* 8:58–65.

Munz, Peter. 1977. *The Shapes of Time: A New Look at the Philosophy of History*. Middletown, CN: Wesleyan University Press.

Naitō Torajirō. 1949. *Shina Shigakushi* (History of Chinese historiography). Tokyo: Kōbundō.

Needham, Joseph. 1959. *Science and Civilization in China*. Cambridge: Cambridge University Press.

Ng, On-cho. 1984. "Private Historiography of the Late Ming: Some Notes on Five Works." *Ming Studies* 18:46–68.

———. 1993a. "Revisiting Kung tzu-chen's (1792–1841) *Chin-wen* (New Text) Precepts: An Excursion in the History of Ideas." *Journal of Oriental Studies* 31, 2:237–263.

———. 1993b. "A Tension in Ch'ing Thought: 'Historicism' in Seventeenth- and Eighteenth-Century Chinese Thought." *Journal of the History of Ideas* 54, 4:561–583.

———. 1994. "Mid Ch'ing New Text (*chin-wen*) Classical Learning and Its Han Provenance: The Dynamics of a Tradition of Ideas." *East Asian History* 8:1–32.

———. 1995. "Interpreting 'Qing Thought' in China as a 'Period Concept': On the Construction of an Epochal System of Ideas." *Semiotica* 107, 3–4:237–264.

———. 1996. "Worldmaking, *Habitus* and Hermeneutics: A Re-reading of Wei Yuan's (1794–1856) New Script (*chin-wen*) Classicism." In *Worldmaking*, edited by William Pencak. New York: Peter Lang.

———. 2003. "The Epochal Concept of 'Early Modernity' and the Intellectual History of Late Imperial China." *Journal of World History* 14, 1:37–61.

Niu, Runzhen. 1999. *Han zhi Tang chu shiguan zhidu de yanbian* (The change of official historical culture from the Han to the Tang). Shijiazhuang: Hebei jiaoyu chubanshe.

Nivison, David S. 1966. *The Life and Thought of Chang Hsueh-ch'eng*. Stanford: Stanford University Press.

Ono, Kazuko. 1967. *Kō Sōgi* (Huang Zongxi). In *Chūgoku jimbutsu sōsho*, second series, no. 9. Tokyo: Jimbutsu ōraisha.

Ōtani, Toshio. 1971. "Gi Gen keisei shisō kō" (An investigation into Wei Yuan's statecraft thought). *Shirin* 54.6:33–75.

———. 1978. "Tai Meisei danzai jiken no seiji teki haikai" (The political background of the affairs of putting Dai Mingshi on trial). *Shirin* 64.1:1–37.

Ouyang, Xiu. 2004. *Historical Records of the Five Dynasties*. Translated by Richard L. Davis. New York: Columbia University Press.

Park, Chua-wu (Piao, Zaiyu). 1994. *Shiji Hanshu bijiao yanjiu* (Comparative study of the *Records of the Historian* and the *Han History*). Beijing: Zhongguo wenxue chubanshe.

Pearce, Scott, Audrey Spiro, and Patricia Ebrey, eds. 2001. *Culture and Power in the Reconstitution of the Chinese Realm*. Cambridge MA: Harvard University Press.

Peng, Zhongde, and Li Lin. 2001. "Li Zhi de shilun ji qi yingxiang" (Li Zhi's historical discourse and its influence). *Zhongguo wenhua yuekan* 261:35–47.

Peterson, C. A. 1979. "Court and Province in mid and late T'ang." In *The Cambridge History of China*, Vol. 3, edited by Denis Twitchett. London: Cambridge University Press.

Peterson, Willard. 1979. *Bitter Gourd: Fang I-chih and the Impetus for Intellectual Change.* New Haven: Yale University Press.

Pines, Yuri. 2002. *Foundations of Confucian Thought: Intellectual Life in the Chunqiu Period, 722–453 B.C.E.* Honolulu: University of Hawai'i Press.

Priest, Quinton G. 1986. "Portraying Central Government Institutions: Historiography and Intellectual Accommodation in the High Ch'ing." *Late Imperial China* 7, 1:27–49.

Puett, Michael J. 2001. *The Ambivalence of Creation: Debates Concerning Innovation and Artifice in Early China.* Stanford: Stanford University Press.

Pulleyblank, Edwin G. 1961. "Chinese Historical Criticism: Liu Chih-chi and Ssuma Kuang." In *Historians of China and Japan,* edited by W. G. Beasley and E. G. Pulleyblank. London: Oxford University Press.

———. 1964. "The Historiographical Tradition." In *The Legacy of China,* edited by Raymond Dawson. London: Oxford University Press.

———. 1979. "The An Lu-shan Rebellion and the Origins of Chronic Militarism in Late T'ang China." In *Essays on T'ang Society: The Interplay of Social, Political and Economic Forces,* edited by John Curtis Perry and Bardwell L. Smith. Leiden: E. J. Brill.

Qian, Maowei. 1999. "Lun Li Zhi dui yili shixue de xitong pipan" (On Li Zhi's systematic critique of moral historical learning). *Xueshu yuekan* 7:82–88.

———. 2001. "Lun Ming zhongye shixue fengqide bianhua" (On the change of trends in historical learning in the mid Ming). *Shixueshi yenjiu* 2:26–35.

Qian, Mu. 1964. *Zhongguo jin sanbai'nian xueshushi* (A history of the intellectual developments in the past three hundred years). 2 Vols. Taipei: Commercial Press.

Qu, Lindong. 1999a. "Liangsong shixue piping de chengjiu" (Achievements in historical criticism in the two Song dynasties). *Hebei xuekan* 2:82–89.

———. 1999b. *Zhongguo shixueshi gang* (Outline history of Chinese historiography). Beijing: Beijing Chubanshe.

Rao, Zongyi. 1977. *Zhongguo lishi shang de zhengtong lun* (The legitimacy theory in Chinese historiography). Hong Kong: Longmen.

Rogers, Michael C., trans. 1968. *The Chronicle of Fu Chien: A Case of Exemplar History.* Berkeley: University of California Press.

Said, Edward. 1979. *Orientalism.* New York: Vintage Books.

Sargent, Clyde B. 1944. "Subsidized History: Pan Ku and the Historical Records of the Former Han Dynasty." *The Far Eastern Quarterly* 3, 2 (February): 119–143.

Sato, Masayuki. 1991. "Comparative Ideas of Chronology." *History and Theory* 30, 3:275–301.

Satō, Taketoshi. 1997. *Shiba Sen no Kenkyū* (Study of Sima Qian). Tokyo: Kyūko Shoin.

Schaberg, David. 2001. *A Patterned Past: Form and Thought in Early Chinese Historiography.* Cambridge MA: Harvard University Press.

Schama, Simon. 1999. *Rembrandt's Eyes.* New York: Alfred A. Knopf.

Schirokauer, Conrad. 1989. "Zhu Xi." In *Great Historians from Antiquity to 1800: An International Dictionary,* edited by Lucian Boia et al. New York: Greenwood Press.

———. 1993. "Chu Hsi's Sense of History." In *Ordering the World: Approaches to State and Society in Sung Dynasty China,* edited by Robert P. Hymes and Conrad Schirokauer. Berkeley: University of California Press.

———. 2004. "Hu Hung as historian." In *The New and the Multiple: Sung Senses of the Past,* edited by Thomas H. C. Lee. Hong Kong: The Chinese University Press.

Schwartz, Benjamin. 1985. *The World of Thought in Ancient China.* Cambridge MA: The Belknap Press of Harvard University Press.

Shangshu (Classic of Documents). 1993. In *Sishu wujing* (Four books and five classics), 113–146. Annotated by Wu Genyou. Beijing: Zhongguo youyi chuban gongsi.

Shaughnessy, Edward. 1997. *Before Confucius: Studies in the Creation of the Chinese Classics.* Albany: State University of New York Press.

Shibaki, Kunio. 1979. "Ōyō Shu no shigaku shisō" (The historical thinking of Ouyang Xiu). In *Kaga hakushi taikan kinen: Chūgoku bunshi tetsugaku ronshū.* Tokyo: Kodansha.

Shigezawa, Toshio. 1972. "Ōyō Shū no seitō ron" (Ouyang Xiu's discourse on legitimate succession). In *Tōhōgaku ronshu.* Tokyo: Tōhō gakkai.

Shiji. 1988. Sima Qian. *Shiji (Records of the Historian).* Changsha: Yuelu shushe.

Shimada, Kenji. 1969. "Rekishi teki risei hihan—'Rikkei minna shi' no setsu" (Critique of historical reasoning—the notion of "the Six Classics are histories"). *Iwanami kōza tetsugaku* 123–157.

Shitong. 1978. Liu Zhiji, *Shitong tongshi* (Perspectives on historiography: a comprehensive annotation). Annotated by Pu Qilong. 2 Vols. Shanghai: Shanghai guji chubanshe.

Shixueshi. 1983. *Zhongguo lishi dacidian—shixueshi* (A great dictionary of Chinese history—history of historiography). Shanghai: Shanghai cishu chubanshe.

Solomon, Bernard S., trans. 1955. *The Veritable Records of the T'ang Emperor Shun-tsung (February 28, 805–August 31, 805) Han Yü's Shun-tsung Shih lu.* Cambridge MA: Harvard University Press.

Song, Xi. 1988. "Difangzhi yu lishixue" (Local gazetteers and the study of history). *Guoshiguan guankan* (new series) 5:1–5.

Song, Yanshen et al., eds. 1987. *Zhongguo lishi yaoji jieshao ji xuandu* (An introduction to and selected readings of important texts on Chinese history). Changqun: Dongbei shifan daxue.

Struve, Lynn A. 1988a. "The Early Ch'ing Legacy of Huang Tsung-hsi: A Reexamination." *Asia Major* (new series) 1:83–122.

———. 1988b. "Huang Zongxi in Context: A Reappraisal of His Major Writings." *Journal of Asian Studies* 47, 3:474–502.

———. 1989. "Early Qing Officials as Chronicles of the Conquest." *Late Imperial China* 10, 1:1–26.

Suishu. 1973. Wei Zheng, *Suishu (Sui history).* Beijing: Zhonghua shuju.

Suzuki, Torao. 1955. "Gen I-shan no shishi" (The historical poetry of Yuan Haowen) *Kwaitoku* 26:36–54.

Tang, Gang, Wang Hongjiang, and Fu Gueijiu. 1983. "Mingshi de zuanxiu ji shixue sixiang" (The compilation of the *Ming History* and its historical thought) *Mingshi yanjiu luncong* 2:302–329.

Tang, Qinfu. 1998a. "Zhu Xi yu *Tongjian ganmu*" (Zhu Xi and the *Outline of the Comprehensive Mirror*). *Shixueshi yanjiu* 2:45–50.

———. 1998b. "Zhu Xi zhishi jiazhilun chanwei" (An in-depth exposition of Zhu Xi's view on the value of historical studies). *Jianghai xuekan* 5:129–135.

———. 1999. "Zhu Xi shixue sixiang zai Songdai shixue shang de diwei" (The role of Zhu Xi's historical thought in the historiography of the Song period). *Xueshu yuekan* 7:75–81.

Tang, Zhijun. 1980. "Qingdai jing jinwenxue de fuxing" (Revival of the New Script classical learning in the Qing period). *Zhongguoshi yanjiu* 2:145–156.

Tang Huiyao. 1955. Wang Pu, *Tang Huiyao* (*Gathering of Essentials of the Tang*). Beijing: Zhonghua shuju.

Tao, Fanbing. 1987. *Zhongguo gudai shixueshi lue* (A brief historiography of traditional China). Changsha: Hunan renmin.

Tao, Yuanzhen. 1944. "Wanli qijuzhu" (The diary of activity and repose of the Wanli reign). *Wenshi zazhi* 4, 7–8: 54–56.

Teng, S. Y. 1968. "Wang Fu-chih's Views on History and Historical Writing." *Journal of Asian Studies* 28, 1:111–123.

Tillman, Hoyt Cleveland. 1982. *Utilitarian Confucianism: Ch'en Liang's Challenge to Chu Hsi.* Cambridge: Harvard University Press.

———. 1992. *Confucian Discourse and Chu Hsi's Ascendancy.* Honolulu: University of Hawai'i Press.

———. 1995a. "Confucianism under the Chin and the Impact of Sung Confucian Tao-hsüeh." In *China under Jurchen Rule: Essays on Chin Intellectual and Cultural History,* edited by Hoyt Cleveland Tillman and Stephen H. West. Albany: State University of New York Press.

———. 1995b. "An Overview of Chin History and Institutions." In *China under Jurchen Rule: Essays on Chin Intellectual and Cultural History,* edited by Hoyt Cleveland Tillman and Stephen H. West. Albany: State University of New York Press.

———. 2004. "Textual Liberties and Restraints in Rewriting China's Histories: The Case of Ssu-ma Kuang's Re-construction of Chu-ko Liang's Story." In *The New and the Multiple: Sung Senses of the Past,* edited by Thomas H. C. Lee. Hong Kong: The Chinese University Press.

Tongdian. 1988. Du You, *Tongdian* (*Comprehensive compendium*). Beijing: Zhonghua shuju.

Tsien, Tsuen-hsuin. 1962. *Written on Bamboo and Silk: The Beginnings of Chinese Books and Inscriptions.* Chicago: University of Chicago Press.

Tu, Wei-ming. 1993. *Way, Learning, and Politics: Essays on the Confucian Intellectual.* Albany: State University of New York Press.

Twitchett, Denis. 1961. "Chinese Biographical Writing." In *Historians of China and Japan,* edited by W. G. Beasley and E. G. Pulleyblank. London: Oxford University Press.

———. 1992. *The Writing of Official History under the T'ang.* Cambridge: Cambridge University Press.

Vermeer, Eduard. 1995. "Notions of Time and Space in the Early Ch'ing: The Writings of Ku Yen-wu, Hsü Hsia-k'o, Ku Tsu-yü and Chang Hsüeh-ch'eng." In *Time and Space in Chinese Culture* edited by Chun-chieh Huang and Erik Zürcher. Leiden: E. J. Brill.

Wang, Aihe. 2000. *Cosmology and Political Culture in Early China.* Cambridge: Cambridge University Press.

Wang, Deyi. 1997. "Songdai Jiangxi de shixue" (Historical learning in Jiangxi in the Song Dynasty). *Taidai lishi xuebao* 21:147–173.

Wang, Gaoxin. 1998. "Zhu Xi he shixue" (Zhu Xi and historical learning). *Shixueshi yanjiu* 3:43–50.

Wang, Gungwu. 1957. "The *Chiu Wu-tai Shih* and History-writing during the Five Dynasties," *Asia Major* (new series) 6, 1:1–22.

———.1962. "Feng Tao: An Essay on Confucian Loyalty." In *Confucian Personalities,* edited by Arthur F. Wright and Denis Twitchett. Stanford: Stanford University Press.

———. 1973. "Some Comments on the Later Standard Histories." In *Essays on the Sources for Chinese History* edited by Donald D. Leslie, Colin Mackerras, and Wang Gungwu. Columbia: University of South Carolina Press.

Wang, Guowei. 1997. "Shi shi" (Interpreting the *shi*). In *Wang Guowei xueshu jingdian ji* (Anthology of the classic works by Wang Guowei). Vol. 2. Nanchang: Jiangxi renmin chubanshe.

Wang, Jiajian. 1993. "Wei Yuan de shixue yu jingshi shiguan" (Wei Yuan's historical learning and historical view on statecraft). *Taida lishi xuebao* 21:155–172.

Wang, Mingsun. 1988. "Jin xiu guoshi ji Jinshi yuanliu" (The national histories compiled during the Jin and the origins and developments of Jin historiography). *Shumu jikan* 22.1:47–60.

———. 1989. "Liao Jin zhi shiguan yu shiguan" (The History Bureau and history officials in the Liao and the Jin). *Guoshiguan guankan* (new series) 6:15–28.

———. 2000. "Jindai shiren zhi lishi sixiang" (The historical thinking of the literati of the Jin period). *Zhongxing daxue lishi xuebao* 11:1–24.

Wang, Q. Edward. 1995. "Time Perception in Ancient Chinese Historiography." *Storia della Storiografia* 28:69–86.

———. 1999. "History, Space, and Ethnicity: The Chinese Worldview." *Journal of World History* 10, 2:285–305.

———. 2000a. "Historical Writings in Twentieth Century China: Methodological Innovation and Ideological Influence." In *Assessment of 20th Century Historiography,* edited by Rolf Torstendahl. Stockholm: The Royal Academy of Letters, History and Antiquities.

———. 2000b. "Objectivity, Truth, and Hermeneutics: Re-reading the *Chunqiu.*" In *Classics and Interpretations: The Hermeneutic Tradition in Chinese Culture,* edited by Ching-i Tu. New Brunswick: Transaction Publishers.

———. 2001. *Inventing China through History: The May Fourth Approach to Historiography.* Albany: State University of New York Press.

———. 2002. "Time, History, and Dao: Zhang Xuecheng and Martin Heidegger." *Dao: A Journal of Comparative Philosophy* 1, 2:251–226.

Wang, Shumin. 1997. *Zhongguo shixueshi gangyao* (An outline history of Chinese historiography). Beijing: Zhonghua shuju.

Watson, Burton. 1958. *Ssu-ma Ch'ien: Grand Historian of China.* New York: Columbia University Press.

———. 1969. *Records of the Historian: Chapters from the Shih chi of Ssu-ma Ch'ien.* New York: Columbia University Press.

———, trans. 1989. *The Tso Chuan: Selections from China's Oldest Narrative History.* New York: Columbia University Press.

Wechsler, Howard J. 1985. *Offerings of Jade and Silk: Ritual and Symbol in the Legitimation of the T'ang Dynasty.* New Haven: Yale University Press.

Wei, Hong. 1998. "Qian Daxin lishi kaozheng fangfa shulun" (Explanations and comments on Qian Daxin's method of historical investigation and verification). *Shixueshi yanjiu* 4:53–60.

Wenxin diaolong. 1983. *The Literary Mind and the Carving of Dragons.* Translated by Vincent Yu-chung Shih. Hong Kong: The Chinese University Press.

West, Stephen H. 1995. "Chilly Seas and East-Flowing Rivers: Yüan Hao-wen's Poems of Death and Disorder, 1233–35." In *China under Jurchen Rule: Essays on Chin Intellectual and Cultural History,* edited by Hoyt Cleveland Tillman and Stephen H. West. Albany: State University of New York Press.

White, Hayden. 1966. "The Burden of History." *History and Theory* 5:113–134.

———. 1987. *The Content of the Form: Narrative Discourse and Historical Representation.* Baltimore: The Johns Hopkins University Press.

Wilson, Thomas A. 1994. "Confucian Sectarianism and the Compilation of the *Ming History.*" *Late Imperial China* 15, 2:53–84.

———. 1995. *Genealogy of the Way: The Construction and Uses of the Confucian Tradition in Late Imperial China.* Stanford: Stanford University Press.

———. 1996. "The Ritual Formation of Confucian Orthodoxy and the Descendants of the Sage." *Journal of Asian Studies* 55, 3:559–584.

Wong, Young-tsu. 2001. "Xifang shijia dui suowei 'Rujia shixue' de renshi yu wujie" (Understanding and Misunderstanding of 'Confucian Historiography' in the West). *Taida lishi xuebao* 27:125–149.

Woolf, D. R., ed. 1998. *A Global Encyclopedia of Historical Writings.* New York: Garland Publishing.

Wright, Mary C. 1958. "What's in a Reign Name: The Uses of History and Philology." *Journal of Asian Studies* 18:103–106.

Wu, K. T. 1942–1943. "Ming Printers and Printing." *Harvard Journal of Asiatic Studies* 7: 203–260.

Wu, Tianren. 1989. "Liu Zhiji yu Zheng Qiao shixue zhi tantao" (An investigation of the historical learning of Liu Zhiji and Zheng Qiao). *Dongfang zazhi* (new series) 22.9:20–28.

Wu, Ze. 1962. "Wei Yuan de bianyi sixiang he lishi jinhua guannian" (The idea of change and the view of historical evolution in Wei Yuan's philosophy). *Lishi yanjiu* 9.5: 33–59.

Xie, Guei'an. 1999. "Ruizong Chongzhen ji nan Ming zhuchao shilu zuanxiu kaoshu" (An investigation of the compilation of the Veritable Records of the various reigns of Ruizong, Chongzhen, and the Southern Ming). *Shixueshi yanjiu* 2:57–61.

Xu, Guansan. 1980. "Gong Wei zhi lishi zhexue yu bianfa sixiang" (Gong Zizhen and Wei Yuan's philosophy of history and their ideas of political reform). *Zhonghua wenshi luncong* 1:69–104.

Xu, Hong. 1997. *"Mingshi jishi benmo* 'Yan Song yongshi' jiaodu" (A critical reading of [the chapter of] 'Yan Song's Domination' [in the] *Records of Events from beginning to End in Ming History). Jida xuebao* 1, 1:17–60.

Yamanoi, Yū. 1954. "Mimmatsu Shinsho ni okeru keisei chiyō no gaku" (On the learning for the ordering of the world in the late Ming and early Qing). *Tōhōgaku ronshu* 1:135–150.

Yang, Lien-sheng. 1947. "A Theory about the Titles of the Twenty-Four Dynastic Histories." *Harvard Journal of Asiatic Studies* 10, 1: 41–47.

———. 1961. "The Organization of Chinese Official Historiography: Principles and Methods of the Standard Histories from the T'ang through the Ming Dynasty." In *Historians of China and Japan,* edited by W. G. Beasley and E. G. Pulleyblank. London: Oxford University Press.

Yang, Yanqiu. 1998. "Ming *Guangzong shilu Sanchao yaodian* de bianxiu" (The compilation of the *Veritable Records of [the Reign of] Guangzong* and the *Main Documents of Three Reigns). Shixueshi yanjiu* 4:48–52.

———. 2001. "Ming zhonghouqi de shixue sichao" (The tides of thought in historical learning in the latter part of mid Ming). *Shixueshi yanjiu* 2: 36–44.

Yang, Yaokun, and Wu Yechun. 1998. *Chen Shou, Pei Songzhi pingzhuan* (Critical biographies of Chen Shou and Pei Songzhi). Nanjing: Nanjing daxue chubanshe.

Yao, Xinzhong. 2000. *An Introduction to Confucianism.* Cambridge: Cambridge University Press.

Yi, Da, ed. 1985. *Zhongguo shixue fanzhan shi* (A history of the development of Chinese historical learning). Zhongzhou, Henan: Zhongzhou guji.

Yü, Ying-shih. 1975. "Some Preliminary Observations on the Rise of Ch'ing Intellectualism." *Tsing Hua Journal of Chinese Studies* 11:105–146.

———. 1976a. *Lun Dai Zhen yu Zhang Xuecheng* (On Dai Zhen and Zhang Xuecheng). Hong Kong, Longmen shudian.

———. 1976b. "Qingdai sixiangshi de yige xinjieshi" (A new interpretation of the history of thought of the Qing period). In *Lishi yu sixiang* (History and thought), edited by Yü Ying-shih. Taipei: Lianjing chubanshe.

———. 1980. *Zhongguo zhishi jieceng shilun—gudai pian* (History of the Chinese intellectual class: ancient period). Taipei: Lianjing.

———. 1982. "Tai Chen and the Chu Hsi Tradition." In *Essays in Commemoration of the Golden Jubilee of the Fung Ping Shan Library,* edited by Chan Pingleung. Hong Kong: Fung Ping Shan Library of the University of Hong Kong.

———. 1985. "Individualism and the Neo-Taoist Movement in Wei-Chin China." In *Individualism and Holism: Studies in Confucian and Taoist Values,* edited by Donald Munro. Ann Arbor: University of Michigan Press.

Zeng, Yifen. 1998. "Qian Daxin de lishi wenxian xue" (Qian Daxin's studies on historical bibliographies and documents). *Shixueshi yanjiu* 1:64–71.

———. 1999. "Quan Zuwang de shixue yu 'qijiao' 'sanjian' " (Quan Zuwang's historical learning and his "seven redactions" and "three comments"). *Shixueshi yanjiu* 2:62–69.

———. 2000. "Sui Tang shiqi sibu fenfa de queli" (The establishment of the four

divisions in bibliography during the Sui and Tang period) *Shixueshi yanjiu*
3:46–52.

Zhang, Dake. 1994. *Sima Qian pingzhuan* (A critical biography of Sima Qian). Nanjing: Nanjing daxue chubanshe.

Zhang, Dake, Yu Zhanghua, et. al. 1995. *Sima Qian yijia yan* (Sima Qian's creation
of his own tradition). Xi'an: Shanxi renmin jiaoyu chubanshe.

Zhang, Sanxi. 1992. *Pipan shixue de pipan: Liu Zhiji jiqi* Shitong *yanjiu* (A critique of
critical historiography: A study of Liu Zhiji and his *Comprehensive Historiography*). Taipei: Wenjin chubanshe.

Zhang, Shou'an. 1979. "Gong Ding'an yu Changzhou Gongyangxue" (Gong Zizhen
and the Gongyang learning of Changzhou). *Shumu jikan* 13, 2:3–20.

Zhang, Suqing. 1998. *Xushi yu jieshi:* Zuozhuan *jingjie yanjiu* (Narrative and interpretation: a study of the hermeneutics in the *Zuo Commentary*). Taipei: Shulin
chuban gongsi.

Zhang, Xu. 1968. "Wan Jiye yu Mingshi" (Wan Sitong and the *Ming History*). In
Mingshi bianzuan kao (Investigations into the compilations of the *Ming History*).
Taipei: Xuesheng shuju.

Zhang, Yuan. 1975. "Songdai lixuejia de lishiguan" (The historical views of the
scholars of the school of principle in the Song period). Ph. D. dissertation,
National Taiwan University.

Zhao, Lingyang. 1982. "Lun Gong Zizhen dui shi zhi guannian" (On Gong Zizhen's
conception of history). In *Xianggang daxue Feng Pingshan tushuguan jinxi jinian
lunwenji* (Collected commemorative essays on the fiftieth anniversary of the
Fung Ping-shan library at the University of Hong Kong), edited by Chan Pingleung et al. Hong Kong: Xianggang daxue Feng Pingshan tushuguan.

Zhao, Shengqun. 2000. Chunqiu *jingzhuan yanjiu* (Study of the classic and commentary of the *Spring and Autumn*). Shanghai: Shanghai guji chubanshe.

Zhou, Shaochuan. 2001. *Yuandai shixue sixiang yanjiu* (A study of historical thought
in the Yuan period). Beijing: Shehui kexue wenxian.

Zhou, Yutong, and Tang Zhijun. 1962. "Zhang Xuecheng liujing jieshi shuo chutan"
(Preliminary investigation into Zhang Xuecheng's idea that "the six classics
are all history"). *Zhunghua wenshi luncong* 1:211–227.

Zhuang, Cangyi. 2001. "Sima Guang Zizhi tongjian de Wei shu lun" (A discussion
on Sima Guang's according legitimacy to the Wei in the *Comprehensive Mirror*).
Zhongguo wenhua yuekan 258:106–126.

Zuozhuan (Zuo commentary). 1993. In *Sishu wujing* (Four books and five classics).
Annotated by Wu Genyou. Beijing: Zhongguo youyi chuban gongsi.

Zürcher, Erik. 1972. *The Buddhist Conquest of China: The Spread and Adaptation of Buddhism in Early Medieval China.* 2nd edition. 2 Vols. Leiden: E. J. Brill.

Index

About the Authors

On-cho Ng is associate professor of history and religious studies at Pennsylvania State University. He is author of *Cheng-Zhu Confucianism in the Early Qing: Li Guangdi (1642–1718)* and *Qing Learning* (2001), and coeditor of *Imagining Boundaries: Changing Confucian Doctrines, Texts, and Hermeneutics* (1999).

Q. Edward Wang is professor of history at Rowan University. He is author of *Inventing China through History: The May Fourth Approach to Historiography* (2001) and coeditor of *Turning Points in Historiography: A Cross-Cultural Perspective* (2002).

Production Notes for Ng and Wang /*Mirroring the Past*
Cover design by Santos Barbasa Jr.
Text design by UH Press production staff with text in Baskerville
and display in Avant Garde
Text composition by Tseng Information Systems, Inc.
Printing and binding by Integrated Book Technology, Inc.
Printed on 55 lb. Antique Natural Cream, 366 ppi